AF702131

Poor and Rich in James

Bulletin for Biblical Research Supplements

Editor

Richard S. Hess, Denver Seminary

Associate Editor

Craig L. Blomberg, Denver Seminary

Advisory Board

Leslie C. Allen
Fuller Theological Seminary
Donald A. Carson
Trinity Evangelical Divinity School
Donald A. Hagner
Fuller Theological Seminary
Elmer A. Martens
Mennonite Brethren Biblical Seminary
Bruce K. Waltke
Knox Theological Seminary

Poor and Rich in James

A Relevance Theory Approach to James's Use of the Old Testament

by

Nelson R. Morales

Eisenbrauns | University Park, Pennsylvania

Library of Congress Cataloging-in-Publication Data

Names: Morales, Nelson R., author.
Title: Poor and rich in James : a relevance theory approach to James's use of the Old Testament / by Nelson R. Morales.
Description: University Park, Pennsylvania : Eisenbrauns, [2018] | Series: Bulletin for Biblical research | Includes bibliographical references and index.
Summary: "Employing Relevance Theory as a methodological framework, examines how the book of James uses the Old Testament in passages on wealth and poverty"—Provided by publisher.
Identifiers: LCCN 2018017524 | ISBN 9781575067827 (cloth : alk. paper)
Subjects: LCSH: Bible. James—Criticism, interpretation, etc. | Bible. James—Relation to the Old Testament. | Poverty—Biblical teaching. | Wealth—Biblical teaching.
Classification: LCC BS2785.6.P65 M67 2018 | DDC 227/.9106—dc23
LC record available at https://lccn.loc.gov/2018017524

Copyright © 2018 The Pennsylvania State University
All rights reserved
Printed in the United States of America
Published by The Pennsylvania State University Press,
University Park, PA 16802-1003

Eisenbrauns is an imprint of The Pennsylvania State University Press.

The Pennsylvania State University Press is a member of the Association of University Presses.

It is the policy of The Pennsylvania State University Press to use acid-free paper. Publications on uncoated stock satisfy the minimum requirements of American National Standard for Information Sciences—Permanence of Paper for Printed Library Material, ANSI Z39.48–1992.

To Xenia, my beloved wife

Contents

List of Tables

Preface

I have been a professor of New Testament, Greek, and Hermeneutics at the Seminario Teológico Centroamericano (SETECA) since 1995. I was assigned to teach the exegesis of James in 2004. Since then my heart has been attached to the wonderful book of James, as I have taught it many times. During the years of my doctoral studies I wanted to learn a new approach and use the book of James as a study case. Don Carson introduced me to the world of the NT use of the OT, and Gene Green invited me to explore Relevance Theory as a discourse analysis tool. With these ideas in mind, I decided to explore in my dissertation how James uses the Old Testament, with Relevance Theory as my discourse analysis lens. The epistle is five chapters long, but that was too much to explore. So I decided to focus on one of its most pertinent themes for Latin American discussion, the passages where James deals with poverty and wealth. In that way, I could explore how James builds his ethics on this issue. Grant Osborne accepted the invitation to be my mentor. His guidance and insights strengthened the project. Te Li Lau, as second reader, gave me very useful criticism and insights that resulted in stronger research. Finally, Craig Blomberg thoroughly reviewed the dissertation and gave me new ideas for adapting it into this book.

I completed my Ph.D. at Trinity International University in Deerfield, Illinois. Many people and organizations made this dream possible. First of all, the triune God gave me the blessing to study. My seminary, the Seminario Teológico Centroamericano, supported me before and after I went to Trinity. John Stott Ministries, Langham Partnership, Lamb Foundation, and ScholarLeaders International spiritually and financially contributed to the project. Finally, my wife, Xenia Pereira de Morales, and other friends helped me in many different ways. Among those who were crucial in this research, I should name Jules and Ana Martínez, Andrew Abernethy, Gene Green, Bryan Harmelink, Gary Williams, Nathan Purtzer, Alvin Thompson, and Michael Makidon.

List of Abbreviations

AB	Anchor Bible
ABC	Ariel's Bible Commentary
ABR	*Australian Biblical Review*
AH	Alektor-Hochschulschriften
ALBA	Abundant Life Bible Amplifier
ALGNT	*Analytical Lexicon to the Greek New Testament*
AnBib	Analecta Biblica
AOAT	Alter Orient und altes Testament
AsTJ	Asbury Theological Journal
ATJ	*Ashland Theological Journal*
AUSS	*Andrews University Seminary Studies*
AYBRL	Anchor Yale Bible Reference Library
BAR	*Biblical Archaeology Review*
BBR	*Bulletin for Biblical Research*
BDAG	Bauer, Danker, Arndt, Gingrich, eds., *A Greek-English Lexicon of the New Testament and Other Early Christian Literature*
BDB	Brown, Driver, Briggs, eds., *Hebrew and English Lexicon*
BEB	*Baker Encyclopedia of the Bible*
BECNT	Baker Exegetical Commentary on the New Testament
BETL	Bibliotheca Ephemeridum Theologicarum Lovaniensium
BFT	Biblical Foundations in Theology
BHL	Blackwell Handbooks in Linguistics
BHT	Beiträge zur historischen Theologie
BI	Biblical Interpretation (Series)
Bib	*Biblica*
BibInt	*Biblical Interpretation*
BibSac	*Bibliotheca Sacra*
BN	*Biblische Nötizen*
BNTC	Baker New Testament Commentary
BR	*Biblical Research*
BRS	Biblical Resource Series
BT	*The Bible Translator*
BTB	*Biblical Theology Bulletin*
BTL	Blackwell Textbooks in Linguistics
BTNT	Biblical Theology of the New Testament
BTS	Biblisch-theologische Studien
BVB	Beiträgen zum Verstehen der Bibel
BZ	*Biblische Zeitschrift*
BZNW	Beihefte für die Zeitschrift für die neutestamentliche Wissenschaft
CB	*Christian Bioethics*
CBC	Cornerstone Biblical Commentary

CBQ	*Catholic Biblical Quarterly*
CBR	*Currents in Biblical Research*
CNT	Commentaire du Nouveau Testament
Conc	*Concilium*
ContBS	Continuum Biblical Studies
CRINT	Compendia Rerum Iudaicarum ad Novum Testamentum
CSL	Cambridge Studies in Linguistics
CTR	*Criswell Theological Review*
CuadT	*Cuadernos Teológicos*
CurBS	*Currents in Biblical Studies*
DCL	Deuterocanonical and Cognate Literature
DGENT	*Diccionario Griego-Español del Nuevo Testamento*
DJG	*Dictionary of Jesus and the Gospels*
DLNTD	*Dictionary of the Later New Testament and Its Developments*
DPL	*Dictionary of Paul and His Letters*
DTIB	*Dictionary of Theological Interpretation of the Bible*
EB	*Estudios Bíblicos*
EBC	*Expositor's Bible Commentary*
EBT	Explorations in Biblical Theology
EDEJ	*Eerdmans Dictionary of Early Judaism*
ESEC	Emory Studies in Early Christianity
ESV	English Standard Version
EvQ	*Evangelical Quarterly*
FM	*Faith and Mission*
GP	Gospel Perspectives
GTB	Gütersloher theologische Beiträge
HABES	Heidelberger althistorische Beiträge und epigraphische Studien
HBT	*Horizons in Biblical Theology*
HCSPTH	Holy Cross Studies in Patristic Theology and History
HTR	*Harvard Theological Review*
HTS	*Hervormde Teologiese Studies*
IBS	*Irish Biblical Studies*
ICC	International Critical Commentary
IJL	*Italian Journal of Linguistics*
Int	*Interpretation*
ITSS	Invitation to Theological Studies Series
IVPNTC	InterVarsity Press New Testament Commentary Series
JAJ	*Journal of Ancient Judaism*
JAJSup	Journal of Ancient Judaism Supplement Series
JBL	*Journal of Biblical Literature*
JBQ	*Jewish Biblical Quarterly*
JETS	*Journal of the Evangelical Theological Society*
JJS	*Journal of Jewish Studies*
JL	Janua Linguarum
JMM	*Journal of Markets and Morality*
JNSL	*Journal of Northwest Semitic Languages*
JOTT	*Journal of Translation and Textlinguistics*

JPrag	*Journal of Pragmatics*
JPSTC	Jewish Publication Society Torah Commentary
JRA	*Journal of Roman Archaeology*
JRE	*Journal of Religious Ethics*
JRT	*Journal of Religious Thought*
JSJSup	Journal for the Study of Judaism Supplements
JSNT	*Journal for the Study of the New Testament*
JSNTSup	Journal for the Study of the New Testament Supplements
JSOT	*Journal for the Study of the Old Testament*
JTI	*Journal of Theological Interpretation*
JTSA	*Journal of Theology of Southern Africa*
KJV	King James Version
L&N	Louw and Nida, eds., *Greek-English Lexicon of the New Testament: Based on Semantic Domains*
LBD	*Lexham Bible Dictionary*
LEH	Lust, Eynikel, and Hauspin, eds., *Greek-English Lexicon of the Septuagint*
LNTS	*Library of New Testament Studies*
LXX	Septuagint
MITECS	Massachusetts Institute of Technology Encyclopedia of the Cognitive Sciences
MNTS	McMaster New Testament Studies
MSJ	Master's Seminary Journal
MT	Masoretic Text
NAC	New American Commentary
NBBC	New Beacon Bible Commentary
NCBC	New Cambridge Bible Commentary
NCBCNT	New Collegeville Bible Commentary: New Testament
NEchtB	Neue Echter Bibel
Neot	*Neotestamentica*
NICNT	New International Commentary on the New Testament
NIDOTTE	*New International Dictionary of Old Testament Theology and Exegesis*
NIGTC	New International Greek Testament Commentary
NIVAC	New International Version Application Commentary
NovT	*Novum Testamentum*
NRSV	New Revised Standard Version
NSBT	New Studies in Biblical Theology
NT	New Testament
NTC	New Testament in Context
NTM	New Testament Monographs
NTS	*New Testament Studies*
OBO	Orbis Biblicus et Orientalis
OBT	Overtures to Biblical Theology
OEBI	Oxford Encyclopedia of Biblical Interpretation
OT	Old Testament
OTL	Old Testament Library
OTP	*Old Testament Pseudepigrapha*

PAS	*Proceedings of the Aristotelian Society*
PBNS	Pragmatics and Beyond New Series
PEGLMBS	*Proceedings of the Eastern Great Lakes and Midwest Biblical Societies*
PengC	Penguin Classics
PHC	People's History of Christianity
PhR	*Philosophical Review*
PIBA	Proceedings of the Irish Biblical Association
PNTC	Pillar New Testament Commentary
Prag	*Pragmatics*
Presb	*Presbyterion*
PSPLC	Palgrave's Studies in Pragmatics, Language, and Cognition
RB	*Revue Biblique*
ResQ	*Restoration Quarterly*
RevExp	*Review and Expositor*
RevistB	*Revista Bíbilica*
RIBLA	*Revista de Interpretación Biblica Latinoamericana*
RLED	*Revista Latinoamericana de Estudios del Discurso*
RSR	*Religious Studies Review*
SB	Sources Bibliques
SBG	Studies in Biblical Greek
SBJT	*Southern Baptist Journal of Theology*
SBL	Society of Biblical Literature
SBLAB	Society of Biblical Literature Academia Biblica
SBLDS	Society of Biblical Literature Dissertation Series
SBLSP	Society of Biblical Literature Seminar Papers
SBLSymS	Society of Biblical Literature Symposium Series
SBS	Stuttgarter Bibelstudien
SDSSRL	Studies in the Dead Sea Scrolls and Related Literature
SIL	Summer Institute of Linguistics
SJT	*Scottish Journal of Theology*
SNTSMS	Studiorum Novi Testamenti Societas Monograph Series
SP	Sacra Pagina
SPS	Studies in Peace and Scripture
SSA	Semantic and Structural Analyses
ST	*Studia Theologica*
SUNT	Studien zur Umwelt des Neuen Testaments
SupNovT	Supplements to Novum Testamentum
TBD	*The Bible Dictionary*
ThEd	*Theological Educator*
Them	*Themelios*
THKNT	Theologischer Handkommentar zum Neuen Testament
TNTC	Tyndale New Testament Commentary
TOTC	Tyndale Old Testament Commentary
TR	*Theological Review*
TRu	*Theologische Rundschau*
TS	*Theological Studies*
TTCABS	T&T Clark Approaches to Biblical Studies

TynBul	*Tyndale Bulletin*
UCLWPL	*University College London Working Papers in Linguistics*
VE	*Vox Evangelica*
VTG	Vetus Testamentum Graecum
VTSup	Vetus Testamentum Supplements
WATSA	What Are They Saying About? WBC Word Biblical Commentary
WBC	Word Biblical Commentary
WTJ	*Westminster Theological Journal*
WUNT	Wissenschaftliche Untersuchungen zum Neuen Testament
WW	*Word and World*
ZAW	*Zeitschrift für die alttestamentliche Wissenschaft*
ZECNT	Zondervan Exegetical Commentary on the New Testament

Chapter 1

Introduction

The epistle of James was for years a forgotten book in academic circles. In recent decades, however, a renewed focus on early Judaism has generated interest in looking at James with new eyes.[1] In this context, different studies, monographs, and commentaries have been written. Poverty and wealth in the epistle continues to be a point of interest. Other topics, however, are still to be explored. One of those topics is the rhetorical study of the use of the Old Testament in the book. The present investigation focuses on how James uses the OT in those passages where he deals with poverty and wealth. In particular, it focuses on how he builds his ethics of poverty and wealth. The following pages present a bibliographic survey that includes the issue of poverty and wealth in James and the use of the OT in the epistle. Next, this chapter presents a brief discussion of the author, his addressees, and the date of the letter, followed by the passages under study, the research problem, the hermeneutical approach, methodology, constraints, and the significance of the present research.

Poor and Rich in James

In James poverty and wealth is an important theme.[2] Commentaries and studies have been dedicated to this topic with different assumptions and from different perspectives. Two main views appear: "poor" and "rich" are

1. Four important reviews provide a helpful overview of recent scholarship on James: Peter H. Davids, "The Epistle of James in Modern Discussion," in *Principat 25,5* (New York: Walter de Gruyter, 1988), 3621–45; F. Hahn and P. Müller, "Der Jakobusbrief," *TRu* 63 (1998): 1–73; Todd C. Penner, "The Epistle of James in Current Research," *CurBS* 7 (1999): 257–308; Mati Myllykoski, "James the Just in History and Tradition: Perspectives of Past and Present Scholarship (Part I)," *CBR* 5 (2006): 73–122; Mati Myllykoski, "James the Just in History and Tradition: Perspectives of Past and Present Scholarship (Part II)," *CBR* 6 (2007): 11–98.

2. Davids counts 47 verses out of 105, 45% of the letter, as dedicated to this topic. The passages he considers are 1:9–11, 27; 2:1–13, 14–26; 4:2, 13–17; and 5:1–6 and 7–11. Peter H. Davids, "The Test of Wealth," in *Missions of James, Peter, and Paul: Tensions in Early Christianity*, ed. Bruce Chilton and Craig A. Evans, SupNovT 115 (Leiden: Brill, 2005), 354. Other scholars consider fewer passages. For example, René Krüger considers 1:9–11, 27; 2:1–13, 14–17; 4:13–17; and 5:1–6. René Krüger, *Pobres y ricos en la epístola de Santiago: El desafío de un cristianismo profético* (Buenos Aires: Lumen, 2005), 93. Warden considers 1:9–11, 2:1–12, and 4:13–5:6. Duane Warden,

metaphorical descriptions; "poor" and "rich" represent socioeconomic categories. Representative scholars and their contributions in each decade from 1960 to 2010 appear in the following pages.

Without a doubt, the most prominent scholar on James in the last century is Martin Dibelius. A section of his commentary on the topic of the poor and the rich has been very influential in later approaches to this issue.[3] He recognizes a clear animosity against the rich in the letter. He explains this animosity by defining the concepts "poor" and "rich" in light of the idea of "the pious poor." He builds the concept from the Old Testament, Second Temple history and literature, and his reconstruction of Jesus's ministry and early church history. In his analysis, by the time of the Second Temple, "[t]he pious thought of themselves as the poor because poverty had become a religious concept."[4] Jesus's ministry develops among poverty-stricken groups with a strong eschatological hope, and the letter of James evidences this poverty-stricken apocalyptic strain of Christianity.[5] As a result, Dibelius infers that for James "being poor and being Christian were coincidental concepts."[6] Also, the rich are "the enemies of the Christians." As a consequence of this *Armenfrömmigkeit* and James's clear opposition to the rich and the world, Dibelius thinks that James "wanted to be a 'poor man,' that is, a pious man who did not participate in the world. Further, he wanted all Christians to continue to belong to the 'poor.'"[7]

In the 1960s, some scholars followed Dibelius's idea, while others differed. In his commentary, Franz Mussner dedicates an excursus to the topic of *Armenfrömmigkeit*, in which he briefly explores the concept in the OT and Second Temple literature, and concludes that almost every element of the piety of the poor observed in Second Temple literature is also present in the epistle of James.[8] He goes one step further than Dibelius by considering the situation of the poor described in the letter as idealized. For him, the rich are Jewish communities persecuting believers, the poor.[9] On the other hand, many scholars understood "poor" and "rich" as socioeconomic

"The Rich and Poor in James: Implications for Institutionalized Partiality," *JETS* 43 (2000): 249.

3. It was first published in 1921 in German. The 11th edition was translated into English in 1976. Martin Dibelius, *James: A Commentary on the Epistle of James* (Philadelphia: Fortress, 1976), 39–45.

4. Ibid., 40.

5. David Edgar goes further and argues that οἱ πτωχοί are a group of marginal early Christian prophets, and the rich are God's enemies. David H. Edgar, *Has God Not Chosen the Poor? The Social Setting of the Epistle of James*, JSNTSup 206 (Sheffield: Sheffield Academic, 2001), 95–136.

6. Dibelius, *James*, 44.

7. Ibid., 48.

8. Franz Mussner, *Der Jakobusbrief*, 3rd expanded ed. (Freiburg: Herder, 1975), 80.

9. Ibid., 80–2. René Krüger criticizes both these assumptions. He thinks that Mussner strongly weakens the idea of poor and rich in James by designating the piety of the poor as ideal. He also points out there is no basis in the historical reality of the communities in James for equating rich and Jewish.

categories. For example, J. W. Roberts considers that some passages in the epistle of James refer to the Christian rich (1:10–11) and the Jewish non-Christian rich (2:7; 4:13–5:6).[10] In the same vein, for R. C. H. Lenski "rich" refers to the Christian rich (1:10–11; 4:13–17) and the Jewish non-Christian rich (2:7; 5:1–6).[11] Although Bo Reicke does not define the poor and the rich in his commentary, he suggests his perspective by translating ὁ δὲ πλούσιος in 1:10 as "and the rich brother,"[12] titling the paragraph in 5:1–6 "judgment on the unrighteous rich,"[13] and explaining those sections in socioeconomic terms.

In the 1970s, very few publications on James dealt with the issue of poverty and wealth, but the predominant view was to consider "poor" and "rich" as socioeconomic distinctions.[14] In his commentary, James Adamson partially follows Dibelius in his understanding of the poor. For him, the concept "poor" in James has a socioeconomic dimension but also includes a religious flavor.[15] Regarding the rich, he thinks that James presents the typical rich and "those of the rich that are not possessed by their wealth."[16] In this sense, he considers as Christians those depicted in 1:9–10 and 4:10, 15. For him, 1:11, 2:1–13, and 5:1–6 portray the typical rich, some patently non-Christians (2:7).[17] Later in his influential work *James: The Man and His Message,*

10. J. W. Roberts, *A Commentary on the General Epistle of James* (Austin, Tex.: R. B. Sweet, 1963), 51–6.

11. R. C. H. Lenski, *The Interpretation of the Epistle to the Hebrews and the Epistle of James* (Minneapolis: Augsburg, 1966), 533–6, 638–9. Both Roberts and Lenski consider the rich to be mostly Sadducees. Ibid., 568, 644–5; Roberts, *James*, 94. Bent Noack, who analyzes Jas 4:13–5:6, agrees with Dibelius about the connection of James's epistle with di*e Armenfrömmigkeit,* but he thinks that in James the social emphasis is clear. Bent Noack, "Jakobus wider die Reichen," *ST* 18 (1964): 10–25.

12. Bo Reicke, *The Epistles of James, Peter, and Jude: Introduction, Translation, and Notes*, AB (Garden City, N.Y.: Doubleday, 1963), 15.

13. Ibid., 50. Roy Ward makes the case that the term πλούσιος is reserved in the letter for the outsider. Roy B. Ward, "Partiality in the Assembly: James 2:2–4," *HTR* 62 (1969): 96–7.

14. See, e.g., Hans Eberhard von Waldow, "Social Responsibility and Social Structure in Early Israel," *CBQ* 32 (1970): 182–204; Rodolfo Obermüller, "¿Contaminación? En torno a una definición de religión (Sant 1,27)," *RevistB* 34 (1972): 13–9; Rodolfo Obermüller, "Hermeneutische Themen im Jakobusbrief," *Bib* 53 (1972): 234–44; Rodolfo Obermüller, "Santiago: La iglesia en minoría," *CuadT* 1.4 (1972): 11–31; Luis Fernando Rivera, "Sobre el socialismo de Santiago (Sant 2,1–13)," *RevistB* 34 (1972): 3–9; Luis Fernando Rivera, "La epístola de Santiago como modelo de halakha cristiana," *CuadT* 1.4 (1972): 32–48; Roberto Sartor Bressan, "Culto y compromiso social según la epístola de Santiago," *RevistB* 34 (1972): 21–32; Albert S. Geyser, "The Letter of James and the Social Condition of His Addressees," *Neot* 9 (1975): 25–33.

15. Following Dibelius, Adamson thinks that in NT times "the social problem had become a religious issue." As a result, "poverty and piety, wealth and wickedness ha[d] become almost synonymous." In the same vein, James's readers "were apparently drawn from the 'poor,' whose affinities were with the an*awim.*" James B. Adamson, *The Epistle of James*, NICNT (Grand Rapids, Mich.: Eerdmans, 1976), 29.

16. Ibid.

17. Ibid., 29–31.

he expands his ideas by connecting James's epistle with its socioeconomic background. He associates the rich with specific first-century Palestinian Jewish groups: farmers, traders and merchants, and financiers.[18] He points out: "James never regards wealth as a sign of God's favor."[19] Other scholars see those categories exclusively as socioeconomic terms. In his commentary, D. Edmond Hiebert understands "poor" as Christian poor, and "rich" similarly to Lenski's view.[20] Francis X. Kelly writes a dissertation on this topic, in which he criticizes Dibelius's concept of *Armenfrömmigkeit*. He makes the case that the poor in the epistle are economically poor and rejects Dibelius's idea that in James, "poor" and "Christian" are coincidental terms.[21]

During the 1980s, the topic developed with force. It is hard to summarize all the ideas regarding poor and rich. The works of four scholars are still very influential: Peter Davids, Ralph Martin, Pedrito Maynard-Reid, and Elsa Tamez. Their work is not limited to this decade. In particular, Davids, Maynard-Reid, and Tamez contributed to the discussion in the following decades as well.

Peter Davids published his commentary on James in 1982. He continued some ideas on poverty and wealth previously presented in his studies on Luke.[22] He applies the same concept of "pious poor" to explain the issue of poverty and wealth in his influential commentary.[23] Although he recognizes that "the major pressure upon the community [of James] is economic pressure," the term "poor" is "virtually identical in his [James's] mind with

18. James B. Adamson, *James: The Man and His Message* (Grand Rapids, Mich.: Eerdmans, 1989), 228–58. For him, "the term 'poor' had acquired a peculiar meaning by NT times; and that is the meaning that James employs, signifying not merely a social, economic, or material condition but also a certain religious temper." Ibid., 256.

19. Ibid., 237.

20. For Hiebert, "the poor" refers to financially poor Christian. "The rich" indicates economical rich Jewish Christians (1:9–11, 4:13–17), and Christ-rejecting Jews (2:7; 5:1–6). D. Edmond Hiebert, "Unifying Theme of the Epistle of James," *BibSac* 135 (1978): 229; D. Edmond Hiebert, *James* (Chicago: Moody Press, 1979), 93, 159–61, 282–94.

21. Kelly centers his investigation on Jas 1:9–12, 2:1–9, and 4:13–5:13, and analyzes literature from the OT, Second Temple period, the NT, and early Christianity. Francis X. Kelly, "Poor and Rich in the Epistle of James" (Ph.D. diss., Temple University, 1973), v-vi. In the same vein, several articles published in Spanish reinforce the idea of socioeconomic concerns in James's epistle: Obermüller, "¿Contaminación?," 13–9; Obermüller, "La iglesia en minoría," 11–31; Rivera, "Sant 2, 1–13," 3–9; Sartor Bressan, "Culto y compromiso social," 21–32.

22. In his article on the issue in Luke, Davids draws the conclusion, among others, that Luke's focus on the poor as primary recipients of the Gospel "partly reflects the historic actuality of the results of the preaching of Jesus and his followers, and it is partly a development of the Old Testament tradition of the pious poor." Peter H. Davids, "The Poor Man's Gospel," *Them* 1 (1976): 40.

23. Davids introduces the theme in his introduction with the title "Poverty-Piety." Peter H. Davids, *The Epistle of James: A Commentary on the Greek Text*, NIGTC (Grand Rapids, Mich.: Eerdmans, 1982), 42.

'Christian,' probably due to the community's circumstances and the traditional piety-poverty link."[24] In this way, Davids follows the path of Dibelius. The same is true regarding the rich. For him, οἱ πλούσιοι are "the wealthy persecutors of the church." This group does not include some wealthy Christians present in the community.[25]

Davids's thoughts regarding wealth and poverty in James have gradually changed in recent years. In his essay "Palestinian Traditions in the Epistle of James," he still understands James's community as "the poor" and the outsiders as "the rich."[26] In his essay "James's Message: The Literary Record," he points out two possible sources of the references to the poor and the rich in the letter. One could be the literary world of James, which is "modeled on scriptural oppression of the poor by the rich," and the other, an external historical phenomenon, concrete experiences of the addressees.[27] A clear change is observed in his essay "The Test of Wealth,"[28] where he compares James's and Paul's approaches to the issue of wealth, discussing their thoughts on charity, poverty and its blessing, and the rich and their position. He perceives a call to charity throughout James's epistle, especially in 2:14–26. In this essay, Davids does not link the poor to the *Armenfrömmigkeit*. Rather, he points out that James does not romanticize the poor, and that in his community there are poor people. In the epistle, it also "appears that the believers are pictured as at least identifying with the poor and perhaps as themselves being the oppressed poor. These poor are the righteous, believers, those waiting for the coming of the Lord, those about to receive a far different outcome than 'the rich.'"[29] The rich parallel the role of the wicked in the OT. For that reason he concludes: "James consistently describes the wealthier people within the Christian community negatively, while 'the rich' (outside the community) are roundly condemned."[30] In his last writing on James's theology, Davids clearly presents the poor and the rich as financial

24. Ibid., 45. When analyzing Jas 1:12, 2:5, and 5:7, Davids concludes: "[E]ach passage identifies the community with the poor and oppressed group."

25. Ibid., 46.

26. Peter H. Davids, "Palestinian Traditions in the Epistle of James," in *James the Just and Christian Origins*, ed. Bruce Chilton and Craig A. Evans, SupNovT 98 (Leiden: Brill, 1999), 33–57.

27. Peter H. Davids, "James's Message: The Literary Record," in *The Brother of Jesus: James the Just and His Mission*, ed. Bruce Chilton and Jacob Neusner (Louisville: Westminster John Knox, 2001), 66–87.

28. Davids, "The Test of Wealth," 355–84.

29. Ibid., 373. Davids points out that one source of suffering in the epistle is the oppression the poor experience. Peter H. Davids, "Why Do We Suffer? Suffering in James and Paul," in *Missions of James, Peter, and Paul*, ed. Bruce Chilton and Craig A. Evans, SupNovT 115 (Leiden: Brill, 2005), 437–8. Davids develops a similar argument regarding the rich in F. F. Bruce et al., *Hard Sayings of the Bible* (Downers Grove, Ill.: InterVarsity Press, 1996), 701–3.

30. Davids, "The Test of Wealth," 379. In this sense, for him, the rich depicted in Jas 4:13–17 and even in 2:1–6, are Christian. Davids, *James*, 46.

categories. For him, James confronts two worldviews, one from God's eschatological perspective and the other from the world's standards.[31]

In his commentary, Ralph Martin follows a path similar to Dibelius's *Armenfrömmigkeit,* but in more financial terms. He thinks the situation of the poor and the rich in the letter fits well with the economic and social background of Palestine prior to James's death in A.D. 62.[32] The book of James presents different classes of poor: "those who were disadvantaged and neglected through no fault of their own, widows and fatherless; those who were economically victimized, workers whose sad state was due to their employers' greed and indifference; and those who were reduced to dire straits of poverty and wretchedness, perhaps because they had no legal rights."[33]

In his opinion, each of these classes of poor has trusted in God for help. As a result, they represent a type of poor in spirit, or the pious ones, although he calls only the last category "the afflicted of the Lord, the *'anawim*."[34] Regarding the rich, he considers that the term οἱ πλούσιοι refers to non-Christian wealthy people, including those mentioned in James 4:13–17.[35]

Pedrito Maynard-Reid has contributed to the topic by introducing sociological analysis of the epistle's background.[36] He situates James and his readers over against the Greco-Roman social stratification. For him, "[t]o separate the economical poor and oppressed from the pious in James's community seems to be wrong." However, he is clear that James's emphasis

31. Peter H. Davids, *A Theology of James, Peter, and Jude: Living in the Light of the Coming King*, BTNT 6 (Grand Rapids, Mich.: Zondervan, 2014).

32. Ralph P. Martin, *James*, WBC 48 (Waco, Tex.: Word Books, 1988), lxxxiv.

33. Ibid., lxxxv.

34. Ibid.

35. Martin refers to them as godless merchants and wealthy and oppressing farmers, and links them with the Sadducees. He, however, is open to consider those mentioned in 4:13–17 as Christians. In any case, the decision does not greatly affect his exegesis. Martin, *James*, ciii, 25–6, 162, 5. Carlton Winbery offers a similar view on the rich, although he considers those mentioned in Jas 1:10–11 as Christians. Carlton L. Winbery, "The Attitude toward Wealth in the Letter of James," *ThEd* 34 (1986): 26–34.

36. Maynard-Reid's book was based on his dissertation. His work was the first of three dissertations written on this topic in the early eighties in North America. The other two: Charlie W. Boggan, "Wealth in the Epistle of James" (Ph.D. diss., The Southern Baptist Theological Seminary, 1982); Cain Hope Felder, "Wisdom, Law, and Social Concern in the Epistle of James" (Ph.D. diss., Columbia University, 1982). Charlie Boggan focuses on wealth in the OT, Second Temple literature, and early Christianity. He studies the concept of πτωχός, and contrary to Dibelius, makes the case that this term is not used in the NT as a technical one to refer to Christians. He applies these results to the study of Jas 5:1–6, 1:9–11, and 2:1–13. For him, early Christianity was a middle-class movement. In light of 5:1–6, Christians are accumulating riches. James corrects this situation, pointing out the temporary nature of wealth (1:9–11), and the need for solidarity with the poor (2:1–13). Cain Felder's main foci are wisdom and Law as leitmotifs in the epistle. He dedicates a few pages to analyzing and discussing James's social concerns present in 5:1–6. He depicts the rich as forming part of James's addressees.

is on the social aspect.[37] For Maynard-Reid, the economically rich are not part of James's community. Christian or non-Christian, "all rich fall in the same category."[38]

Elsa Tamez wrote *Santiago: Lectura latinoamericana de la epístola* in 1985. It was translated into English in 1992 and revised in 2002 under the title *The Scandalous Message of James: Faith without Works Is Dead*. She develops her reading of the epistle from three angles: oppression-suffering, hope, and praxis.[39] For her, "in James the relationship is clear among poverty, oppression, exploitation, and violence."[40] In the letter, the oppressed were the laborers, the poor, the widows and orphans, women, "many of whom ... belonged to Christian communities."[41] On the other hand, the oppressors were the rich. "The rich ... in the letter do not belong to the Christian community, or at least the author does not think they should belong to it."[42]

She expands her ideas in recent publications. In her article "I Timothy and James on the Rich, Women, and Theological Disputes," Tamez contrasts and compares the situation of these two letters. In her opinion, both letters disapprove "of the presence of rich people in the community."[43] In her book *No discriminen a los pobres: Lectura latinoamericana de la carta de Santiago* (2008), Tamez summarizes the ideas of her *The Scandalous Message* and comments on the letter of James section by section, focusing on the oppressed.[44] Finally, in her article "James: A Circular Letter for Immigrants" (2011) she rereads the letter from the perspective of migration, from the point of view of believers

37. Pedrito U. Maynard-Reid, *Poverty and Wealth in James* (Eugene, Ore.: Wipf & Stock, 1987, 2004), 40–1. François Vouga follows a similar approach in *L'épître de saint Jacques*, CNT XIIIa (Geneva: Labor et Fides, 1984), 25–6. Robert Williams studies the topic and centers on the ethical dimension of poverty in the letter. His reconstruction of the *Sitz im Leben* is similar to Martin's reconstruction above. Robert Lee Williams, "Piety and Poverty in James," *WTJ* 22 (1987): 37–55.

38. Maynard-Reid, *Poverty and Wealth*, 44. Maynard-Reid's commentary on James follows these same distinctions. Pedrito U. Maynard-Reid, *James: True Religion in Suffering*, ALBA (Boise: Pacific, 1996), 56–62.

39. Elsa Tamez, *The Scandalous Message of James: Faith without Works Is Dead*, rev. ed. (New York: Crossroad, 2002), 11.

40. Ibid., 15.

41. Ibid., 18.

42. Ibid., 25. Tamez presents a similar idea in Elsa Tamez, "Elementos que iluminan el camino de la comunidad cristiana: Un ejercicio hermenéutico de la carta de Santiago," *RIBLA* 1 (1988): 61.

43. The reason, Tamez says, is that "in 1 Timothy, ... they [the rich] try to take over the community through their influence and power and sympathize with outside ideas; in James it is because there is no room in the community for them." The difference between the two letters is that in 1 Timothy the presence of the rich in the community is considered inevitable, and the author advises them. On the contrary, James "rejects any overbearing presence of rich people." Elsa Tamez, "I Timothy and James on the Rich, Women, and Theological Disputes," *Conc* 1 (2002): 53.

44. Elsa Tamez, *No discriminen a los pobres: Lectura latinoamericana de la carta de Santiago* (Estella: Verbo Divino, 2008).

in the dispersion. She analyzes the problems of patronage, discrimination, and oppression, considering James's addressees as immigrants. For example, she points out: "The Christian communities to which James wrote were conforming to prevailing norms of Roman society. What is surprising is not the attitude immigrants adopted toward the wealthy or their discrimination against the poor ([Jas] 2:19), but the letter's radical critique of those foreign values."[45]

The decade of the 1990s is prolific on the topic of poverty and wealth in James. In one way or another, a number of papers, essays, dissertations, monographs, and commentaries include a section on poverty and riches in James.[46] Some of the most significant contributors were Luke Timothy Johnson, Hubert Frankemölle, Wesley Wachob, and Patrick Hartin.

45. Elsa Tamez, "James: A Circular Letter for Immigrants," *RevExp* 108 (2011): 373.

46. Some of them in chronological order are Justo L. González, *Faith and Wealth: A History of Early Christian Ideas on the Origin, Significance, and Use of Money* (San Francisco: Harper Collins, 1990); George M. Stulac, "Who Are 'the Rich' in James?," *Presb* 16.2 (1990): 89–102; Robert W. Wall, "James as Apocalyptic Paraenesis," *ResQ* 32 (1990): 11–22; John Hall Elliott, "The Epistle of James in Rhetorical and Social Scientific Perspective: Holiness-Wholeness and Patterns of Replication," *BTB* 23 (1993): 71–81; Patrick J. Hartin, "'Come Now, You Rich, Weep and Wail…' (James 5:1–6)," *JTSA* 84 (1993): 57–63; Wesley Hiram Wachob, "'The Rich in Faith' and 'the Poor in Spirit': The Socio-Rhetorical Function of a Saying of Jesus in the Epistle of James" (Ph.D. diss., Emory University, 1993); Duane F. Watson, "James 2 in Light of Greco-Roman Schemes of Argumentation," *NTS* 39 (1993): 94–121; Pablo Nogueira, "O grito do salário: Conflito no mundo do trabalho en Tiago 4,13–5,6," *EB* 44 (1994): 77–86; Charles Frank Ziglar, "The Social Orientation of the Implied Community in James" (Ph.D. diss., The Southern Baptist Theological Seminary, 1994); Matthias Ahrens, *Der Realitäten Widerschein oder Arm und Reich im Jakobusbrief: Eine sozialgeschichtliche Untersuchung*, AH (Berlin: Alektor-Verlag, 1995); Luke Timothy Johnson, "The Social World of James: Literary Analysis and Historical Reconstruction," in *Social World of the First Christians: Essays in Honor of Wayne A. Meeks*, ed. L. Michael White and O. Larry Yarbrough (Minneapolis: Fortress, 1995), 178–97; Lauri Thurén, "Risky Rhetoric in James?," *NovT* 37 (1995): 262–84; Nancy J. Vyhmeister, "The Rich Man in James 2: Does Ancient Patronage Illumine the Text?," *AUSS* 33 (1995): 265–83; Siow-Heng Ong, *A Strategy for a Metaphorical Reading of the Epistle of James* (Lanham, Md.: University Press of America, 1996); Robert Davidson, "The Imagery of Isaiah 40:6–8 in Tradition and Interpretation," in *Quest for Context and Meaning: Studies in Biblical Intertextuality in Honor of James A. Sanders*, ed. Craig A. Evans and Shemaryahu Talmon (Leiden: Brill, 1997), 37–55; José Adriano Filho, "El pobre y el rico en Santiago y en el Pastor de Hermas," *RIBLA* 31 (1998): 144–58; Matthias Konradt, *Christliche Existenz nach dem Jakobusbrief: Eine Studie zu seiner soteriologischen und ethischen Konzeption*, SUNT (Gottingen: Vandenhoeck & Ruprecht, 1998); Pedro Lima Vasconcellos, "Los pobres y el reino: Santiago y la recreación de las sentencias de Jesús," *RIBLA* 31 (1998): 136–43; Nestor Míguez, "Ricos y pobres: Relaciones clientelares en la carta de Santiago," *RIBLA* 31 (1998): 86–98; Pablo Nogueira, "La dignidad del pobre en una sinagoga cristiana de la diáspora: Un ejemplo de seguimiento de la Torá en el cristianismo primitivo," *RIBLA* 31 (1998): 99–109; Frank Pimentel, "Codicia, resistencia y proyecto alternativo: Un acercamiento socio-lingüístico y actualizante a la carta de Santiago," *RIBLA* 31 (1998): 68–85; Patrick A. Tiller, "The Rich and Poor in James: An Apocalyptic Proclamation," in *SBL Seminar Papers*, ed. David J. Lull, SBLSP 37 (Atlanta: Scholars, 1998), 909–20; Alicia J. Batten, "An Asceticism of Resistance in James," in *Asceticism and the New Testament* (New York: Routledge, 1999), 355–70; Craig L. Blomberg, *Neither Poverty*

Luke Timothy Johnson has significantly contributed to James studies.[47] In his commentary (1995), he deals with the issue of poverty and wealth.[48] He analyzes the different perspectives on the identity of the rich in James and concludes that it is more probable that the rich are people outside the community, part of the "rich oppressors" attacked in 5:1–6.[49] The economically poor are part of the Christian community, but the congregation as a whole is a marginalized community that has suffered from the acts of favoritism "by which the wheels of the world are greased."[50]

On his part, in his commentary, Hubert Frankemölle suggests caution in directly linking the social stratification in the letter and the real audience. He presents three layers of readers: the poor, the more or less fortunate in the community, and the rich.[51] Throughout the letter, he points out, James's sharpest attacks are directed against the third group because it lacks Christian brotherhood.[52] James also criticizes the middle group for their lack of solidarity. In this sense, he differs from Sirach and other wisdom literature.

Nor Riches: A Biblical Theology of Material Possessions, NSBT (Grand Rapids, Mich.: Eerdmans, 1999), 148–60; John S. Kloppenborg, "Patronage Avoidance in James," *HTS* 55 (1999): 755–94.

47. Among Johnson's works are Luke Timothy Johnson, *The Literary Function of Possessions in Luke-Acts*, SBLDS 39 (Missoula, Mont.: Scholars Press, 1977); "The Use of Leviticus 19 in the Letter of James," *JBL* 101 (1982): 391–401; "James 3:13–4:10 and the Topos ΠΕΡΙ ΦΘΟΝΟΥ," *NovT* 25 (1983): 327–47; "The Mirror of Remembrance (James 1:22–25)," *CBQ* 50 (1988): 632–45; "The Social World of James," 178–97; *The Letter of James: A New Translation with Introduction and Commentary*, AB 37A (New Haven: Yale University Press, 1995); *The Writings of the New Testament: An Interpretation, Revised Edition* (Minneapolis: Fortress, 1999); "An Introduction to the Letter of James," *RevExp* 97 (2000): 155–67; *Brother of Jesus, Friend of God: Studies in the Letter of James* (Grand Rapids, Mich.: Eerdmans, 2004); "Making Connections: The Material Expression of Friendship in the New Testament," *Int* 58 (2004): 158–71; *Among the Gentiles: Greco-Roman Religion and Christianity*, AYBRL (New Haven: Yale University Press, 2009); *Sharing Possessions: What Faith Demands*, 2nd ed. (Grand Rapids, Mich.: Eerdmans, 2011).

48. In an article published the same year, analyzing the social world of James, Johnson concludes: "James is not simply a compendium of wisdom themes or a free-floating piece of parenesis, but a vivid exhortation that emerges from and addresses real human beings in specific social settings. Everything in the letter and everything lacking from the letter help confirm the impression that this social world was that shared by a leader of the Jerusalem church and Jewish messianists of the diaspora during the first decades of the Christian movement." Johnson, "Social World of James," 196–7.

49. Johnson, *James*, 190–1.

50. Ibid., 229.

51. Hubert Frankemölle, *Der Brief des Jakobus, Kapitel 1*, GTB 517 (Gütersloh: Echter, 1994), 253–4. Dale Allison follows the same stratification with minor differences. Dale C. Allison, *A Critical and Exegetical Commentary on the Epistle of James*, ICC (New York: Bloomsbury, 2013), 46.

52. Frankemölle, *Der Brief des Jakobus*, 254. Ahrens presents a similar approach to the issue. He criticizes Dibelius's and Mussner's concept of Ar*menfrömmigkeit. He* proposes a socio-historical approach to the topic instead. Ahrens, *Der Realitäten Widerschein*. In the same vein, Manabu Tsuji argues for Christian and non-Christian rich in James's community. Manabu Tsuji, *Glaube zwischen Vollkommenheit und Verweltlichung: Eine Untersuchung zur literarischen Gestalt und zur inhaltlichen Kohärenz des Jakobusbriefes*, WUNT 2 93 (Tübingen: J. C. B. Mohr, 1997), 135–71.

Instead of taking the hortatory or ethical approach of this type of literature, as Frankemölle highlights, James criticizes this group with theological arguments.[53]

Wesley Wachob presented his influential work as a dissertation in 1993, which was published later in 2000.[54] He centers his analysis on James 2:1–13. Although his main contribution is in intertextuality, he sees the social background as essential to the rhetoric of the letter.[55] As he says regarding James 2:1–13, "to get inside the discourse . . . to probe the social implications of the situation it evokes, should provide significant clues both to the social location of its thought and also to its intended social function within its argumentative situation."[56] He follows Dibelius's concept of *Armenfrömmigkeit* to explain the poor and the rich in the epistle, but he slightly differs from Dibelius by affirming that "the poverty of the 'elect poor' cannot be limited to the religious dimension." For him, "the possessions, power/ability, and status of those whom God has chosen are 'poor.'"[57]

Wachob further introduces the concepts of honor, limited good and patron-client relationships in order to explain the rhetoric of the text, and in particular the conflict between poor and rich in James.[58] For him poor and rich are not mere socioeconomic labels but "achieved states." The "poor" are "the elected poor," the Christian community; and the "rich" are the powerful outsiders, who are "aligned with the 'world.'"[59] Like Dibelius and Davids, for him the community includes wealthy people, who are part of the "elect poor."[60]

Patrick Hartin has also contributed to James studies.[61] Regarding the theme of the poor and the rich, he distances himself from Dibelius's

53. Frankemölle, *Der Brief des Jakobus*, 258.

54. Wesley Hiram Wachob, *The Voice of Jesus in the Social Rhetoric of James*, SNTSMS 106 (Cambridge: Cambridge University Press, 2000).

55. Ibid., 154–93. He presents how "the rhetoric of James 2:1–13 exploits the 'beliefs, assumptions and values' of the author, the audience, and the broader culture in an effort to persuade the audience that acts of partiality are incompatible with Jesus' faith." Ibid., 194.

56. Ibid., 155. S. H. Ong follows a slightly different approach. He analyzes the epistle rhetorically under the use of metaphors as instrument of discourse cohesion. He argues that "the major metaphoric concept of trials is crucial for the thematic unity of the epistle. The epistle, from start to end, develops the metaphor that life is a divine trial." Ong, *A Metaphorical Reading*, 5. He explains poor/rich as secondary metaphors under the conceptual metaphor of "life is a divine trial." Ibid., 73. There is an open contrast of pious poor vs. rich impious. Poor refers to economically poor Christians. Rich are economically rich non-Christian. Ibid., 73–92, 106–12. He concludes that the secondary metaphors of poor and rich describe the severity of the trials for the poor and the judgment for the rich. For him, poverty is a form of a test of faith. Ibid., 81–2.

57. Wachob, *The Voice of Jesus*, 83.

58. Ibid., 178–82.

59. Ibid., 152–3.

60. Ibid., 169.

61. Among his discussions of this topic are Hartin, "James 5:1–6," 57–63; "Call to Be Perfect through Suffering (James 1,2–4): The Concept of Perfection in the Epistle of James and the

approach. He sees poor and rich as economic categories. In his article "'Come Now, You Rich, Weep and Wail . . .' (James 5:1–6)," he sees James's addressees as "a community which embraces mainly the poor."[62] To him, the rich are wealthy outsiders, except those addressed in James 1:10–11.[63] In his article "The Poor in the Epistle of James and the Gospel of Thomas," he argues that "the Gospel of Thomas and the Epistle of James reflect traditional sayings that endorse a similar ethos of radical discipleship."[64] He focuses on the topic in light of James's attitude toward "the world." James appeals to his addressees "not to forget the poor, the traditional focus of their concern, and to distance themselves from the evil intentions and actions of the rich."[65] For Hartin, "[w]ealth is that aspect of the world that leads one away from God."[66]

Hartin points out that James uses the relationship between the poor and the rich as a rhetorical instrument to challenge his addressees' tenets. In James 2:1–13, emulating "the Greek rhetorical structure of the perfect argument," he challenges "the accepted values of his world where honour is always given to the rich and powerful."[67] The woes in James 4:13–5:6 warn the community of a worldly attitude toward wealth.[68] "Like the Hebrew prophets of the Old Testament, James's focus is on his own community while he uses the rich outside his community as a foil to communicate his message."[69]

It is hard to decide what to include in the last fifteen years of research on James. Many publications follow some of the approaches on poverty and wealth pointed out above. Two recent contributions from Alicia Batten and Darian Lockett shed new light on this issue.

Sermon on the Mount," *Bib* 77 (1996): 477–92; "The Poor in the Epistle of James and the Gospel of Thomas," *HTS* 53 (1997): 146–62; *James*, SP 14 (Collegeville, Minn.: Liturgical Press, 2003); *James of Jerusalem: Heir to Jesus of Nazareth* (Collegeville, Minn.: Liturgical Press, 2004); "'Who Is Wise and Understanding among You?' (James 3:13): An Analysis of Wisdom, Eschatology, and Apocalypticism in the Letter of James," in *Conflicted Boundaries in Wisdom and Apocalypticism*, ed. Benjamin G. Wright III and Lawrence M. Wills, SBLSymS 35 (Atlanta: Society of Biblical Literature, 2006), 149–68; "The Letter of James: Its Vision, Ethics, and Ethos," in *Identity, Ethics, and Ethos in the New Testament*, ed. J. G. Van der Watt and F. S. Malan, BZNW 141 (Berlin: Walter de Gruyter, 2006), 445–71; *James, First Peter, Jude, Second Peter*, NCBCNT 10 (Collegeville, Minn.: Liturgical Press, 2006); "The Religious Context of the Letter of James," in *Jewish Christianity Reconsidered: Rethinking Ancient Groups and Texts*, ed. Matt Jackson-McCabe (Minneapolis: Fortress, 2007), 203–31, 326–8; "James and the Jesus Tradition: Some Theological Reflections and Implications," in *Catholic Epistles and Apostolic Tradition*, ed. Karl-Wilhelm Niebuhr and Robert W. Wall (Waco: Baylor University Press, 2009), 55–70.

62. Hartin, "James 5:1–6," 58.

63. Ibid., 59. Regarding the identity of his addressees and the rich oppressors, Hartin comments: "If the hearers/readers of this letter are Christian Jews living in Jewish ghettoes, it is quite possible that the rich oppressors are themselves Jewish." Hartin, *James*, 27.

64. Hartin, "The Poor," 146.

65. Ibid., 151.

66. Ibid., 148.

67. Hartin, "The Letter of James," 466.

68. Hartin, "Wisdom and Apocalypticism," 154.

69. Hartin, "The Letter of James," 467.

Alicia Batten has made an important contribution to James studies, particularly with reference to the issue of poverty and wealth.[70] In her article "An Asceticism of Resistance in James," she not only presents an economic understanding of poverty and wealth in James, but also introduces another sociological implication of that tension. She says: "[James] praises and reassures the poor, but he also challenges the scheme of power relations based upon status distinctions."[71] In her view, James builds a new reality "that opposes wealth and patronage and all the accompanying behaviors that assist in the perpetration of such evil."[72] In her article "God in the Letter of James: Patron or Benefactor?" she proposes that James challenges the patronage system and presents God as an ideal benefactor.[73] She deepens this concept in her *Friendship and Benefaction in James*.[74]

In her "Ideological Strategies in James," she summarizes and deepens many of her previous ideas by analyzing James 1:9–11, 2:1–13, and 5:1–6 from the perspective of ideological criticism. She points out that in the letter the categories of poverty and wealth are not only economic but also refer "to the ability to maintain and gain honour and status, as in the case of the rich, or the loss of honour and status, with the poor."[75] It is highly probable that the majority of James's addressees were neither poor nor rich, she says.[76] James's rhetorical strategy, "by casting the rich as the 'other,'" is to "construct... a positive identity and ideology for his audience as the honourable poor who must care for the poor among them."[77] In this sense, "James uses the dishonorable depictions of the rich and their future demise as a contrast to his audience's identity as the honourable poor, who must continue to support one another and withstand the trials of carving out an existence without patronal support."[78]

70. Among her works are Batten, "An Asceticism of Resistance," 355–70; "God in the Letter of James: Patron or Benefactor?," *NTS* 50 (2004): 257–72; "Ideological Strategies in the Letter of James," in *Reading James with New Eyes*, ed. Robert L. Webb and John S. Kloppenborg, LNTS 342 (London: T&T Clark, 2007), 6–26; *What Are They Saying about the Letter of James?* WATSA (New York: Paulist Press, 2009); *Friendship and Benefaction in James*, ESEC 15 (Dorset: Deo, 2010); "The Jesus Tradition and the Letter of James," *RevExp* 108 (2011): 381–90.

71. Batten, "An Asceticism of Resistance," 364.

72. Ibid., 365.

73. Batten, "Patron or Benefactor?," 257–72.

74. Batten, *Friendship and Benefaction in James*. Edgar has a similar socio-scientific approach to patron-client relationships in James. Edgar, *Has God Not Chosen the Poor?*, esp. 95–136, 62–76.

75. Batten, "Ideological Strategies," 14.

76. Ibid., 12.

77. Ibid., 10. For Batten, "James's ideology consists in part... of the notion of an honourable poor.... It is not to suggest that every member of the community to which James writes is of identical social status, but that together as a unity—as 'the poor'—they are honourable in contrast to the rich." Ibid., 24.

78. Ibid., 25.

Darian Lockett addresses the topic of poverty and wealth in James from a socio-rhetorical perspective.[79] Dealing with the social categories of purity and worldview, he considers that the language used in the denunciation of the rich in James 5:1–6 "does not reflect the social-historical character of the audience, rather it is affective rhetoric."[80] In the same vein, James's affective rhetoric evidences that "the primary tension [in the letter] is not between a community and its enemies, but rather the audience's ascribed identity over against the values, attitudes, and actions associated with the dominant culture."[81] For that reason, "[t]hough rich and poor are not entirely empty of social connotation neither are they entirely socio-economic terms. Rather, they are social types exhibiting humility and dependence upon God for salvation in the case of the poor and pride and reliance upon wealth and status in the case of the rich."[82]

For him, it is clear that any conclusion about the identity of the poor and the rich in James is "shaped by the methodology one uses to frame the question."[83] From the perspective of rhetorical analysis, he concludes, "[w]hatever the social identity of the 'rich', the author of James, inprophetic

79. Among Lockett's writings are Darian Lockett, "The Spectrum of Wisdom and Eschatology in the Epistle of James and 4QInstruction," *TynBul* 56 (2005): 131–48; "'Unstained by the World': Purity and Pollution as an Indicator of Cultural Interaction in the Letter of James," in *Reading James with New Eyes*, ed. Robert L. Webb and John S. Kloppenborg, LNTS 342 (London: T&T Clark, 2007), 49–74; "Structure or Communicative Strategy? The 'Two Ways' Motif in James' Theological Instruction," *Neot* 42 (2008): 269–87; *Purity and Worldview in the Epistle of James*, LNTS 366 (London: Clark, 2008); "God and 'the World': Cosmology and Theology in the Letter of James," in *Cosmology and New Testament Theology*, ed. Jonathan T. Pennington and Sean M. McDonough, LNTS 355 (London: T&T Clark, 2008), 144–56; "Strong and Weak Lines: Permeable Boundaries between Church and Culture in the Letter of James," *RevExp* 108 (2011): 391–405; *An Introduction to the Catholic Epistles*, TTCABS (New York: T&T Clark, 2012).

80. Lockett, *Purity and Worldview*, 158. He presents a similar but more condensed argument in Lockett, "Unstained by the World," 49–74.

81. Lockett, *Purity and Worldview*, 166. In similar terms, Batten points out: "James has not only exposed the ancient obsession with honour and wealth as corrupt and contrary to the traditions which his audience presumably shared; he has replaced it by stressing the poor as honourable, and shown how this notion of the honourable poor is the true understanding of the tradition (which include some of Jesus's teachings)." Batten, "Ideological Strategies," 24.

82. Lockett, *Purity and Worldview*, 165. Luke Cheung adopts a similar position. For him, "poor" and "rich" are stereotyped polarities used as rhetorical devices. Luke L. Cheung, *The Genre, Composition, and Hermeneutics of the Epistle of James* (Eugene, Ore.: Wipf & Stock, 2006), 260. For Wachob, these are categories used by the author to contrast the righteous (the pious poor) and the unrighteous (the rich). Wachob, *The Voice of Jesus*, 153. But these categories do not deny the existence of socially poor and wealthy within the Jamesian community. "James's rhetoric opens the door for those with plenty to assume an even more honorable status within the elect community. . . . They are to become the honored patrons of their impoverished community members." Wesley Hiram Wachob, "The Apocalyptic Intertexture of the Epistle of James," in *Intertexture of Apocalyptic Discourse in the New Testament*, ed. Duane F. Watson (Atlanta: Society of Biblical Literature, 2002), 182.

83. Lockett, *Catholic Epistles*, 31. Here, Lockett gives a broad picture of recent nonclassical approaches to James, in particular focusing on socio-rhetorical and postcolonial approaches.

tone, sharply announces judgment on this group and urges the readers to identify with the attitude (and perhaps the socio-economic status) of the 'poor.'"[84]

Some conclusions surface from this survey. It is clear that Dibelius's concept of *Armenfrömmigkeit* has almost been relegated to a secondary plane. Although the religious concept of pious poor seems to be present in the epistle, socioeconomic distinctions are predominant. The letter reflects an implied audience that includes different types of poor. Discussion regarding the rich continues. For some scholars, James's audience includes wealthy Christians. For others, it does not. In any case, the implied audience seems to reflect three groups: the poorest, a middle group (the more or less fortunate), and the rich (present or absent, insiders or outsiders).

More recent approaches to the topic shed new light on the discussion. Sociological approaches to the letter permit analyzing the concept of poverty and wealth from different angles. The dynamics of honor, power relations, patronage, and benefaction in Greco-Roman and Jewish societies contribute to the analysis. New implications and nuances and rhetorical effects of the texts about the poor and the rich enter into the discussion. These diverse tools open a new door to explore how James builds his ethics of poverty and wealth.

The Old Testament in James

The history of the study of the use of the OT in James is significantly different from what is observed above. Although Todd Penner wrote an excellent review of recent work on the OT in James, it lacks a discussion of monographs on the subject prior to 1999.[85] Nevertheless, some works deal with James's use of the OT.[86]

He gives an excursus on "Poor-Rich in James," and also talks about patron-client relations related to that topic. Ibid., 25–40.

84. Ibid., 31. In the same vein, Dale Allison argues that the letter presents three groups: "those who are, in his [the author of the letter's] view, mistreated and suffering, those who mistreat them, and those, belonging to neither of the first groups, whose sympathy he wishes to augment." Allison wonders whether "our author intended 'the poor' to function as a sort of code word for his Christian group." Allison, *James*, 46, 50. René Krüger arrives at similar conclusions using semiotic analysis. René Krüger, *Der Jakobusbrief als prophetische Kritik der Reichen: Eine exegetische Untersuchung aus lateinamerikanischer Perspektive*, BVB 12 (Münster: Lit, 2005).

85. Penner, "The Epistle of James in Current Research," 257–308. Anthony Hanson and Wiard Popkes have noticed the same phenomenon. Anthony T. Hanson, *The Living Utterances of God: The New Testament Exegesis of the Old* (Darton: Darton, Longman and Todd, 1983), 146; Wiard Popkes, "James and Scripture: An Exercise in Intertextuality," *NTS* 45 (1999): 214–5.

86. Commentaries usually deal with the OT, but mainly from author-oriented approaches and following historical-critical methods. Some others are more concerned with readers, for

Commentaries usually deal with OT passages related to James's epistle. Joseph Mayor's commentary is still a reference in this regard. He dedicates a chapter to the relation of the epistle to earlier writers, including the canonical books of the OT.[87] Dibelius deals with some OT passages in his commentary, and in a few cases he considers the rhetorical use of them.[88] In the introduction to his commentary, Johnson includes a brief summary of the topic, focusing on the Law, Prophecy, and wisdom literature.[89] He is most concerned with James and Law, in particular Leviticus 19.[90] In this regard, he points out: "Like all NT writings, James can be regarded as a reinterpretation of the symbolic world of Torah in light of the confession of Jesus as Messiah and Lord."[91]

Some works focus on particular passages or topics, mainly from an author-centered perspective.[92] Davids analyzes the four OT characters mentioned

example, Johnson and Scot McKnight, who do not consider the rhetorical effect of the OT in the letter. Johnson, *James*; Scot McKnight, *The Letter of James*, NICNT (Grand Rapids, Mich.: Eerdmans, 2011). In the case of Witherington, although he focuses on rhetorical issues, he does not consider the rhetorical effects of the use of the OT in the letter of James. Ben Witherington III, *Letters and Homilies for Jewish Christians: A Socio-Rhetorical Commentary on Hebrews, James, and Jude* (Downers Grove, Ill.: IVP Academic, 2007), 383–555.

87. Mayor sees links between Jas and Gen, Exod, Lev, Num, Deut, Josh, 1 Kgs, Pss, Prov, Eccl, Isa, Jer, Ezek, Hos, Joel, Amos, Jonah, Micah, Zech, and Mal. Nevertheless, he does not analyze James's use of them. Joseph B. Mayor, *The Epistle of St. James: The Greek Text with Introduction, Notes, and Comments*, 2nd ed. (London: Macmillan, 1897), lxix-lxxxiii. David Jones presents a similar list. David A. Jones, *Old Testament Quotations and Allusions in the New Testament* (Bellingham, Wash.: Logos Research Systems, 2009), Logos edition (not available in hard copy). Anthony Hanson writes the report of a working group that deals with chapters 1–3. They find use of the OT in only nine passages (1:2–8, 8, 9–11, 13–14, 25; 2:1–13, 25; 3:6–8, 17–18). The report sheds light on the possible presence of midrashic use of Pss and Isa. It, nevertheless, is extremely succinct and does not deal with how James uses the OT in his discourse. Anthony T. Hanson, "Seminar Report: Report on Working Group on 'The Use of the Old Testament in the Epistle of James,' Tübingen, 1977; Châtenay-M, 1978," *NTS* 25 (1979): 526–7.

88. For example, he discusses the use of Isa 40:6–8 in Jas 1:10–11, Lev 19:18 in 2:8–11, Abraham and Rahab in 2:20–26, and Prov 3:34 in 4:6. Dibelius, *James*, 86–7, 160–74, 225.

89. Johnson, *James*, 29–34. In his dissertation, Cain Felder also explores wisdom and Law in James. He sees several parallels with OT wisdom literature, in particular with Ben Sirach. He argues that wisdom and Law are leitmotifs in the epistle, and both "bear upon James's social concern." Felder, "Wisdom, Law, and Social Concern in the Epistle of James," 162. See also Cain Hope Felder, "Partiality and God's Law: An Exegesis of James 2:1–13," *JRT* 39.2 (1983): 51–69. Frankemölle also sees links between Ben Sirach and James. Hubert Frankemölle, "Zum Thema des Jakobusbriefes im Kontext der Rezeption von Sir 2,1–18 und 15,11–20," *BN* 48 (1989): 21–49.

90. For him, Lev 19 is not only evoked/quoted, but also is the background for the entire letter. See Johnson, *James*, 30–1; Johnson, "The Use of Leviticus 19 in the Letter of James," 391–401.

91. Johnson, *James*, 29. Later in his commentary, Johnson deals with the use of the OT in some passages, but he mainly focuses on identifying OT sources or parallel themes.

92. In an author-centered approach, "any significant verbal parallel is counted as an OT citation." Christopher R. Bruno, "Readers, Authors, and the Divine Author: An Evangelical Proposal for Identifying Paul's Old Testament Citations," *WTJ* 71 (2009): 313. In the same vein,

in the epistle. He concludes that James uses canonical and extracanonical sources when citing OT characters and events. As a corollary, the author of the epistle "needs the readers to supply the traditional embellishments of the biblical account to fully understand the passage."[93] Esther Yue Ng argues that James builds his Father-God language on the OT (in particular on Gen 9; Pss 68, 136; Jer 3).[94] John J. Schmitt studies a possible OT background of James 4:4.[95] Karen Jobes describes and analyzes the presence of the Minor Prophets in James.[96] Mariam Kamell makes a strong case that Jeremiah 31:27–34 is not only alluded to in James 1:18, 21, but also is the background for James's soteriology; it helps to understand more deeply James's use of

---

Popkes adds that a study of the OT in James "should not only list (possible) cross-connections but also ask further questions about the media of transmission and about the needs and intentions at the receiving end." Popkes, "James and Scripture," 215.

93. Peter H. Davids, "Tradition and Citation in the Epistle of James," in *Scripture, Tradition, and Interpretation: Essays Presented to Everett F. Harrison by His Students and Colleagues in Honor of His Seventy-Fifth Birthday*, ed. W. Ward Gasque and William Sanford LaSor (Grand Rapids, Mich.: Eerdmans, 1978), 121. Richard Bauckham argues that James uses these characters as ethical and religious paradigms. Richard Bauckham, "James, 1 and 2 Peter, Jude," in *It Is Written: Scripture Citing Scripture*, ed. D. A. Carson and H. G. M. Williamson (Cambridge: Cambridge University Press, 1988), 306–8. Other scholars focus on specific characters. See, e.g., J. Byron, "Living in the Shadow of Cain: Echoes of a Developing Tradition in James 5:1–6," *NovT* 48 (2006): 261–74; Ronald Charles, "Rahab: A Righteous Whore in James," *Neot* 45 (2011): 206–20; Beate Ego, "Abraham's Faith in the One God: A Motif of the Image of Abraham in Early Jewish Literature," in *Biblical Figures in Deuterocanonical and Cognate Literature*, ed. H. Lichtenberger and U. Mittmann-Richert, DCL (Berlin: de Gruyter, 2009), 337–54; Anthony T. Hanson, "Rahab the Harlot in Early Christian Tradition," *JSNT* 1 (1978): 53–60; Irving Jacobs, "Midrashic Background for James 2:21–3," *NTS* 22 (1976): 457–64; Richard N. Longenecker, "'Faith of Abraham' Theme in Paul, James, and Hebrews: A Study in the Circumstantial Nature of New Testament Teaching," *JETS* 20 (1977): 203–12; David Marcus, "Prolepsis in the Story of Rahab and the Spies (Joshua 2)," in *Bringing the Hidden to Light: Essays in Honor of Stephen A. Geller*, ed. Kathryn F. Kravitz and Diane M. Sharon (Winona Lake, Ind.: Eisenbrauns, 2007), 149–62; Aquiles Ernesto Martínez, "Imágenes feministas en Santiago: Óptica de género y destellos de liberación," *Apuntes* 18.3 (1998): 67–79; Kurt A. Richardson, "Job as Exemplar in the Epistle of James," in *Hearing the Old Testament in the New Testament*, ed. Stanley E. Porter (Grand Rapids, Mich.: Eerdmans, 2006), 213–29; Robert W. Wall, "The Intertextuality of Scripture: The Example of Rahab (James 2:25)," in *Bible at Qumran: Text, Shape, and Interpretation*, ed. Peter W. Flint, SDSSRL (Grand Rapids, Mich.: Eerdmans, 2001), 217–36; Roy Bowen Ward, "Works of Abraham: James 2:14–26," *HTR* 61 (1968): 283–90.

94. Esther Yue L. Ng, "Father-God Language and Old Testament Allusions in James," *TynBul* 54 (2003): 41–54.

95. John J. Schmitt, "You Adulteresses! The Image in James 4:4," *NovT* 28 (1986): 327–37.

96. Although the tone of the epistle is frequently associated with the Minor Prophets, in particular with Hosea, Amos, and Malachi, Jobes does not manage to convincingly demonstrate any strong connection. Karen H. Jobes, "The Minor Prophets in James, 1 & 2 Peter, and Jude," in *Minor Prophets in the New Testament*, ed. Maarten J. J. Menken and Steve Moyise, LNTS 377 (London: T&T Clark, 2009), 135–53.

the concepts of λόγος and νόμος.[97] For Wiard Popkes, James uses the OT indirectly as a secondary source.[98]

In his book, Robert Wall partially considers the rhetoric of the OT in James's discourse.[99] He considers that the author of James undertakes a midrashic reading of the OT. For him, the primary indicator of this biblical midrash is "a text's 'intertextuality,' when the reader of a biblical text recognizes its citation, allusion, or echo of another, earlier biblical text which then completes and commends its meaning."[100] The purpose of this intertextuality, for him, is "to construct a fuller biblical context within which the strong interpreter reflects upon the theological meaning of the passage under analysis."[101] For that reason, he concludes: "I have come to read James as the literary product of an author whose 'canon consciousness' first elevates the status of his Bible as the central symbol of his religious life and then routinely appeals to it, sometimes in subtle ways, to justify the moral authority of what he advises his readership to be and do."[102]

Dale Allison makes an important contribution to this discussion in his *ICC* commentary.[103] For him, the letter gives the impression that James

97. Mariam J. Kamell, "The Soteriology of James in Light of Earlier Jewish Wisdom Literature and the Gospel of Matthew" (Ph.D. diss., University of Saint Andrews, 2010), 134–46; Mariam J. Kamell, "Incarnating Jeremiah's Promised New Covenant in the 'Law' of James," *EvQ* 83 (2011): 19–28. Kamell's position convincingly contradicts Matt Jackson-McCabe's idea that logos and law in James come from Greek wisdom traditions. See Matt A. Jackson-McCabe, *Logos & Law in the Letter of James: The Law of Nature, the Law of Moses, & the Law of Freedom*, SupNovT (Leiden: Brill, 2001); Jackson-McCabe, "The Law of Freedom (James 1:25): Light from Early Exegesis," *PEGLMBS* 21 (2001): 33–44.

98. Popkes's argument is unconvincing. Without interacting with contrary opinions, he assumes a lack of coherence in the letter; he argues that James uses a kind of *Zettelkasten of* biblical citations and a dependence on Jewish pseudo-epigraphic traditions. Popkes, "James and Scripture," 213–29. When dealing with the use of the OT, he repeats his assumptions in his commentary. Wiard Popkes, *Der Brief des Jakobus*, THKNT 14 (Leipzig: Evangelische Verlagsanstalt, 2001). Allison adds: "The regular appearance of Septuagintalisms [in the letter] stands against positing nothing but a second-hand knowledge of scripture." Allison, *James*, 52 n. 289.

99. Robert W. Wall, *Community of the Wise: The Letter of James*, NTC (Valley Forge, Pa.: Trinity, 1997). Wachob also analyzes the explicit quotations in Jas 2:1–13 and their contribution to James's discourse. Wachob, *The Voice of Jesus*, 98–113. John Schmitt studies the OT image of "adulteresses" in Jas 4:4. Schmitt, "You Adulteresses!," 327–37.

100. Wall, *Community of the Wise*, 21.

101. Ibid.

102. Ibid. Later, in the book, Wall tries to connect OT passages as subtexts of James's discourse. On occasion, he analyzes the theological contribution of OT texts he considers relevant to a passage. For example, when dealing with Jas 1:9–11, he links the passage with Jer 9:23, by pairing them through the topic/ideology of wealth and wisdom. Ibid., 55. However, except for dealing with the explicit OT quotations, his work with specific OT allusions and echoes is scarce. In his paper on Rahab, he analyzes the rhetorical contribution of her mention in James's discourse. Wall, "The Example of Rahab," 217–36. His insights are used later in the present work.

103. Allison argues in his commentary that the author of James uses five sources: the LXX, extracanonical Jewish tradition, popular Hellenistic philosophy, the Jesus tradition, and other

was well versed in the OT, in particular a heard or read version close to the LXX. He points out clear allusions from the Pentateuch, Former Prophets, Latter Prophets, and Psalms and wisdom literature.[104] Like Davids (as mentioned above), Allison also notices that the author assumes his audience's familiarity with the OT.[105] In this regard, he comments: "This circumstance makes it likely that at least some of James's borrowing from the LXX is intended to be noticed; that is, certain lines are designed to function as allusions and so don divine authority."[106] Allison additionally points out that when the author uses phrases such as "the twelve tribes," "the Lord of Sebaoth," "the day of slaughter," and so on, he "tacitly commends himself to those steeped in the Jewish scriptures."[107] This familiarity with the Scriptures would come from memory and not necessarily from written texts. As Allison explains, "[t]he ability to quote texts does not entail their physical presence. It requires only hearing them often enough so that they become memories."[108]

The major work on the use of the OT in James is D. A. Carson's contribution in the *Commentary on the New Testament Use of the Old Testament*.[109] In his work, he deals with the context of the citation, the OT context from which the citation is drawn, the use of the citation in Second Temple literature, and textual factors surrounding James's use of the citation. With this information in mind, he tries to understand James's use of the citation. Finally, he includes theological reflections on James's use of the OT in light of the NT.[110] Although his contribution to the understanding of the passages is very important, in his analysis he does not include the effect on or the response of the audience, nor the rhetorical effect of the citations in

early Christian traditions and texts. His assumption about the use of early Christian traditions and texts is highly debatable though, because it depends on the date of the letter. He dates James to A.D. 100–120. Allison, *James*, 29, 51.

104. Ibid., 51–2. In Allison's perspective, among the texts alluded to or quoted are Gen 1:1, 26–27, 15:6, 22:1–19; Lev 19:15; Isa 5:7–9, 40:6–7; Jer 5:24; Prov 3:34; LXX Wis 2; Ecclus 2.

105. Allison argues: "This is why he can summarize in the briefest manner stories about Abraham (2.22–23), Rahab (2.25), Job (5.11), and Elijah (5.17–18): in each case, a few words should suffice to call to mind a known episode. James says as much in 5.11: 'you have heard of the steadfastness of Job'. In like fashion, our author presumes readers know something about God's gift of the Torah to Moses on Sinai when he writes: 'For the one who said, "Do not commit adultery," also said, "Do not murder"' (2.11). Without such knowledge, the line, with its unspecified ὁ εἰπών, is an enigma." Ibid., 52.

106. In his commentary, Allison deals with the rhetorical implication of some of these allusions; for example, to Isa 40 in Jas 1:9–10. Ibid., 52, 194–9.

107. Ibid., 53.

108. Ibid.

109. D. A. Carson, "James," in *Commentary on the New Testament Use of the Old Testament*, ed. G. K. Beale and D. A. Carson (Grand Rapids, Mich.: Baker, 2007), 997–1013. Hanson does similar but brief work on eight passages of the epistle (1:25; 2:1–8, 21–25; 3:6–8, 18; 4:5–6; 5:11 and 16–18). Hanson, *Living Utterances*, 146–55.

110. Carson almost always follows this pattern. A handful of references are just presented in a more generic discussion, especially those he considers less certain allusions.

the discourse. Carson points out that in general James's source of the OT is the LXX, his handling of themes resembles the wisdom literature of the OT, he "shares vocabulary and concepts with early Jewish literature of the Second Temple period," and his wisdom teaching is close to or echoes Jesus's teachings, in particular the Sermon on the Mount. He concludes from these features: "[O]ne suspects that sometimes James is using biblical categories that have been filtered through the common heritage of the early church's teaching and preaching."[111]

In general terms, the use of the OT in James still remains fertile soil for study. The presence of OT quotations, allusions, echoes, imagery, and other tropes has been recognized. A great percentage of the studies are author-centered. Few works have explored reader-centered analysis. As mentioned above, one of the main topics of the letter is the issue of poverty and wealth. Commentaries and other works mention OT connections with this issue, but almost none of them explores how OT texts contribute to James's rhetoric. This lack of discussion opens a door of opportunity to explore how James uses the OT in those passages that deal with poverty and wealth. In particular, there is an opportunity to explore how James builds his ethics of poverty and wealth. In fact, each time he deals with poverty and wealth, he intertwines the OT and Jesus's teaching with his own discourse.

Author, Addressees, and Date

The letter of James names its author as Ἰάκωβος θεοῦ καὶ κυρίου Ἰησοῦ Χριστοῦ δοῦλος (Jas 1:1). Traditionally, the name Ἰάκωβος refers to James, the Lord's brother. There has been, however, no agreement among scholars in this regard.[112] Dan McCartney presents a summary of the four commonly espoused views regarding authorship of the letter:[113]

1. The letter was written by the historical James prior to the Galatians controversy, and even before the apostolic council in Jerusalem noted in Acts 15, thus probably in the mid- to late 40s.
2. The letter was written by James in response to Paulinism of some sort, specifically correcting the idea that righteousness can be acquired simply by acknowledging certain theological propositions.
3. The letter is pseudonymous, written at the end of the first century or early in the second century by a proponent of Jewish (non-Pauline) Christianity.

111. Carson, "James," 997.

112. Davids groups scholars who support the main views on authorship and date of the letter. See Davids, *James*, 4.

113. Dan G. McCartney, *James*, BECNT (Grand Rapids, Mich.: Baker, 2009), 14.

4. Much of the material of the letter goes back to James, but has been edited and assembled after his death by someone with Greek literary training.

In academic circles, the traditional position, represented by options 1 and 2 above, has recovered strength. The arguments against it have been compellingly refuted.[114] Among the arguments for the traditional view are the following:[115]

1. The letter claims James as its author.
2. The text is thoroughly Jewish in tone and at points seems to reflect acquaintance with Palestine or even Galilee.
3. Our epistle exhibits significant overlaps with the speech attributed to James in Acts 15:13–21 as well as the letter of Acts 15:23–30.
4. Although James displays knowledge of the Jesus tradition, the book shows no familiarity with Matthew, Mark, Luke, or John. This is consistent with an early date.
5. Some have urged that knowledge of the letter was early, well known, and authoritative, as attested by use of it in 1 Clement and Hermas, or even in Paul and 1 Peter.
6. The social and religious circumstances reflected in James mirror the Christian situation in Palestine before 70.
7. The letter's fairly accomplished Greek is no longer an argument against James's authorship.
8. The fact that the author does not refer to himself as the brother of Jesus argues against pseudonymity.
9. The relatively slow acceptance of the letter into the canon of the universal church could be due to its being originally written to a

114. See, e.g., Adamson, *James: The Man and His Message*, 3–52; Johnson, *James*, 89–123; McCartney, *James*, 14–32; McKnight, *James*, 13–38. Allison presents and refutes six arguments supporting James's authorship. Then, he presents and evaluates seven arguments supporting a pseudepigraphal author. He thinks that "although not all of the arguments marshaled to deny authorship by the brother of Jesus have merit, (ii)-(v), taken together, tip the scale." Even having said that, he admits: "One can indeed slot James into pre-70 Palestine if so inclined." Allison, *James*, 3–13. The different arguments in favor of James's authorship taken together also "tip the scale," as McCartney convincingly demonstrates.

115. Allison, *James*, 6–8. As mentioned in the preceding note, Allison presents and evaluates the first six points in favor of James's authorship, although he regards James as pseudepigraphal. His arguments against these six points are not convincing. For points 7 to 9 and a defense and variations of points 1–6, see, e.g., Adamson, *James: The Man and His Message*, 3–52; Johnson, *James*, 89–123; McCartney, *James*, 14–31; McKnight, *James*, 13–33; Douglas J. Moo, *The Letter of James*, PNTC (Grand Rapids, Mich.: Eerdmans, 2000), 9–22. For arguments in favor of pseudonymity, see, e.g., Allison, *James*, 13–32; Dibelius, *James*, 11–21; Frankemölle, *Der Brief des Jakobus*, 45–54; Popkes, *Der Brief des Jakobus*, 64–9; Tsuji, *Glaube*, 38–44.

> minority population, Jewish Christians of eastern Mediterranean regions, in the infancy of Christianity.[116]

This research concludes that James, the Lord's brother, was the author of the letter.[117] However, the date of composition is not clear. Evidence is scarce and inconclusive. Some evidence points to the possibility of a date between the late 40s and the late 50s.[118]

The letter presents the addressees as αἱ δώδεκα φυλαί αἱ ἐν τῇ διασπορᾷ (1:1) and ἀδελφοί μου (1:2). This salutation is used to refer to Jews living outside Palestine (*Ps. Sol.* 9:2). In particular, the expression αἱ δώδεκα φυλαί is a designation for Israel (*Ps. Sol.* 17:26–28; *Syb. Or.* 3:249), or an expression of hope for the eschatological restoration of Israel (1QS 8:1). However, a similar salutation appears in 1 Peter 1:1–2, addressed to Gentile Christians. The identity of the addressees of the letter is closely linked to the question of author and date. If James is the author, and the letter is early, the implied readers would be a mostly Jewish-Christian audience.[119] McCartney convincingly argues

116. Karen H. Jobes, *Letters to the Church: A Survey of Hebrews and the General Epistles* (Grand Rapids, Mich.: Zondervan, 2011), 177.

117. This decision does not affect the conclusions of the present work. Even a pseudepigraphic Jewish-Christian author living in first-century Palestine would have a similar cognitive environment. As shown later, the context accessed in the interpretation process is built on a set of assumptions about the world shared by an author and her addressees. This set of assumptions is called the cognitive environment. See more details below and more broadly in the next chapter. The setting of Palestine at the end of the first century or in the second century suffered strong changes, so if a second-century Jewish-Christian author were in view—as Allison speculates—the set of considered assumptions would be very different from what the book of James seems to reflect. Allison, *James*, 13.

118. Allison presents a good summary of diverse proposed dates found in commentaries and monographs, ranging from the early 40s to the early second century. Ibid., 28–9. Dating the letter is intimately linked to the discussion about authorship. Bruce Wilkinson and Kenneth Boa present a good summary of points in favor of an early date, around A.D. 45: "(1) There is no mention of Gentile Christians or their relationship to Jewish Christians as would be expected in a later epistle. (2) Apart from references to the person of Christ, there is practically no distinctive theology in James, suggesting an early date when Christianity was viewed in terms of Messianic Judaism. (3) The allusions to the teachings of Christ have such little verbal agreement with the synoptic Gospels that they probably preceded them. (4) James uses the word "synagogue" (assembly, 2:2) in addition to "church" and indicates a very simple organization of elders and masters, that is, teachers (3:1; 5:14), which was patterned after the early synagogue. (5) James does not mention the issues involved in the Acts 15 Council in Jerusalem (A.D. 49)." Bruce Wilkinson and Kenneth Boa, *Talk thru the Bible* (Nashville: T. Nelson, 1983).

119. Hartin, *James*, 25–7; McKnight, *James*, 38. Some scholars make the case for a more specific audience but with unconvincing arguments. See, e.g., Dale C. Allison, Jr., "The Fiction of James and Its *Sitz im Leben*," *RB* 108 (2001): 529–70; Edgar, *Has God Not Chosen the Poor?* 95–136; Geyser, "Social Condition," 25–33; Martin, *James*, lxxviii. For scholars who see the letter as pseudepigraphal tend to understand the audience as Gentiles; see, e.g., Dibelius, *James*, 21–34; Popkes, *Der Brief des Jakobus*, 16–26; Vouga, *L'épître de saint Jacques*, 24–6. Allison, on his

it is highly probable that this Jewish-Christian audience included a fraction of Gentiles.[120] If the letter is early, Christians would have been mainly Jews, but almost from the beginning there were Gentiles in the church, mainly "God-fearers." In Acts 15, the "tent of David" includes Gentiles; probably, so does James's audience.[121]

The location of the addressees is less clear than their identity. In the first century, the concept of διάσπορα is used literally to describe Jewish communities outside Palestine and metaphorically to describe the idea of still living in exile even in Palestine itself.[122] So, following Scot McKnight's caution, "[i]t is . . . reasonable to think the letter was sent from Jerusalem to a number of churches/synagogues of messianic Jews in the Diaspora and that any more specific setting outstrips the evidence."[123]

Passages to Consider

This work focuses on passages dealing with poverty and wealth in James. Scholars do not agree about what passages to include. As mentioned in note 2 above, Davids counts 47 verses of 105: 1:9–11, 27; 2:1–13, 14–26; 4:2, 13–17; 5:1–6; and 7–11.[124] Other scholars have different lists. For example, McKnight

---

part, considers the audience to be a group of mainly non-Christian Jews. Allison, "The Fiction of James," 529–70; *Allison, James*, 32–50.

120. McCartney, *James*, 32–6. As mentioned in the preceding note, Allison includes non-Christian Jews among the addressees.

121. McCartney also asserts: "[T]he presence of Gentile converts may also have opened the door for the pagan disconnection between religion and ethics to have crept into the church even before Paul's mission, and thus there is no need to suppose a form of 'Paulinism' as the background for James 2." In any case, the presence of Gentiles "does not call into question the 'Jewish' flavor of James." Ibid., 36.

122. See, e.g., 1QS 8:12–14, 1QM 1:2–3, 4Q372 1, Jub. 1:7–18. For the study of this and other evidence, see Martin G. Abegg, "Exile and the Dead Sea Scrolls," in *Exile: Old Testament, Jewish, and Christian Conceptions*, ed. James M. Scott (Leiden: Brill, 1997), 111–25; James M. Scott, "Exile and the Self-Understanding of Diaspora Jews in the Greco-Roman Period," in *Exile: Old Testament, Jewish, and Christian Conceptions*, ed. James M. Scott (Leiden: Brill, 1997), 173–218; James C. VanderKam, "Exile in Jewish Apocalyptic Literature," ibid., 89–109. See also Douglas S. McComiskey, "Exile and Restoration from Exile in the Scriptural Quotations and Allusions of Jesus," *JETS* 53 (2010): 673–96; N. T. Wright, *The New Testament and the People of God* (London: SPCK, 1992), 268–70.

123. McKnight, *James*, 38. Some scholars point to more specific places. For example, Carson and Douglas Moo understand Phoenicia, Cyprus, and Antioch as possible; Edgar indicates Syria-Palestine; and Laws prefers Rome. See D. A. Carson and Douglas J. Moo, *An Introduction to the New Testament*, 2nd ed. (Grand Rapids, Mich.: Zondervan, 2005), 628–9; Edgar, *Has God Not Chosen the Poor?*, 224–7; Sophie S. Laws, *A Commentary on the Epistle of James*, BNTC 16 (San Francisco: Harper & Row, 1980), 25–6.

124. Davids, "The Test of Wealth," 354. Although Davids includes Jas 4:2, it is not directly associated with the focus of this research. He includes it because he considers those passages that deal with wealth and its use. In this case, the link is with covetousness.

points out 1:9–11, 26–27; 2:1–4, 5–7, 14–17; and 4:13–5:6.[125] Ulrich Berges and Rudolf Hoppe study 1:9–11, 2:1–6, 4:13–17, and 5:1–6.[126] James 1:9–11 speaks about the reversal of the situation of the poor and the rich. James 1:26–27 depicts the pure religion, which includes the care of orphans and widows. James 2:1–13 deals with discrimination against the poor as a transgression of the law. James 2:14–26 presents the relationship between works and faith in the context of helping the poor. The passage in James 4:13–17 shows the wealthy, who do not consider God in their plans. James 5:1–6 presents a strong prophetic denunciation against the corrupt wealthy farmers. Finally, the passage in James 5:7–11 is an appeal for the addressees to hope in the Lord's coming in light of that denunciation. Thus, this research considers these passages: 1:9–11, 26–27; 2:1–13, 14–26; 4:13–17; 5:1–6, 7–11. In order to analyze James's use of the OT in those passages, it is necessary to consider the grammatical unit, i.e., the paragraph where the topic of poverty and wealth appears.[127] So the analysis also includes the co-text for each passage.

Research Problem and Hermeneutical Approach

Approaches to the study of the use of the OT in James follow the same lines observed in the study of its use in the rest of the NT. Until now all the work on the NT use of the OT has been explicitly or implicitly done under the framework of the code model of communications with its limitations.[128] The main perspectives are author-centered and reader/hearer-centered approaches. Many scholars working with those approaches consider them mutually exclusive. Also, there is an ongoing debate on meaning/significance in the use of the OT in the NT. According to some scholars, a NT author, when using the OT, gives to the OT text a new significance but preserves the original meaning. He respects the OT context, and the meaning depends on the OT authorial intention, not on his creative understanding. However,

125. McKnight, *James*, 46.

126. Ulrich Berges and Rudolf Hoppe, *Arm und Reich*, NEchtB 10 (Würzburg: Echter, 2009), 106–15.

127. See a detailed structural analysis in George Hart and Helen Hart, *A Semantic and Structural Analysis of James*, SSA (Dallas: SIL International, 2001); Mark E. Taylor, *A Textlinguistic Investigation into the Discourse Structure of James*, LNTS 311 (New York: T&T Clark, 2006); Ralph Bruce Terry, "Some Aspects of the Discourse Structure of the Book of James," *JOTT* 5 (1992): 106–25.

128. Essentially, the code model understands communication as a process of encoding and decoding messages. "The basic premise of the code model is that a communicator's thoughts are contained within the socially-constructed code and the code produces a duplication of those thoughts in the mind of the hearer or reader." Gene L. Green, "Relevance Theory and Biblical Interpretation," in *Linguist as Pedagogue*, OEBI (Sheffield: Sheffield Phoenix, 2009), 219. The next chapter of this research presents and evaluates this model.

according to others, the NT author, although aware of the OT context, follows an already begun trajectory of interpretation.[129]

As previously mentioned, the topic of poverty and wealth is important in James's discourse. Every time it is present in the epistle, the OT also appears. This connection has been noticed by some of the above-mentioned works. James seems to found his teaching and authority on the OT. However, there are few direct quotations. Allusions and echoes are recurrent. Although much helpful work has been done with the code model, some questions still remain unanswered. For example: How is the author using the OT? How does this usage contribute to his discourse? Is the author directly utilizing the OT and its original meaning, or is he filtering the meaning of the OT passage through Second Temple Jewish understandings? In what way does his intended audience influence his use of the OT? How does the socio-economic context of the author and his addressees influence the way he addresses them? How does this context inform our understanding of the letter? How does the OT contribute to James's ethics of poverty and wealth?

The use of Relevance Theory (RT) not only helps to answer these questions but also provides the opportunity to explore the biblical text and its cognitive environments in a more integrated way (through pragmatics/semantics), while searching for the author's intended meaning.[130] That is, it permits one to simultaneously take into account the author's and the reader's/hearer's perspectives in the study of citations. The next chapter presents a more complete description of RT and how the present research applies it. Here a brief summary shows the main ideas of the model.

There is a difference in approach between the code model and an inferential model of communication. The code model of communication is signal oriented. An author encodes her thoughts into a signal. The reader/hearer decodes the signal and recovers the meaning by using an identical copy of the code.[131] However, this model does not take into account the inferential nature of language nor how context contributes to the meaning. RT is an inferential model of communication and cognition. As such, it considers the code fundamental to communication, but merely as evidence of the thoughts

129. The next chapter presents a broader discussion of these issues.

130. The next chapter presents a detailed treatment of this theory. RT "is a psycholinguistic model which provides analytic tools to explain the nature of the mechanisms underlying human overt and intentional, that is ostensive, communicative behaviour." Maria Jodłowiec, "Relevance Theory and Degrees of Understanding," in *Relevance Round Table I*, ed. Ewa Mioduszewska and Agnieszka Piskorka (Warsaw: Warsaw University Press, 2008), 24. As Jeannine Brown summarizes, "Relevance Theory at its center claims that (1) an utterance requires hearers to infer more than is provided in the linguistic features of the utterance itself, and (2) hearers will select from among a host of contextual inputs those that are most relevant for understanding a particular utterance." Jeannine K. Brown, *Scripture as Communication: Introducing Biblical Hermeneutics* (Grand Rapids, Mich.: Baker, 2007), 35.

131. Deirdre Wilson and Dan Sperber, "Relevance Theory," in *Handbook of Pragmatics*, ed. Gregory Ward and Laurence Horn, BHL 16 (Oxford: Blackwell, 2004), 607.

of an author. Authors also convey intentions. From the RT perspective, a reader/hearer infers from the code and context the meaning explicit and implicit in the utterance. In this way, the reader/hearer infers the meaning of an author's utterance. He fills the gap between utterance and sentence meaning through an interpretive process. RT explains both sides of that communicative process, the author's side and the reader's/hearer's side.

The communicative process is more complex in written texts than in oral communication. A written text involves not only an author and her primary readers/hearers, but also several other types of readers. The primary readers are those addressed directly by the author. Secondary readers are those who read the text even though it was not necessarily intended for them. A secondary reader could approach the text through the literary construct of "the implied reader." As Grant Osborne points out, "the actual reader is called on by the text to read it from the standpoint of these implied readers and to identify with the problems and message intended for them."[132]

Both oral and written communication is a two-way process. An author communicates ostensively. That is, she wants her intention to communicate to be recognized.[133] The reader/hearer infers from the evidence provided what the author's intent was. This is possible because "[h]umans possess the ability to represent their own thoughts through the linguistic sign system but also metarepresent the thoughts of others and ascribe intentions to them."[134] This ability is not limited to verbal communication but is present also in literary interpretation.[135] In fact, this human ability is crucial in the use and recognition of quotations, allusions, and echoes.[136] An author may metarepresent her own thoughts or the thoughts of others in different ways, including written texts. On his part, a reader/hearer may understand an author and also the her connections with former texts.[137]

132. Grant R. Osborne, *The Hermeneutical Spiral: A Comprehensive Introduction to Biblical Interpretation*, 2nd ed. (Downers Grove, Ill.: InterVarsity Press, 2006), 211. The next chapter of this research presents more details and a brief discussion on the concept of the implied reader and its implication for the methodology used here.

133. In this regard, Wilson and Sperber say: "[T]he goal of inferential pragmatics is to explain how the hearer infers the speaker's meaning on the basis of the evidence provided." Wilson and Sperber, "Relevance Theory," 607.

134. Gene L. Green, "Relevance Theory and Biblical Interpretation," OEBI (Oxford: Oxford University Press, 2013), 267.

135. Green, "Relevance Theory and Biblical Interpretation," 42–7; Robyn Carston, *Thoughts and Utterances: The Pragmatics of Explicit Communication* (Oxford: Blackwell, 2002).

136. Adrian Pilkington, *Poetic Effects: A Relevance Theory Perspective*, PBNS 75 (Amsterdam: John Benjamins, 2000); Adrian Pilkington, "Metaphor Comprehension: Some Questions for Current Accounts in Relevance Theory," in *Explicit Communication: Robyn Carston's Pragmatics*, ed. Belén Soria and Esther Romero, PSPLC (Basingstoke, England: Palgrave Macmillan, 2010), 156–72; Deirdre Wilson, "Relevance Theory and the Interpretation of Literary Works," *UCLWPL* 23 (2011): 47–68.

137. The concept of metarepresentation is presented later in detail. At this point it is enough to say that "to metarepresent" is the human ability of representing the thoughts of another

In the interpretive process, code and context concur. RT recognizes the essential role of the code in communication, but at the same time it considers indispensable the role of context in recovering the meaning of an utterance.[138] The context of an utterance is understood as a subset of the cognitive environment common to the author and her reader/hearer that is accessed in the communication of an utterance.[139] In biblical interpretation, defined in this way, the context of an utterance is not exactly the Greco-Roman world, or the Jewish environment, or written texts present in the first-century milieu, or even the co-text. It is, rather, the information that is accessed in the communication process. Each one of these aspects of the context forms part of the cognitive environment shared by an author and her reader/hearer. In the communication process, however, each utterance triggers the access to different components of this cognitive environment. As a result, those specific components become the context of the utterance. This process is guided by the two principles of relevance: the cognitive principle and the communicative principle.

Relevance Theory understands communication as an ostensive-inferential process guided by these two principles.[140] The cognitive principle points out that human cognition tends to be geared to the maximization of relevance. The communicative principle states that an author's utterance conveys its own presumption of optimal relevance, in that it is relevant enough to be worth the reader/hearer's cognitive effort and that it is the most relevant utterance compatible with the author's abilities and preferences. Here "relevance" is understood in technical terms related to cognitive effect. "Relevance" relates to the modifications of a reader's/hearer's cognitive environment and the processing effort invested in that change. "An assumption is relevant to an individual at a given time if and only if it has some positive cognitive effects in one or more of the contexts accessible to him at that time."[141] Thus, the

---

person or of oneself at another time. So, in this sense, simplistically speaking, a metarepresentation of the OT in the NT is a NT author's or his audience's representation of an OT author. See Deirdre Wilson, "Metarepresentation in Linguistic Communication," *UCLWPL* 11 (1999): 127–62. According to her, representation is "anything used in such a way that it can be construed as being ab*out s*omething (as having me*aning)* as opposed to just being itself; aboutness may be truth-based or resemblance-based" (her emphasis). See also Eun-Ju Noh, *Metarepresentation: A Relevance-Theory Approach*, PBNS 69 (Amsterdam: John Benjamins, 2000).

138. Other approaches also consider the importance of context, but they do not have a model that explains how context contributes to meaning. Scholars of socio-cognitive approaches have made some preliminary efforts in that direction. See, e.g., Carston, *Thoughts and Utterances*, 380. For other preliminary pragmatic models, see Teun A. van Dijk, *Discourse and Context: A Sociocognitive Approach* (Cambridge: Cambridge University Press, 2008); Etsuko Oishi and Anita Fetzer, eds., *Context and Contexts: Parts Meet Whole?*, PBNS 209 (Amsterdam: John Benjamins, 2011).

139. Dan Sperber and Deirdre Wilson, *Relevance: Communication and Cognition*, 2nd ed. (Oxford: Blackwell, 1995), 132–42.

140. Ibid., 260.

141. Carston, *Thoughts and Utterances*, 380.

greater the cognitive effects, the greater the relevance, and also the lesser the processing effort to obtain those effects, the greater the relevance.[142]

A reader/hearer fills the gap between author meaning and utterance meaning in a particular context through a process led by the search for relevance. At an explicit level, a reader/hearer looks for ambiguities to clarify, references to assign, ellipses to interpret, and so on. At a higher level of explicitness, such as the level where irony functions, he infers attitudes, resolves illocutionary indeterminacies, and so on. RT calls these tasks the recovery of *explicatures*. At the implicit level, he also discerns implicated premises and derives implicated conclusions. This process is called the recovery of *implicatures*. The search for relevance leads both processes.[143] A reader/hearer follows the same process with the understanding of metarepresentations in general, and quotations, allusions, and echoes in particular. When there are OT metarepresentations intended by an author, the search for relevance may guide the reader/hearer to make some intertextual connections. In that case, making connections with an OT metarepresentation will lead to more cognitive effects than making them with other aspects of his cognitive environment.

In order to illustrate these concepts, note this example:[144] in James 2:11, without much preamble, James declares:

> (1) Because the one who said, "do not commit adultery," also said, "do not murder."

In this sentence, James assumes his readers/hearers know whom he is talking about. There is no explicit referent for the subject of both occurrences of the verb "said." What is said in both cases corresponds to two famous commandments of the Ten Words of the Torah. So James guides his readers to recognize those imperatives. They recognize them as part of the Ten Words. Then they access their encyclopedic knowledge about the story of the Ten Words and recognize God as the one who said them. All this pragmatic process is the recovery of the referent of the participle ὁ εἰπών and the subject of the verb εἶπεν. It is the recovery of an explicature. An implicit conclusion here could be

> (2) Someone who violates a commandment sins against the author of the Law, God.

142. Sperber and Wilson, *Relevance: Communication and Cognition*, 260–78.

143. Robyn Carston says that "[a]n assumption (proposition) communicated by an utterance is an 'explicature' of the utterance if and only if it is a development of (a) a linguistically encoded logical form of the utterance, or of (b) a sentential subpart of a logical form." Carston, *Thoughts and Utterances*, 124. On the other hand, "[a]ny assumption communicated [by an utterance] but not explicitly so, is implicitly communicated: it is an im*plicature*." Sperber and Wilson, *Relevance: Communication and Cognition*, 182.

144. Later, chapter 2 presents a more extensive explanation and examples.

Later, in chapter 4, this text is analyzed. It is clear that another implicature strongly communicated here is

(3) Discrimination is as heinous as adultery or murder.

A biblical interpreter today reads the text as a secondary audience. Current interpreters have to decide what aspects of the cognitive environment of the author and her intended audience—recovered by historical-critical methods—are to be considered in the interpretation process. The search for relevance also guides this process. Incorrect assumptions lead to inadequate or less probable interpretations. For that reason, exhaustiveness, plausibility, and unity must lead to "the optimally relevant interpretation of the text as a whole."[145]

In particular, discerning OT metarepresentations is a challenge. In many instances, there are competing interpretations or possible allusions to OT passages. Subjectivity and probability concur in the evaluative process. The first four of Richard Hays's tests for assessing claims of OT metarepresentations help to evaluate the evidence: (1) availability, (2) volume, (3) recurrence, and (4) thematic coherence.[146] However, the search for relevance, and the evaluation of cognitive effects, also contribute to the validation process. If a particular OT passage contributes more cognitive effects to an interpretation of a NT passage than other factors of the cognitive environment or another OT competing passage, this could be an indicator that the author actually used that passage inside the fence posts of the mutual cognitive environment and the search for optimal relevance. This leads to a cautious approach to quotations.

In conclusion, Relevance Theory is a robust framework. It permits exploring the evidence retrieved by traditional historical-critical methods, more effectively integrating the relationship between text, context, author, and readers. By working with RT, this research explores how the use of the OT traditions and the cognitive environment of James and his addressees

145. Anne M. Furlong, "Relevance Theory and Literary Interpretation" (Ph.D. diss., University College London, 1995), 196. For a detailed definition of these concepts, see the next chapter.

146. Richard B. Hays presents seven criteria for discerning echoes of the OT in the NT in his very influential *Echoes of Scripture in the Letters of Paul* (New Haven: Yale University Press, 1989), 29–32. His first four criteria relate in different ways to RT. "Availability" relates to what RT calls encyclopedic knowledge and mutual cognitive environment. "Volume" relates to what RT calls metalinguistic and interpretive resemblance of metarepresentations. "Recurrence" relates to mutual cognitive environment. "Thematic coherence" relates to implicatures and cognitive effects. For a positive evaluation of the seven criteria, see G. K. Beale, *Handbook on the New Testament Use of the Old Testament: Exegesis and Interpretation* (Grand Rapids, Mich.: Baker, 2012), 33–5. For an adverse evaluation, see Stanley E. Porter, "Allusions and Echoes," in *As It Is Written: Studying Paul's Use of Scripture*, ed. Stanley E. Porter and Christopher D. Stanley, SBLSymS 50 (Atlanta: Society of Biblical Literature, 2008), 36–9.

contribute to understanding the passages in the letter addressing poverty and wealth as well as James's ethics related to these themes. What is clear from the research is that James intertwines the OT and Jesus's teachings with his own discourse. In this way, he builds his ethics of poverty and wealth by interpretively metarepresenting the OT and Jesus's teachings.

Research Methodology and Constraints

This research uses RT as its methodological framework. It uses historical-critical methodology and some tools of socio-rhetorical approaches and linguistics (semantics and pragmatics). The next chapter details the methodological approach espoused by this work. Due to the nature of any investigation, some constraints are present: the study of James's use of the OT focuses on those passages that deal with the poor and rich. Some other passages are mentioned in passing. Also, the intertextual work centers on the OT, although echoes of the Jesus tradition are mentioned in passing.

Significance of the Project

This research contributes to NT studies in three ways. In the first place, it adds to the discussion of poverty and wealth in James through the integration of the study of the use of the OT in the NT and discourse analysis using RT. Second, it contributes to the use of RT in biblical studies. Finally, it has the potential to provide new insights into the discussion of poverty and wealth in general and in Latin America in particular.

Summary of Chapters

Chapter 2 presents the methodology used in this research. First, it explains the main perspectives and approaches to OT quotations in the NT. It describes author- and reader-centered approaches as well as intertextuality and rhetorical approaches. It also evaluates the code model of communication and its relationship with these approaches to a quotation. After that, it presents a summary of Relevance Theory. It includes a précis of RT, RT and quotations, and some contributions of RT to the present research. Finally, the methodology used in the study of the relevant passages is explained in detail.

Chapter 3 applies the method to the first group of texts: James 1:9–11 and 26–27. In each case, the method contributes to understanding how James uses the OT. The chapter shows the variety of forms in which James drives his addressees to make connections with the OT and derive implicatures from their own social perspectives. A conclusion summarizes the main findings in this chapter.

Chapter 4 studies James 2:1–26. The passage is divided into two segments, 2:1–13 and 14–26. This chapter makes clear that James not only uses the OT but also evokes the Jesus tradition, in particular in 2:1–13. In this way, James builds his ethics of poverty and wealth by interpretively metarepresenting the OT and Jesus's teachings. Across chapter 2 of the epistle James uses the OT in a variety of ways. He alludes to different OT texts, quotes specific passages, and uses examples from the OT in order to strengthen his argument. A conclusion summarizes the results of the analysis.

Chapter 5 deals with the third group of texts: James 4:13–17 and 5:1–6 and 7–11. Again, the method contributes to understanding how James is using the OT. Jesus tradition appears in 5:7–11. Some ways of using the OT detected in chapters 3 and 4 reappear in this chapter. Others confirm James's recurrent interpretive metarepresentation of the OT. In this way, the research shows a pattern. James builds his ethics of poverty and wealth by interpretively metarepresenting the OT and Jesus's teachings. A conclusion summarizes the results of the analysis.

Chapter 6 recapitulates the results of the research. It summarizes each previous chapter, including the main findings of each studied text, describes six characteristics of James's use of the OT, presents James's ethics of poverty and wealth, and summarizes RT contributions to the research.

Chapter 2

Overall Methodology

New Testament authors use the Old Testament in different ways. This fact has attracted scholars for decades. Different aspects have received attention, such as the OT texts used, Jewish exegetical patterns, and appropriation techniques utilized.[1] Some studies, in particular, have focused on how to recognize the presence or absence of an OT reference in a NT passage, and how this contributes to the discourse. These works can be grouped into two main perspectives. This chapter presents a brief description of these perspectives and suggests another alternative, namely, the use of a different reference framework called Relevance Theory. Finally, it explains the methodology used in this research.

Perspective and Approaches to a Quotation

Scholars try to understand how an OT citation functions in a NT passage. Some of them define criteria for discerning citations.[2] Fundamental to this discernment is the perspective or point of view considered. The main perspectives are reader/hearer- and author-centered approaches.[3] A reader/

1. See, e.g., D. A. Carson and H. G. M. Williamson, eds., *It Is Written: Scripture Citing Scripture; Essays in Honour of Barnabas Lindars* (Cambridge: Cambridge University Press, 1988); Leonhard Goppelt, *Typos: The Typological Interpretation of the Old Testament in the New* (Grand Rapids, Mich.: Eerdmans, 1982); Richard N. Longenecker, *Biblical Exegesis in the Apostolic Period*, 2nd ed. (Grand Rapids, Mich.: Eerdmans; Regent College, 1999).

2. Some scholars define criteria or principles as guides to evaluate potential allusions or quotations in a NT passage. Not all agree on what aspects or evidences are to be considered. For example, Thompson defines eleven criteria, Hays seven, Osborne five, and Belli four. Michael Thompson, *Clothed with Christ: The Example and Teaching of Jesus in Romans 12:1–15:13*, JSNTSup 59 (Sheffield: JSOT, 1991), 28–36; Richard B. Hays, *Echoes of Scripture in the Letters of Paul* (New Haven: Yale University Press, 1989), 29–32; Grant R. Osborne, *The Hermeneutical Spiral: A Comprehensive Introduction to Biblical Interpretation*, 2nd ed. (Downers Grove, Ill.: InterVarsity Press, 2006), 167–9; Filippo Belli, *Argumentation and Use of Scripture in Romans 9–11*, AnBib 183 (Rome: Gregorian & Biblical Press, 2010), 37–8. For pragmatic reasons, "citation" in the present work is used as the broadest concept that includes quotations, allusions, and echoes.

3. Dennis L. Stamps, "The Use of the Old Testament in the New Testament as a Rhetorical Device: A Methodological Proposal," in *Hearing the Old Testament in the New Testament*, ed. Stanley Porter (Grand Rapids, Mich.: Eerdmans, 2006), 16–7. Hays mentions three more possible loci of "intertextual fusion": the text itself (which he recognizes as a heuristic fiction), "my act of

hearer-centered approach focuses on the receiver of the NT book. It pursues an answer to the question, Could the reader have recognized this OT citation?[4] In an author-centered approach, however, any significant written similarity is considered an OT citation.[5]

Many scholars regard these approaches to be mutually exclusive. Stanley Porter opposes an audience-oriented approach. He thinks that it is "questionable whether it provides the proper basis for establishing the author's use of the Old Testament."[6] In a more recent article, he seems to admit that an audience-oriented approach has a certain validity, although he affirms that "making the success of citation dependent upon the audience runs the risk of determining literary success on the basis of the level of ignorance or information of the audience, rather than on how the author crafts the work."[7] On the other hand, a risk of extreme forms of author-centered studies is to deny the variations in meaning that are found in the NT use of the OT.[8]

There is an ongoing debate on the meaning/significance of the use of the OT in the NT. Essentially, there are two predominant perspectives on

reading," and "a community of reading." These last two are related to present readers "with a text not addressed to them." Hays, *Echoes of Scripture*, 26–7. Christopher Bruno proposes a "divine author" approach as an evangelical proposal. At the end of the day, his is basically a canonical approach that tries to resolve the problem of unconscious allusions made by a human author. It is a kind of *sensus plenior* approach. See more details in Christopher R. Bruno, "Readers, Authors, and the Divine Author: An Evangelical Proposal for Identifying Paul's Old Testament Citations," *WTJ* 71 (2009): 311–21.

4. Stanley presents a stricter reader-oriented approach that "classifies as citation only those passages that give the reader at least some indication that a quotation is indeed present." These markers include "explicit introductory formulae, interpretive comments, or a literary style that differs markedly from the surrounding verses." Christopher D. Stanley, *Paul and the Language of Scripture: Citation Technique in the Pauline Epistles and Contemporary Literature*, SNTSMS 74 (Cambridge: Cambridge University Press, 1992), 34. This way of finding citations leaves out unmarked quotations, and allusions, as Stanley recognizes and Porter also points out. Stanley E. Porter, "The Use of the Old Testament in the New Testament: A Brief Comment on Method and Terminology," in *Early Christian Interpretation of the Scriptures of Israel*, ed. Stanley E. Porter (Sheffield: Sheffield Academic, 1997), 93; Stanley, *Paul and the Language of Scripture*, 34. Richard Hays and Dietrich Koch also use this approach. Hays, *Echoes of Scripture*; D. A. Koch, *Die Schrift als Zeuge des Evangeliums: Untersuchungen zur Verwendung und zum Verständnis der Schrift bei Paulus*, BHT 69 (Tübingen: Mohr Siebeck, 1986).

5. Bruno, "Readers, Author, and the Divine Author," 313.

6. Porter, "The Use of the Old Testament," 92–5.

7. Stanley E. Porter, "Further Comments on the Use of the Old Testament in the New Testament," in *The Intertextuality of the Epistles: Explorations of Theory and Practice*, ed. Thomas L. Brodie, Dennis R. MacDonald, and Stanley E. Porter, NTM 16 (Sheffield: Sheffield Phoenix, 2006), 105–6. In his most recent book, Porter is more open to considering the contribution of a reader-centered approach, but he still considers the author-centered approach as the foundational perspective. Stanley E. Porter, *Sacred Tradition in the New Testament: Tracing Old Testament Themes in the Gospels and Epistles* (Grand Rapids, Mich.: Baker Academic, 2016), esp. 1–124.

8. See, e.g., Robert L. Thomas, "The New Testament Use of the Old Testament," *MSJ* 13 (2002): 79–98; Robert L. Thomas, "The Principle of Single Meaning," *MSJ* 12 (2001): 33–47.

how NT authors use the OT. Some scholars, such as Greg Beale, affirm that when a NT author uses the OT in a new context, he gives the OT text new significance, not new meaning. NT authors respect the OT context in their use of it. Also the meaning of the OT passage derives from authorial intention not from the creative processes of the readers. On the other hand, some scholars, such as Steve Moyise, emphasize that NT authors give new meaning to OT references in their interpretations of them. They are aware of the OT context of those references, but in their interpretation of them they follow an already begun trajectory of interpretation. They are thus not completely free to "create meaning."[9]

For some scholars, the problem with reader-centered approaches is our ignorance of the audience's level of competence in discerning OT allusions. For example, Dennis Stamps considers it to be virtually impossible to assess "the level of audience understanding and perception."[10] Both Porter and Stamps, among many others, prefer an author-oriented approach.[11]

9. See, e.g., the discussion in G. K. Beale, ed., *The Right Doctrine from the Wrong Texts? Essays on the Use of the Old Testament in the New* (Grand Rapids, Mich.: Baker Academic, 1994); G. K. Beale, *John's Use of the Old Testament in Revelation*, JSNTSup 166 (Sheffield: Sheffield Academic, 1998), 41–59; G. K. Beale, "Questions of Authorial Intent, Epistemology, and Presuppositions and Their Bearing on the Study of the Old Testament in the New: A Rejoinder to Steve Moyise," *IBS* 21 (1999): 152–80; Steve Moyise, "The Old Testament in the New: A Reply to Greg Beale," *IBS* 21 (1999): 54–8; Steve Moyise, "Intertextuality and the Study of the Old Testament in the New Testament," in *Old Testament in the New Testament: Essays in Honour of J. L. North* (Sheffield: Sheffield Academic Press, 2000), 14–41; Steve Moyise, "Respect for Context Once More," *IBS* 27 (2006): 24–31; Steve Moyise, *Evoking Scripture: Seeing the Old Testament in the New* (London: T&T Clark, 2008); Jon Paulien, "Dreading the Whirlwind: Intertextuality and the Use of the Old Testament in Revelation," *AUSS* 39 (2001): 5–22; Jon Paulien, "New Testament Use of the Old Testament," in *"For You Have Strengthened Me": Biblical and Theological Studies in Honor of Gerhard Pfandl in Celebration of His Sixty-Fifth Birthday*, ed. Martin Pröbstle (St. Peter am Hart, Austria: Seminar Schloss Bogenhofen, 2007), 167–88; Kevin J. Vanhoozer, *Is There a Meaning in This Text? The Bible, the Reader, and the Morality of Literary Knowledge* (Grand Rapids, Mich.: Zondervan, 1998). Furthermore, there are different approaches to the issue of authorial intention and citation; cf. Peter Enns, "Apostolic Hermeneutics and an Evangelical Doctrine of Scripture: Moving beyond a Modernist Impasse," *WTJ* 65 (2003): 263–87; Peter Enns, *Inspiration and Incarnation: Evangelicals and the Problem of the Old Testament* (Grand Rapids, Mich.: Baker Academic, 2005), 113–65; Jonathan Lunde and Kenneth Berding, eds., *Three Views on the New Testament Use of the Old Testament* (Grand Rapids, Mich.: Zondervan, 2007), 45–231.

10. Dennis Stamps points out that even "optimal 'readers/hearers'" or implied/ideal readers is a product within the author's text. The optimal reader/hearer "represents the informed reader who responds appropriately to all literary constructs and devices the author uses." Stamps, "The Use of the Old Testament," 17. However, Stanley, although he limits his work to explicit marked quotations, illustrates how a first-century audience could interact with the text and understand OT quotations. Christopher D. Stanley, *Arguing with Scripture: The Rhetoric of Quotations in the Letters of Paul* (New York: T&T Clark, 2004).

11. A huge number of works in the study of the use of the OT in the NT are author-oriented. See, e.g., the essays in Craig A. Evans and H. Daniel Zacharias, eds., *Early Christian Literature and Intertextuality*, vol. 1, *Thematic Studies*, LNTS 391 (London: T&T Clark, 2009); Craig A. Evans, ed.,

Nevertheless, the differences between authors in their use of citations in the Gospels, for example, cannot be reduced just to their individual preferences or styles. There seems to be a correlation between the (implied) audience's competence in discerning the OT and the author's election of the OT material. In this regard, Moyise points out that "Matthew is much more concerned than Mark to link incidents in Jesus' life with explicit Old Testament texts."[12] This use of the OT could be in part due to his perceived Jewish implied audience.[13] The implied audience, in one way or another, influences the mode in which NT authors use the OT.[14]

Scholars have noted this in James's use of the OT. Wiard Popkes comments in this regard: "Evidently James can presuppose enough knowledge and understanding on the part of his readers to keep the references brief."[15] This phenomenon illustrates that an approach that focuses only on the writer's perspective is not adequate to understand what happens in the text.

Some recent literary approaches, such as intertextuality and rhetorical analysis, have taken readers/hearers more into account. Moyise points out that "intertextuality is not a method but a theory (or a group of theories) concerning the production of meaning. . . . Intertextuality suggests that meaning of a text is not fixed but is open to revision as new texts come along and

From Prophecy to Testament: The Function of the Old Testament in the New (Peabody, Mass.: Hendrickson, 2004).

12. Steve Moyise, *The Old Testament in the New: An Introduction*, ContBS (London: Continuum, 2001), 43.

13. In this regard, Osborne says, "Matthew specially had the Jewish Christian church and the Jewish people in mind. With the preponderance of OT fulfillment quotations . . . , the rabbinic style of the reasoning in several passages . . . , the centrality of Jesus' fulfilling the law in the Sermon on the Mount . . . , and the way Jesus relates to the Jewish people throughout, it seems clear that Jewish issues are uppermost." Grant R. Osborne, *Matthew*, ZECNT 1 (Grand Rapids, Mich.: Zondervan, 2010), 31.

14. Christopher D. Stanley, "Paul's 'Use' of Scripture: Why the Audience Matters," in *As It Is Written: Studying Paul's Use of Scripture*, ed. Stanley E. Porter and Christopher D. Stanley, SBLSymS 50 (Atlanta: Society of Biblical Literature, 2008), 125–55. Contrary to the suggestion here, Richard Bauckham makes the case that the four Gospels were originally intended for a broad audience and not a specific community or groups of communities. Richard Bauckham, "For Whom Were Gospels Written?," in *Gospels for All Christians: Rethinking the Gospel Audiences* (Grand Rapids, Mich.: Eerdmans, 1998), 9–48. Among other scholars in the same volume, Craig Blomberg disagrees with Bauckham's proposal and argues that "[t]he Gospels were written for specific communities but also in hopes that they would eventually reach as many Christians as possible." Craig L. Blomberg, "The Gospels for Specific Communities and All Christians," in *Audience of the Gospels: The Origin and Function of the Gospels in Early Christianity*, ed. Edward W. Klink, LNTS 353 (London: T&T Clark, 2010), 133.

15. Popkes continues: "No explanation need to be given about the 'sacred history', its lawgiver and judge, its document(s), quotable as ἡ γραφή, and the grand old partisans, one of them even a woman of questionable status. His readers will appreciate these arguments and experiences from their own religious background." Wiard Popkes, "James and Scripture: An Exercise in Intertextuality," *NTS* 45 (1999): 216.

reposition it."[16] On his part, Osborne points out that "intertextuality is best used as a study of the reuse of an Old Testament passage in a NT context, considering exactly how the dialogue between original meaning (Old Testament context) and the new meaning (New Testament context) develops."[17]

These two definitions illustrate that intertextuality nowadays is a broad term. Different emphases result in divergent approaches. Some works of intertextuality have focused more on the text and semiotics, even denying the possibility of finding an authorial intention.[18] Scholars like Porter criticize these extremes.[19] Moyise shows that both the historical-critical method

16. Steve Moyise, "Intertextuality, Historical Criticism, and Deconstruction," in *The Intertextuality of the Epistles: Explorations of Theory and Practice*, ed. Thomas L. Brodie, Dennis R. MacDonald, and Stanley E. Porter (Sheffield: Sheffield Phoenix Press, 2006), 24. Moyise speaks about at least five types of intertextuality: intertextual echo, narrative intertextuality, exegetical intertextuality, dialogical intertextuality, and postmodern intertextuality. Steve Moyise, "Intertextuality and Biblical Studies: A Review," *VE* 23 (2002): 418–31. See also Michael A. Fishbane, "Types of Biblical Intertextuality," in *Congress Volume: Oslo 1998*, ed. André Lemaire and Magne Sæbø, VTSup 80 (Leiden: Brill, 2000), 39–44.

17. Osborne, *The Hermeneutical Spiral*, 331. See a brief presentation of this dialogue in Osborne's summary of the use of the OT in Revelation in Grant R. Osborne, "Recent Trends in the Study of the Apocalypse," in *The Face of New Testament Studies: A Survey of Recent Research*, ed. Scot McKnight and Grant R. Osborne (Grand Rapids, Mich.: Baker, 2004), 491–5. This dialogue considers not just the cited OT verses, but also the biblical context of the citation. As Moyise says, "a quotation brings with it more than just the cited words; it also brings connotations and associations from the surrounding verses." Steve Moyise, *Paul and Scripture: Studying the New Testament Use of the Old Testament* (Grand Rapids, Mich.: Baker Academic, 2010), 111. In the same vein as historical-critical approaches, an intertextual analysis considers the tradition or traditions of interpretations associated with an OT passage. See, e.g., the essays in Craig A. Evans and James A. Sanders, eds., *Paul and the Scriptures of Israel*, JSNTSup (Sheffield: JSOT Press, 1993); Maarten J. J. Menken and Steve Moyise, eds., *Deuteronomy in the New Testament*, LNTS 358 (London: T&T Clark, 2007). For that reason, Craig Evans says that one has to listen not just for echoes of Scripture but also for echoes of interpreted Scripture. Craig A. Evans, "Listening for Echoes of Interpreted Scripture," in *Paul and the Scriptures of Israel*, ed. Craig A. Evans and James A. Sanders, JSNTSup 83 (Sheffield: JSOT Press, 1993), 47–51. In this regard, Susanne Gillmar-Bucher points out that "all biblical texts are always embedded into a tradition of teaching and religious doctrine as well as a text tradition and a tradition of translations. The text another text refers to thus might not be the original text, but an interpretation of the original text current at the time the new text was written." Susanne Gillmayr-Bucher, "Intertextuality: Between Literary Theory and Text Analysis," in *The Intertextuality of the Epistles: Explorations of Theory and Practice*, ed. Thomas L. Brodie, Dennis R. MacDonald, and Stanley E. Porter (Sheffield: Sheffield Phoenix, 2006), 17.

18. Moyise recognizes that this is a risk in extreme forms of intertextuality. See, e.g., the essays in Steve Moyise, "Intertextuality and Historical Approaches to the Use of Scripture in the New Testament," *VE* 26 (2005): 447–58. See also George Aichele and Gary A. Phillips, "Intertextuality and the Bible," *Semeia* 69–70 (1995): 1–305; Richard B. Hays, Stefan Alkier, and Leroy Andrew Huizenga, *Reading the Bible Intertextually* (Waco: Baylor University Press, 2009); Aldo Adriano Ranieri, "La intertextualidad como perspectiva hermenéutica: Un desafío para la exégesis bíblica," in *Palabra viva y actual*, ed. Carlos Galli and Héctor Fernández (Buenos Aires: San Benito, 2005), 99–111.

19. Porter, "The Use of the Old Testament," 84–5.

and intertextuality have limitations, but used together, they have a great potential for exegesis.[20] This integration can be observed in other works that take historical-critical concerns more into account.[21]

Very close to intertextuality are rhetorical approaches. These methods consider what an author does with the text in order to persuade his readers/hearers to accept his interpretation.[22] David deSilva proposes some questions to consider when analyzing citations: "How do the intertextual resources enhance the hearers' experience of the new text? How do they contribute to the topics being developed? What would be lost if the quotation, reference or allusion was not there? What specific rhetorical goals are advanced by the introduction of these resources and by the author's shaping of them?"[23]

Christopher Stanley analyzes quotations in some Pauline letters from a rhetorical perspective.[24] He tries to understand how Paul's different audiences could have perceived his quotations.[25] Roy Ciampa, for example,

20. Moyise adds: "Historical criticism has many important tasks, such as establishing the availability and form of texts, delineating the most likely meanings in their cultural context and establishing the most likely influences in light of linguistic similarities. But it goes astray when its ideology of single authorial meaning is to the fore. Intertextuality requires such historical 'fences' to contain the otherwise infinite number of possible influences but reminds the reader that meaning can never be isolated from other phenomena." Moyise, "Intertextuality and Historical Approaches," 457.

21. See, e.g., the essays in Thomas R. Hatina, *The Gospel of Luke*, vol. 3 of *Biblical Interpretation in Early Christian Gospels*, LNTS 376 (New York: T&T Clark, 2010); D. Sänger, ed., *Gottessohn und Menschensohn: Exegetische Studien zu zwei Paradigmen biblischer Intertextualität*, BTS (Neukirchen-Vluyn: Neukirchener, 2004).

22. Moyise, *Paul and Scripture*, 111. See also Steve Moyise, "How Does Paul Read Scripture?," in *Early Christian Literature and Intertextuality,* vol. 1, *Thematic Studies*, ed. Craig A. Evans and H. Daniel Zacharias, LNTS 391 (London: T&T Clark, 2009), 184–96. Stamps makes the case that NT authors use the OT as a rhetorical device. He focuses on Hellenistic rhetoric with an author-centered approach. Stamps, "The Use of the Old Testament," 23–35.

23. David A. deSilva, *An Introduction to the New Testament: Contexts, Methods, and Ministry Formation* (Downers Grove, Ill.: InterVarsity Press; Apollos, 2004), 800–1. He applies these criteria in, e.g., David A. deSilva, "Final Topics: The Rhetorical Functions of Intertexture in Revelation 14:14–16:21," in *Intertexture of Apocalyptic Discourse in the New Testament*, ed. Duane F. Watson, SBLSymS 14 (Atlanta: Society of Biblical Literature, 2002), 215–41.

24. Stanley's main concerns are "(1) [H]ow do Paul's quotations serve to advance the developing arguments of his letters? and (2) how well does Paul's strategy of biblical argumentation cohere with what we can surmise about the capabilities and inclinations of his audience?" Stanley, *Arguing with Scripture*, 171.

25. Stanley presents a typology of four different potential audiences: "(1) People who knew the original context of every verse that Paul quoted and agreed with all his interpretations of Scripture (clear and ideal type); (2) people whose knowledge of Scripture was broad enough, whether from prior experience in the synagogue or personal study, to enable them to recognize most but not all of Paul's references to the biblical text; (3) people who possessed precisely the level of biblical literacy that Paul presumed in his letters, but not more; and (4) people who were generally ignorant of the content of the Jewish Scriptures." In the case of Paul's audience, Stanley assumes that most of the people would have fallen into categories 3 and 4, and a few

studies how Paul uses the OT in Galatians 1–2. Using ancient rhetorical categories, he focuses his work not just on explicit quotations but also on allusions and echoes, using rhetorical analysis and intertextuality.[26] With a similar methodology, Filippo Belli studies how the Scriptures contribute to the development of Paul's argument in Romans 9–11.[27] Nevertheless, neither Ciampa nor Belli considers the audience in his analysis.

Although these main perspectives on the use of the OT in the NT are mutually exclusive, they appear to have something in common. Scholars using these approaches seem to operate under the code model of communication. Perry Blackburn presents a historical development of the code model. This is a result of the integration of three constituent models: the conduit metaphor, Saussure's speech circuit model, and Shannon's information theoretic model of communication as adapted by Weaver.[28] Basically, "a *code* . . . is a system which pairs messages with signals, enabling two information-processing devices (organisms or machines) to communicate. A *message* is a representation internal to the communicating devices. A *signal* is a modification of the external environment which can be produced by one device and recognised by the other."[29]

This model considers language as a signal.[30] The thoughts of the speaker/writer are encoded into a signal. The hearer/reader, using the same language,

into category 2, especially those with Jewish background. On this basis, he works with three potential readers/hearers: "the informed audience," "the competent audience," and "the minimal audience." Ibid., 67–9.

26. Ciampa makes the case that "Paul uses Scripture to reinforce his ethos and credibility as an authority to be reckoned with." Roy E. Ciampa, *The Presence and Function of Scripture in Galatians 1 and 2*, WUNT 2 102 (Tübingen: Mohr Siebeck, 1998), 295.

27. Belli, *Argumentation and Use of Scripture*.

28. Perry L. Blackburn, *The Code Model of Communication, A Powerful Metaphor in Linguistic Metatheory* (Dallas: SIL International, 2007), 27.

29. Dan Sperber and Deirdre Wilson, *Relevance: Communication and Cognition*, 2nd ed. (Oxford: Blackwell, 1995), 3–4.

30. Even to Saussure, who makes a distinction between general language (*langue*) and individual particular use of it (*parole*), language is still a signal (without a clear connection with context). When describing his speech circuit model of communication, he says: "If we could embrace the sum of word-images stored in the minds of all individuals, we could identify the social bond that constitutes language. It is a storehouse filled by the members of a given community through their active use of speaking, agrammatical system that has a potential existence in each brain, or, more specifically, in the brains of a group of individuals. For language [*langue*] is not complete in any speaker; it exists perfectly only within a collectivity." He adds: "In separating language [*langue*] from speaking [*parole*] we are at the same time separating: (1) what is social from what is individual; and (2) what is essential from what is accessory and more or less accidental." In the same vein, he points out that language [*langue*] "is not a function of the speaker; it is a product that is passively assimilated by the individual. . . . Speaking [*parole*], on the contrary, is an individual act. It is willful and intellectual. Within the act, we should distinguish between: (1) the combinations by which the speaker uses the language code for expressing his own thought; and (2) the psychophysical mechanism that allows him to exteriorize those combinations." Ferdinand de Saussure, *Course in General Linguistics*, trans. Wade Baskin (New York:

decodes the signal and recovers the thoughts of the speaker/writer. So, "communication is achieved by encoding and decoding messages."[31] Essentially, the understanding is reduced to know the code.[32]

The different variants of this model found in linguistic literature share these presuppositions:

1. Natural languages are codes defining the correspondence between sound and meaning.
2. Languages (i.e., codes) are systematic, distinctive, and have an existence independent of any given speaker or hearer.
3. Speaker and hearer must share a code in order for successful communication to proceed.
4. The text conveys meaning.
5. The speaker/author of the text encodes a message when he produces the text.
6. Those receiving the text decode the message when they hear/read the text.
7. Communication may be inhibited by noise.
8. The speaker and hearer are connected via the channel of communication.
9. Communication requires intention by the speaker and response by the hearer.
10. The linguists' problem lies (primarily) in defining the code and (secondarily) in defining the processes of transmission and reception.[33]

Philosophical Library, 1957), 13–4. This distinction between *langue* and *parole* has become foundational for modern linguistic theory. It is very helpful, for example, when considering idiolect in interpretation. Nevertheless, one important problem in this distinction, as Porter points out, is that it does not consider the social factors in language usage, and as a result these factors do not "enter into Saussurian estimation of *parole*." Stanley E. Porter, "Is Critical Discourse Analysis Critical? An Evaluation Using Philemon as a Test Case," in *Discourse Analysis and the New Testament: Approaches and Results*, ed. Stanley E. Porter and Jeffrey T. Reed, JSNTSup 170 (Sheffield: Sheffield Academic Press, 1999), 53. Also, Saussure misses at least three important pragmatic issues. First, in defining *parole,* Saussure doesn't distinguish between sentences and utterance. Second, although some scholars, such as Hugh White, see the inclusion of context in the definition of *parole,* in *Course of Linguistics,* there is no discussion of how context relates to *parole.* Finally, Saussure does not include the process of inference in his model of communication. Hugh C. White, "The Joseph Story: A Narrative Which 'Consumes' Its Content," *Semeia* 31 (1985): 49.

31. Anne M. Furlong, "Relevance Theory and Literary Interpretation" (Ph.D. diss., University College London, 1995), 20; Joseph D. Fantin, *The Greek Imperative Mood in the New Testament: A Cognitive and Communicative Approach*, SBG 12 (New York: Peter Lang, 2010), 40–8. Maybe the best-known hermeneutical movement that explicitly applied this method was the old structuralism of the 1960s and 1970s.

32. Gene L. Green, "Relevance Theory and Biblical Interpretation," in *Linguist as Pedagogue*, OEBI (Sheffield: Sheffield Phoenix, 2009), 219.

33. Blackburn, *The Code Model*, 82.

11. Although this way of understanding communication has been useful and widespread,[34] it has some important limitations. Among others, it gives no account for communicative intentions, and it "cannot accommodate or explain the role of context in communication."[35] In fact, as Gene Green says, "[w]hat a speaker or writer communicates is always something much larger than what is encoded in the sign system. What we communicate is a combination of explicit and implicit information."[36] This information is highly context-dependent.

The code model has been used explicitly and implicitly in the study of the NT use of the OT. Author-oriented perspectives tend to focus on the transmitter of the signal (speaker/writer), and reader-oriented perspectives tend to focus on the receiver of the signal (hearer/reader).[37] Scholars working under this model are conscious that contextual information is essential to interpretation but do not have a theoretical model that permits them to integrate this pragmatic dimension of communication with their interpretation of the text.[38] Also, some of the above approaches do not consider how readers may affect the way an author chooses to present OT citations, while others completely miss the author's contribution.

Relevance Theory offers a robust model that integrates context and text into the interpretive process.[39] Dan Sperber and Deirdre Wilson proposed this theory of cognition and communication originally in 1986, as a reaction to H. P. Grice's works on pragmatics. In particular, they diverge on Grice's cooperative principle and the maxims of *quality*, *quantity*, *relation*, and *manner*.[40] They made some important improvements to their theory in

34. The work of Blackburn makes manifest that "*most* contemporary linguists have used the code model, regardless of the theories they may employ in accounting for lower level issues. It seems to have mattered little whether they were formalists or functionalists, grammarians or sociolinguists." Ibid., 5 (his emphasis).

35. Furlong, "Relevance Theory and Literary Interpretation," 22. Although defending the code model, in his evaluation, Blackburn explains and proposes alternatives to four limitations that he sees in the code model: variation, abstraction, meaning, and discourse. He also sees limitations in the code model regarding intention and context, and includes them in his category of problems with meaning. Blackburn, *The Code Model*, 183–209.

36. Gene L. Green, "Relevance Theory and Theological Interpretation: Thoughts on Metarepresentation," *JTI* 4 (2010): 78.

37. Even here there is a variation in emphasis. Some approaches focus on the real reader today, while others center on the implied reader of the first century.

38. Green, "Relevance Theory and Biblical Interpretation," 217. See an exhaustive analysis of the *status quaestionis* on the study of context, explicit theories of contexts, and the way they relate to discourse and communication in Teun A. van Dijk, *Discourse and Context: A Sociocognitive Approach* (Cambridge: Cambridge University Press, 2008), vii-xii, 1–55.

39. Sperber and Wilson, *Relevance: Communication and Cognition.*

40. H. P. Grice's first work, "Meaning," was published in 1957. H. P. Grice, "Meaning," *PhR* 66 (1957): 377–88. This prolific author still influences pragmatics through Gricean and neo-Gricean approaches. For more details, see Dan Sperber and Deirdre Wilson, "Introduction:

the second edition of their book in 1995. Since then, the theory has reached different fields, from linguistics to neuroscience, theory of mind, and translations. RT has been applied to the study of multiple languages, from English to Japanese, Sissala, and Spanish. It has woken up a worldwide interest in its study and use, from Europe to Asia, Africa, and the Americas,[41] and scholars have recently begun to use it in biblical studies.[42]

Besides the way that RT integrates text and context explained in the next section, RT considers both the writer's and the reader's perspective. According to RT, readers/hearers are not alone in the interpretation process, nor are writers/speakers disconnected from their readers/hearers. This inferential communication model helps the reader/hearer bridge the gap between the linguistic meaning and the speaker's/writer's meaning. As Wilson and Sperber say, "[t]he central claim of relevance theory is that the expectations of relevance raised by an utterance are precise and predictable enough to guide the hearer toward the speaker's meaning."[43]

With regard to the locus of meaning, RT is in the vein of recent holistic hermeneutical methods. Paraphrasing Osborne, it presents a trialogue between the author, the text, and the reader all seated at the table of context.[44] As some scholars point out, as different hermeneutical models have appeared, the locus of meaning has moved in the last two centuries from the author to the text to the reader.[45] In the last two decades, new methods

---

Pragmatics," in *Meaning and Relevance*, ed. Deirdre Wilson and Dan Sperber (Cambridge: Cambridge University Press, 2012), 1–27; Deirdre Wilson and Dan Sperber, "Relevance Theory," in *Handbook of Pragmatics*, ed. Gregory Ward and Laurence Horn, BHL 16 (Oxford: Blackwell, 2004), 607–31.

41. This extensive spectrum of applications could be seen in the wide bibliography of Francisco Yus, "Relevance Theory Online Bibliographic Service," http://www.ua.es/personal/francisco.yus/rt.html.

42. See, e.g., Tim Meadowcroft, "Relevance as a Mediating Category in the Reading of Biblical Texts: Venturing beyond the Hermeneutical Circle," *JETS* 45 (2002): 611–27; Harriet Hill, *The Bible at Cultural Crossroads: From Translation to Communication* (Manchester, England: St Jerome, 2006); Margaret G. Sim, "A Relevance Theoretical Approach to the Particle [*sic*] ἵνα in Koine Greek" (Ph.D. diss., University of Edinburgh, 2006); Jeannine K. Brown, *Scripture as Communication: Introducing Biblical Hermeneutics* (Grand Rapids, Mich.: Baker, 2007); Karen H. Jobes, "Relevance Theory and the Translation of Scripture," *JETS* 50 (2007): 773–97; Gene L. Green, "Lexical Pragmatics and Biblical Interpretation," *JETS* 50 (2007): 799–812; Green, "Relevance Theory and Biblical Interpretation," 217–40; Joseph D. Fantin, *Lord of the Entire World: Lord Jesus, a Challenge to Lord Caesar?* (Sheffield: Sheffield Phoenix Press, 2011); Fantin, *The Greek Imperative Mood*; Margaret G. Sim, "Particles and Participles: A Helpful Partnership," in *Discourse Studies & Biblical Interpretation: A Festschrift in Honor of Stephen H. Levinsohn*, ed. Steven E. Runge (Bellingham, Wash.: Lexham, 2011), 226–44. Additionally, the "Relevance Theory and Biblical Interpretation" group has met yearly at the SBL International Meeting since 2003. Green, "Relevance Theory and Biblical Interpretation," 234 n. 35.

43. Wilson and Sperber, "Relevance Theory," 607.

44. Osborne, *The Hermeneutical Spiral*, 516.

45. E.g., Brown, *Scripture as Communication*, 57–78; Tremper Longman III, "Literary Approaches to Biblical Interpretation," in *Foundations of Contemporary Interpretation*, ed. Moisés

have attempted to move toward a more holistic hermeneutical approach to meaning by including the three factors of author, text, and reader in a more balanced way.[46] New models avoid the excess of the historical positivism of Schleiermacher and Dilthey and the intentional fallacy associated with it. As Jeannine Brown says, "the more modest goal in this case is to access only those authorial intentions that are communicated via the text in its setting, not to re-create the motives of the author that lie outside the boundaries of textual meaning."[47] Furthermore, some of these new approaches give a prominent place to the text,[48] avoiding the excessive independence from its author given to it by the New Criticism. Although the place each method gives to the reader varies,[49] in general terms, there is more awareness of the reader's role in interpretation.[50] Nevertheless, it is hard to find room in these

Silva (Grand Rapids, Mich.: Zondervan, 1996), 103–23. Also, Manfred Oeming presents and evaluates seventeen hermeneutical methods. He classifies them as methods focused on author, text, reader, and the reality behind the text. He proposes a broad dialogue that permits a methodological plurality, but he does not suggest any particular method. Manfred Oeming, *Contemporary Biblical Hermeneutics: An Introduction*, trans. Joachim Vette (Aldershot, England: Ashgate, 2006). Randolph Tate presents an integrated approach that includes the world behind the text, the world within the text, and the world in front of the text. He summarizes in four appendices several methods that focus on each "world," or on more than one "world." W. Randolph Tate, *Biblical Interpretation: An Integrated Approach*, 3rd ed. (Peabody, Mass.: Hendrickson, 2008). Craig Bartholomew presents a similar but more theological approach. Craig G. Bartholomew, *Introducing Biblical Hermeneutics: A Comprehensive Framework for Hearing God in Scripture* (Grand Rapids, Mich.: Baker Academic, 2015). See also the exhaustive analysis of the problem of meaning and his proposal in Osborne, *The Hermeneutical Spiral*, 465–521.

46. This has been more evident since the publication of the influential work of Vanhoozer, *Is There a Meaning in This Text?* As Klein says, "any appraisal of 'meaning,' then, must take into consideration this complex coalition of text, author, and audience." William W. Klein, Craig L. Blomberg, and Robert L. Hubbard, *Introduction to Biblical Interpretation* (Nashville: Thomas Nelson, 2004), 9.

47. Brown, *Scripture as Communication*, 61.

48. For example, describing his method of trialogue between author, text, and reader, Osborne explains: "The author has produced the *text* and given *it* certain meanings that are intended to be understood by the reader. The *text* then guides the reader by producing certain access points that point the reader to the proper language game for interpreting that particular *illocutionary act*. The reader thereby aligns him- or herself with the *textual world* and propositional content, thus coming to understand the intended meaning of the *text*." Osborne, *The Hermeneutical Spiral*, 516 (emphasis added).

49. For example, just to name a few works, Osborne is aware of this and gives significant space to the reader in his model. Osborne, *The Hermeneutical Spiral*, 516–21. Graeme Goldsworthy is aware of the importance of reader and text, but is less clear in how he includes them in his Christological model. Graeme Goldsworthy, *Gospel-Centered Hermeneutics: Foundations and Principles of Evangelical Biblical Interpretation* (Downers Grove, Ill.: InterVarsity Press, 2006). Andreas Köstenberger and Richard Patterson give limited consideration to the reader in their model. They seem to see the locus of meaning in the author. Andreas J. Köstenberger and Richard D. Patterson, *Invitation to Biblical Interpretation: Exploring the Hermeneutical Triad of History, Literature, and Theology*, ITSS (Grand Rapids, Mich.: Kregel, 2011), 118.

50. In this regard, Brown says: "Every reader has an interpretive 'location' that influences his or her understanding of the biblical text. This location includes the reader's theological

models for the inferential character of communication and for a theoretical model of context.[51] An exception to this tendency is the proposal of Brown in her *Scripture as Communication*.[52]

Relevance Theory is a good companion to the historical-critical methods. As Harriet Sim points out, RT is an aid in exegesis.[53] This can be seen in concrete examples in the biblical field. Some scholars using Relevance Theory deal with the NT use of the OT. Stephen Pattemore interacts with intertextuality from an RT point of view in his book on Revelation.[54] David Hoe uses RT for understanding intertextual echoes of apocalyptic motifs in 2 Peter and "how the audience might have understood the discourse."[55] Steve Smith use RT for understanding the temple motif in Luke-Acts in Jesus's lament over Jerusalem and Steven's discourse.[56] The advantage of these works is that the three of them more consciously consider the author, readers/hearers, and context, in order to discern meaning and authorial intention. To enhance understanding of the contributions RT makes to the enterprise of studying how the NT uses the OT, the next section presents the basics of this theory.

---

tradition, cultural and social location, and pre-understandings brought to specific texts and Scripture in general. To claim that the reader's location does not significantly influence interpretation is no longer possible, given the work of Heidegger, Gadamer, and others. In addition, the idea that meaning occurs in the interplay of text and reader is now a standard one in hermeneutics." Brown, *Scripture as Communication*, 69.

51. An example of this tendency is the work of Köstenberger and Patterson, *Invitation to Biblical Interpretation*. The only clear place in their method where they deal with "non-linguistic features of discourse" is in the section on discourse analysis. Nevertheless, they limit the inferential aspect of language basically to cases of interpersonal communication or dialogue. Ibid., 599–600. When explaining the importance of the situation of a discourse, they use the good but outdated work of Cotterell and Turner, who build their work partially on the first version of Relevance Theory. Peter Cotterell and Max Turner, *Linguistics and Biblical Interpretation* (Downers Grove, Ill.: InterVarsity Press, 1989). On the other hand, as mentioned before, van Dijk emphasizes in his works the lack of a theory of context and gives examples of the recent attempts to provide one. He presents the basis for his proposal in Teun A. van Dijk, *Sociedad y discurso: Cómo influyen los contextos sociales sobre el texto y la conversación* (Barcelona: Editorial Gedisa, 2011); van Dijk, *Discourse and Context*. The next section of this chapter presents a relevance-theoretic model of context.

52. Brown consciously integrates RT and Speech Act Theory in her communication model of hermeneutics. Brown, *Scripture as Communication*, 29–56. She defines meaning as "the complex pattern of what an author intends to communicate with his or her audience for purposes of engagement, which is inscribed in the text and conveyed through use of both shareable language parameters and background-contextual assumptions." Ibid., 47.

53. Sim, "Particles and Participles," 226–7.

54. Stephen W. Pattemore, *The People of God in the Apocalypse: Discourse, Structure, and Exegesis*, SNTSMS 128 (Cambridge: Cambridge University Press, 2004).

55. David H. K. Hoe, "Apocalyptic Discourse in Second Peter" (Ph.D. diss., Dallas Theological Seminary, 2008), 10.

56. Steve Smith, *The Fate of the Jerusalem Temple in Luke-Acts: An Intertextual Approach to Jesus' Laments over Jerusalem and Stephen's Speech*, LNTS 553 (London: T&T Clark, 2016).

Relevance Theory

"An essential feature of most human communication, both verbal and non-verbal, is the expression and recognition of intentions."[57] From this human characteristic, Wilson and Sperber built Relevance Theory. This is an inferential theory of human cognition and communication. "[It] focuses on intentional (not accidental) overt (not covert) communication. Its proper domain is ostensive-inferential communication."[58] In the next sections, a précis of Relevant Theory, how it understands quotations, and its contribution to the discussion of the use of the OT in the NT are presented.

Précis of Relevance Theory

Relevance Theory "provides a comprehensive theory of communication which shows how authors, readers, texts, and contexts interact in the communication of meaning and, as such, provides a rich model for understanding the interpretive task."[59] RT studies a speaker's/writer's communication and a hearer's/reader's cognition. It analyzes how both the hearer/reader and the speaker/writer are involved in the comprehension process. Also, it defines the *context* differently than how it has been defined in biblical studies, and considers the text as the record of a real communicative event. All these aspects are developed below.

Relevance and the Speaker/Writer

As mentioned above, RT is interested in ostensive-inferential communication. In this case, in order to communicate, not only must a speaker/writer make her intention clear to inform the audience about something, but the audience also must perceive her intention.[60] For that reason, in an overt

57. Deirdre Wilson and Dan Sperber, "Relevance Theory," *UCLWPL* 14 (2002): 249. This is one of the central claims of Paul Grice, *Studies in the Way of Words* (Cambridge, Mass.: Harvard University Press, 1989).

58. Green, "Relevance Theory and Biblical Interpretation," 223. Deirdre Wilson points out that RT differs from other Gricean approaches in three main respects: "It does not treat communication as necessarily cooperative in Grice's sense: for communication to be successful, the only goal that speaker and hearer need to share is that of understanding and being understood. It is not maxim-based: the communicative principle of relevance is not a maxim that speakers need to know, but a generalization about acts of inferential communication. It follows that deliberate maxim-violation, which is central to Gricean pragmatics, has no role in relevance-theoretic comprehension." Deirdre Wilson, "Relevance Theory," in MIT Encyclopedia of the Cognitive Science, edited by Robert A. Wilson and Frank C. Keil (Cambridge, MA: MIT Press, 2001), 720.

59. Green,"Relevance Theory and Biblical Interpretation," 267.

60. Wilson and Sperber say that "for communication to be truly overt, the communicator's informative intention must become not merely manifest to the audience (i.e. capable of being

communication, "the communicator intentionally provides evidence that he intends the audience to arrive at certain conclusions."[61] As Green notes, "[c]ommunication is ostensive in the sense that the speaker/author wants her intention to communicate to be recognized. On the other hand, from the perspective of the hearer/reader it is inferential in that he must infer from the evidence provided what the speaker/author's intent was."[62]

When a person communicates ostensively, she creates in her audience the expectancy of relevance. "[T]he communicator... encourages her audience to presume that it is relevant enough to be worth processing."[63] For that reason, the *communicative principle of relevance* (or just *the principle of relevance*) points out that "[e]very ostensive stimulus conveys a presumption of its own optimal relevance."[64] Now, this *presumption of optimal relevance* involves the perspective of both the hearer/reader and the speaker/writer: "a. The ostensive stimulus is relevant enough to be worth the audience's processing effort. b. It is the most relevant one compatible with the communicator's abilities and preferences."[65]

---

recognized and accepted as true, or probably true), but mutually manifest to communicator and audience." Wilson and Sperber, "Relevance Theory," 628 n. 5. The informative intention is the intention to inform an audience of something, "to make manifest a set of assumptions." Green, "Relevance Theory and Theological Interpretation," 78 n. 7. Wilson and Sperber point out that "understanding is achieved when the communicative intention is fulfilled—that is, when the audience recognizes the informative intention. (Whether the informative intention itself is fulfilled depends on how much the audience trusts the communicator)." Wilson and Sperber, "Relevance Theory," 611.

61. Christoph Unger, *Genre, Relevance, and Global Coherence: The Pragmatics of Discourse Type*, PSPLC (Basingstoke, England: Palgrave Macmillan, 2006), 11.

62. Green, "Relevance Theory and Biblical Interpretation," 223. Sperber and Wilson say that communication is ostensive-inferential if and only if "the communicator produces a stimulus which makes it mutually manifest to communicator and audience that the communicator intends, by means of this stimulus, to make manifest or more manifest to the audience a set of assumptions (I)." Sperber and Wilson, *Relevance: Communication and Cognition*, 63. In other words, RT sees two levels or layers of intention: (1) the informative intention, to make manifest or more manifest to an audience a set of assumptions (I), and (2) the communicative intention, to make mutually manifest the informative intention. Deirdre Wilson, "Metarepresentation in Linguistic Communication," *UCLWPL* 11 (1999): 140. The way RT defines intentions is not what W. K. Wimsatt and Beardsley criticize as the "intentional fallacy." They argue that at least in poetry "the design or intention of the author is neither available nor desirable as a standard for judging the success of a work of literary art." W. K. Wimsatt and Monroe C. Beardsley, "The Intentional Fallacy," in *The Verbal Icon: Studies in the Meaning of Poetry*, ed. W. K. Wimsatt (Lexington: University of Kentucky Press, 1954), 3. As Green points out, "[a]lthough we may not have access to a poet's or any other author's motivations, in all human communication, a speaker/author intends to convey information as well as to inform others of her intent to convey information." Green, "Relevance Theory and Theological Interpretation," 78 n. 7.

63. Wilson and Sperber, "Relevance Theory," 611.

64. Ibid., 612.

65. Ibid. This definition corresponds to the revised version of the Principle of Relevance in Sperber and Wilson, *Relevance: Communication and Cognition*, 270.

This theory assumes both the speaker/writer and the reader/hearer are rational. In this sense, the writer wants to communicate something. As Wilson and Sperber say, "[e]ven a self-interested, deceptive or incompetent communicator manifestly intends her audience to assume that her stimulus is relevant enough to be worth processing."[66] In the case of biblical authors, obviously, they are adequate communicators. They want their audience to act in accordance with what they write to them. In any case, even a competent communicator or an attentive reader/hearer can find misunderstanding. RT helps to understand not only successful communication but also misunderstandings.[67]

Relevance and the Hearer/Reader

When engaging in an ostensive communication, a speaker/writer encourages her audience to be involved with her in this process. Relevance drives this ostensive-inferential communication. Now, the concept of relevance, in technical terms, is not merely synonymous with applicability or pertinence. Rather, it is related to cognitive changes in a hearer/reader and the cognitive effort necessary for those changes. RT considers that any stimulus (such as observable phenomena, thoughts, memories, conclusions of inferences) may be relevant to an individual "when it connects with background information he has available to yield conclusions that matter to him: say, by answering a question he had in mind, improving his knowledge on a certain topic, settling a doubt, confirming a suspicion, or correcting a mistaken impression. According to relevance theory, an input is relevant to an individual when its processing in a context of available assumptions yields a *positive cognitive effect*."[68]

On its part, cognitive effect is "[t]he result of a fruitful (i.e. relevant) interaction between a newly impinging stimulus and a subset of the assumptions already in the cognitive system; there are three main kinds of contextual (cognitive) effects: supporting and so strengthening existing assumptions, contradicting and eliminating assumptions, combining inferentially with them to produce new conclusions."[69]

66. Wilson and Sperber, "Relevance Theory," 611.

67. See a good analysis and different types of misunderstandings in Francisco Yus, "Misunderstandings and Explicit/Implicit Communication," *Prag* 9 (1999): 487–517.

68. Wilson and Sperber, "Relevance Theory," 608 (their emphasis). RT understands *assumption* as "thoughts treated by the individual as representations of the actual world (as opposed to fictions, desires, or representations of representations)." Sperber and Wilson, *Relevance: Communication and Cognition*, 2.

69. Robyn Carston, *Thoughts and Utterances: The Pragmatics of Explicit Communication* (Oxford: Blackwell, 2002), 377. Some scholars still use the concepts of cognitive and contextual effects as synonyms. Nevertheless, Sperber and Wilson changed from using "contextual" to "cognitive" effects in all the articles published after 1986. In the second edition of *Relevance, Communication*

This interaction demands a cognitive processing effort, namely, "the effort which a cognitive system must expend in order to arrive at a satisfactory interpretation of incoming information."[70] The relevance of an utterance may be assessed in terms of cognitive effects and processing effort. As Sperber and Wilson say

a. Other things being equal, the greater the positive cognitive effects achieved by processing an input, the greater the relevance of the input to the individual at that time.
b. Other things being equal, the greater the processing effort expended, the lower the relevance of the input to the individual at that time.[71]

In summary, for information to be relevant to an individual, it has to provoke cognitive benefits in relation to the effort expended to achieve them.

This relevance may vary depending on the circumstances. Some inputs may be more relevant than others, or the same input may be more relevant on one occasion than another depending on the circumstances. The same is true of contextual assumptions and cognitive effects. On a given occasion a contextual assumption may be more or less salient or a cognitive effect easier or harder to derive. In any case, humans tend to process information in a context that maximizes its relevance. For that reason, the *cognitive principle of relevance* affirms that "[h]uman cognition tends to be geared to the maximization of relevance."[72]

In the case of a written text, several types of readers come into consideration. There are the first readers, those whom the writer addresses (synchronic communication situations); there are also subsequent or secondary readers, those who read the text although it was not intended necessarily for them (diachronic communication situations).[73] Stephen Pattemore points out regarding synchronic and diachronic communication situations that

---

and Cognition, they explicitly define "cognitive effect as a contextual effect occurring in a cognitive system (e.g. an individual)." Sperber and Wilson, *Relevance: Communication and Cognition*, 265.

70. This interpretation "involve[s] factors such as the accessing of an appropriate set of contextual assumptions and the inferential work involved in integrating the new information with existing assumptions." Carston, *Thoughts and Utterances*, 379.

71. Wilson and Sperber, "Relevance Theory," 609. The second affirmation does not imply necessarily that if there is a high processing effort there automatically is less relevance. Relevance is assessed simultaneously in terms of cognitive effects and processing effort. As Harriet Hill points out, "[i]f the cognitive effects are high, even if there are high processing costs, the net effect may be more relevant than communication that requires less processing effort but has less effects. " Hill, *The Bible at Cultural Crossroads*, 6.

72. Wilson and Sperber, "Relevance Theory," 610.

73. In narrative texts, there are also many levels of communication, e.g., between characters, between narrator and narratees, between implied author and implied readers. The *cognitive principle of relevance* applies in each level and for each type of reader. See a brief discussion on this issue in Pattemore, *The People of God in the Apocalypse*, 23–4.

"the problem in each case is to establish whether there is a mutual cognitive environment within which the search for relevance can be seen to guide both author and audience."[74] The focus of this research is the author and her first readers and their mutual cognitive environment.[75]

There are at least two ways to understand the communication between the author and the intended audience, and in particular how this audience understands the metarepresentation of the OT.[76] Stanley argues that in the case of Pauline literature, one option is to consider his different audiences and how they could have understood his quotations. This alternative has to deal with the diversity and limitations of Pauline audiences and many of "the different 'meanings' for Paul's biblical quotations, reflecting the diverse literary capabilities and experiences of the many people in his churches."[77] The other option is to consider the literary construct of the implied reader.[78] Although James's audience is not very diverse, this second option seems better. As mentioned in chapter 1, this research assumes that James's first readers/hearers were mainly Jewish Christians. It will be clearer in chapters 3 to 5 that the addressees can be socioeconomically considered as three groups: the poor, the rich, and those in between. James focuses on each group in different portions of his discourse. Hence, it seems better not to consider one implied reader as representing the entire audience, but rather one for each social stratum. For example, in 1:9 James focuses on the poor, in 1:10–11 he addresses the rich, and in 1:26–27 and 2:1–26, he highlights the responsibilities and problems of the main group, those "in between." In 4:13–5:6, the focus is on the rich. However, even when he focuses on one group, he uses the same text to address the rest of the congregation as well, so that each group of the church receives James's instructions.

Here are some reasons for using the figure of the implied reader: (1) Since today there is no total certainty concerning how diverse an ancient audience was, it is hard to analyze exhaustively the different possible scenarios of interpretation.[79] (2) The text provides important evidence about how an

74. Ibid., 29.

75. Even though one cannot avoid completely the real reader. This research, for example, does not consider the different audiences reading the text today or other reader response concerns.

76. The concept of metarepresentation is presented later in detail. At this point, as mentioned in the preceding chapter, it is enough to say that "to metarepresent" is the human ability of representing the thoughts of another person or oneself at another time. In this sense, simplistically speaking, a NT author's or his audience's representation of an OT author is a metarepresentation of the OT.

77. Christopher D. Stanley, "'Pearls before Swine': Did Paul's Audiences Understand His Biblical Quotations?," *NovT* 41 (1999): 142. He applies to 1 Cor, 2 Cor, Gal, and Rom this distinction of different possible audiences and their interpretations of Paul's quotations in Stanley, *Arguing with Scripture*, 75–183.

78. Stanley, "Pearls before Swine," 142.

79. In his analysis, Stanley defines and uses three types of readers (the optimal, the competent, and the minimal audience). Stanley, *Arguing with Scripture*, 68–9. Nevertheless, other

author considered his audience. In RT terms, an author writes with his audience in mind in order to be optimally relevant to them. As Ian MacKenzie points out, "[w]hile readers are not obliged to follow the roles marked out for them in texts, many readers clearly *do* attempt to become part of the authorial audience whose hypothetical knowledge and beliefs determined the author's use of explicatures and implicatures."[80]

The implied reader, or better the implied audience, could be understood as the "persona constructed from the narrative text that responds appropriately to the text's rhetorical devices and thus fulfills the goals of the text."[81] This device permits one to derive a resemblance of the first readers from the text, at least as the author perceives them. Following the ideas of Mark Powell, an implied reader has five types of knowledge: (1) knowledge of the language of the text, (2) knowledge that might be considered universal, (3) knowledge of what is revealed within the text, (4) knowledge of what is presupposed by the spatial, temporal, and social setting of the text, and (5) knowledge of other literature that is cited (by reference or allusion) within the text.[82]

In a real audience, there is a degree of knowledge, including, in the case of James's addressees,[83] biblical knowledge. Thus some of James's addressees—probably the most experienced or the teachers of the congregation—could have the characteristics of the implied reader. They could teach and explain

---

factors could be considered to build a typology, e.g., male readers, female readers, widows, slaves, rich, poor, and so on.

80. Ian Mackenzie, *Paradigms of Reading: Relevance Theory and Deconstruction* (New York: Palgrave Macmillan, 2002), 39 (his emphasis). In the same vein, Stanley comments: "What makes the 'implied reader' concept so useful is not what it says (if anything) about the original audience of a text, but what it reveals about the author's perception of that audience, including how that perception shaped the author's strategies for communicating with the intended audience." Stanley, "Pearls before Swine," 142–3.

81. Jeannine K. Brown, *The Disciples in Narrative Perspective: The Portrayal and Function of the Matthean Disciples*, SBLAB 9 (Leiden: Brill, 2002), 123. This constructed reader has been defined and labeled in different ways. For a good summary of the discussion, see Robert M. Fowler, "Who Is 'The Reader' in Reader Response Criticism," *Semeia* 31 (1985): 5–23; Brown, *The Disciples in Narrative Perspective*, 123–33. For a critical evaluation of the role of the reader in general, and the "implied reader" in particular, in interpretation, see Vanhoozer, *Is There a Meaning in This Text?*, 148–96.

82. Mark Allan Powell, "Expected and Unexpected Readings of Matthew: What the Reader Knows," *AsTJ* 48.2 (1993): 31–51. Christopher Stanley, quoting Stanley Fish, points out that the implied reader is "the reader whose education, opinions, concerns, linguistic competence, etc., make him capable of having the experience the author wished to provide." Stanley, "Pearls before Swine," 142; Stanley E. Fish, "Interpreting the Variorum," in *Reader-Response Criticism: From Formalism to Post-structuralism*, ed. Jane P. Tompkins (Baltimore: Johns Hopkins University Press, 1980), 174.

83. For an exhaustive analysis of James's implied and real addressees, see David H. Edgar, *Has God Not Chosen the Poor? The Social Setting of the Epistle of James*, JSNTSup 206 (Sheffield: Sheffield Academic, 2001), 95–136.

the letter to the rest of the congregation, the less informed ones.[84] In RT terms, they could supply the adequate encyclopedic knowledge to make the letter more relevant and guide the congregation to the recovery of its *explicatures* and *implicatures*.

Relevance and the Process of Comprehension

Both the speaker/writer and the hearer/reader are involved in the process of comprehension. As mentioned earlier, in any ostensive communicative event, anutterance is more than what is linguistically encoded. There is a gap between sentence meaning and utterance meaning, which is filled by inference. What a speaker/writer communicates has an explicit and an implicit content that the hearer/reader has to infer from the code and context. The information encoded by the utterance and the implicit information tied to it and recovered by reference assignment, disambiguation, and enrichment is called *explicature*.[85] In more technical terms, Robyn Carston says that "[a]n assumption (proposition) communicated by an utterance is an 'explicature' of the utterance if and only if it is a development of (a) a linguistically encoded logical form of the utterance, or of (b) a sentential subpart of a logical form."[86] The rest of the implicit content is called *implicature*.[87] In other words, an *implicature* is any "communicated assumption which is derived solely via a process of pragmatic inference."[88]

In an ostensive communication, a hearer/reader infers the speaker's/writer's meaning by doing several pragmatic subtasks. At the explicit level, inany utterance, there are ambiguities to clarify, references to assign, ellipses to interpret, and so on. At a higher level of explicitness, there are attitudes to discern, and illocutionary indeterminacies to resolve, among other tasks. Relevance Theory defines these tasks as the recovery of *explicatures*. But interpretation/comprehension does not stop there. There are implicated premises, and implicated conclusions, to derive. This process is called the

84. Stanley proposes something similar with respect to the problem created by the assumption that "Paul's audiences could and did routinely supply for themselves the background and context of Paul's many quotations, allusions, and other references to the Jewish Scriptures." One of the alternatives he proposes as viable is that "Paul addressed his letters primarily to the literate members of his churches." They were familiar with the OT and could read and explain the letters and his OT references to the less educated members. Stanley, "Pearls before Swine," 133.

85. Robyn Carston, "Relevance Theory and the Saying/Implicating Distinction," in *Handbook of Pragmatics*, ed. Gregory Ward and Laurence Horn, BHL 16 (Oxford: Blackwell, 2004), 633–56; Robyn Carston and Alison Hall, "Implicature and Explicature," in *Cognitive Pragmatics*, ed. H-J. Schmid and D. Geeraerts (Berlin: Mount de Gruyter, 2011), 1–30; Green, "Relevance Theory and Biblical Interpretation," 266–73.

86. Carston, *Thoughts and Utterances*, 124.

87. Sperber and Wilson, *Relevance: Communication and Cognition*, 182.

88. Carston, *Thoughts and Utterances*, 377.

recovery of *implicatures*.[89] Wilson and Sperber say: "The Communicative Principle of Relevance and the definition of optimal relevance suggest a practical procedure for performing these subtasks and constructing a hypothesis about the speaker's meaning. The hearer should take the linguistically encoded sentence meaning; following a path of least effort, he should enrich it at the explicit level and complement it at the implicit level until the resulting interpretation meets his expectation of relevance."[90]

In synthesis, the hearer's goal "is to construct a hypothesis about the speaker's meaning that satisfies the presumption of relevance conveyed by the utterance."[91]

Consider next some examples that illustrate this process of comprehension, which focus first on the cognitive effect, and then on the processing effort:[92]

1. Peter: Did John pay back the money he owed you?
2. Mary: No. He forgot to go to the bank.

In order for Peter to understand Mary's utterance, he has some tasks to do. First of all, he assumes that Mary's utterance is optimally relevant to him by answering his question. Second, he takes the sentence "He forgot to go to the bank" and enriches it at the explicit level. In order to do this, he needs to assign the reference of the pronoun "he." In this case, it is clear that the referent is "John." Also, he needs to disambiguate the concept "bank." The concept "bank" could refer to a financial institution ($bank_1$), a river bank ($bank_2$), a steep slope of a hill ($bank_3$), and so on. In this situation, it is clear that "bank" denotes a financial institution that deals with private individuals. Also, the encyclopedic knowledge about the various type of banks helps the hearer to understand that the phrase "go to the bank" does not mean just

89. It should be mentioned here that when scholars debate the meaning of a verse, usually they debate at the level of explicatures. Rarely, the discussion is about higher levels of explicitness, such as the speech acts performed in a text. In exceptional cases, discussions revolve around implicatures. Another important focus of discussion is about what aspects of the cognitive environment are salient in a specific point of the discourse, or behind the complete work, such as the different types of *Sitzen im Leben*. Later in the research, these distinctions will be apparent.

90. Wilson and Sperber, "Relevance Theory," 613.

91. Ibid., 615. Wilson and Sperber say here that this process of comprehension/interpretation can be expressed as a development of several subtasks: "a. Constructing an appropriate hypothesis about explicit content (in relevance-theoretic terms, EXPLICATURES) via decoding, disambiguation, reference resolution, and other pragmatic enrichment processes. b. Constructing an appropriate hypothesis about the intended contextual assumptions (in relevance-theoretic terms, IMPLICATED PREMISES). c. Constructing an appropriate hypothesis about the intended contextual implications (in relevance-theoretic terms, IMPLICATED CONCLUSIONS)."

92. Taken and adapted from Wilson and Sperber, "Relevance Theory," 615–7.

something like "visiting a bank," but rather "visiting a bank in order to get money from a banking account."[93] So, the explicature recovered could be

3. John forgot to go to the $bank_I$.

Third, he complements explicature (3) at the implicit level. An implicit premise in this case could be

4. Forgetting to go to the $bank_I$ may make one unable to repay the money one owes.

With the explicature (3) plus the implicated premise (4), the implicated conclusion is

5. John was unable to repay Mary the money he owes because he forgot to go to the bank.

An extra weak implicature derived from (5) that also satisfies the expectation of relevance could be

6. John may repay Mary the money he owes after his next visit to the $bank_I$.

In certain circumstances, Mary could also present a higher-level explicature expressing her attitude, such as

7. Mary regrets that John forgot to go to the $bank_I$.

Also, she could imply other implicit premises and implicit conclusions. For example:

8. Someone who does not pay his debts is irresponsible.
9. John is irresponsible.

Implicatures can be communicated with a different degree of strength.[94] As Diane Blakemore says, "[t]he strongest implicatures are those fully

93. The example here is oversimplified. In fact, from the encyclopedic knowledge about banks today, "go to the bank" could mean, "go to an ATM." This phenomenon in RT is called narrowing or broadening the encoded meaning. Lexical narrowing/broadening is highly context-dependent. For a deeper discussion, see Carston, *Thoughts and Utterances*, 320–75; Manuel Hernández Iglesias, "*Ad Hoc* Concepts and Metaphor," in *Explicit Communication: Robyn Carston's Pragmatics*, ed. Belén Soria and Esther Romero, PSPLC (Basingstoke, England: Palgrave Macmillan, 2010), 173–82.

94. This variation of strength is also called "differing in saliency" or "more or less determinate." Deirdre Wilson and Dan Sperber, "Outline of Relevance Theory," *Hermes* 5 (1990): 48.

determinate implicated conclusions and premises that the hearer is forced to derive in order to obtain an interpretation consistent with the principle of relevance. The tighter the constraint the speaker imposes on the hearer's choice of contextual assumptions, the stronger the resulting implicatures. The less tight the constraint, the weaker the resulting implicatures."[95]

In this regard, Sperber and Wilson point out that there is no cutoff point between strongly and weakly implicated inferences. Nevertheless, "a point is reached at which the hearer receives no encouragement at all to supply any particular premise and conclusion, and he takes the entire responsibility for supplying them himself."[96] In this example, the implicature (5) is more strongly communicated than (6) or (9).

On the other hand, Sperber and Wilson call *poetic effect* the effect "of an utterance which achieves most of its relevance through a wide range of weak implicatures."[97] In this case, the speaker/writer gives more responsibility to the hearer/reader in deriving conclusions. See the next example:[98]

10. Richard is a gorilla.

Assuming that Richard is the name of a human being, some of the implicatures of (10) could be:

11. Richard is fierce.
12. Richard is nasty.
13. Richard is prone to violence.

Metaphors, irony, and other tropes or figures of speech involve poetic effect.[99]

The other component of the process of interpretation is processing effort. As mentioned above, Wilson and Sperber point out that the greater the processing effort, the less the relevance. See the next example, used by Regina Blass:[100]

95. Diane Blakemore, *Understanding Utterances: An Introduction to Pragmatics*, BTL 6 (Oxford: Blackwell, 1992), 129.

96. Sperber and Wilson, *Relevance: Communication and Cognition*, 199.

97. Ibid., 222.

98. Taken from Adrian Pilkington, *Poetic Effects: A Relevance Theory Perspective*, PBNS 75 (Amsterdam: John Benjamins, 2000), 94.

99. See more details in Blakemore, *Understanding Utterances*, 155–79; Pilkington, *Poetic Effects*; Adrian Pilkington, "Metaphor Comprehension: Some Questions for Current Accounts in Relevance Theory," in *Explicit Communication: Robyn Carston's Pragmatics*, ed. Belén Soria and Esther Romero, PSPLC (Basingstoke, England: Palgrave Macmillan, 2010), 156–72.

100. Blass refers to "implicated premises" as "contextual assumption," and "implicated conclusion" as "contextual implications." Regina Blass, *Relevance Relations in Discourse: A Study with Special Reference to Sissala*, CSL 55 (Cambridge: Cambridge University Press, 1990), 50–2.

14. Jane: Do I look strange in my cover cloth?
15. Janice: Everybody wears them around here.

In order for Jane to see the relevance of Janice's answer, she has to derive at least one implicated premise:

16. People do not look strange wearing what everybody else is wearing.

So, in this context, she can derive the implicated conclusion:

17. She does not look strange in her cover cloth.

Now, consider a slightly different answer:

18. Jane: Do I look strange in my cover cloth?
19. Janice: We are in Africa.

In this case, Jane has to derive at least two implicated premises—(20) and (21)—to arrive at the same implicated conclusion (17).

20. Many women in Africa wear cover cloths.
21. Jane does not look strange wearing what many other women are wearing.

Thus, in comparison, answer (15) takes less processing effort to understand than (19). In other words, (15) is more relevant than (19). On some occasions, major cognitive effects compensate for the major cognitive efforts applied in the interpretive process. It is not difficult to imagine a context where (19) could bring more cognitive effects than (15) and, as a result, would be more relevant.

Relevance and Context

Until this point, the description of the participation of the speaker/writer, the hearer/reader, and the process of comprehension show how central the context is in an ostensive-inferential communication. Nevertheless, it has not been defined. One of RT's contributions to biblical studies is the way it defines context. It is not a third type of context in addition to socio-historical and literary contexts. Rather, it is a different way to conceive context. As mentioned above, in the RT perspective, utterances provide evidence of a speaker's/writer's meaning and trigger the hearer's/reader's inferential interpretive process. Furthermore, it is well recognized that words and utterances can have different meanings depending on the context in which they are communicated. So, context and utterances are intimately linked in any communicative event. In biblical studies, for example, Joel Green says:

> The term [context] is often used of (1) the sociohistorical setting within which a text was generated, within which the events to which a text provides witness took place, or within which the traditions that came finally to expression in a text were shaped and handed down. Context can mean (2) the portions of something written that precede and follow a word or passage in a text. It can also refer to (3) the situation of the reader, understood in sociohistorical as well as theological terms, which helps to shape how the reader accesses and construes the significance of a text.[101]

This definition does not include how a particular reader uses these different aspects of context in the process of interpreting the biblical text.[102] In defining context, RT focuses on the speaker/writer and the hearer/reader. As Maria Jodłowiec says, "[t]he inferential relevance-oriented processing that lies at the heart of human verbal comprehension is believed to be highly context-sensitive. It is highly context-sensitive, firstly, due to the fact that communicative intentions are made manifest in—and therefore inevitably belong to—the context in which a given ostensive act is performed, and secondly, because the background assumptions brought to bear in the interpretation process determine the meaning recovered by the interpreter."[103]

In other words, the context is not secondary but an essential part in order for a hearer/reader to understand a speaker's/writer's utterance. "Context is a subset of all the salient or available information to the communicator and the addressee which is accessed in the communication of an utterance."[104] In other words, in an ostensive-inferential communication, context is part of the *mutual cognitive environment* of the communicator and the addressee.[105]

101. Joel B. Green, "Context," *DTIB* 130. Eugene Nida recognizes the centrality of context in defining meaning. However, in his article, he does not provide an explicit method or theory that permits the interpreter to decide which factors of the context he/she has to consider. Eugene Albert Nida, "The Role of Context in the Understanding of Discourse," in *Discourse Analysis and the New Testament: Approaches and Results*, ed. Stanley E. Porter and Jeffrey T. Reed, JSNTSup 170 (Sheffield: Sheffield Academic, 1999), 20–7. As mentioned before, van Dijk presents some preliminary efforts toward a theory of context from the perspective of a socio-cognitive approach in van Dijk, *Studies in the Pragmatics of Discourse*, JL 101 (Mouton: The Hague, 1981); Teun A. van Dijk, "Algunos principios de una teoría del contexto," *RLED* 1 (2001): 69–81; van Dijk, *Discourse and Context*; van Dijk, *Sociedad y discurso*.

102. Gene Green points out that in biblical studies "[c]ontext is viewed very broadly and imprecisely as 'all that out there' beyond the specific text under consideration, including both the immediate literary context of the discourse (the 'cotext'), the larger literary corpus of a particular author, the body of biblical literature itself (the canon), as well as the cultural context shared by both the writer and the readers." Green, "Relevance Theory and Biblical Interpretation," 226.

103. Maria Jodłowiec, "How the Context Emerges," in *In the Mind and across Minds: A Relevance-Theoretic Perspective on Communication and Translation*, ed. Ewa Wałaszewska, Marta Kisielewska-Krysiuk, and Agnieszka Piskorka (Cambridge: Cambridge Scholars Publishing, 2010), 135.

104. Green, "Relevance Theory and Biblical Interpretation," 268.

105. A *cognitive environment* is "a set of assumptions that are manifest to an individual at a given time," and a *mutual cognitive environment* is "a cognitive environment which is shared by a

It is a psychological construct.[106] It is not a static preestablished set of assumptions before communication happens. Instead, it is dynamic. As Green points out, "[c]ontext does not stand as a pre-set, unmoving, unchanged whole, but is woven or shaped as the discourse continues. In this way, the context is constantly shifting and changing in accordance with the purposes of the speaker or writer who plays on the interaction of the text with its context in order to make known her informative intent. Not all the potential contexts are accessed at once but only the contextual information which will be needed in the process of communication."[107]

The next examples, used by Regina Blass, illustrate how context influences the understanding of an utterance.[108]

22. He went to McDonald's. The quarter pounder sounded good and he ordered it.
23. The river had been dry for a long time. Everyone attended the funeral.

Blass points out that a Western reader would probably have no difficulties understanding (22), but (23) may seem incomprehensible. On the contrary, for a speaker of Sissala (spoken in Burkina Faso and Ghana) the opposite would be the case. In both instances, the contextual assumptions (or implicated premises) are respectively

22. He went to a place where food is prepared and cooked called McDonald's. There he saw ground meat, which is formed into patties, fried, and placed between two pieces of bread.
23. If a river has been dry a long time, then a river spirit has died. Whenever a spirit dies there is a funeral. The river had been dry for a long time.

Now, the sources of *context* are threefold: "the physical environment of communicator and addressee, the discourse in which an utterance is embedded, and the encyclopedic knowledge shared by the communicator and

---

group of individuals and in which it is manifest to those individuals that they share it with each other; every manifest assumption in a mutual cognitive environment is 'mutually manifest.'" Carston, *Thoughts and Utterances*, 376, 8.

106. To Sperber and Wilson, context is "the set of premises used in interpreting an utterance (apart from the premises that the utterance in question has been produced).... A context is a psychological construct, a subset of the hearer's [and speaker's] assumptions about the world." In this sense, "expectation about the future, scientific hypotheses, religious beliefs, anecdotal memories, general cultural assumptions, beliefs about the mental state of the speaker, may play a role in interpretation." Sperber and Wilson, *Relevance: Communication and Cognition*, 15–6. In the same vein, Harriet Hill says: "The [speaker's] utterance does not evoke the audience's entire cognitive environment. It only evokes certain assumptions, and these form the *context* in which the utterance is processed." Hill, *The Bible at Cultural Crossroads*, 14.

107. Green, "Relevance Theory and Biblical Interpretation," 229.

108. Blass, *Relevance Relations in Discourse*, 85–6.

addressee."[109] The mutual cognitive environment in first-century Christian circles includes "an array of other texts (oral and written) to which the author can assume the audience has access."[110]

A biblical interpreter today reads the text as a secondary audience.[111] So, in order to understand a biblical utterance, he or she must pay attention to "the means by which text and context work together in communication and the principles which came into play to distinguish which contexts are appropriate in our reading of a text."[112] In that sense, the diverse aspects of the cognitive environment recovered by historical-critical methods help the interpretive process by trying to resemble the cognitive environment of the writer and first readers.[113] The biblical interpreter, nevertheless, "must also ask which aspects of their [the writer and addressees'] cognitive environment (drawn from discourse and memory) would allow for a particular utterance to achieve relevance."[114] It is clear that not every aspect of the first-century Greco-Roman world, or Second Temple literature, or social relationships, and so on is present or more salient in the mutual cognitive environment of authors and their addressees. The question is which of these assumptions "the biblical authors would have expected their readers to be capable of representing."[115] As a result, "the search for relevance constrains the interpretive process."[116] RT strengthens the historical-critical methods by helping the interpreter to evaluate the different aspects of the cognitive environment. It guides the exegete to decide what are the most probable converging contexts in the interpretation of a text. It helps to integrate text and context in a more consistent way.

109. Green, "Relevance Theory and Biblical Interpretation," 227.

110. Pattemore, *The People of God in the Apocalypse*, 29–30.

111. A secondary communication is a "communication in which a message designed for one audience is given to another, secondary audience," in this case, an audience separated "by vast quantities of time and space." Hill, *The Bible at Cultural Crossroads*, 28–9 and n. 13.

112. Green, "Relevance Theory and Biblical Interpretation," 235. This is what Joseph Fantin implies when he says: "I am attempting to re-create as much of the relevant context as possible to help the reader hear the text as the original readers would have heard it." Fantin, *Lord of the Entire World*, 8.

113. As Harriet Hill points out, biblical translation performs a similar task. She says: "To understand the intended meaning, receptors need the intended context. Communication of Scripture succeeds to the extent that the cognitive environment the secondary audience believes it shares with the biblical author resembles that of the first audience's. Unlike primary communication situations, the original author is no longer active, and so cannot repair the communication. This places the onus on the secondary receptors to adjust the mutual cognitive environment they perceive they share with the biblical author so that it resembles that of the first audience's. Over time, they can acquire the relevant parts of this mutual cognitive environment as their own and access the intended contextual assumptions rapidly and without undue effort. When this happens, the processing costs of understanding Scripture are reduced and relevance increases." Hill, *The Bible at Cultural Crossroads*, 29.

114. Green, "Relevance Theory and Biblical Interpretation," 236.

115. Ibid., 238.

116. Ibid., 232. Furlong calls this interpretation "literary interpretation." This interpretation, she says, "is geared to picking out the optimally relevant interpretation of the text as a whole." Furlong, "Relevance Theory and Literary Interpretation," 196.

Anne Furlong proposes three criteria that help the interpreter in this search for the relevance of the text that can be helpful in this research.[117] She says that the goals of a literary interpretation should be exhaustiveness, plausibility, and unity. An interpreter must deal with all the evidence, namely, all the elements of the text. "The literary reader . . . rather than stopping when he has a fragmentary interpretation that is relevant enough, will make an effort at integrating the result with other evidence provided by the text, achieving a richer, more wide-ranging interpretation." This is exhaustiveness. Also, the reader "should make sure that his interpretation is warranted by the text, and by any other evidence he can discover." This is plausibility. Finally, in the process of interpretation, the reader spends much processing effort in deriving the cognitive effects of the different segments of the text. "The resulting effects must interact with each other, rather than remaining isolated, fragmentary leading to nothing beyond themselves." This is unity. These goals, namely, exhaustiveness, plausibility, and unity, lay in the way RT considers a text.

The Relevance of a Text

Relevance Theory considers a text, a written discourse, as the record of a real communication.[118] As a result, RT analyzes it as a complex ostensive stimulus.[119] Christoph Unger makes the case that a reader looks for the overall relevance of a text in a similar way that a hearer looks for the relevance of an utterance. In this sense, "each utterance may create its own expectation of relevance, which may be constrained and calibrated by the expectation of the relevance created for the sequence as a whole."[120] This way of understanding the text helps in the interpretive process. As Furlong says, the interpreter "attempts to account for all the evidence provided in the work; he tries to explore the range of assumptions intentionally made manifest; and his aim is to derive an interpretation which is reinforced and extended on the basis of assumptions made manifest throughout the work."[121]

Now, utterances of a text contribute in different ways to the overall relevance.[122] Some contribute as background information for later utterances

117. Furlong, "Relevance Theory and Literary Interpretation," 196–7.

118. Pattemore, *The People of God in the Apocalypse*, 46–7.

119. Unger, *Genre, Relevance, and Global Coherence*, 109–11. See also similar conclusions in Diane Blakemore, *Relevance and Linguistic Meaning: The Semantics and Pragmatics of Discourse Markers*, CSL 99 (Cambridge: Cambridge University Press, 2002); Jane Rita Caetano da Silveira, "Cognição, relevância e textualidade," in *Tópicos em teoria da relevância*, ed. Jorge Campos and Fábio José Rauen (Porto Alegre, Brazil: EDIPUCRS, 2008), 68–95.

120. Unger, *Genre, Relevance, and Global Coherence*, 111.

121. Furlong, "Relevance Theory and Literary Interpretation," 198.

122. This concept is an elaboration of the Wilson and Sperber understanding of background and foreground implications. Unger, *Genre, Relevance, and Global Coherence*, 113; Sperber and Wilson, *Relevance: Communication and Cognition*, 202–17.

by giving contextual assumptions that reduce the processing effort of following utterances or by "creating more specific expectations about the cognitive effects to be achieved in later utterances."[123] Others contribute directly to cognitive effects as foreground implicatures "by carrying information which is relevant in its own right."[124] Authors control the recovery of explicatures and implicatures of a text in order to guide their readers in the search for relevance.[125] Readers, on their part, assume the author is being relevant. They read trying to understand what the writer wants to communicate. Authors can use different literary resources such as genre,[126] register considerations, or style (the use of poetic effect, rhetorical patterns, quotations, etc.).[127] In particular, NT authors use the OT in different ways. They insert biblical references in their discourses, use OT imagery, and so on. These references contribute in different ways to the relevance of the whole discourse. It is necessary, then, to describe briefly how RT understands quotations.

Relevance Theory and Quotations

A person may use written and oral sources in a variety of ways.[128] In biblical studies, there is an ongoing discussion on this issue.[129] RT understands quo-

123. Unger, *Genre, Relevance, and Global Coherence*, 114.

124. Sperber and Wilson, *Relevance: Communication and Cognition*, 217.

125. Ibid., 217–24. From the perspective of RT, for example, Seiji Uchida explains the use of two literary devices. He explains that authors delay some of the subtasks of recovering explicatures (disambiguation, referent assignment, and enrichment) to create "suspense" or control the strong and weak implicatures to create a "twist" in a story. See other examples in Seiji Uchida, "Text and Relevance," in *Relevance Theory: Applications and Implications*, ed. Robyn Carston and Seiji Uchida, PBNS 37 (Amsterdam: John Benjamins, 1998), 161–78.

126. The definition of "genre" and its influence in interpretation have been widely discussed. For a discussion, see Grant R. Osborne, "Genre," *DTIB* 252–3; Unger, *Genre, Relevance, and Global Coherence*, 1–10.

127. For more details regarding how these literary characteristics interact with relevance, see Unger, *Genre, Relevance, and Global Coherence*; Pilkington, *Poetic Effects*, esp. chap. 5.

128. For a discussion on theories of quotations, see Herman Cappelen and Ernie Lepore, "Varieties of Quotation," *Mind* 106 (1997): 429–50; Herman Cappelen and Ernie Lepore, "Using, Mentioning, and Quoting: A Reply to Saka," *Mind* 108 (1999): 741–50; Herman Cappelen and Ernie Lepore, *Language Turned on Itself: The Semantics and Pragmatics of Metalinguistic Discourse* (Oxford: Oxford University Press, 2007); Paul Saka, "Quotation: A Reply to Cappelen & Lepore," *Mind* 108 (1999): 751–4; François Recanati, *Oratio Obliqua, Oratio Recta: An Essay on Metarepresentation* (Cambridge, Mass.: MIT Press, 2000); François Recanati, *Truth-Conditional Pragmatics* (Oxford: Oxford University Press, 2010), 219–302. For an evaluation from an RT perspective of different theories, see Eun-Ju Noh, *Metarepresentation: A Relevance-Theory Approach*, PBNS 69 (Amsterdam: John Benjamins, 2000). See also Stanley's evaluation of different literary theories of the function of quotations in written texts, Stanley, *Arguing with Scripture*, 16–31.

129. See, e.g., G. K. Beale, *The Book of Revelation: A Commentary on the Greek Text*, NIGTC (Grand Rapids, Mich.: Eerdmans, 1999), 76–97; G. K. Beale and D. A. Carson, eds., *Commentary on the New Testament Use of the Old Testament* (Grand Rapids, Mich.: Baker, 2007); Steve Moyise,

tations from a slightly different perspective. Quotations are a subcategory of metarepresentation.

Metarepresentation

Oral or written utterances are representations of a person's thoughts.[130] Also, people are able to represent the thoughts of others or themselves at another time. This use of a representation to represent another representation is called metarepresentation.[131] Humans have the ability to engage in metarepresentation, "the ability to represent the content of representations or to have concept about concepts."[132] From this perspective, quotations are a particular case of metarepresentation: linguistic metarepresentation.

RT emphasizes that a quotation metarepresents an original by resemblance (even merely to some degree).[133] "Two representations resemble each other (in a context) to the extent that they share logical and contextual implications [*implicatures*]. The more implications they have in common, the more they resemble each other."[134] In that sense, identity (namely, verbatim reproduction) is a particular case of resemblance. Resemblance, Wilson says, involves shared properties.[135] Two types of resemblance are the main concern of this research: metalinguistic and interpretive. Metalinguistic use is the exploitation of resemblance in linguistic form. Interpretive use is the utilization of the saliency of semantic, logical, or propositional form; it is

---

"Quotations," in *As It Is Written: Studying Paul's Use of Scripture*, ed. Stanley Porter and Christopher D. Stanley, SBLSymS 50 (Atlanta: Society of Biblical Literature, 2008), 15–28; Moyise, *Evoking Scripture*; Moyise, *Paul and Scripture*; Jon Paulien, "Elusive Allusions: The Problematic Use of the Old Testament in Revelation," *BR* 33 (1988): 37–53; Jon Paulien, "Elusive Allusions in the Apocalypse: Two Decades of Research into John's Use of the Old Testament," in *The Intertextuality of the Epistles: Explorations of Theory and Practice*, ed. Thomas L. Brodie, Dennis R. MacDonald, and Stanley E. Porter (Sheffield: Sheffield Phoenix, 2006), 61–8; Stanley, *Arguing with Scripture*, 32–66.

130. Oral or written utterances are particular cases of linguistic representation. Carston points out that representation is "anything used in such a way that it can be constructed as being *about* something (as having *meaning*) as opposed to just being itself." Carston, *Thoughts and Utterances*, 380 (her emphasis).

131. Eun-Jo Noh indicates that "metarepresentation is defined as the use of one representation to represent another in virtue of some resemblance between them, whether in content or form." Noh, *Metarepresentations*, 5.

132. Green, "Relevance Theory and Theological Interpretation," 82.

133. Wilson points out that in some literature about quotations, "it has been assumed that identity rather than resemblance is the normal or typical case." Also, it is clear that even "the degree of accuracy required in verbatim reporting depends on culture and circumstance." Wilson, "Metarepresentation in Linguistic Communication," 142.

134. Ibid., 143.

135. "The resemblances may be of just any type: perceptual, linguistic, logical, mathematical, conceptual, sociolinguistic, stylistic, typographic." Ibid.

resemblance in content.[136] A NT author uses metalinguistic resemblance, for example, when he evokes an OT text and then explains it or derives teaching from it.[137] On the other hand, NT authors create an interpretive resemblance of an OT text when they use an example, as James does (Abraham, Rahab, Elijah, Job). The author does not need to quote extensive sections of text. A couple of words are enough, a name, in order to trigger in the reader a variety of evocations. The author resembles the original, but uses it in his own context.[138] A combination of both types of metarepresentation is also common. Depending on the degree of similarity, Noh points out, resemblance can be a "literal or less-than-literal (loose) representation."[139] Also, the metarepresentation may be accompanied by expressions of the speaker's/writer's "attitude to the original thought or utterance being metarepresented."[140]

A NT author using the OT occasionally changes a word, or a phrase when using the LXX.[141] His quotation/allusion resembles the original (or originals); in general terms, it is a faithful one. Now, if the change is intentional, he wants to communicate something different from the original. He could expect for his addressees to detect the change, or trust in his usage of the sacred text. In this case, the change can contribute to cognitive effects, and so to the relevance of that utterance. Hays's criteria of validation mentioned in chapter 1 may help in discerning the probability of intentional use. On the other hand, if the change is unintentional—a problem of memory, for example—and the audience perceives it, then there could be a problem

136. Ibid. Direct quotation is a case of metalinguistic use, and indirect quotation is a case of interpretive use. Mixed quotations exploit both uses, metalinguistic and interpretive. See the next section below.

137. In Hebrews this use is recurrent. See, e.g., Heb 1:2–14; 2:5–8; 3:7–13; 10:35–39.

138. D. Dimant proposes a similar category. She calls it "compositional use." Devorah Dimant, "Use and Interpretation of Mikra in the Apocrypha and Pseudepigrapha," in *Mikra: Text, Translation, Reading, and Interpretation of the Hebrew Bible in Ancient Judaism and Early Christianity*, ed. Martin J. Mulder and Harry Sysling, CRINT 2 (Philadelphia: Fortress, 1988), 379–419. Paulien applies this concept to study allusions in Revelation. Paulien, "Dreading the Whirlwind," 5–22.

139. Noh, *Metarepresentations*, 74–5. Given this variation in resemblance, Wilson points out: "In interpreting a quotation, or more generally a linguistic metarepresentation, the hearer must make some assumption about the type and degree of resemblance involved. According to the relevance-theoretic comprehension procedure, he should not expect strict identity between representation and original: following a path of least effort, he should start with the most salient hypothesis about the intended resemblances, compute enough implications to satisfy his expectation of relevance, then stop." Wilson, "Metarepresentation in Linguistic Communication," 143.

140. Noh, *Metarepresentations*, 75.

141. This assumes that the scholars are using the sources today available or something similar. An author also makes changes when conflating sources. If the source of a NT author is the MT, all the words are always changed as they are translated from Hebrew into Greek, the first stage of the metarepresentation. I give thanks to Craig Blomberg for this last insight.

of communication of unintended *implicatures*. Another issue always present is the lack of total certainty about what source was used by a NT author. A different written source (from the MT or LXX versions available today) with that recension or variant is still a possibility.[142]

The book of James has a few cases of just metalinguistic or interpretive resemblance. In fact, there are no pure metalinguistic metarepresentations in James. For example, James 2:8 says: Εἰ μέντοι νόμον τελεῖτε βασιλικὸν κατὰ τὴν γραφήν· ἀγαπήσεις τὸν πλησίον σου ὡς σεαυτόν, καλῶς ποιεῖτε.[143] The prepositional phrase κατὰ τὴν γραφήν introduces a direct quotation from Leviticus 19:18b [LXX]. Here, James exploits a metalinguistic resemblance, a resemblance in linguistic form. Also, in this case, this resemblance is a literal representation of Leviticus 19:18b. Each word of the LXX appears in James's text. However, he uses this quotation in his own discourse to highlight discrimination as a violation of the law. So, he combines metalinguistic and interpretive resemblance.

Furthermore, there are a few cases of interpretive use. For example, James 2:25 says: ὁμοίως δὲ καὶ Ῥαὰβ ἡ πόρνη οὐκ ἐξ ἔργων ἐδικαιώθη ὑποδεξαμένη τοὺς ἀγγέλους καὶ ἑτέρᾳ ὁδῷ ἐκβαλοῦσα; Here, James exploits an interpretive resemblance, a resemblance in content of Joshua 2:1–16. It is also a loose representation of LXX Josh 2:1–16.[144] Namely, he takes a few words of that chapter to evoke the entire section. It is an interpretive resemblance because he uses the words in his own discourse. In this case, he uses them as an example of his thesis, that one cannot have faith without deeds. As will be seen in the next chapters, James mainly uses the OT by combining metalinguistic and interpretive resemblance. In fact, James builds his ethics of poverty and wealth by interpretively metarepresenting the OT and Jesus's teachings, even in those cases where he combines metalinguistic and interpretive resemblance.

Linguistic metarepresentations can achieve relevance in at least two ways. Reported speech achieves relevance mainly "by informing the hearer[/reader] about the content of the original."[145] In other occasions, the interpretation of an utterance "achieve[s] relevance by informing the reader of the fact that the speaker has in mind what so-and-so said, and has a certain attitude to it: the speaker's interpretation of so-and-so's thought is relevant itself.

142. See, e.g., assumptions #6 and #7 in Stanley, *Arguing with Scripture*, 52–7.

143. Other examples are Jas 2:11, 23; 4:6.

144. Other examples could be Jas 2:21; 4:5; 5:11, 17–18. The case of Jas 4:5 is highly problematic, among other issues, regarding the OT reference there. For more discussion, see Richard Bauckham, "The Spirit of God in Us Loathes Envy: James 4:5," in *Holy Spirit and Christian Origins: Essays in Honor of James D. G. Dunn*, ed. Graham N. Stanton, Bruce W. Longenecker, and Stephen C. Barton (Grand Rapids, Mich.: Eerdmans, 2004), 270–81; C. B. Carpenter, "James 4.5 Reconsidered," *NTS* 47 (2001): 189–205.

145. Wilson, "Metarepresentation in Linguistic Communication," 148.

When interpretations achieve relevance in this way, we will say that they are *echoic*."[146] Consider this example:[147]

24. [A person writing to an ex-classmate, remembers a phrase used by her teacher]
25. The teacher used "the rod of love" to make us learn better.

The person simultaneously asserts that the teacher used a rod and alludes to the words the teacher used.[148] The phrase "rod of love" contributes to her utterance. So, the reader could understand it and search for relevance at the text level. In this way, he expends some effort and obtains some cognitive effects. Nevertheless, if the reader makes the connection the writer is assuming is mutually known, then the extra effort expended in recognizing the allusion is compensated with some additional cognitive effects, as *implicature*: for example, the reader may remember the teacher's violence without good cause. Furthermore, in this case, the writer could even be using irony in the phrase, as an echoic metarepresentation. As a result, at a higher level of explicitness she could be communicating her attitude of dissociation or disagreement with the phrase.

Linguistic metarepresentations vary in a continuum from the fully explicit to the fully inferred. A marked quotation is fully explicit.[149] In contrast, unmarked (not overtly marked) quotations are left to the speaker to infer. In this case, the pragmatic inference is "governed by consideration of relevance,"[150] as in the next example:[151]

26. Mary: So what did Jane say about the party?
27. Peter: a. She said that it was fantastic.
28. b. It was fantastic.

In answer (a) it is manifest that the phrase "it was fantastic" metarepresents Jane's opinion. In the second case, answer (b) could be understood as Peter's opinion of the party or his report of Jane's reaction. Assuming that

146. Sperber and Wilson, *Relevance: Communication and Cognition*, 238 (their emphasis). Wilson points out: "The attitudes conveyed by echoic utterances are very rich and varied: the speaker may indicate that she agrees or disagrees with the original, is puzzled, angry, amused, intrigued, sceptical, etc., or any combination of these." Wilson, "Metarepresentation in Linguistic Communication," 148.

147. Taken and adapted from Noh, *Metarepresentations*, 85.

148. Noh points out that in this case "the speaker borrows the original expression for her own use: that is why the same part of the utterance both metarepresents another representation and contributes to a truth-conditional description of the speaker's." Ibid.

149. Most languages have different quotational devices, such as hearsay words, particles, noun-phrases, and so on. Wilson, "Metarepresentation in Linguistic Communication," 146.

150. Noh, *Metarepresentations*, 77.

151. Taken and adapted from ibid.

Peter's assertion is relevant by answering Mary's question, the sentence in (b) metarepresents Jane's utterance. This is a case of an inferred metarepresentation. As this example illustrates, considerations of relevance play a role in discerning the metarepresentation. See this biblical example:

29. Rev 1:7 (ESV) Behold, he is coming with the clouds, and every eye will see him, even those who pierced him, and all tribes of the earth will wail on account of him. Even so. Amen.

If John intentionally evokes the OT, he is not using any quotational device. So, he lets his addressees infer the text. In this case, he is metarepresenting Daniel 7:13 and Zechariah 12:10.[152]

Furthermore, this description of linguistic metarepresentation marks a difference in the way intertextual approaches deal with texts. As Rachel Malik emphasizes in her work, intertextual approaches such as those of Bakhtin or Kristeva do not make a distinction between intertextual production and reception and tend to collapse reading as writing. In this regard, RT makes a clear distinction between production and reception of the linguistic metarepresentation.[153] Concerning the speaker/writer, "the choice of the metarepresentational form, and more generally, the intended degree of resemblance, may be dependent on the speaker's abilities or preferences, as the assumption of optimal relevance predicts."[154] Concerning the hearer/reader, the words of Cynthia Edenburg are appropriate. Studying the role of memory in intertextuality, she points out that "intertextuality indicates the association evoked in one's mind between one text and another. To a certain extent, all association between texts is triggered by memory. Even if the association is triggered by something a reader perceives in a written text, the associative impulse calls up the memory of another text, which the reader is not immediately perusing."[155]

This account of linguistic metarepresentation is very close to Richard Hays's description of what he calls intertextual echo. Speaking of the variation of intertextual echoes, he says: "Quotation, allusion, and echo may be

152. For details on the use of these OT texts here, see Grant R. Osborne, *Revelation*, BECNT (Grand Rapids, Mich.: Baker, 2002), 75–6.

153. RT considers both the speaker/writer as producer of intertextuality and the speaker/reader as receptor of intertextuality. Both intertextual processes are guided by the *principle of relevance.* Rachel Malik, "Fixing Meaning: Intertextuality, Inferencing, and Genre in Interpretation" (Ph.D. diss., Middlesex University, 2003), 1–173.

154. Noh, *Metarepresentations*, 84. This understanding considers that first-century authors would use the techniques and styles of writing, and quoting appropriate to the literature of their time.

155. Although Edenburg's study does not use Relevance Theory, her conclusions are in total agreement with RT's observations. Cynthia Edenburg, "Intertextuality, Literary Competence, and the Question of Readership: Some Preliminary Observations," *JSOT* 35 (2010): 137.

seen as points along a spectrum of intertextual reference, moving from the explicit to the subliminal. As we move farther away from overt citation, the source recedes into the discursive distance, the intertextual relations become less determinate, and the demand placed on the reader's listening powers grows greater."[156]

The search for relevance guides this process of association. Wilson points out that, on one hand, "[t]he task of the speaker [or writer] is to make the intended interpretation accessible enough to be picked out." On the other hand, "[a] hearer following the relevance-theoretic comprehension procedure should consider interpretive hypotheses in order of accessibility. Having found an interpretation that satisfies his expectation of relevance, he should stop."[157] Of course, a secondary audience never could be 100% certain. However, each time an interpreter looks for connections, he/she invests cognitive effort and obtains cognitive benefits. So he/she stops when he/she satisfies his/her own expectation of relevance, as Furlong points out in her criteria of literary interpretation.[158] Now, recognizing a quotation (especially in aural communication) "costs the hearer [/reader] a certain amount of extra effort, which is offset by some additional cognitive effects. . . . If the hearer [/reader] cannot recognize the original source, the cognitive effects would be considerably reduced."[159] This process is particularly important when dealing with the NT use of the OT.[160]

A biblical author may intentionally lead the reader through this intertextual process. For example, in an overt quotation, the author uses linguistic

156. Hays, *Echoes of Scripture*, 23. This ability of recognition assumes the hearer's knowledge of the OT. This assumption cannot always be granted, as Stanley clearly argues in Stanley, "Pearls before Swine."

157. Wilson, "Metarepresentation in Linguistic Communication," 145.

158. Furlong, "Relevance Theory and Literary Interpretation," 196–7.

159. Noh, *Metarepresentations*, 85. In this regard, Edenburg says that even when what one reads in a text has triggered the intertextuality, "[a]t a later stage the association may be clinched after locating a copy of the other text and visually comparing the two. In the case of oral and aural association, the role of memory is all the more critical since one must retain the memory of a text as it is performed, while searching through long term memory in order to retrieve the recollection of the other text evoked by the association." Edenburg, "Some Preliminary Observations," 137.

160. This approach to the reader's success in identifying the quotation helps to alleviate Stanley Porter's concerns. On one hand, he recognizes that "[b]eing able to judge audience understanding of a citation would be highly desirable, since it would give us a sense of how and in what way the audience interpreted and understood both the cited and the citing passage." On the other hand, he adds: "However, making the success of citation dependent upon the audience runs the risk of determining literary success on the basis of the level of ignorance or information of the audience, rather than on how the author crafts the work." Porter, "Further Comments," 105–6. Precisely, RT takes both sides into account: the author and the audience. By focusing on the mutual cognitive environment, the present work also considers the issue of accessibility to the OT text and audience limitations pointed out by Stanley, "Pearls before Swine," 124–44.

devices to guide the reader toward the search for relevance. In this way, although the reader finds some *explicatures* and *implicatures* in the text, the author drives him to look for more *implicatures* in the source text. As a result, the reader uses less cognitive effort in linking the current text with the source text, and obtains more cognitive effects (such as more implications coming from the source, widening the mutual cognitive environment via redefining a theological framework, and so on).

In an unmarked quotation, allusion, or echo, the issue is a little more complex. An author could be intentionally using an OT passage. In this case, "the audience may reasonably assume that the author wishes them to explore the source context for further implicatures."[161] As a result, finding more cognitive effects (through studying the OT passage in its own context) can be a clue that this author intended the reader to make the connections.[162] It is also possible, however, that this connection was unseen by the author, and making the association is the entire responsibility of the reader.[163] This could be due to different reasons, such as unintended parallels with other works, and the general mind-set, such as OT Jewish thought. As Hays says, "as we near the vanishing point of the echo, it inevitably becomes difficult to decide whether we are really hearing an echo at all, or whether we are only conjuring things out of the murmurings of our own imaginations."[164] In any case, RT may guide the interpreter's process of deciding if an OT passage is intended to be used or not. If a particular OT passage contributes more cognitive effects to an interpretation of a NT passage than other factors of the cognitive environment or another OT competing passage, this could be an indicator that the author actually used that passage inside the fence posts of the mutual cognitive environment and the search for optimal relevance. This leads to a cautious approach to allusions. As Pattemore says, "[c]ognitive environments defined by prior texts must always be evaluated alongside those defined by local situations to determine which yields the most positive cognitive effects for the least processing effort."[165]

161. This is what Pattemore calls "contextually evoked" text. Pattemore, *The People of God in the Apocalypse*, 40.

162. Pattemore emphasizes that at pragmatic levels there could be no strong differences between an explicit quotation and an unmarked quotation. He says: "[I]f an allusion is deliberate and recognizable, then it is equivalent to a quotation because it conveys propositions like 'I have taken this idea from the former text' and 'the former text has something to contribute to your understanding of my meaning' as cognitive effects. Even a formal quotation may convey no more than this, in terms of communicative intents." Ibid.

163. As mentioned above, there is a point when *implicatures* are the entire responsibility of the hearer/reader. This is the case with this type of associations.

164. Hays, *Echoes of Scripture*, 23.

165. Pattemore, *The People of God in the Apocalypse*, 40. Although this is frequently the case, in some situations, the greater processing effort in recognizing the OT passage is compensated with higher or stronger cognitive effects.

This approach to the issue does not eliminate the subjectivity of deciding whether an OT passage is used or not but at least reduces it. As Pattemore says, "Relevance Theory suggests a way of understanding intertextual allusion that respects the original context without making prior assumptions about the way it is being used. It gives access to the author's probable intentions, not as though they can be directly read off the text, but by assuming that the author has communicated ostensively and that human communication is guided by the quest for optimal relevance."[166] Also, Pattemore makes it clear that "our investigation of the (synchronic) relevance found by the first readers will necessarily be limited by our ignorance of their cognitive environment."[167] On one hand, the interpreter could find optimal relevance in a text not necessarily accessible to the first-century readers/hearers. One interpretation of 2 Thessalonians 2:3 precisely illustrates this point.[168] Charles Wanamaker, in his commentary on 2 Thessalonians 2:3, argues that "the lawless one" is a title given to the Roman general Pompey in the Psalms of Solomon 17:11. He makes the case that "the lawless one" to whom Paul refers recalls this person. He also sees other parallels between Psalms of Solomon 17 and 2 Thessalonians 2.[169] Besides the critical problems mentioned by Green, "we would have to ask whether the Thessalonians would have been capable of representing this assumption, especially given the fact that the vast majority of the Christians in that city were recent converts from paganism (1 Thess. 1.9) and not likely to have any knowledge of the *Psalms of Solomon*."[170]

In this case, Wanamaker finds relevance in his cognitive environment by disambiguating "the lawless one" with information salient to him, but highly probable to have been unknown to the first readers. This example, additionally, shows that "RT not only describes what occurs in successful but also in unsuccessful communication."[171] Finally, on the other hand, the interpreter could miss a connection because of his/her ignorance of the alluded text. This could be the case of the quotation in James 4:5 if, in fact, James alludes to a specific text.[172]

166. Ibid., 42.

167. Ibid.

168. Quoted by Green, "Relevance Theory and Biblical Interpretation," 236.

169. Charles A. Wanamaker, *The Epistles to the Thessalonians: A Commentary on the Greek Text*, NIGTC (Grand Rapids, Mich.: Eerdmans, 1990), 245–6.

170. Green, "Relevance Theory and Biblical Interpretation," 236. See more details in Gene L. Green, *The Letters to the Thessalonians*, PNTC (Grand Rapids, Mich.: Eerdmans, 2002), 306–9.

171. Green, "Relevance Theory and Biblical Interpretation," 269.

172. As mentioned above, for more discussion on Jas 4:5, see Bauckham, "James 4:5"; Carpenter, "James 4.5 Reconsidered."

Types of Quotations

Within the broad field of investigation of the NT use of the OT, citations and how NT authors use them are still under discussion and analysis.[173] From the perspective of RT, reported speech and thoughts (namely, direct, indirect, and free indirect quotations) are considered metarepresentations of attributed utterances and thoughts.[174] Mixed quotations are considered metarepresentations of attributed expressions.[175] In this case, "[t]he speaker[/writer] borrows the original expression for her own use: that is why the same part of the utterance both metarepresents another representation and contributes to a truth-conditional description of the speaker's."[176] Traditionally, in biblical studies, this category includes unmarked/nonformal quotations, allusions and echoes.[177] In this work, for practical reasons, if it is necessary to make distinctions, the broad definitions by Osborne will be enough: "[W]e will consider a *quotation* to be a near verbatim rendering of a passage, an *allusion* to be the use of several words or phrases, and an *echo* the use of a theme or a couple of terms from a passage."[178]

A NT author could consciously or unconsciously use the OT. When writing, an author's language could be "religious," sounding like the OT.[179] It is clear in James that he profusely uses the OT throughout his letter. Consideration of relevance could help to determine with high probability whether

173. The discussion on unmarked quotations, allusions, and echoes has revolved around semantic grounds. Definitions, and particularly the criteria to distinguish them, vary greatly. See the exhaustive evaluation by Porter, "The Use of the Old Testament," 79–96; Porter, "Further Comments," 98–110; Stamps, "The Use of the Old Testament," 9–37.

174. Eun-Jo Noh points out that "[a]ll three types of quotation are used to represent an attributed utterance or thought on the basis of shared properties. They differ in what these shared properties are. Direct quotations are metalinguistic; they metarepresent an utterance or thought in virtue of shared formal properties. Indirect quotations are interpretive: they metarepresent an utterance or thought in virtue of shared content.... Free indirect quotations are both metalinguistic and interpretive: they metarepresent their original in both content and form." Noh, *Metarepresentations*, 84.

175. A mixed quotation is a combination of a direct and an indirect quotation.

176. Noh, *Metarepresentations*, 85.

177. As mentioned above, defining these categories is still problematic. But it is not an essential issue for the analysis of discourse in the present work. As Pattemore points out, "whether the relationship of a statement to a previous text is an 'informal quotation,' an 'allusion,' or an 'echo' is scarcely relevant. What is relevant is whether the author has made manifest only the assumptions expressed by the statement (its explicatures) and those implicatures entailed by the immediate context, or in addition, the assumption that she used a particular source for her language. This distinction is to be made on the criterion of optimizing relevance." Pattemore, *The People of God in the Apocalypse*, 41.

178. Osborne, *The Hermeneutical Spiral*, 543 n. 1.

179. See a good discussion on this issue in Gordon J. Wenham, "The Date of Deuteronomy: Linch-Pin of Old Testament Criticism," *Them* 10 (1985): 15–20; F. Young and D. F. Ford, *Meaning and Truth in 2 Corinthians*, BFT (London: SPCK, 1987), 60–84.

the author is consciously using the OT or not. Hays's validation criteria (availability, volume, recurrence, and thematic coherence) contribute in the same enterprise. If an author consciously uses the OT, a reader's/hearer's extra effort in making the connection to the OT is compensated with more cognitive effects. Therefore, in doing the analysis, these factors can help to determine a conscious allusion with a good amount of certainty.

Contributions of Relevance Theory

Some may argue that RT does not add anything significant that is not already being done in historical-critical exegesis.[180] Nevertheless, RT contributes to the discussion in at least two ways: its understanding of *context*, and the

180. Probably because it is relatively new in the neighborhood, until now there has been no criticism of biblical studies using RT. See, e.g., the good description of RT and biblical interpretation in W. Randolph Tate, *Handbook for Biblical Interpretation: An Essential Guide to Methods, Terms, and Concepts* (Grand Rapids, Mich.: Baker, 2012), 384–6. Also see RT and translation in Stanley E. Porter, "Assessing Translation Theory: Beyond Literal and Dynamic Equivalence," in *Translating the New Testament: Text, Translation, Theology*, ed. Stanley E. Porter and Mark J. Boda, MNTS (Grand Rapids, Mich.: Eerdmans, 2009), 134–7. Nevertheless, some criticism has appeared in the related field of biblical translation. See, e.g., the criticism of E. R. Wendland, "On the Relevance of 'Relevance Theory' for Bible Translation," *BT* 47 (1996): 126–37; E. R. Wendland, "A Review of 'Relevance Theory' in Relation to Bible Translation in South-Central Africa, Part 1," *JNSL* 22 (1996): 91–10; E. R. Wendland, "A Review of 'Relevance Theory' in Relation to Bible Translation in South-Central Africa, Part 2," *JNSL* 23 (1997): 83–108. He mainly reacts to Ernst-August Gutt, *Translation and Relevance: Cognition and Context* (Cambridge: Cambridge University Press, 1991). His main concerns are with the validity of RT as an interpretive tool, with the application of the theory to biblical translation, and what he considers "its distinctive terminology" as a "formidable, perhaps impossible, barrier to overcome, at least for ordinary translators." Wendland, "On the Relevance," 134. His evaluation of RT misrepresents it and, as Pattemore clearly points out, is unwarranted. Pattemore, *The People of God in the Apocalypse*, 34–6, 46. On the other hand, SIL has recently published RT works in simple language for translators' training. See, e.g., Harriet Hill and Margaret Hill, *Translating the Bible into Action: How the Bible Can Be Relevant in All Languages and Cultures* (Carlisle: Piquant Editions, 2008); Harriet Hill et al., *Bible Translation Basics: Communicating Scriptures in a Relevant Way* (Dallas: SIL International, 2011).

In his description of RT, Randahl Buth points out an important consideration. Although he does not represent very well the essentials of RT, he notices that assuming the text as communication between a writer and his addressees could be complicated for the interpretive process. Randall Buth, "Language, Linguistics," *DTIB* 434. In texts with multiple audiences, such as the Gospels, or different layers of composition, such as the Psalms, RT could have the difficulty of recognizing these different contexts, authors, editors, and audiences. However, RT explains the process of communication-cognition. It could help in understanding how the different audiences of a text perceive the text and derive explicatures and implicatures. It is clear, nonetheless, that this task is easier in some corpora of texts than others, but this fact does not diminish its utility.

way it deals with intertextuality.[181] First of all, RT considers "the text as the record of a real communication event and, as a consequence, emphasizes the importance of context for understanding."[182] As mentioned earlier, the principle of relevance and the way RT conceives *context* help the interpreter prioritize different potential sources of the cognitive environment. Specifically, the interpreter may decide if these potential sources are more or less probably manifest at the time of the communicative event by assessing the cognitive effects and the processing effort.[183] Again, in the case of the evaluation of possible allusions or echoes, considerations of relevance are key for deciding if a potential candidate that fulfills Hays's four criteria is more relevant than other input in the cognitive system. In other words, it gives more cognitive benefits that compensate the processing effort in making the connection than other competing aspects of the cognitive environment. In this sense, RT is not a "stand-alone model" but rather adds to historical-critical approaches by emphasizing that the speaker's/writer's meaning is more than what is explicitly communicated. It includes also what is implicit, and both aspects should be contextually recovered.[184]

Furthermore, RT contributes to the discussion in the way it deals with intertextuality. From the perspective of RT, the former written texts and traditions evoked in a text are part of the cognitive environment of the speaker/writer and hearers/readers. Intertextuality, as it pertains specifically to this research, focuses on the evocation of former biblical texts (and traditions). As a result, intertextuality is analyzed in light of the principle of relevance. This manner of dealing with intertextuality makes positive contributions to this research: the way RT understands intertextuality helps to constrain the

181. Although Malik finds weaknesses in the principle of relevance and what she considers a too-rational character of "Relevance-person" theory, she uses it in her thesis, by integrating it with some intertextual theories in her methodology of intertextual analysis. In fact, the way RT deals with the text-context relation and the control it gives to "the constitutive polysemy or ambiguity of the utterance" are fundamental to her methodological approach. Malik, "Fixing Meaning," 129–72.

182. Pattemore, *The People of God in the Apocalypse*, 46.

183. The socioeconomic world of the first century, Jewish traditions, the OT, assumptions about honor, patronage, etc. are part of this cognitive environment of James and his readers/hearers. However, at the time of the interpretation of a specific utterance only some of these aspects are part of the context. They are the set of assumptions that are manifest (or more manifest) to the reader/hearer at this time. In this sense, the RT's understanding of *context* and the principle of relevance help to prioritize those aspects of the cognitive environment that are more probably manifest at the time of the communicative event. They are particularly helpful in discerning between those competing aspects in a specific text (e.g., deciding between a potential use of an OT passage and a first-century popular concept).

184. Wilson, "Metarepresentation in Linguistic Communication," 143. Historical-critical approaches still have an essential role in the interpretation process. As Furlong says, "one of the aims of historical scholarship is, of course, to make more accessible to present-day readers what assumptions the communicator might have envisaged." Furlong, "Relevance Theory and Literary Interpretation," 112 n. 37.

polyvalence of a text found in other intertextual approaches.[185] Also it makes a distinction between intertextual production and reception.[186] Finally, it is a bridge between author-centered and reader-centered approaches.

Specific Methodology

The goal of this project is to understand James's use of the OT through the reconstruction of the cognitive environment, and the recovery of *explicatures* and *implicatures*.[187] For this reason, the methodology develops through the following logical steps.

Establishment of the Text

What is the text one is dealing with? The main focus in this research is semantics and pragmatics. Nevertheless, it is necessary to determine the working text. This research follows the NA[28] Greek text. There are no major textual problems in those texts where James quotes or alludes to the OT. In general terms, the text is stable. So, in order to establish the working text, textual issues are addressed as they arise to the extent that they contribute to decision-making.[188]

Elucidation of the Co-text

The principal evidence for the recovery of *explicatures* and *implicatures* of a text is its co-text. Here, co-text "refers to the location of an utterance within a string of linguistic data, the sentences, paragraphs, and chapters surrounding and related to a text and within which an utterance finds its meaning."[189]

185. I owe this insight to Steve Smith, who worked with RT and intertextuality in his doctoral thesis on judgment over Jerusalem and the Temple in Luke-Acts under Steve Moyise at the University of Chichester, UK. As mentioned above in note 56, his thesis appears in the LNTS series as Smith, *The Fate of the Jerusalem Temple*.

186. In the RT perspective, there are strong and weak implicatures. The author creates strong implicatures, but some of the weak implicatures are entirely the responsibility of the reader. Also, in contrast to intertextual approaches (e.g., Bakhtin, Kristeva), as Malik points out, in RT there is a clear distinction between production and interpretation, and so between intertextual production and intertextual reception. Malik, "Fixing Meaning," 1–34.

187. This methodology follows and adapts Pattemore's steps. See more details in Pattemore, *The People of God in the Apocalypse*, 47–50.

188. Ibid., 47. Other issues proper to text criticism such as "the history of interpretation, literary layers in the production of texts, theologically or ethically motivated changes, and the impact of canon on textual issues" are not considered in the research. But see Peter R. Rodgers, "Textual Criticism," *DTIB* 784.

189. Green, *DTIB* 132.

For that reason, discourse analysis focuses on how the co-text contributes to the relevance of the analyzed passage.[190]

In a letter as intricate as James's epistle, themes develop throughout the letter.[191] For example, the theme of speech control (1:19–21; 3:1–12, 13–17; 5:9, 12) and the theme of word/law (1:18, 19–25; 2:1–13; 4:11–12) are recurrent topics of the letter. As a result, not only is the co-text around the section in consideration analyzed, but the way earlier parts can contribute to cognitive effects and/or diminish the processing effort of latter parts also receives great attention. In particular, the topic of rich and poor becomes a major focus, although other themes are taken into account to the extent that they have an impact on the relevance of the text under consideration.[192]

Description of the General Cognitive Environment

What aspects of the cognitive environment are more probable in function? In particular, what assumptions of the encyclopedic knowledge are salient? In order to interpret a particular passage, it is also necessary to pay attention to other aspects, such as the socio-cultural and the historical setting, and how these aspects can contribute to that passage. Given the fact that RT considers context as dynamic, in each case it is necessary to decide what aspects are more pertinent to the interpretation. Recurrent aspects are treated in detail the first time they appear. Later on, they are just mentioned. As in any other historical-critical approach, it is clear that it is impossible to exhaustively reproduce the complete cognitive environment of James and his first readers. As Joseph Fantin says, "[o]f course, we cannot fully place ourselves in the shoes (or sandals) of these people. Nevertheless, we must do whatever possible to attempt to gain a glimpse (albeit a somewhat blurred glimpse)

190. See more details in Unger, *Genre, Relevance, and Global Coherence*, esp. 107–42.

191. For a discussion on the structure of James, see, e.g., Timothy B. Cargal, *Restoring the Diaspora: Discursive Structure and Purpose in the Epistle of James*, SBLDS 144 (Atlanta: Scholars, 1993); Mark E. Taylor, "A Textlinguistic Investigation into the Discourse Structure of James" (Ph.D. diss., Southwestern Baptist Theological Seminary, 2001); Darian R. Lockett, "Structure or Communicative Strategy? The 'Two Ways' Motif in James' Theological Instruction," *Neot* 42 (2008): 269–87.

192. One of these themes is the eschatology of the book. As Penner says, "[t]he theme of eschatology . . . , although it stands out most clearly in the opening and closing sections of the main body, is not limited to the framework alone for it both undergirds and influences the actual community instruction." Todd C. Penner, *The Epistle of James and Eschatology: Re-reading an Ancient Christian Letter*, JSNTSup 121 (Sheffield: Sheffield Academic Press, 1996), 217. In the same vein are Ernst Baasland, "Der Jakobusbrief als Neutestamentliche Weisheitsschrift," *ST* 36.2 (1982): 122–4; Dan G. McCartney, *James*, BECNT (Grand Rapids, Mich.: Baker, 2009), 70; Patrick A. Tiller, "The Rich and Poor in James: An Apocalyptic Proclamation," in *SBL Seminar Papers*, ed. David J. Lull, SBLSP 37 (Atlanta: Scholars, 1998), 909–20; Patrick A. Tiller, "The Rich and Poor in James: An Apocalyptic Ethic," in *Conflicted Boundaries in Wisdom and Apocalypticism*, ed. Benjamin G. Wright III and Lawrence M. Wills, SBLSymS 35 (Atlanta: Society of Biblical Literature, 2005), 169–79.

of the world of the first-century Christian."[193] So, the goal is to describe the aspects of the cognitive environment and the encyclopedic knowledge that may have been accessed in the search for optimal relevance.

Identification of Possible OT Texts and Traditions Evoked

Potential OT references are considered and analyzed as part of the cognitive environment. This section of the methodology follows Beale's and Carson's useful procedure to study the NT use of an OT passage. The co-text of the citation in the NT, the OT co-text from which the citation is drawn, the use of the citation in Second Temple literature, and textual factors of the citation are considered.[194] Hays's first four criteria for validation of possible allusion help in the evaluation process: availability, volume, recurrence, and thematic coherence.

Evaluation of the Accessibility of the Cognitive Environment

The different aspects of the cognitive environment are analyzed in terms of cognitive effort and effects, and the search for optimal relevance. It is not enough to point out potential OT passages. It is necessary to evaluate them in comparison with other factors in the cognitive environment that can be contributing to the interpretation process. In this way, the potential OT passage is analyzed without assuming priority over other factors of the context.

Interpretation of the Text within a Prioritized Cognitive Environment

This step is where RT will be the most evident. The collected evidence from steps 2 to 5 helps analyze the passage under study. The interpretive process focuses on the recovery of *explicatures* and *implicatures*, namely, "the likely interpretation of the text which provides the audience with good contextual effects for minimal processing effort."[195]

Summary of How James Uses the OT

Finally, the contribution of the OT passage to James's discourse is analyzed. This step also focuses on how James's use of the OT contributes to his ethics of poverty and wealth. In each analyzed passage, some issues are pointed out. But, later on, the work presents a more comprehensive summary of the findings. Throughout the study, a pattern appears. James builds his ethics of

193. Fantin, *Lord of the Entire World*, 18.

194. G. K. Beale and D. A. Carson, "Introduction," in *Commentary on the New Testament Use of the Old Testament*, ed. G. K. Beale and D. A. Carson (Grand Rapids, Mich.: Baker, 2007), xxiv–xxv.

195. Pattemore, *The People of God in the Apocalypse*, 50.

poverty and wealth by interpretively metarepresenting the OT and Jesus's teachings.

Conclusions

This chapter presents a summary of the different perspectives of works that deal with the presence and use of OT citations in the NT. A brief discussion on the author-centered and reader-centered approaches shows that it is necessary to include both the author and the reader in the analysis of any text. Also, it is apparent in the review that both approaches seem to operate under the code model of communication. This model gives no account for communicative intentions nor is it a model that integrates contextual information with the interpretation of the text. This work presents Relevance Theory (RT) as a solution in that direction.

This chapter introduces RT and how this theory deals with metarepresentations. RT offers a robust model that integrates context and text into the interpretive process. Additionally, it takes into account not only the explicit content of the text but also what is implicitly communicated. It considers both the writer's and the reader's perspective. This theory is a good companion for historical-critical methods.

This research builds its methodology on how RT understands quotations. As mentioned above, metarepresentation is a person's representation of another person's representation (or of himself or herself at another time). In this vein, quotations are a type of linguistic metarepresentation. These metarepresentations can be interpretive or linguistic. Both types are present in James. This research focuses on quotations that are written representations of an OT author's or Jesus's words.

Lastly, this chapter describes the methodology applied in the research. Seven steps develop the methodology. These steps combine historical-critical tools and RT principles in order to understand James's use of the OT and Jesus's words. In synthesis, RT provides a robust model for the integration of author, text, reader, and context in the search for meaning. It provides a framework for the inferential character of language and a theory for context. In this sense, RT is a helpful supplement to historical and literary investigation. As Pattemore says, "RT does not supplant semantic, syntactic, structural or literary analysis. It both undergirds and guides them."[196] In particular, RT is a useful framework for the study of the NT use of the OT.

196. Ibid., 36.

Chapter 3

James 1:9–11, 26–27

James writes his letter with several concerns. He wants his addressees to strengthen their faith in Jesus Christ and have a consistent Christian life. The letter reflects that there is incongruence between their faith and their treatment of the poor. James builds his teaching on poverty and wealth upon the OT and Jesus's teachings. From the beginning, he guides his addressees to metarepresent the OT.[1] He develops the theme throughout the epistle. Using a Relevance Theory analysis, this chapter studies James's teaching and his use of the OT in those passages where he deals with the issue of poverty and wealth. In particular, James 1:9–11 and 26–27 are considered. First, an outline of the epistle is offered, and then the methodology is applied to each text.

Outline

This chapter explores James 1:9–11 and 26–27. In order to define the co-text of each it is necessary, first of all, to define the outline or structure where these verses fit. However, the complexity of offering an outline for the epistle is well known. Almost every work on James's epistle has its own proposal.[2] Approaches go from no structure at all to intricate chiastic outlines.[3]

1. Detailed explanation of metarepresentation appears in chapter 2. Here, it is enough to say that "to metarepresent" is the human ability of representing the thoughts of another person or oneself at another time. In this sense, simplistically speaking, a NT author's or his audience's representation of an OT author is a metarepresentation of the OT.

2. In this regard, see some good summaries in Scot McKnight, *The Letter of James*, NICNT (Grand Rapids, Mich.: Eerdmans, 2011), 47–55.

3. Timothy B. Cargal, *Restoring the Diaspora: Discursive Structure and Purpose in the Epistle of James*, SBLDS 144 (Atlanta: Scholars, 1993); Robert B. Crotty, "The Literary Structure of the Letter of James," *ABR* 40 (1992): 45–57; Hubert Frankemölle, "Das semantische Netz des Jakobusbriefes: Zur Einheit eines umstrittenen Briefes," *BZ* 34 (1990): 161–97; René Krüger, *Pobres y ricos en la epístola de Santiago: El desafío de un cristianismo profético* (Buenos Aires: Lumen, 2005), 111–36; Darian R. Lockett, "Structure or Communicative Strategy? The 'Two Ways' Motif in James' Theological Instruction," *Neot* 42 (2008): 269–87; Benjamin J. Pehrson, "Mitigation and Intensitifaction of Persuasive Discourse in a Koine Greek Letter: Coherent Macrostructure in the Letter of James" (master's thesis, Graduate Institute of Applied Linguistics, 2010), 25–61; Wiard Popkes, *Adressaten, Situation und Form des Jakobusbriefes*, SBS 125/126 (Stuttgart: Katholisches Bibelwerk, 1986); Mark E.

Craig Blomberg and Mariam Kamell adequately summarize the four main approaches to the structure of the epistle:[4]

1. James has no overarching outline in view.
2. James intends a broad topical or thematic structure.
3. James weaves his smaller units together into larger fabrics of thought and uses his overall structure to prioritize his key themes.
4. James adopts Greco-Roman rhetorical structures or modern discourse analysis.

So, aware of this diversity, the present work considers a structure between alternatives 2 and 3 above. There is an introduction of the main issues (1:2–18) revolving around of how to live the daily Christian life. This theme is developed later in the letter in three major sections (1:19–4:12, 4:13–5:11, and 5:12–20). This way of seeing the text uses the next outline as a basis for analysis:

I. Greetings (1:1)
II. The daily Christian life should reflect faith in God in the midst of trials and temptations (1:2–18)
  A. Endurance under trials (1:2–4)
  B. Wisdom and faith in trials (1:5–8)
  C. Eschatological reversal of fortunes: poor and rich (1:9–11)
  D. Trials and temptation (1:12–14)
  E. God as benefactor (1:15–18)
III. The daily Christian life should reflect the presence of the implanted word (1:19–4:12)
  A. Living the word (1:19–27)
    1. Hearers of the word (1:19–21)
    2. Doers of the word (1:22–25)
    3. True religion (1:26–27)
  B. True faith: no discrimination but deeds (2:1–26)
    1. True faith does not discriminate against the poor (2:1–13)
      a. Example of discrimination (2:1–7)
      b. Discrimination as a violation of God's law (2:8–11)
      c. God's retribution (2:12–13)
    2. True faith does deeds (2:14–26)
      a. True faith is sensitive to the needy (2:14–17)
      b. True faith performs deeds (2:18–19)
      c. Abraham and Rahab examples of true faith (2:20–26)

Taylor, "Recent Scholarship on the Structure of James," *CurBS* 3 (2004): 86–115; Mark E. Taylor and G.H. Guthrie, "The Structure of James," *CBQ* 68 (2006): 681–705; Ralph Bruce Terry, "Some Aspects of the Discourse Structure of the Book of James," *JOTT* 5 (1992): 106–25.

4. Craig L. Blomberg and Mariam J. Kamell, *James*, ZECNT 16 (Grand Rapids, Mich.: Zondervan, 2008), 23–6.

C. Relationships in the community (3:1–4:12)
1. Taming the tongue (3:1–12)
2. God's wisdom vs. earthly wisdom (3:13–18)
3. Calling for friendship with God (4:1–10)
4. Slander and judging (4:11–12)

IV. The daily Christian life should reflect a correct attitude toward wealth (4:13–5:11)
A. Merchants' arrogance (4:13–17)
B. Farmers' sins (5:1–6)
C. Christian patient endurance (5:7–11)

V. Final exhortations: The daily Christian life should reflect care for one another (5:12–20)
A. Oaths (5:12)
B. Suffering and prayer (5:13–18)
C. Restoring the wanderer (5:19–20)

Although in one way or another the structure of a discourse contributes to its meaning, the Relevance Theory method used in this research focuses on how each segment of a co-text contributes to the relevance of a particular passage. So instead of looking for a general structure, the main concern in this chapter and in the next two is to understand how James uses the OT in each pericope. A global coherence is assumed.[5]

Methodology Applied to 1:9–11

This is the first mention of the issue of poverty and wealth. James presents two exhortations in an antithetical parallelism. He uses language that sounds and evokes the OT. Next, the analysis of the text, the possible allusions, and their contribution to James's discourse is presented.

Elucidation of the Co-text

This pericope is part of the introduction to the letter, 1:2–18.[6] In our outline, the section 1:2–18 is divided into 1:2–4, 5–8, 9–11, 12–14, and 15–18. One of the

5. Christoph Unger, *Genre, Relevance, and Global Coherence: The Pragmatics of Discourse Type*, PSPLC (Basingstoke, England: Palgrave Macmillan, 2006); Luke Timothy Johnson, *The Letter of James: A New Translation with Introduction and Commentary*, AB37A (New Haven: Yale University Press, 1995), 11–5; Pehrson, "Coherent Macrostructure in the Letter of James." In the same vein, Bauckham and Allison note the coherence of thoughts in James's arguments. Richard Bauckham, *James: Wisdom of James, Disciple of Jesus the Sage* (London: Routledge, 1999), 67; Dale C. Allison, *A Critical and Exegetical Commentary on the Epistle of James*, ICC (New York: Bloomsbury, 2013), 77.

6. See the discussion of the introduction of the letter in Mark E. Taylor, *A Textlinguistic Investigation into the Discourse Structure of James*, LNTS 311 (New York: T&T Clark, 2006), 99–106.

questions relevant to this research is how the text of 1:9–11 interacts with the ideas in the introduction. Luke Cheung shows four typical ways to see the connection between 1:9–11 and the precedent passages:[7]

1. They are unrelated.
2. 1:9–11 is a reprise of the teaching in 1:2–4 as a special application of the teaching of rejoicing in trial.
3. It is a warning to those who are rich, that wealth is a test of true faith.
4. 1:9–11 tells the correct estimate of life by the tried.

The last three options seem to be interwoven. As Marie Isaacs points out,

> Verses 9–11 introduce the assurance that, with the coming of the End-time, there will soon be a reversal in the current fortunes of the faithful. This (contra Dibelius) is no digression. Rather, it supplies the second reason for the opening exhortation: Rejoice in the face of trials (v. 2) (a) because they produce steadfastness that leads to spiritual maturity (vv. 3–4); and (b) because there will be a reversal in your fortunes at the eschaton (vv. 9–11). This picks up from the preceding verse the theme of divine judgment. Yet, whereas in vv. 6–8 it is the doubter who is contrasted with the faithful, here it is the rich man (*plousios*) whose fate is contrasted with that of the humble/lowly (*tapeinos*).[8]

Cheung concludes that James presents a program of life in 1:2–4. This program requires wisdom in order to achieve it (1:5–8). In this context, James shows in 1:9–11 an example of the wisdom perspective required in concrete life realities.[9] On his part, Scot McKnight is a little more emphatic on thematic connections. He thinks that the theme of poverty and wealth is implicitly developed from 1:2 on; the socioeconomic oppression is one of the reasons for praying for wisdom in 1:5–8; but comes up clearly in 1:9–11.[10] Thus, it is clear that these verses are intimately related to the previous segment of James's discourse. Some thematic ideas are in nuce as McKnight infers. This consideration is important for the analysis below.

7. Luke L. Cheung, *The Genre, Composition, and Hermeneutics of the Epistle of James* (Eugene, Ore.: Wipf & Stock, 2006), 63. For option 1, see, e.g., Sophie S. Laws, *A Commentary on the Epistle of James*, BNTC 16 (San Francisco: Harper & Row, 1980), 62; Douglas J. Moo, *The Letter of James*, PNTC (Grand Rapids, Mich.: Eerdmans, 2000), 66. For option 2, see James Hardy Ropes, *A Critical and Exegetical Commentary on the Epistle of St. James*, ICC (New York: C. Scribner's Sons, 1916), 144. For option 3, see Ralph P. Martin, *James*, WBC 48 (Waco, Tex.: Word Books, 1988), 22–3. For option 4, see D. Edmond Hiebert, *James* (Chicago: Moody Press, 1979), 88.

8. Marie E. Isaacs, *Reading Hebrews and James: A Literary and Theological Commentary* (Macon, Ga.: Smyth and Helwys, 2002), 185.

9. Cheung, *Epistle of James*, 63. Allison sees an introduction to the whole letter in chapter 1, but no great connections between topics in it. Allison, *James*, 79, 195.

10. McKnight, *James*, 94. He seems to overstate his case, though.

Description of the General Cognitive Environment

James and his addressees lived in a Greco-Roman context with clear connections with Palestine and its culture. The text of James 1:9–11 assumes an encyclopedic knowledge on some issues. There is a mention of poverty and wealth, an eschatological reversal, and vegetation and the sun's effects upon it. When reading or hearing the text, the first readers/hearers accessed these components of their encyclopedic knowledge in order to understand James's message. Thus, studying these topics sheds light on their comprehension process and on the diverse competing factors when discerning the presence of the OT in James's discourse.

Poverty and Wealth

This pericope presents an antithetical parallelism between ὁ ταπεινός and ὁ πλούσιος. Both words evoke in James's readers/hearers the encyclopedic knowledge of "poverty and wealth." This is a recurrent topic in the book, and in the present research. At this point some important ideas are introduced. Later in the work other aspects will be included, depending on the saliency of particular issues in each passage.

The first sentence of this pericope is addressed toward ὁ αδελφὸς ὁ ταπεινός. Many authors relate this syntagma to the concept of *Armenfrömmigkeit* (Dibelius, Davids, others). Later in the present research, it is apparent that although there is a component of this idea, the financial and social distinctions are predominant in the text. The contrast between ὁ ταπεινός and ὁ πλούσιος helps to define the semantic range of the former. The idea of "humble, low" is closer to "poor."[11] But who are the poor and the rich in the epistle?

James uses the words πτωχός and πλούσιος only a few times in the letter but in key points. The noun πτωχός appears only in 2:1–13, James's discourse against discrimination (2:2, 3, 5, 6). It refers to a poor person who enters into their synagogue (2:2–3), God's election of the poor (2:5), and the addressees' dishonor of them (2:6). The noun πλούσιος appears five times (1:10–11; 2:5, 6; 5:1). Once, it refers to the poor (to be rich in faith and heirs of God's kingdom, 2:5). The rest of the time, it refers to the financially rich. As the review of literature in chapter 1 shows, there is no agreement among scholars on

11. Allison, *James*, 201; Bauckham, *James*, 185–203; Craig L. Blomberg, *Neither Poverty Nor Riches: A Biblical Theology of Material Possessions*, NSBT (Grand Rapids, Mich.: Eerdmans, 1999), 149; D. A. Carson, "James," in *Commentary on the New Testament Use of the Old Testament*, ed. G. K. Beale and D. A. Carson (Grand Rapids, Mich.: Baker, 2007), 993; Cheung, *Epistle of James*, 258–60; Mariam J. Kamell, "The Economics of Humility: The Rich and the Humble in James," in *Engaging Economics: New Testament Scenarios and Early Christian Reception*, ed. Bruce W. Longenecker and Kelly D. Liebengood (Grand Rapids, Mich.: Eerdmans, 2009), 157–75; Pedrito U. Maynard-Reid, *Poverty and Wealth in James* (repr., Eugene, Ore.: Wipf & Stock, 2004). The implicatures of the use of ταπεινός are discussed below, in the interpretation of the text.

whether or not the rich should be classified as Christians. However, James seems to be intentionally ambiguous about both the poor and the rich. For example, when depicting the pure and undefiled religion in 1:26–27, James mentions the orphans and widows without specifying whether they belong to the community or not. The poor person depicted in 2:2–4 seems to be an outsider. Conversely, the poor mentioned in 1:9, 2:5–6, and more explicitly in 2:15–16 are part of the Christian community. In a similar vein, in 1:10–11 or in 4:13–17, the rich seem to be part of the community, but those depicted in 2:2–7 and in 5:1–6 seem to be outsiders.[12] In this way, for rhetorical reasons, James could deal with the issue of poverty and wealth. As is shown later, using the same discourse, James may give hope to the Christian poor and warn the rich Christian via implicatures.

The description and identity of James's addressees come from the literary evidence of "the world of James," as Luke Timothy Johnson calls it.[13] It is hard to define whom the poor and the rich are in the epistle. There is a high amount of speculation in doing this enterprise of discerning who they are.[14] Furthermore, Bruce Longenecker prevents us from making generalizations regarding distinctions between πτωχός and πένης. He points out that the evidence we have from the NT times shows instability in the use of terms to describe poverty and the way people conceptualize it. What the evidence presents, instead, is that there is a tendency to use one term to connote a range of poverties instead of using different expressions to describe them. For that reason, "each reference to 'poverty' and 'the poor' must be read in its particular case-specific context, precisely in view of ancient and modern 'fuzziness of the language about and meaning of poverty.'"[15]

Both terms "poor" and "rich" are relative concepts. Several studies show a financial range among the urban and rural population of the Roman Empire. Although it is impossible to know the exact socioeconomic distribution of

12. For a discussion on these passages, see the respective chapters in the present research.

13. Luke Timothy Johnson, *Brother of Jesus, Friend of God: Studies in the Letter of James* (Grand Rapids, Mich.: Eerdmans, 2004), 101–22.

14. For example, Edgar thinks the poor are itinerant Christian preachers. David H. Edgar, *Has God Not Chosen the Poor? The Social Setting of the Epistle of James*, JSNTSup 206 (Sheffield: Sheffield Academic, 2001), 95–136. Martin, on his part, sees the rich as the Sadducees in Palestine pre–A.D. 70. Martin, *James*, 156, 62. Dibelius thinks the poor are the Christians, the pious poor. Martin Dibelius, *James: A Commentary on the Epistle of James* (Philadelphia: Fortress, 1976), 39–45. For more details, see the review of the literature on Poor and Rich in James in chapter 1.

15. Bruce W. Longenecker, *Remember the Poor: Paul, Poverty, and the Greco-Roman World* (Grand Rapids, Mich.: Eerdmans, 2010), 37–9. See also Denise Kimber Buell, "'Be Not One Who Stretches Out Hands to Recieve but Shuts Them When It Comes to Giving': Envisioning Christian Charity when Both Donors and Recipients Are Poor," in *Wealth and Poverty in Early Church and Society*, ed. Susan R. Holman, HCSPTH (Grand Rapids, Mich.: Baker, 2008), 39.

James's addressees, Steven Friesen and Bruce Longenecker propose similar distributions of wealth that shed some light on this issue.[16]

In the letter, the different people mentioned could be classified using these scales. Friesen thinks the audience of James's letter is mostly between PS_4 and PS_7. "The audiences live near the level of subsistence (PS5–6), probably with some destitute (PS7) and some with moderate surplus resources (PS4), but no one from the wealthy elites (PS1–3)."[17] In this spectrum, in Longenecker's scale, it is possible to find ES_4 or ES_5 people. Adamson points out three groups of "rich" in the letter: farmers (5:1–6), traders and merchants (4:13–17), and financers (2:6–7). After analyzing each group, he concludes: "The oppressors against whom James inveighs were not Roman but Jewish magnates."[18] Another rich person present in the epistle is the golden-ringed man mentioned in 2:2, probably an ES_4 person. Conversely, there are also some discernible ES_7 groups: widows and orphans (1:27), the filthy man (2:2–5), the brother and sister lacking in daily food and cloth (2:15), and the harvesters/peasants whose wages are being withheld (5:2–5). Most of the audience seems to lie between these two extremes, in categories ES_5 and ES_6. So, the referent of "the humble brother" of 1:9 is probably a person between ES_5 and ES_7, and the referent of "the rich" of 1:10 is probably people between ES_4 and ES_5.[19] Both groups are mainly Jewish and could include insiders and outsiders of the Christian community, as it will be argued later.

Eschatological Connections/Hopes

Eschatological expectation frames the letter and is a shared knowledge between James and his addressees.[20] James calls his addressees αἱ δώδεκα

16. Steven J. Friesen, "Injustice or God's Will: Explanations of Poverty in Proto-Christian Texts," in *Christian Origins*, ed. Richard A. Horsley, PHC 1 (Minneapolis: Fortress, 2005), 20–1; Longenecker, *Remember the Poor*, 53. The table comes from Helen Rhee, *Loving the Poor, Saving the Rich: Wealth, Poverty, and Early Christian Formation* (Grand Rapids, Mich.: Baker, 2012), 9–10. Following Lenski, Saldarini presents a slightly different classification in a pre–A.D. 70s Palestinian society. Anthony J. Saldarini, *Pharisees, Scribes, and Sadducees in Palestinian Society: A Sociological Approach*, BRS (Grand Rapids, Mich.: Eerdmans, 2001), 39–45.

17. Friesen, "Injustice of God's Will," 247.

18. James B. Adamson, *James: The Man and His Message* (Grand Rapids, Mich.: Eerdmans, 1989), 239–54.

19. See also Allison, *James*, 46; Hubert Frankemölle, *Der Brief des Jakobus, Kapitel 1*, GTB 517 (Gütersloh: Echter, 1994), 253–4; Martin, *James*, lxxv; Elsa Tamez, *The Scandalous Message of James: Faith without Works Is Dead*, rev. ed. (New York: Crossroad, 2002), 18.

20. See, e.g., Cheung, *Epistle of James*, 241–71; Matt A. Jackson-McCabe, "A Letter to the Twelve Tribes in the Diaspora: Wisdom and 'Apocalyptic' Eschatology in the Letter of James," *SBLSP* 35 (1996): 504–17; Mariam J. Kamell, "Incarnating Jeremiah's Promised New Covenant in the 'Law' of James," *EvQ* 83 (2011): 19–28; René Krüger, "El vuelco irritante y definitivo: Santiago 1:9–11 y el anuncio de la inversión total de la situación," *CuadT* 23 (2004): 45–77; Todd C. Penner, *The Epistle of James and Eschatology: Re-reading an Ancient Christian Letter*, JSNTSup 121 (Sheffield: Sheffield Academic Press, 1996); Patrick A. Tiller, "The Rich and Poor in James: An Apocalyptic Proclamation," in *SBL Seminar Papers*, ed. David J. Lull, SBLSP 37 (Atlanta: Scholars, 1998),

Table 3.1. Comparison of population categories in the urban context of the Roman Empire according to the Poverty Scale (PS) of Friesen (2004) and the Economic Scale (ES) of Longenecker (2010)

Scale (Friesen/ Longenecker)	**Categories**	**Groups included**	**Percent of population (Friesen)**	**Percent of population (Longenecker)**
PS_1/ES_1	Imperial elites	Imperial dynasty, Roman senatorial families, a few retainers, local royalty, a few freedpersons	0.04%	ES_{1-3} 3% (the same percentage for the total elite groups; no further breakdown given)
PS_2/ES_2	Regional or provincial elites	Equestrian families, provincial officials, some retainers, some decurial families, some freedpersons, some retired military officers	1%	(See above)
PS_3/ES_3	Municipal elites	Most decurial families, wealthy men and women who do not hold office, some freedpersons, some retainers, some veterans, some merchants	1.76%	(See above)
PS_4/ES_4	Moderate surplus resources	Some merchants, some traders, some freedpersons, some artisans (especially those who employ others), and military veterans	7% (estimated)	15% (adding two particular groups: *Apparitores* and *Augustales*)
PS_5/ES_5	Stable near subsistence level (with reasonable hope of remaining above the minimum level to sustain life)	Many merchants and traders, regular wage earners, artisans, large shop owners, freedpersons, some farm families	22% (estimated)	27%
PS_6/ES_6	At subsistence level (and often below minimum level to sustain life)	Small farm families, laborers (skilled and unskilled), artisans (especially those employed by others), wage earners, most merchants and traders, small shop/tavern owners	40%	30%
PS_7/ES_7	Below subsistence level	Some farm families, unattached widows, orphans, beggars, disabled, unskilled day laborers, prisoners	28%	25%

φυλαί αἱ ἐν τῇ διασπορᾷ (Jas 1:1). This title seems to evoke in his readers/hearers the eschatological hope of God's gathering of the twelve tribes.[21] This hope is rooted in the OT (Isa 11:10, 49:6, 54:7, 56:8; Jer 3:18; Ezek 37:15–28, 47:13; Sir 36:10–16, 48:10), and it is implicit in Jesus's teaching (Matt 15:24; Luke 22:24–30//Matt 17:27–29) and in the NT (Rev 7:4–8; 14:1, 3). Also it recurs in Second Temple literature (Pss. Sol. 17:21–34; Tob. 13:5; 4 Ezra 13:1–13, 14:7; 2 Apoc. Bar. 78:6–7; 1QM 1.1–2, 2.2–3, 3.14–16; 1QS 8.1–2; 1QSa 1.15–19; 11Q19 18.14–16). Consequently, it is highly probable that it is part of the cognitive environment shared by James and his addressees.

This eschatological hope not only frames James's thoughts on faith, suffering, and trials (1:2–4) but also guides all his ethical instructions.[22] As Hartin points out, James's eschatology "provides the worldview in which the Letter of James lives and breathes. In effect, it demonstrates the outcome of the consequences for the ethical instructions."[23] Todd Penner convincingly demonstrates that "the themes and motifs which predominate in James 1.2–12 and 4.6–5.12 are largely drawn from the prophetic literature of the Old Testament with significant parallels in texts of early Judaism, and that these themes and motifs are placed in an explicitly Christian eschatological context."[24] In this way, this type of inclusio sets the main content of the whole epistle into an eschatological frame.[25]

Some eschatological topics and the way they are presented in the epistle permit one to infer that James and his addressees share this encyclopedic knowledge. Some of them are analyzed in this work later. The letter mentions an eschatological reversal (1:9–11), rewards and punishment (1:12, 21; 2:5, 13; 4:10; 5:1–6, 20), believers as "the firstfruits of God's redemption" (1:18), the inheritance of the kingdom (2:5), future evaluation (3:1; 4:12; 5:9), and the Lord's coming (5:7–9). All of these topics are explicitly mentioned but not fully developed. This characteristic illustrates how many eschatological

909–20; Patrick A. Tiller, "The Rich and Poor in James: An Apocalyptic Ethic," in *Conflicted Boundaries in Wisdom and Apocalypticism*, ed. Benjamin G. Wright III and Lawrence M. Wills, SBLSymS 35 (Atlanta: Society of Biblical Literature, 2005), 169–79; Wesley Hiram Wachob, "The Apocalyptic Intertexture of the Epistle of James," in *Intertexture of Apocalyptic Discourse in the New Testament*, ed. Duane F. Watson (Atlanta: Society of Biblical Literature, 2002), 165–85; Robert W. Wall, "James as Apocalyptic Paraenesis," *ResQ* 32 (1990): 11–22.

21. Frankemölle, *Der Brief des Jakobus*, 130–2; Patrick J. Hartin, "James and Eschatology: Place and Function of Eschatology within a Letter to the 'Twelve Tribes in the Dispersion,'" in *Eschatology of the New Testament and Some Related Documents*, ed. J. G. Van der Watt, WUNT 2 315 (Tübingen: Mohr Siebeck, 2011), 460; Jackson-McCabe, "Wisdom and 'Apocalyptic' Eschatology," 504–17; Wiard Popkes, *Der Brief des Jakobus*, THKNT 14 (Leipzig: Evangelische Verlagsanstalt, 2001), 71–3.

22. Wachob, "Apocalyptic Intertexture," 177–8; Wall, "James as Apocalyptic Paraenesis," 11–22.

23. Hartin, "James and Eschatology," 466.

24. Penner, *The Epistle of James*, 158–9.

25. Ibid., 121.

assumptions James and his addressees share.[26] For example, when arguing in 2:1–7, James presents a rhetorical question in 2:5 that assumes that his reader/hearer knows that the poor are heirs of the kingdom.

Vegetation and the Sun's Effects on It

Any person living in the first-century Palestine should be aware of vegetation and the sun's effects on it. As John W. Klotz mentions, "[t]here are about 460 different kinds of grasses found in the Holy Land. The six grasses most abundant in Bible times were *Aegilops variabilis*, *Alopecurus anthoxanthoides*, *Avena sterilis*, *Eragrostis megastachya*, *Nardurus orientalis*, and *Polypogon monspeliensis*. All of these were native grasses quite common to the Holy Land, and were undoubtedly familiar to both OT and NT writers."[27]

The sun's effects on Palestinian vegetation, particularly its heat, seem to be a common image in the Bible (cf. Mark. 4:6; Matt 20:12).[28] Many commentators relate καύσων in 1:11 to the east wind called the sirocco.[29] The use of this metaphor in James could evoke in his readers/hearers "(1) the complete and swift destructiveness of the wind; and (2) the inevitability of its coming."[30] This wind and its effects on vegetation is also a recurring image in the OT (Gen 41:6; Ps 103:15–16; Isa 27:8, 49:10; Jer 4:11, 18:17; Hos 13:5). This usage also appears in Qumran literature (4Q185 1.10–11) and Philo (*Spec. Laws* 1.311).

Identification of Possible OT Texts and Traditions Evoked

Greg Beale defines allusion as "a brief expression consciously intended by an author to be dependent on an OT passage."[31] Is there any allusion in James 1:9–11? In order to answer this question, criteria of validation for possible allusions are necessary. As mentioned above, Hays's first four criteria for validating possible allusions can be considered here in light of an RT perspective: (1) availability, (2) volume, (3) recurrence, and (4) thematic coherence.[32]

26. Allison, *James*, 93; Wachob, "Apocalyptic Intertexture," 183.

27. John W. Klotz, "Plants," *BEB* 1713.

28. See a good summary of this usage in Allison, *James*, 207–10; Peter H. Davids, *The Epistle of James: A Commentary on the Greek Text*, NIGTC (Grand Rapids, Mich.: Eerdmans, 1982), 77–8.

29. Moo considers this a viable translation; Osborne considers the phrase possibly referring to the sirocco. Martin, *James*, 27; Moo, *James*, 67; Grant R. Osborne, "James," in *James, 1–2 Peter, Jude, Revelation*, CBC 18 (Carol Stream, Ill.: Tyndale House, 2011), 30.

30. Martin, *James*, 27.

31. G. K. Beale, *Handbook on the New Testament Use of the Old Testament: Exegesis and Interpretation* (Grand Rapids, Mich.: Baker, 2012), 31.

32. Richard B. Hays, *Echoes of Scripture in the Letters of Paul* (New Haven: Yale University Press, 1989), 29–32. For a positive evaluation of the seven criteria, see Beale, *Handbook*, 34–5. For an adverse evaluation, see Stanley E. Porter, "The Use of the Old Testament in the New Testament: A Brief Comment on Method and Terminology," in *Early Christian Interpretation of the Scriptures of Israel*, ed. Stanley E. Porter (Sheffield: Sheffield Academic, 1997), 83–4.

After saying that the humble must boast in his exaltation, James says that the rich must boast in his humiliation and give reasons for that (1:10b–11). These reasons seem to be alluding to the OT, in particular the phrases ὅτι ὡς ἄνθος χόρτου παρελεύσεται in 1:10 and τὸ ἄνθος αὐτοῦ ἐξέπεσεν καὶ ἡ εὐπρέπεια τοῦ προσώπου αὐτοῦ ἀπώλετο in 1:11.

Opinions among scholars are diverse regarding a possible OT allusion here, from no connection to several options. One of the reasons for this divergence is that James could be using a traditional metaphor rather than any specific OT text(s). Carson sees in these verses only echoes of "transitoriness" that are present in many passages of the OT (e.g., Job 14:2; Ps 37:2, 90:5–6; Isa 40:6–8; 2 Bar. 82:7).[33] Moo argues something similar. For him, "the annual death of vegetation provides a natural metaphor for this purpose [to illustrate the transitoriness of all human wealth and status], and draws on a rich biblical tradition when he uses it here."[34] Moo points out that the most famous passage is Isaiah 40:6–8, but it is not necessarily being explicitly used here.[35] Davids thinks that James has in mind both Isaiah 40:6–8 and Psalm 103:15–16 (102:14–15 LXX), and adds: "[P]erhaps some rough allusion to these two passages is intended... but one cannot press this."[36] After that, he concludes: "James quite naturally more or less conforms his citation of the proverb to the biblical style."[37] David Jones includes Psalm 102:4, 11 (101:5, 12 LXX) as a possible candidate.[38] McKnight mentions Psalm 90:3–6 (89:3–6 LXX).[39] NA[28] mentions Job 14:2 and Isaiah 40:6–7 as possible allusions here.[40]

Carson is right in pointing out that the idea of transitoriness is common in the OT (Job 14:2, 15:30–33; Pss 37:2, 129:6 [128:6 LXX]). Also it is clear that vegetation is a recurrent source for metaphors within this issue (Hos 13:15; Isa 28:1–4, 51:12). However, the concern here is to discern whether or not James is alluding to a specific OT text.

Hays's first criterion is availability. It is hard to know how much of the OT was available to James and his addressees. It is highly probable that those

33. Bauckham, *James*, 67.

34. Carson, "James," 998.

35. Moo, *James*, 67.

36. Davids, *James*, 77. Davids admits later, though, that this is more probably a quotation of Isa 40:6b–7. Ibid., 261.

37. Cheung, *Epistle of James*, 63–4.

38. David A. Jones, *Old Testament Quotations and Allusions in the New Testament* (Bellingham, Wash.: Logos Research Systems, 2009), Logos edition, James, "chapter 1."

39. McKnight, *James*, 101. Williams proposes an intertextual reading of Jas 1:9–11 in light of Jer 9:23–24. But, although there are thematic connections between both passages, it is not the type of intertextuality in which this present research is interested. H. H. D. Williams, "Of Rags and Riches: The Benefits of Hearing Jeremiah 9:23–24 within James 1:9–11," *TynBul* 53 (2002): 273–82.

40. Barbara Aland et al., *Nestle-Aland Novum Testamentum Graece*, 28th ed. (Stuttgart: Deutsche Bibelgesellschaft, 2012), 685.

who were raised Jewish would have heard it all read many times and some of them would have had large chunks of it committed to memory.[41] But at least James assumes his reader/hearers know Job's story (5:11). Psalms and Isaiah are highly quoted in the NT. In Mayor's list of OT texts in James, Job, Psalms, and Isaiah are quoted or alluded to several times.[42] Therefore, under this criterion all the passages mentioned above (Job 14:1–2; Pss 89:3–6 [LXX]; 101:5, 12 [LXX]; 102:14–15 [LXX]; Isa 40:6–7) are possible candidates.

The second criterion is volume. This criterion looks for the amount of similar words or syntactical patterns between the potential OT source and the NT text. The more similarities that exist between passages, the more support there is for an intentional use. Table 3.2 contrasts the possible OT passage and James 1:10b–11.[43]

It is clear that Job 14:1–2 and Psalms 89:3–6; 101:5, 12; and 102:14–15 have only thematic connections with James. In other words, a conceptual relationship exists between these passages and the use of the same metaphor to express human transience (cf. Pss 37:2, 90:5–6, 92:7, 102:5, 129:6). But regarding similar wording, the text of Job 14:1–2 shares with James 1:10–11 only the noun ἄνθος and the verb ἐξέπεσεν. Psalm 89:3–6 shares the noun ταπείνωσις with James but contains different prepositions and the verb παρέρχομαι in different tenses. Psalm 101 shares the noun χόρτος and the verb ξεραίνω; however, the verb appears in a different voice. Psalm 102 shares the same noun with James, and also differs in its use of the phrase ἄνθος τοῦ ἀγροῦ instead of ἄνθος χόρτου.

On the other hand, the closeness of Isaiah 40 to James 1 is high. The passage in Isaiah 40 shares verbs and other forms, as table 3.3 shows. Furthermore, as Allison convincingly argues, James 1:9–11 also reflects the language of Isaiah 40:2–9.[44] So, under the second criterion, Isaiah 40:6–7 is a good candidate. Conversely, the other mentioned passages share few words with James 1:10–11.

The third criterion is recurrence. The author (or other NT authors) uses the same OT text or surrounding texts in his writing(s). NT authors and early

41. I owe this insight to Craig Blomberg.

42. Mayor mentions Job 5:17; 7:19; 13:28; 24:24; 27:21; 33:23, and "the general moral of this book." Also he considers Pss 7:14; 12:2; 24:4; 50:20; 83:13–14; 85:9; 103:8; 119:45; 126:5; 126:6; and 140:3. Finally, he points out Isa 1:11–17; 5:7–9; 9:18; 10:17–18; 13:6; 32:17; 40:6–7; 41:8; 50:9; 54:5–8; and 61:1. Joseph B. Mayor, *The Epistle of St. James: The Greek Text with Introduction, Notes, and Comments*, 2nd ed. (London: Macmillan, 1897), lxxi-lxxiii.

43. All the quotations from the LXX come from the Göttingen edition: Joseph Ziegler, ed., *Septuaginta*, vol. 14, *Isaias*, VTG, Auctoritate Academiae Scientiarum Gottingensis editum (Göttingen: Vandenhoeck & Ruprecht, 1983), 264; Alfred Rahlfs, ed., *Septuaginta*, vol. 10, *Psalmi cum Odis*, VTG, Auctoritate Academiae Scientiarum Gottingensis editum (Göttingen: Vandenhoeck & Ruprecht, 1979), 238, 56–57; Joseph Ziegler, ed., *Septuaginta*, vol. 11, *Iob*, VTG, Auctoritate Academiae Scientiarum Gottingensis editum (Göttingen: Vandenhoeck & Ruprecht, 1982), 270.

44. Allison, *James*, 197–8.

Table 3.2. Comparison between different mentioned texts from the LXX and James 1:10–11

Job 14:1–2 βροτὸς γὰρ γεννητὸς γυναικὸς ὀλιγόβιος καὶ πλήρης ὀργῆς ἢ ὥσπερ **ἄνθος** ἀνθῆσαν **ἐξέπεσεν**, ἀπέδρα δὲ ὥσπερ σκιὰ καὶ οὐ μὴ στῇ.	ὅτι ὡς ἄνθος χόρτου παρελεύσεται. ἀνέτειλεν γὰρ ὁ ἥλιος σὺν τῷ καύσωνι καὶ ἐξήρανεν τὸν χόρτον καὶ τὸ **ἄνθος** αὐτοῦ **ἐξέπεσεν** καὶ ἡ εὐπρέπεια τοῦ προσώπου αὐτοῦ ἀπώλετο·
Ps 89:3–6 μὴ ἀποστρέψῃς ἄνθρωπον εἰς **ταπείνωσιν**. καὶ εἶπας Ἐπιστρέψατε, υἱοὶ ἀνθρώπων. ὅτι χίλια ἔτη ἐν ὀφθαλμοῖς σου ὡς ἡ ἡμέρα ἡ ἐχθές, ἥτις διῆλθεν, καὶ φυλακὴ ἐν νυκτί. τὰ ἐξουδενώματα αὐτῶν ἔτη ἔσονται. τὸ πρωὶ ὡσεὶ χλόη **παρέλθοι**, τὸ πρωὶ ἀνθήσαι καὶ **παρέλθοι**, τὸ ἑσπέρας ἀποπέσοι, σκληρυνθείη καὶ ξηρανθείη.	ὁ δὲ πλούσιος ἐν τῇ **ταπεινώσει** αὐτοῦ, ὅτι ὡς ἄνθος χόρτου **παρελεύσεται.** ἀνέτειλεν γὰρ ὁ ἥλιος σὺν τῷ καύσωνι καὶ ἐξήρανεν τὸν χόρτον καὶ τὸ ἄνθος αὐτοῦ ἐξέπεσεν καὶ ἡ εὐπρέπεια τοῦ προσώπου αὐτοῦ ἀπώλετο·
Ps 101:5 ἐπλήγην ὡσεὶ **χόρτος** καὶ **ἐξηράνθη** ἡ καρδία μου, ὅτι ἐπελαθόμην τοῦ φαγεῖν τὸν ἄρτον μου. 101:12 αἱ ἡμέραι μου ὡσεὶ σκιὰ ἐκλίθησαν, καὶ ἐγὼ ὡσεὶ **χόρτος** **ἐξηράνθην**.	ὅτι ὡς ἄνθος χόρτου παρελεύσεται. ἀνέτειλεν γὰρ ὁ ἥλιος σὺν τῷ καύσωνι καὶ **ἐξήρανεν** τὸν **χόρτον** καὶ τὸ ἄνθος αὐτοῦ ἐξέπεσεν καὶ ἡ εὐπρέπεια τοῦ προσώπου αὐτοῦ ἀπώλετο·
Ps 102:14–15 **ὅτι** αὐτὸς ἔγνω τὸ πλάσμα ἡμῶν· μνήσθητι ὅτι χοῦς ἐσμεν. ἄνθρωπος, ὡσεὶ **χόρτος** αἱ ἡμέραι αὐτοῦ· ὡσεὶ **ἄνθος τοῦ ἀγροῦ**, οὕτως ἐξανθήσει·	**ὅτι** ὡς **ἄνθος χόρτου** παρελεύσεται. ἀνέτειλεν γὰρ ὁ ἥλιος σὺν τῷ καύσωνι καὶ ἐξήρανεν **τὸν χόρτον** καὶ τὸ **ἄνθος** αὐτοῦ ἐξέπεσεν καὶ ἡ εὐπρέπεια τοῦ προσώπου αὐτοῦ ἀπώλετο·
Isa 40:6–7 φωνὴ λέγοντος Βόησον· καὶ εἶπα Τί βοήσω; Πᾶσα σὰρξ **χόρτος**, καὶ πᾶσα δόξα ἀνθρώπου **ὡς ἄνθος χόρτου· ἐξηράνθη ὁ χόρτος, καὶ τὸ ἄνθος ἐξέπεσε**,	ὅτι **ὡς ἄνθος χόρτου** παρελεύσεται. ἀνέτειλεν γὰρ ὁ ἥλιος σὺν τῷ καύσωνι καὶ **ἐξήρανεν τὸν χόρτον καὶ τὸ ἄνθος** αὐτοῦ **ἐξέπεσεν** καὶ ἡ εὐπρέπεια τοῦ προσώπου αὐτοῦ ἀπώλετο·

Table 3.3. Comparison of Isaiah 40 and James 1:9–11

Isa 40:2–4	ταπείνωσις . . . ταπεινωθήσεται
Jas 1:9–10	ταπεινός . . . ταπεινώσει
Isa 40:6	χορτός . . . ὡς ἄνθος χόρτου
Jas 1:10	ὡς ἄνθος χόρτου
Isa 40:7	ἐξηράνθη ὁ χόρτος καὶ τὸ ἄνθος ἐξέπεσεν
Jas 1:11	ἐξήρανεν τόν χόρτος καὶ τὸ ἄνθος αὐτοῦ ἐξέπεσεν
Isa 40:9	ὑψηλόν . . . ὕψωσον . . . ὑψώσατε
Jas 1:9	ὕψει

Table 3.4. New Testament's use of Isaiah 40

Isaiah	New Testament
40:3	Matt 3:3; Mark 1:3; Luke 1:76; John 1:23
40:3–5	Luke 3:4–6
40:13	Rom 11:34; 1 Cor 2:16

Table 3.5. NA^{28}'s suggested allusions to Isaiah 40

Isaiah	New Testament	Isaiah	New Testament
40:1	Luke 2:25	40:17	Acts 19:27
40:2	Rev 1:5, 18:6	40:18	Mark 4:30; Acts 17:29
40:5	Luke 2:30; Acts 28:28	40:26	Rom 1:20; Eph 1:19, 6:10
40:8	Matt 24:35; Luke 21:33	40:28	Rom 1:20; Heb 3:4
40:9	John 12:15	40:29	Rev 12:14
40:10	Rev 22:7–12		

Christian writers use or allude to Isaiah 40, but not the other mentioned texts.[45] The text of 1 Peter 1:24–25 quotes Isaiah 40:6–8. Other NT authors use other verses of Isaiah 40. NA^{28} suggests allusions to Isaiah 40 in several NT passages.

Early Christian authors also quote from Isaiah 40 (Barn. 16 [Isa 40:12], Justin, *Dial.* 50 [Isa 40:1–17], Irenaeus, *Adv. Haer.* 5.33.4 [Isa 40:6], and 1 Clem 34 [Isa 40:10]). With this clear evidence, it is highly probable that the text of Isaiah 40 was part of the shared encyclopedic knowledge of James and his addressees.

Some scholars think that James has more than one passage in mind. Osborne sees Isaiah 40:6–7 and Psalm 103:15–16 behind the metaphor in James 1:10–11.[46] However, following Hays's criteria, it is not possible to demonstrate a conscious use of other texts apart from Isaiah 40:6–7, even though there are some thematic relationships. The second criterion increases the case for a conscious use of Isaiah 40:6–7 but demonstrates that the conscious use of other candidates cannot be as confidently determined. The third criterion points toward the conscious use of Isaiah 40:6–7, but makes the presence of the other texts improbable. The fourth criterion, thematic coherence, is discussed later.

45. Job 14:1–2 and Psalms 101:5 and 102:14–15 are not quoted or alluded to in Second Temple literature, the NT, or early Christian authors. Close to these other OT passages are Ps 101:26–28 (LXX) in Heb 1:10–12, and Job 14:4–5 in 1 Clem. 17.

46. Osborne, "James," 30.

Isaiah 40:6–7 in Its Own OT Context

The author(s) and addressees of the book of Isaiah and their contexts are hard to determine. The discussion in commentaries and monographs demonstrates the difficulty of this issue.[47] Many agree on an exilic context. But it is not clear enough. This complexity contributes to a degree of uncertainty in the interpretive process. If James is using Isaiah 40:6–7, it is important to know the context of the OT passage. In this way, it could be seen whether the meaning of the OT passage thematically agrees with James's text and sheds light on it.[48]

Isaiah 40:1–11 opens the entire section of chapters 40–55. It is a new commission to the prophet that echoes or recalls the scene in chapter 6. In this regard, Childs points out that "the key to the prologue [Isa 40:1–11] lies in its intertextual reinterpretation of Isaiah 6 and thus serves as a crucial interpretive bridge between First and Second Isaiah. It signals the change from the "old things" of chapters 1–39 to the "new things" of chapters 40ff. The former deals with judgment associated with Assyria, the latter with redemption from Babylon."[49]

Isaiah 40:6–8 is the third of four strophes (40:1–2, 3–5, 6–8, and 9–11). Each one represents a commission: "to comfort, to clear a way, to call out, to shout a message."[50] Many scholars agree that this pericope is a heavenly council scene. Some think this is a call narrative. The council scene fits better, however, because there is a close parallelism between Isaiah 6 and 40, with both chapters sharing imagery of a heavenly council. In Isaiah 40, God speaks in plural imperatives, and heavenly voices proclaim his orders. These voices seem to be angelic heralds (vv. 3, 6). In 6:8–13, there is a clear calling to serve and an answer by the prophet, but in 40:1–11, there are only instructions.[51]

This third stanza in inserted in the proclamation of YHWH's liberation of his people from exile. After focusing mainly on God's judgment upon his people (Isa 1–39), this pericope brings hope to those who are in exile in Babylon. In 40:1–2, God tells the prophet and other messengers to comfort the scattered Israel, "my people" in clear covenantal language (your God, my people). God declares that Israel's punishment is about to finish and her restoration is coming. In vv. 3–5, an anonymous voice of a heavenly herald proclaims the King YHWH's return to Zion with his people. "Nothing can

47. See a good summary of the discussion in John Goldingay and David Payne, *Introduction and Commentary on Isaiah 40:1–44:23*, vol. 1 of *A Critical and Exegetical Commentary on Isaiah 40–55*, ICC (New York: T&T Clark, 2006), 25–48.

48. Beale, *Handbook*, 33.

49. Brevard S. Childs, *Isaiah*, OTL (Louisville: Westminster John Knox, 2001), 296. This change of focus from Assyria to Babylon does not necessarily imply a change of author.

50. Goldingay and Payne, *Isaiah 40–55*, 60.

51. See more details in Childs, *Isaiah*, 294–7; Christopher R. Seitz, "The Divine Council: Temporal Transition and New Prophecy in the Book of Isaiah," *JBL* 109 (1990): 229–47.

prevent his swift coming to his people's aid, neither mountains nor valleys."[52] In vv. 6–8, another voice (or the same as in vv. 3–5) instructs: "Proclaim." There is a short dialogue about the proclamation between this voice and the person addressed. In vv. 9–11, a herald of good tidings announces God's arrival not as a judge but as a shepherd.

At the level of explicatures, there are several pragmatic decisions to make. In 40:6, the referents of the phrase that begins the strophe קוֹל אֹמֵר, φωνὴ λέγοντος, "a voice rings out," and the person addressed by the instruction קְרָא, Βόησον, "proclaim," are not clear. It is possible to consider the referent of the voice here as the same anonymous voice of vv. 3–5. Regarding the person addressed, textual problems directly influence the addressee's identity. In the next sentence, the MT reads וְאָמַר, 1QIsa[a] reads ואומרה, LXX (εἶπα) and Vulgate (dixi) support a *Vorlage* וָאֹמַר. Even in the LXX's case, few manuscripts support the third person, εἶπον. If the first person is the original reading, the prophet is the referent of the pronoun or the collective voice of the people.[53] If the third person feminine is read, then Zion could be the referent.[54] If the third masculine is the original reading, there are a couple of alternatives: an indefinite subject, the prophet,[55] or a heavenly being in the council.[56] In any case, "the fact that we remain unsure of the person addressed as well as of the speaker draws attention to the fact that even here the passage focuses on what is said rather than on who speaks."[57]

It is not entirely clear what part of 40:6b–8 MT constitutes the question and what part is the answer. The question could be brief: "What shall I say?" and the answer could be the rest of v. 6 and all of vv. 7 and 8. Or the question could include all of vv. 6 and 7 and the answer v. 8. In the first case, Benjamin Sommer mentions: "[T]he prophet must proclaim that humans are weak (and the Babylonian conquerors will disappear), but God's strength is enduring."[58] In the other case, "these vv. are an objection to acting as conduit for the divine word . . . v. 8 contains the divine response."[59] The former is the more common understanding among scholars.[60] It fits better into the commissioning discourse. "This may be presupposed by 1 Pet 1:24–25 and by

52. John Oswalt, *Isaiah*, NIVAC (Grand Rapids, Mich.: Zondervan, 2003), 445.

53. Terry W. Eddinger, "An Analysis of Isaiah 40:1–11 (17)," *BBR* 9 (1999): 129.

54. Ibid.

55. Goldingay and Payne, *Isaiah 40–55*, 80.

56. Eddinger, "Isaiah 40:1–11," 129.

57. Goldingay and Payne, *Isaiah 40–55*, 80. See also John N. Oswalt, *Isaiah*, NIVAC (Grand Rapids, Mich.: Zondervan, 2003), 445.

58. Benjamin D. Sommer, "Isaiah," in *The Jewish Study Bible*, ed. Adele Berlin and Marc Zvi Brettler (Oxford: Oxford University Press, 2004), 861.

59. Ibid., 861–2.

60. For the first option, see, e.g., Goldingay and Payne, *Isaiah 40–55*, 80–1. For the second option, see, e.g., John D. W. Watts, *Isaiah 34–66*, rev. ed., WBC 25 (Nashville: Thomas Nelson, 2005), 607.

Tg 'all the wicked are like grass.'"[61] If this discourse parallels Isaiah 6:8–13, then like there, the prophet's intervention is short (6:8b), and the message is extensive (6:9–13). The voice asks the prophet to call out (40:6a). The prophet asks: "What shall I cry?" The voice answers with a message of judgment and hope.

At a higher level of explicitness, it is not clear which speech acts this question performs. This could be a rhetorical question that implies doubts about the mission (cf. Exod 3–4; Jer 1).[62] In any case, the text is a vegetal metaphor. There is a contrast between "all flesh" and "the word of God." The LXX reads: "All flesh is grass, and all the glory of man as the flower of the grass. The grass withers and its flower fades, but the word of God remains/stands forever." The words "grass withers, a flower fades, when God's wind/spirit blows on it. Yes/Indeed the people are grass" from MT 40:7 or 40:7b–8a is missing in the LXX and 1QIs^{a}. Some scholars argue for an addition in the MT, and others for an omission for homoioteleuton in the LXX and 1QIs^{a}. In any case, from an RT perspective, if the metaphor is understood as God's punishment by his word, this conclusion is strongly implied in the MT but less strongly so in the LXX and 1QIs^{a}. Krüger points out that Isaiah 40 links expiry with humiliation. Both concepts ταπείνωσις and ταπεινοῦν (LXX) precede this unit (Isa 40:2–4). In this way, God intervenes in both types of humiliation—the end of his people's humiliation and the lowering of the mountains. This divine intervention results in hope for his people.[63] This double message of hope and warning will be important later, when comparing Isaiah's message with James's use of it.

At the level of implicatures, the metaphor in 40:6–8 seems to imply some conclusions:

1. Men and their glory are fragile and ephemeral, in particular those who are not faithful to YHWH (cf. Isa 28:1–4, 51:12).
2. The Babylonian empire is ephemeral (cf. Isa 40:24).
3. There is an imminent reversal of fortunes. God will fulfill his word by both bringing his people back to Zion and punishing their oppressors.

Isaiah 40:6–7 LXX in Second Temple/Jewish Literature

There are three sources that use Isaiah 40:6–8 (MT)/6–7 (LXX): Targum Isaiah 40:6–8; 2 Baruch 82.7; and 4Q185 1:10–11. The first two of them derive their use as the implicatures of the Isaianic text as shown above.[64] The Tar-

61. Goldingay and Payne, *Isaiah 40–55*, 81.

62. Ibid., 80.

63. Krüger, "El vuelco irritante y definitivo," 65.

64. Davidson presents four interpretations of this passage: rabbinic, New Testament, pseudepigraphic, and post–New Testament. The first three are pertinent to the discussion here. Robert Davidson, "The Imagery of Isaiah 40:6–8 in Tradition and Interpretation," in *Quest for*

gum Isaiah understands this metaphor as God's punishment. In particular, it limits the judgment upon the wicked. It reads Isaiah 40:6–8: "The voice of one saying, Prophesy. And one answered and said, What shall I prophesy? All the wicked are as grass, and all their strength as the flower of the field. The grass withered, its flower faded; for the wind from before the Lord had blown upon it; therefore the wicked among the people are counted as grass. The wicked died, his thoughts (or plans) perish; but the word of our God abided forever."[65]

Second Baruch shows a similar interpretation. Giving hope to Israel, 2 Baruch 82.7 seems to apply Isaiah 40:6 to the Gentiles: "And we meditate on the beauty of their gracefulness though they have to do with pollutions, but *as grass that withers shall they fade away*."[66] In the case of 4Q185, the text presents the disaster of those who do not follow God's wisdom. The text seems to allude to Isaiah 40:6–8. It reads: "For see, (man) *sprouts like grass and his loveliness blooms like a flower. His grace makes the wind blow over him and his roots parch, and his leaves the wind scatters*, until hardly anything is in his place."[67] In this case, the similitude with James is closer. Both texts include the idea of beauty and the environmental effects on plants (James uses sun, 4Q185 uses wind).

Evaluation of Accessibility of the Cognitive Environment

In evaluating whether Isaiah 40:6–7 (LXX) is an allusion or not, there are at least three competing aspects of the cognitive environment that are necessary to consider: general vegetation metaphors, general OT proverbs depicting transitoriness, and Isaiah 40 and all its eschatology, which contributes to James's argument.

As mentioned above, people from Palestine were familiar with vegetation metaphors as the diverse agricultural parables in the Gospels illustrate.[68] This is true also in other Greco-Roman contexts (for example, Pliny, *Nat. Hist.* 21.1). James uses other vegetation illustrations: the fire in a forest (3:5), the fruits of the fig tree and the vine (3:12), and the farmer and his work on the field (5:7). This familiarity with botanical imagery makes it highly

Context and Meaning: Studies in Biblical Intertextuality in Honor of James A. Sanders, ed. Craig A. Evans and Shemaryahu Talmon (Leiden: Brill, 1997), 44–55.

65. Eddinger, "Isaiah 40:1–11," 129.

66. Emphasis added in Jones, *Old Testament Quotations and Allusions in the New Testament*. As chapter 4 in the present work shows, the imagery used in 2 Bar 82 is close to that present in Jas 4:13–17.

67. Emphasis added in Florentino García Martínez, *Textos de Qumrán*, 6th ed. (Madrid: Trotta, 2009), 407–8.

68. For example, Jesus teaches about the growing seed (Mark 4:26–29), the wheat and the weeds (Matt 13:24–30, 36–43), the mustard seed (Matt 13:31–32; Mark 4:30–32; Luke 13:18–19), and the barren fig tree (Luke 13:6–9).

probable that James's readers/hearers could make a small amount of effort in order to understand the imagery in 1:10b–11 and derive some implicatures from the metaphors,[69] such as the following:

1. Grass and its flowers are fragile and ephemeral.
2. The sun's heat/the wind quickly withers them.
3. In a similar way, human life is fragile and ephemeral.
4. It is not wise to put complete focus on wealth—taking life for granted.

However, as mentioned above, the metaphor of grass as an example of transience is well attested in the OT (2 Kgs 19:26; Pss 36:2 [LXX], 102:15 [LXX], 128:6 [LXX]). In the OT, the grass imagery (Isa 51:12; Jer 9:21, 12:41, 14:6; Dan 4:15–33; Ezek 17:24 uses trees with the same idea) and the sun's heat/the wind imagery are associated with God's punishment (Hos 12:2, 13:15; Isa 28:1–4, 51:12; Jer 18:17, 28:1; Ezek 17:10, 19:12; Jon 4:8).[70] So it is highly probable that James and his addressees are familiar with these OT associations. In that case, James not only "conforms his citation . . . to biblical style," but also, at least, builds his teaching upon biblical thinking. As a consequence, with a little more cognitive effort, James's readers/hearers could receive more cognitive effects by deriving other implicatures, such as the following:

5. The grass and its flowers are fragile and ephemeral.
6. The sun's heat/the wind quickly withers the grass and its flowers.
7. The Scriptures teach us that human life is similar to the grass and its flowers.
8. The Scriptures teach us that wealth is ephemeral and deceptive.
9. The Scriptures teach us that the wicked trust only in their wealth.
10. The Scriptures teach us that God punishes the person who trusts only in his wealth.
11. God punishes the wicked like the sun's heat/the wind withers the grass.
12. James warns us because the Scriptures teach it.
13. It is not wise to put one's complete focus on wealth—taking life for granted.

In this case, James is metarepresenting by interpretive resemblance. As shown in chapter 2, with an RT view, there are at least two ways of metarepresenting a thought or utterance attributed to someone other than the

69. Davids, *James*, 77. McKnight suggests a connection between "flower" here and the priestly headgear, and for that reason, this verse could be an indirect attack on the wealth of the Jerusalem priestly establishment. However, the assertion is very speculative and hard to falsify. McKnight, *James*, 102–3.

70. In Sir 34:16 and Isa 49:10, God protects those who love him from the wind and sun.

speaker, or to the speaker herself at some other time:[71] metalinguistic and interpretive resemblance. Metalinguistic use is the exploitation of resemblance in linguistic form. Interpretive use is the utilization of the saliency of semantic, logical, or propositional form; it is resemblance in content.[72] In this case, if there is not a specific passage in view but a general OT truth, James guides his readers/hearers to make a loose resemblance of those types of passages. In this way, he reinforces his exhortation by appealing to a general OT teaching.

Now, if James intended his readers/hearers to make intertextual connections with Isaiah 40:6–7 (LXX), the processing or cognitive effort the readers/hearers have to exert is relatively higher than the effort made in the two cases above. The cognitive effects obtained, however, are much higher than those obtained by not making the connections.[73] In particular, apart from the linguistic connection with the Isaianic passage, they may make these links in light of the expectation of relevance created by the eschatological language present since the beginning of the letter and the clear reversal of fortunes expressed in the exaltation of the humble and the humiliation of the rich in James 1:9–10a. These two factors reduce the processing effort of making the association with the OT passage. Furthermore, the adversative connective δέ at the beginning of v. 10 constrains the implicatures of the next sentence by making a clearer contrast between two opposite sides of the situation.[74] In this case, a longer list of implicatures is contextually derived:

14. The grass and its flowers are fragile and ephemeral.
15. The sun's heat/the wind quickly withers the grass and its flowers.
16. What James says that happens to the rich and the humble is the same as what Isaiah says.
17. Isaiah says that human life is similar to the grass and its flowers.
18. People and their glory are fragile and ephemeral, in particular those who are not faithful to God.
19. The Scripture teaches us that wealth is ephemeral and deceptive.
20. The Scriptures teach us that the wicked trust only in their wealth.

71. Eun-Ju Noh, *Metarepresentation: A Relevance-Theory Approach*, PBNS 69 (Amsterdam: John Benjamins, 2000), 74.

72. Deirdre Wilson, "Metarepresentation in Linguistic Communication," *UCLWPL* 11 (1999): 143.

73. Deirdre Wilson and Dan Sperber, "Truthfulness and Relevance," in *Meaning and Relevance*, ed. Deirdre Wilson and Dan Sperber (Cambridge: Cambridge University Press, 2012), 63.

74. On the constraints of procedural markers, see Deirdre Wilson and Dan Sperber, "Linguistic Meaning and Relevance," in *Meaning and Relevance*, ed. Deirdre Wilson and Dan Sperber (Cambridge: Cambridge University Press, 2012), 149–68; Diane Blakemore, *Relevance and Linguistic Meaning: The Semantics and Pragmatics of Discourse Markers*, CSL 99 (Cambridge: Cambridge University Press, 2002).

21. As the Babylonian empire received God's punishment also the wicked rich will be punished as well.[75]
22. In Isaiah, there is an imminent reversal of fortunes. God will fulfill his word by bringing his people back to Zion, but punishing their oppressors.
23. In the same way, the humiliation of the poor has come to its end. God will exalt the poor and punish the wicked.

Furthermore, there could be at least two speech acts derived at a higher level of explicitness as illocutions: hope and warning. James gives hope to the poor by evoking Isaiah 40:6–7. A poor Christian reading/hearing this text finds hope. His or her situation is coming to its end. On the other hand, a rich Christian should consider this as a warning. If God will act upon the wicked rich in such a way, he or she should change his or her attitude toward the poor. Both speech acts could be implicit in James's utterance. The addressees who are in between the poor and the rich, the middle group, could perceive a third type of illocution. They could perceive a different type of warning. In this case, there could be an exhortation to not put their confidence in and look for the patronage of the rich.

If this analysis is correct, vv. 10–11 could be sarcastic. If there is sarcasm, then we are in the presence of a high level of explicitness, something like "I mean you should lament about your humiliation, which is your imminent punishment." There is no agreement among scholars whether there is irony in 1:10–11 or not. Those who see no irony at all tend to consider the rich mentioned here as Christians. As Christians, the rich should humble themselves—"a heroic humility."[76] On the other hand, those who see irony (or even bitter irony) here tend to consider the rich as unbelievers. Thus, the irony is that they should boast in their destruction.[77] However, the irony could be present independently whether the rich are Christians or not. As mentioned above, the illocutionary force varies depending on the audience. The irony is that what seems to be the basis of their pride—wealth—is the source of their damnation (1:11, 5:2–3). The rich should boast in their punishment. The implicit language behind the irony could be similar to 4:9. The implicatures of this text could reinforce the idea of hope for the humble, as a vindication, and the warning for those wealthy Christians and those addressees in between them. As Kamell rightly points out, "James makes clear that everyone will, at some

75. In this regard, Krüger says: "If one continues with this update [of the message of Isa 40:1–8], this means that the rich will be flattened like the mountains and hills." Krüger, "El vuelco irritante y definitivo," 65.

76. See, e.g., Moo, *James*; Blomberg and Kamell, *James*; Kurt A. Richardson, *James*, NAC 36 (Nashville: Broadman & Holman, 2001).

77. See, e.g., Allison, *James*, 204–6; Davids, *James*, 75; Isaacs, *Reading James*, 186; Elsa Tamez, *No discriminen a los pobres: Lectura latinoamericana de la carta de Santiago* (Estella: Verbo Divino, 2008), 41; McKnight, *James*, 98–100.

point or another, be ταπεινός. The question merely is whether this humility is self-chosen (and temporary) or enforced by God (and permanent)."[78]

At this point of the analysis, three alternatives have been considered. The general use of the metaphor contributes with some implicatures revolving around the ephemeral life. A general context from the OT contributes with similar terms, but adds the strength of biblical authority. In fact, the other competing passages (Job 14:1–2; Ps 89:3–6; 101:5, 12; 102:14–15) present the fragility of human life in order to highlight God's care for human beings (Job 14:1–2; Ps 101:5, 12; 102:14–15) or God's punishment (Ps 89:3–6). Under the criteria of global coherence, however, these passages do not seem to fit well in James's context. Furthermore, in RT terms, the effort invested in making the connection with these other passages does not contribute to more cognitive effects in James's discourse. Conversely, making the connection with Isaiah 40:6–7 notably contributes to reinforcing his discourse.

In this case, James is metarepresenting Isaiah 40:6–7 by metalinguistic and interpretive resemblance. The metalinguistic resemblance is clear because James uses phrases and words from Isaiah 40:6–7, as table 3.2 shows. He adds ἀνέτειλεν γὰρ ὁ ἥλιος σὺν τῷ καύσωνι and ἡ εὐπρέπεια τοῦ προσώπου αὐτοῦ ἀπώλετο.[79] He uses Isaiah's words for his own discourse. He exploits the passage's interpretive resemblance with Isaiah 40:6–7. As mentioned in chapter 2, two utterances resemble each other to the degree that they share logical and contextual implications. In this way, the more implications they share, the more they resemble each other.[80] The resemblance in content permits James to attach the eschatological reversal of the Isaianic passage to his own eschatological discourse. In this way, he reinforces his admonition with biblical support.

Isaiah 40:6–7 in James 1:10–11 fits well in Hays's fourth criterion of thematic coherence. It is clear from the analysis of this passage that "the alleged OT allusion is suitable and satisfying in that its meaning in the OT not only thematically fits into the NT writer's argument but also illuminates it."[81] The Isaianic passage illuminates the concept of an eschatological reversal of fortunes by reinforcing it throughout the theme of God's bringing his people back to Zion and punishing his adversaries. An experienced first reader could explain these connections to a lesser-informed audience. So, although it is impossible to affirm with total certainty that James intentionally drove his readers/hearers to make this link, we can assert with confidence that it is highly probable that he did so. On the other hand, as mentioned above, the

78. Kamell, "The Economics of Humility," 169. See also Pedrito U. Maynard-Reid, *James: True Religion in Suffering*, ALBA (Boise: Pacific, 1996), 58–62.

79. Allison notes that in 4Q185 1:10–11, the allusion to Isa 40:7–8 includes the wind's effects on flowers and the idea of beauty. Allison, *James*, 208–10.

80. Wilson, "Metarepresentation in Linguistic Communication," 142.

81. This is Beale's summary of Hays's fourth criterion. Beale, *Handbook*, 33.

other candidate passages (Job 14:1–2; Pss 89:3–6; 101:5, 12; and 102:14–15) do not fit this last criterion.

Interpretation of the Text in James

As mentioned in chapter 2, other parts of a discourse influence what aspects of the mutual cognitive environment are more salient in the current segment. In particular earlier parts contribute with contextual assumptions by reducing the processing effort or creating more specific expectations of the cognitive effects in a particular segment of the discourse. The preceding verses (1:1–8) trigger some aspects of that general cognitive environment—encyclopedic knowledge shared by James and his addressees. As mentioned above, eschatology is a prominent aspect. Wisdom in the midst of trials is also present. Some scholars see poverty as a special case of trials, already presented in 1:2–3.[82] In this sense, this paragraph, 1:9–11, seems to be a particular case of trials/tests (1:2–8). In fact, James 1:12–15 continues the same issue, focusing on trials (1:12) and temptation (1:13–15). Allison states: "In view of all this [the several literary and content connections between 1:5–8 and 1:9–11], and because the units before and after 1.9–11 clearly relate themselves to to vv. 2–4 and the theme of trial, it is natural to connect also vv. 9–11 with that theme. So vv. 2–4 introduce the subject; vv. 5–8 discuss the wisdom that is required for enduring trials; vv. 9–11 put difficulties in eschatological perspective by foretelling the fate of both poor (= oppressed; cf. 2:6; 5:4–6) and rich (= oppressor; cf. 2:6–7; 5:4–6)."[83]

In order to explain this passage, there are several points to make at the level of explicature. The passage begins with a particle δέ. It is a "mild adversative" that joins this paragraph (1:9–11) with the rest of this unit, weaker than δέ in 1:5.[84] The particle δέ in 1:10 introduces a contrast between the two lines. Grammatically, these lines form an antithetical parallelism:

> καυχάσθω δὲ ὁ ἀδελφός ὁ ταπεινὸς ἐν τῷ ὕψει αὐτοῦ,
> ὁ δὲ πλούσιος ἐν τῇ ταπεινώσει αὐτοῦ,

Sociologically, these lines also form a clear chiastic structure of contrast, as Allison notes, between honor and shame:[85]

82. See, e.g., McKnight, *James*, 76. McKnight also thinks that wealthy persons could be a type of double-minded criticized in 1:6–8.

83. Allison, *James*, 195–6.

84. This use of δέ is similar to μέν, as in 1 Tim 5:6 and 2 Tim 2:22. Allison points out that this δέ, like the one in 1:5 and 1:22, "appears . . . to mark the turn from one subject to another," although he recognizes that "[o]ne can . . . also translate the particle with 'but' and draw a contrast with the double-minded of v. 8." Allison, *James*, 200 and n. 38; George Benson, *A Paraphrase and Notes on the Seven (Commonly Called) Catholic Epistles* (London: J. Waugh and W. Fenner, 1756), 31.

85. Allison, *James*, 199.

Shame Let the brother who is lowly
Honor glory in his exaltation
Honor But the rich
Shame in his humiliation

The exhortation presents a contrast, a reversal of the situation of both people. The first one is called "the humble brother." Given the contrast, "humble" should be considered "financially humble," "in humble circumstances," or "poor in the world's perspective" (2:5).[86] In light of the rest of the epistle, the singular ὁ ἀδελφός ὁ ταπεινός represents a variety of poor described in the letter. This person, ὁ ἀδελφός, is part of the community of believers:[87] the widow and the orphan (1:27), the brother and sister lacking clothing or food (2:15), the field workers (5:4), even the filthily dressed one (2:2). Also, the "humble brother" could include, in Longenecker's scale, believers from ES_5 to ES_7.

Those persons, in the midst of their trials, should boast, glory in their high position. The verb καυχάομαι has a positive connotation here (cf. Ps 32 [31 LXX]:11).[88] Furthermore, because of its position at the beginning of the sentence, it is highly emphatic. The illocutionary force of this imperative seems to be encouragement. At a higher level of explicitness, the sentences could be "I encourage you, my beloved humble brother: rejoice, glory in your high position." The phrase "high position," as Johnson points out, has both a future component in light of 1:12, "a crown of life," and a present aspect in light of 2:5, "inheritance of the kingdom."[89] In fact, by the structure of the rhetorical question in 2:5, James assumes that information as part of the encyclopedic knowledge shared with his addressees. Finally, at the level of explicature, the phrase "his high position" implies "his high position given by God."

These implicatures are strongly communicated:

1. The humble brother/sister experiences trials in his/her poverty.
2. God has given a high position to the poor.
3. The one who boasts in his/her exaltation strengthens his/her faith.
4. The one who boasts in his/her exaltation has hope in the midst of trials.
5. The one who boasts in his/her high position has hope in God's future vindication.

86. As Kamell shows, the word ταπεινός could also imply piety. Kamell, "The Economics of Humility," 166–74.

87. Against Allison, who thinks "brothers" here refers to Jewish coreligionists; see his arguments in 1:2. Allison, *James*, 145–6.

88. James uses καυχάομαι/καύχησις with negative connotations in 4:16, also κατακαυχάομαι in 3:14. Osborne, regarding this, says: "Pride in self is a sin, but pride in what Christ is doing in one's life is a Christian privilege." Osborne, "James," 29.

89. Johnson says: "The exaltation can be read as including the future reward of the one who endures, which is promised by 1:12, and therefore be seen as eschatological. . . . But it also has already been realized in God's election of the poor to be 'rich in faith' in the kingdom (2:5)." Johnson, *James*, 185.

An implicature derived in a second reading of the epistle might be the following:

6. The lowly brother/sister should rest in the eschatological hope as an heir of God's kingdom.

The next line, ὁ δὲ πλούσιος ἐν τῇ ταπεινώσει αὐτοῦ (1:10), stands in contrast to the former. At the level of explicature, there is a clear ellipsis of the verb. However, it is not clear whether or not James intends his readers/hearers to supply ὁ ἀδελφός. As a result of this ambiguity, there has been much debate about whether these rich are Christians or not. The noun πλούσιος appears here and in 2:5, 6–7, and 5:1–6. In 2:5, it refers to the poor in the sphere of the word but rich in God's perspective. In 2:6–7 and 5:1–6, it is clearly presented in a negative way.[90] The absence of the syntagma "the brother" permits one to consider here the rich qua rich. The referent of the noun could be both insiders and outsiders of the Jamesian community. The diverse economic statuses of the addressees and the ambiguity of the referent to the rich make it possible for James to intend multiple illocutionary forces. Here there could be a consolation for the poor and an exhortation or warning to the rich Christian. The sentence could be understood as ironic. The implicatures for the readers/hearers illustrate later the diversity of illocutionary forces present in this prophetic proclamation.

James exhorts the rich to glory/rejoice ἐν τῇ ταπεινῶσει αὐτοῦ. The noun ταπείνωσις could be understood as "humble state" or "humiliation." However, "humiliation" is preferred here because of at least three contextual indicators: (1) there is a contrast between the situations of the poor and rich, (2) there is a clear reversal of the situation of the poor, (3) the explanation James gives in 10b–11 clearly points in the direction of an eschatological punishment. As Ben Witherington points out, "the phrase *en tē tapeinōsei* must be parallel to *en tō hypsei*, so it is a reference to a humble position not a humble attitude."[91] This way of describing the rich is in line with Jesus's frequent description of them, particularly in Luke's Gospel (Matt 19:23–24; Mark 10:25, 12:41; Luke 6:24, 12:16, 14:12, 16:19, 18:25).[92]

90. All these passages are discussed later in the present work.

91. Contrary to Witherington's view, though, this humble position implies punishment. See, e.g., Popkes, *Der Brief des Jakobus*, 94–8. Witherington thinks that "the rich person should boast in voluntarily assuming a lower position and more humble circumstances by giving wealth and helping the poor." This interpretation does not consider that the implied warning in 1:11 points toward punishment. He agrees, however, in this eschatological overtone and says: "The point of this lengthy analogy between the rich and their money and the beautiful flower that wilts and is destroyed is that judgment is coming upon such persons who boast in that sort of status." Ben Witherington III, *Letters and Homilies for Jewish Christians: A Socio-Rhetorical Commentary on Hebrews, James, and Jude* (Downers Grove, Ill.: IVP Academic, 2007), 431–2.

92. Johnson, *James*, 185.

James justifies his exhortation of the rich by appealing to the OT. He says: ὅτι ὡς ἄνθος χόρτου παρελεύσεται. This vegetational metaphor is a summary of his idea developed in v. 11. He explains: ἀνέτειλεν γὰρ ὁ ἥλιος σὺν τῷ καύσωνι καὶ ἐξήρανεν τὸν χόρτον καὶ τὸ ἄνθος αὐτοῦ ἐξέπεσεν καὶ ἡ εὐπρέπεια τοῦ προσώπου αὐτοῦ ἀπώλετο. As shown above, the sentence in 1:10b and its explanation in 1:11 evoke Isaiah 40:6–7. Through this connection with Isaiah's message, James reinforces some ideas also present in Jesus's teaching regarding poverty and wealth (Matt 6:19–21; Mark 10:17–27; Luke 6:23–24, 16:19–31) and exaltation and humiliation (Matt 23:12; Luke 14:11, 18:14). It is perfectly possible that these ideas were part of the shared encyclopedic knowledge of James and his community. In this way, James reinforces an assumption by appealing to the OT's authority. In doing this, he also evokes an eschatological reversal present in Isaiah's prophecy. In this regard, after comparing the different backgrounds behind 1:9–11, Krüger points out: "On these different backgrounds, Jas 1:9–11 acquires a clear profile. In no way, do these verses express the notable truth of human mortality, but they have the thematic announcement of the author's position which will be developed later concretely in the epistle at sociological, theological, ecclesiological, financial, and political levels. James surpasses the sapiential pattern by including precisely the severe prophetic criticism about the exploiters and oppressors and by adding an eschatological accent to his denunciation."[93]

James ends his analogy saying: οὕτως καὶ ὁ πλούσιος ἐν ταῖς πορείαις αὐτοῦ μαρανθήσεται. The metaphorical use of this verb triggers several weak implicatures. As Allison points out, "[the presence of μαραίνω here] makes it especially appropriate in the present context. One might think only that the rich are headed for the grave. But the mention of heat prepares for 5.1–6, where they suffer in eschatological fire. Further, it is only the eschatological future that makes real the difference between rich and poor. So 1.9–11 seems to miss its mark without an implicit appeal to the last judgment."[94] In light of the Isaianic passage, some of the implicatures might be the following:[95]

7. The life and business of the rich are ephemeral.
8. The rich could die at any moment.
9. God will punish the wicked rich at any moment.
10. The rich Christian should not put his/her confidence in his/her own financial plans, but in God.
11. The non-rich Christian should not look for security and patronage in the ephemeral rich. (This topic is explicitly exposed in 2:1–13.)

93. Krüger, "El vuelco irritante y definitivo," 66.

94. Allison, *James*, 212–3.

95. Moo argues that this verb does not imply necessarily eschatological punishment. He tends to interpret the idea as the ephemeral life. Moo, *James*, 67–8. But his argument is not convincing, especially in light of Isa 40:6–8, and the eschatological reversal here.

Considering 1:9–11 as a whole, at a higher level of explicitness, it is highly reasonable to understand a double illocution.[96] On one hand, James encourages his addressees and gives them hope, in particular the poorest among them. On the other hand, at the same time, he also exhorts and rebukes some of them, the Christian rich.[97] A sequence of implicatures from this sentence might be the following:

1. The grass and its flowers are fragile and ephemeral.
2. The sun's heat/the wind quickly withers the grass and its flowers.
3. The way in which James describes what happens to the rich and the humble parallels Isaiah's description.
4. Isaiah says that human life is similar to the grass and its flowers.
5. Human beings and their glory are fragile and ephemeral, in particular those who are not faithful to God.
6. The Scriptures teach us that wealth is ephemeral and deceptive.
7. The Scriptures teach us that the wicked trust only in their wealth.
8. As the Babylonian empire received God's punishment, the wicked rich will be punished as well.
9. In Isaiah, there is an imminent reversal of fortunes. God will fulfill his word by bringing his people back to Zion but punishing their oppressors.
10. In the same way, the humiliation of the poor has come to its end. God will exalt the poor and punish the wicked.

Other implicatures derived from this eschatological reversal might be the following:

11. There is hope for the poor. God will vindicate them by punishing their oppressors.
12. There is a warning for the rich Christians. They should abandon all oppression against the poor in order to avoid God's punishment.
13. There is a new status and honor, not based on wealth, for the Christian in the community of believers.

Later in the letter, James explains the results and content of this high position. At this point he creates expectations for the relevance of this sentence.

96. For Allison, the illocutionary forces in this type of text are console, exhort, and rebuke. Allison, *James*, 196. Kamell concludes that James "warns his audience in apocalyptic language of judgment . . . but this vision of judgment is grounded in the God of Israel's self-revelation that he is both 'God of gods and Lord of lords' and one who 'executes justice for the orphan and the widow, and who loves the strangers, providing them food and clothing.' Ultimately, humility or humiliation will come to every person, whether rich or poor." Kamell, "The Economics of Humility," 175.

97. Popkes, *Der Brief des Jakobus*, 99. This reflection is clearer later in Jas 2:1–13.

His readers have to make a cognitive effort that later is compensated by cognitive effects. The same is true regarding the rich. James put all his fire on the rich without explaining whom he is talking about, or what humiliation implies. Later in the development of the letter it is clearer that he has more probably the unbelieving rich in mind, although, as I argued, the rich Christian would read this sentence as a warning/rebuke.

At this point, James's implicatures reveal his ethics of poverty and wealth. The implicated conclusions here form the basis for the theme in the letter. They are the following:

1. The humble brother/sister experiences trials in his/her poverty.
2. God has given a high position to the poor.
3. The one who boasts in his/her exaltation strengthens his/her faith.
4. The one who boasts in his/her exaltation has hope in the midst of trials.
5. The one who boasts in his/her high position has hope in God's future vindication.
6. The lowly brother/sister should rest in the eschatological hope an heir of God's kingdom.
7. The life and business of the rich are ephemeral.
8. The rich could die at any moment.
9. God will punish the wicked rich at any moment.
10. The grass and its flowers are fragile and ephemeral.
11. The sun's heat/the wind quickly withers the grass and its flowers.
12. The way in which James describes what happens to the rich and the humble parallels Isaiah's description.
13. Isaiah says that human life is similar to the grass and its flowers.
14. Human beings and their glory are fragile and ephemeral, inparticular those who are not faithful to God.
15. The Scriptures teach us that wealth is ephemeral and deceptive.
16. The Scriptures teach us that the wicked trust only in their wealth.
17. As the Babylonian empire received God's punishment, the wicked rich will be punished as well.
18. In Isaiah, there is an imminent reversal of fortunes. God will fulfill his word by bringing his people back to Zion but punishing their oppressors.
19. In the same way, the humiliation of the poor has come to its end. God will exalt the poor and punish the wicked.
20. There is hope for the poor. God will vindicate them by punishing their oppressors.
21. There is a warning for rich Christians. They should abandon all oppression against the poor in order to avoid God's punishment.
22. There is a new status and honor, not based on wealth, for the Christian in the community of believers.

23. The rich Christian should not put his/her confidence in his/her own financial plans, but in God.
24. The non-rich Christian should not look for the security and patronage in the ephemeral rich.

Summary of How James Uses the OT in 1:9–11

James paints this passage on an eschatological canvas. From the beginning of the letter, James evokes different eschatological concepts. Here, in 1:9–11, he presents a reversal of fortunes for the poor and the rich. The RT procedure helps to clarify with a high degree of confidence that James uses Isaiah 40:6–7 to reinforce this reversal. He evokes God's vindication of the oppressed and punishment of the wicked. He does this by metarepresenting Isaiah's message through a combination of metalinguistic and interpretive resemblances. He uses some words from Isaiah's text and adapts them for his own discourse. The interpretive resemblance permits him to strengthen his own discourse by evoking vindication and punishment. At the level of explicature, he gives hope and warns his diverse audience. At the level of implicature, he guides his readers to derive eschatological teachings regarding reversal of fortunes, gives a new paradigm of honor/shame, and strengthens his teaching with Isaiah's words.

The methodology applied to this passage helps not only to discern the presence of Isaiah 40:6–7 but also to rule out other possible candidates. The use of Hays's criteria of validation and the principles of relevance help to evaluate also these other LXX passages: Job 14:1–2; Psalms 89:3–6; 101:5, 12; and 102:14–15. Although it is impossible to completely rule out any of these texts, the methodology and the principles of relevance allow one to conclude their presence is unlikely.

Methodology Applied to 1:26–27

This text differs from the above in its use of the OT. Although there are no clearly identifiable allusions, the text is steeped in OT language. James seems to interpretively use the OT in order to reinforce his teaching.

Elucidation of the Co-text

In Osborne's outline, this passage is a subsection of 1:19–27.[98] For Davids, this is part of the closing of the introduction.[99] Taylor also understands

98. Osborne, "James," 17.

99. He presents it as a summary of the second section and a transition toward the next section. Davids, *James*, 27, 100–1.

1:26–27 as transitional. He correctly points out: "[T]he summary character, unusual vocabulary and broad thematic concepts related to true religion of this section offers specific application to the preceding exhortations of 1.21–25 and at the same time anticipates the basic points developed in the rest of the letter."[100] In our outline, this paragraph closes the section 1:19–27. It continues the themes of speech control (1:19) and purity (1:21). It takes up an earlier theme again, the issue of poverty (1:9).

The paragraph is closely related to 1:21–25. Moo sees links through the concepts of law/word. The phrase "accept the word" (v. 21) turns into "do the word" (v. 22), which also becomes "do the law" (v. 25). Verses 26–27 bring this sequence to its climax. Here, James presents three ways one can do the "word/law."[101] These are controlling the tongue, concern for the "helpless," and avoidance of "worldliness."[102] Moo considers that in some way these two verses "set the agenda for the rest of the letter."[103] In fact, some topics of this paragraph are developed later. Speech control is developed in 3:1–12. The impact of a "heavenly wisdom driven life" in 3:13–18 and the ethical demands in 4:1–10 seem to reflect what James means by "keep oneself from being polluted by the world" (1:27 NIV). Other connections are[104] concerns for the marginalized (2:1–13, 14–17) and "the world" (3:6, 4:4).

Description of the General Cognitive Environment

This pericope is rich in social images and cultic imagery. The most prominent are studied next in order to understand James's message and its association with the OT.

Cultic Life

Central to this pericope is the concept of θρησκεία/θρησκός. It is mentioned three times (the adjective once, the noun twice). θρησκεία is mentioned elsewhere once in Colossians 2:18 with the sense of worship and in Acts 26:5 with the sense of religion. In the LXX, it relates to God's worship (4 Macc 5:7, 13) or idol worship (Wis 14:18, 27). The verb is absent in the NT but appears twice in the LXX in connection with worship (Wis 11:15, 14:17). So, it is highly probable that the concept evokes in James's addressees all the issues related to God's cult: temple, cult, ritual, sacrifices, offerings, prayers, synagogue, Lord's Table, and Jerusalem, just to name a few. James qualifies a legitimate religion as καθαρὰ καὶ ἀμίαντος (1:27). Even though there is no specific rite

100. Taylor, *Discourse Structure of James*, 101.

101. Moo, *James*, 95.

102. Ibid. Kurt Richardson sees the connection through the concept of self-deception (1:6–7, 14, 16, 22). Richardson, *James*, 98.

103. Moo, *James*, 96.

104. Allison, *James*, 79.

of Israelite worship, for Hartin, James uses this imagery and language to highlight the separation between "those who belong to God and those who belong to the world."[105] These associations with "religion" are developed later, when explaining the text.

Speech Control

James introduces the topic in 1:19 and develops it in 3:1–12. Here, he relates the theme to true religion. He uses the metaphor χαλιναγωγεῖν τὴν γλῶσσαν (1:26). This rich metaphor evokes horses, riders, strength, control, and so on. The other metaphor he uses is ἀπατεῖν τὴν καρδίαν (1:26). Later, these ideas are explored in the explanation of the verses.

Widows and Orphans

There is no clear number of widows in the first xentury. Bruce Winter points out that "it has been estimated that forty per cent of women between the ages of forty and fifty were widows and that, as a group, they comprised some thirty per cent of women in the ancient world."[106] These percentages illustrate the depth of the problem the Christian community had to deal with.[107] In Jewish communities, the synagogue was the center for helping the widows among them.[108] Outside, in Greco-Roman societies, the family

105. Patrick J. Hartin, *James*, SP 14 (Collegeville, Minn.: Liturgical Press, 2003), 109. For more details on purity and pollution in James, see Darian R. Lockett, "'Unstained by the World': Purity and Pollution as an Indicator of Cultural Interaction in the Letter of James," in *Reading James with New Eyes*, ed. Robert L. Webb and John S. Kloppenborg, LNTS 342 (London: T&T Clark, 2007), 49–74; Darian R. Lockett, *Purity and Worldview in the Epistle of James*, LNTS 366 (London: Clark, 2008); Scot McKnight, "A Parting within the Way: Jesus and James on Israel and Purity," in *James the Just and Christian Origins*, ed. Bruce Chilton and Craig A. Evans, SupNovT 98 (Leiden: Brill, 1999), 83–129.

106. Bruce W. Winter, *Roman Wives, Roman Widows: The Appearance of New Women and the Pauline Communities* (Grand Rapids, Mich.: Eerdmans, 2003), 124. He depends on Jens-Uwe Krause, *Witwen und Waisen im romischen Reich*, HABES 16 (Stuttgart: F. Steiner, 1994), 73.

107. McGinn shows the complexities of studying the issue in the Roman world. T. A. J. McGinn, "Widows, Orphans, and Social History," *JRA* 12 (1999): 617–32. Later, in the fourth century, John Chrysostom mentions three thousand widows and virgins supported by the church in Antioch, and he recognizes that there were more outside. *Hom. Matt. 66*. See a detailed analysis in Efthalia Makris Walsh, "Wealthy and Impoverished Widows in the Writings of St. John Chrysostom," in *Wealth and Poverty in Early Church and Society*, ed. Susan R. Holman, HCSPTH (Grand Rapids, Mich.: Baker, 2008), 183–4.

108. At least in second-century writings and later rabbinic literature there are instructions on this issue. See, e.g., m. Demai 3:1; Pirqe ʾAbot. 5:9; b.t. Meg. 27a; b.t. B. Bat. 8a–9a; b.t. Roš Haš. 4a–5b; b.t. B. Qam. 11:3. In particular, regarding helping widows, see m. Ket. 4:12, 11:1–6, 12:3–4; m. Git. 5:3. Speaking about the organized Jewish charity in local communities, L. T. Johnson says: "[E]ach community would offer a daily 'soup kitchen' for transients and the destitute [which includes widows and orphans], and a 'chest' for meeting the long-term needs." Luke Timothy Johnson, *The Acts of the Apostles*, SP 5 (Collegeville, Minn.: Liturgical Press, 1992), 106. See also Craig S. Keener, *Acts: An Exegetical Commentary, 3:1–14:28* (Grand Rapids, Mich.: Baker Academic, 2013), 1263–68, "Charity and Widows."

was expected to support widows. But there was no enough support.[109] Christian communities early on began to help widows (Acts 6) and continued to do so.[110] One example of this is the treatment of different cases of widows reflected in 1 Timothy 5:3–16.[111]

These two groups, widows and orphans, represent the typical poor. Johnson calls them "the classic recipients of God's help and the object of Israel's care, those who were, in a landed and patriarchal society, the endemically impoverished."[112] Orphans are those without at least their father. In Longenecker's scale, widows and orphans are in ES_7. They were part of "the expendables of society": beggars, unfamilied widows, and orphans. Gerhard Lenski estimates 10–15% of an urban population were in the expendable class.[113] They were vulnerable and socially and legally unprotected. As Arlandson points out, "[t]he expendables are those whom society rejects. If widows (and beggars and orphans) without an οἶκος, did not receive help, then they faded away into obscurity. Laws were passed in Asian and Jewish societies to protect widows, or at least give them some power, but these laws pertained to women of means. The laws were empty if women's hands were empty. Their plight was then potentially life-threatening."[114]

Eschatological Connections

Some scholars see eschatological connections in this passage.[115] As mentioned above, eschatological language and motifs are present from 1:1 on. In 1:9–11, there is an eschatological reversal of fortunes. There, the humble brother receives hope in the midst of his situation. The one who remains steadfast under trial receives the crown of life (1:12). Now, believers should

109. Winter, *Roman Wives, Roman Widows*, 124–7.

110. The testimony of the apostolic fathers gives an account of continuous Christian concern for the widows and orphans (1 Clem. 8:4; Ign. *Smyrn.* 13:1; Ign. *Pol.* 4:1–2, 3; 6:1; Barn. 20:2; Herm. Vis. 2.4.3; Herm. Mand. 8.10; Herm. Sim. 1.8; 9.27.2). The text of Herm. Sim. 1.8 is very close to James's words. For diverse studies on these issues, see, e.g., Susan R. Holman, ed., *Wealth and Poverty in Early Church and Society*, HCSPTH (Grand Rapids, Mich.: Baker, 2008).

111. Some scholars argue for an "order of widows" already present in Pauline communities. The evidence is scarce, however. See more details in M. Cathleen Kaveny, "The Order of Widows: What the Early Church Can Teach Us about Older Women and Health Care," *CB* 11 (2005): 11–34; I. Howard Marshall and Philip H. Towner, *A Critical and Exegetical Commentary on the Pastoral Epistles* (London: T&T Clark International, 1999), 575–81; Manabu Tsuji, "Zwischen Ideal und Realität: Zu den Witwen in 1 Tim 5.3–16," *NTS* 47 (2001): 92–104.

112. Johnson, *James*, 212.

113. Gerhard Emmanuel Lenski, *Power and Privilege: A Theory of Social Stratification* (Chapel Hill: University of North Carolina Press, 1984), 283. Although this percentage is debatable, some scholars consider it close to reality. Keener, *Acts*, ii. widows; Winter, *Roman Wives, Roman Widows*, 124.

114. James Malcolm Arlandson, *Women, Class, and Society in Early Christianity: Models from Luke-Acts* (Peabody, Mass.: Hendrickson, 1997), 112.

115. See, e.g., Hartin, *James*, 102; Laws, *James*, 89–90; Martin, *James*, 53; Penner, *The Epistle of James*, 121–213.

show their pure and undefiled religion before God by visiting widows and orphans in their trials. In the immediate co-text, the themes of salvation of souls (1:21) and the macarism (1:25) also point toward eschatological connections. Even though the word θλίψις per se does not necessarily have eschatological connotations,[116] the context of the letter guides the readers to make those connections. As Allison points out, "the word can, in both Jewish and Christian texts, advert to the woes of the latter days."[117] In RT terms, the preceding text and the later eschatological connections in the letter guide the readers/hearers to disambiguate the concept θλίψις as "eschatological affliction." In this way, the readers/hearers connect afflictions with, for example, hope, temporality, and urgency. As Wall says, "the community's practice of caring for the poor and powerless anticipates the inevitable reversal of their fortunes in the coming Jubilee."[118]

Identification of Possible OT Texts and Traditions Evoked

This passage differs from the former (1:9–11). In this case, James seems not to allude to any specific OT passage. However, his language and teaching are close to the OT. Echoes of the OT resound in James's discourse. The cultic language and the exhortation to visit widows and orphans evoke some OT themes. As mentioned above, the use of θρησκεία/θρησκός "stresses the cultic aspect of religion."[119] Although this cultic language is present, there is not any clear OT allusion in view. However, some echoes of OT teaching regarding prophetic criticism against vain religiousness seem to be behind it. McCartney sees, for example, some echoes of Jeremiah's denunciation of idolatrous religion (Jer 2:5, 8:19, 10:15, 51:58).[120] Malachi 3:1–5, for example, connects God's eschatological refining fire with correct worship, ethics, and care for widows and orphans.

The same happens with the exhortation to visit orphans and widows in their affliction. The theme of helping the widow and the orphan is common in the OT and in Second Temple literature. God is the protector of the widows and orphans (Deut 10:17–18, 24:19–21; Pss 68:5, 94:3–7, 146:9; Prov 15:25). So his people must follow his example (Exod 22:21; Deut 16:14,

116. Dan McCartney thinks that "although James connects suffering and patient endurance with eschatological hope (1:12; 5:7), here he is speaking simply of the economics and social distress that widows and orphans commonly experience." Dan G. McCartney, *James*, BECNT (Grand Rapids, Mich.: Baker, 2009), 129. But it is precisely this eschatological context that strengthens the eschatological urgency to bring help to the widows and orphans. See the discussion below.

117. Allison mentions Dan 12:1 (LXX); Zeph 1:15; Hab 3:16; Matt 24:9; Mark 13:9; Acts 14:22; Col 1:24; Rev 7:14; Herm. Vis. 2.2.7. Allison, *James*, 364.

118. Robert W. Wall, *Community of the Wise: The Letter of James*, NTC (Valley Forge, Pa.: Trinity, 1997), 101.

119. Johnson, *James*, 211.

120. McCartney, *James*, 128.

24:17–21, 26:12–13, 27:19). As Allison points out, "Exodus' prohibition not to harm widows and orphans [Exod 22:21] became, in Jewish and Christian tradition, a positive admonition to do good to them, one often rooted in the imitation of God, guardian of the widows and orphans."[121] Prophets denounce their abuse and exploitation by the wicked (Isa 1:23, 10:2; Jer 7:6, 22:3; Ezek 22:7; Zech 7:10; Eliphaz accuses Job of doing that, Job 22:9) and exhort Judah to care for them (Isa 1:17). Also this issue is present in Second Temple literature. For example, CD A vi.16–18 is an appeal to live an exemplary life, guided by a correct interpretation of the law, which does not consider the widows its spoils and does not kill the orphan.[122] Also Sirach 4:10 encourages the reader/hearer to be a father to the orphans and a husband to the widows. Despite all of this background, there is no clear OT allusion in view here.[123] However, it is possible "to hear" some echoes of the OT.

James's teachings clearly are founded in the OT teaching. In this case, in RT terms, James makes a loose interpretive metarepresentation of the OT. The exhortation to visit orphans and widows loosely resembles in content the OT teaching. In this case, the readers/hearers might make a connection/implication like this:

1. We have to visit orphans and widows in their affliction as the Scriptures say.

In spite of the fact that he does not allude to or quote any specific passage, James builds his exhortation on the Scriptures. He communicates it in such a way that his readers/hearers easily may connect his teaching with the Scriptures. In fact, in the NT, the combination widow/orphan appears only here in James 1:27, although it is relatively common in the OT.[124] Krüger mentions that thirty-four of the thirty-eight occurrences of the combination widow/orphan (sing. or pl.) in the OT (Deuterocanonical included) are "in a social or charitable sense or with reference to situations of need."[125] In terms of RT, James metarepresents an OT teaching through a loose interpretive resemblance. So, it is highly probable that the combination widow/orphan triggers in the readers/hearers access to their encyclopedic knowledge of OT teachings about the care for them. Furthermore, their knowledge about synagogue

121. Allison, *James*, 363.

122. García Martínez, *Textos de Qumrán*, 84. See also Sib. Or. 2.270–71.

123. Allison suggests the command to love thy neighbor as a possibility. Allison, *James*, 363. Nevertheless, even though it is mentioned explicitly later (2:8), there are no indications here that could help to make the connection between Lev 19:18b and Jas 1:27.

124. In total, the combination widow/orphan (sing. or pl.) appears thirty-one times in the canonical OT books (Exod 22:22, 24; Deut 10:18; 14:29; 16:11, 14; 24:17, 19–21; 26:12–13; 27:19; Job 22:9; 24:3; 31:18; Pss 68:5; 94:6; 109:9; 146:9; Isa 1:17, 23; 9:17; 10:2; Jer 7:6; 22:3; 49:11; Lam 5:3; Ezek 22:7; Zech 7:10; Mal 3:5) and seven times in the deuterocanonical (Tob 1:8; Sir 35:17; EpJer 6:38; 2 Macc 3:10; 8:28, 30; 2 Esd 2:20).

125. Krüger, *Pobres y ricos en la epístola de Santiago*, 175.

practices of caring for the needy (and about the Jerusalem Church) would reinforce that connection.

Evaluation of Accessibility of the Cognitive Environment

As mentioned above, no OT passage is clearly alluded to in James 1:26–27. However, James's language sounds in line with OT traditions regarding the care for orphans and widows. For that reason, it is highly probable that James is using a loose interpretive metarepresentation of OT teaching. In this case, in the interpretation process, the readers/hearers could evoke OT teaching to understand the exhortation in 1:27. Passages like Malachi 3:1–5 could be behind James's words. This evocation gives more cognitive effects to the process without much more processing effort than it would take to not make the connections. A sequence of implicatures might be the following:

1. James exhorts us to visit orphans and widows in their affliction.
2. The Scriptures teach us that we have to care for orphans and widows.
3. James exhorts us to do it because the Scriptures teach it.

Interpretation of the Text in James

This pericope functions "as the *axiomatic basis* of the preceding appeal (1:21–25)."[126] In this regard, George and Helen Hart explain: "James assumes that the readers, who are fellow believers, want to worship God rightly and want to be approved by God."[127] Therefore, here, he contrasts the incorrect and the correct worship directed toward God. James Baker thinks rightly that its parallel structure with 1:23 "is intended to signal that what follows in 1:26–27 is another reason for becoming a doer of the word and not remaining a hearer only."[128] The unit has two segments. The first one is a conditional structure in 1:26. It presents an incorrect form of worship, a μάταιος θρησκεία. The second one is a double assertion in 1:27. It presents the correct form of worship, a θρησκεία καθαρὰ καὶ ἀμίαντος. The protasis of the first class conditional structure is an assertion with two adverbial modifiers. The apodosis omits the verb:

Εἴ τις δοκεῖ θρησκὸς εἶναι
μὴ χαλιναγωγῶν γλῶσσαν αὐτοῦ
ἀλλ' ἀπατῶν καρδίαν αὐτοῦ,
τούτου μάταιος ἡ θρησκεία.

126. George Hart and Helen Hart, *A Semantic and Structural Analysis of James*, SSA (Dallas: SIL International, 2001), 56 (their emphasis).

127. Ibid.

128. William R. Baker, *Personal Speech-Ethics in the Epistle of James*, WUNT 68 (Tübingen: J. C. B. Mohr, 1995), 96.

At the level of explicature, several tasks are required. It is necessary to assign the referent to the indefinite pronoun τις. It is possible to understand it as "any one of us" or "any one of you." The other two personal pronouns and the demonstrative have the same referent. The verb δοκέω "is frequently used in the NT for false opinion."[129] It "implies something subjective, based on opinion and not necessarily on fact."[130] The adjective θρησκός is a hapax legomenon. Here it is used for someone who performs a correct form of worship of God or has an adequate relationship with the divine.[131] As Allison points out, "it is the visible side of religious faith, the external manifestation of εὐσεβής."[132] In an implicature of the phrase, regarding the combination of "seems" and "religious," Blomberg and Kamell comment: "[S]hallowness is exactly what James wants to depict here."[133]

The two adverbial modifiers describe the practice of that person. This practice contradicts his/her public worship. That person does not restrain his/her tongue and deceives (indulges?) his/her heart. Both expressions are metaphorical. The first metaphor continues the theme of speech control, βραδὺς εἰς τὸ λαλῆσαι, presented in 1:19. This topic is widely developed later in 3:1–12 and 4:1–12. The metaphor χαλιναγωγεῖν γλῶσσαν emphasizes the control of speech. But at the same time, it permits several weak implicatures derived from the encyclopedic knowledge about "horse control and direction" and "speech." Here, "human speech is compared to a wild horse,"[134] "a runaway horse needing to be reined in lest it do damage."[135] It is not explicit what aspects of the speech are in view here. Scholars mention the following: attribute temptation to God (1:13), anger (1:19–21), speaking without doing (Allison), angry words, maligning another's character (Blomberg and Kamell), criticism (Davids), and inconsistency (Hartin).[136] None is explicit about how they should manifest that control: brevity, silence, wise discourse (Blomberg and Kamell, Johnson), or being careful in what is said (Moo).[137]

129. Johnson mentions as examples of this use Matt 3:9, 6:7, 26:53; Mark 6:49; Luke 8:18, 12:51, 13:2, 19:11, 24:37; John 5:39; and Acts 12:9. Johnson, *James*, 210.

130. Blomberg and Kamell, *James*, 93.

131. Allison, *James*, 355; Dibelius, *James*, 121; Johnson, *James*, 210. Dibelius's assumption that this adjective "would not be presumed in the period of the missionary effort, but rather in the context of churches which have already been consolidated" has no support. Dibelius, *James*, 120. In particular, if the addressees are Jewish Christians, they already have a concept of good religion. Even non-Jewish believers could have their own understanding of how a good religious person looks. Witherington, *Letters and Homilies*, 447.

132. Allison, *James*, 355.

133. Blomberg and Kamell, *James*, 93.

134. Hart and Hart, *Analysis of James*, 56

135. Witherington, *Letters and Homilies*, 147.

136. Allison, *James*, 356; Blomberg and Kamell, *James*, 93; Davids, *James*, 101; Hartin, *James*, 109.

137. Blomberg and Kamell, *James*, 93; Johnson, *James*, 210; Moo, *James*, 96.

All of these ideas seem to be implicit in the metaphor. Some of them are developed later in 3:1–12, 13–18; 4:1–12, 13–17; 5:1–6, 13–18.

The second metaphor is a Hebrew idiom. On one hand, the idea of ἀπατᾶν τὴν καρδίαν is normally understood as "to deceive the heart" as in Testament of Naphtali 3.1: ἐν λόγοις κενοῖς ἀπατᾶν τὰς ψυχὰς ὑμῶν, "do not deceive your souls with empty phrases."[138] In this case, a set of implicatures is derived from the phrase around the concept of "active self-deception."[139] In that vein, McCartney thinks that "to deceive the heart" is a verbal activity, "a corollary to failure to control the tongue."[140] Several cases of self-deception appear previously (1:6–7, 14, 16, 22). These examples could illustrate the type of implicatures derived from the phrase:

1. People who deceive their heart are double-minded.
2. People who deceive their heart fall into temptation.
3. People who deceive their heart just hear the word of God but do not practice it.[141]

On the other hand, Johnson proposes that the verb ἀπατάω also means "give pleasure to."[142] He translates the phrase: "without controlling his tongue and while indulging his heart."[143] Allison considers it as a valid alternative. He concludes: "So, perhaps Johnson is correct to relate v. 26 not to the theme of self-deception in 1.6–7, 14, 16 but rather to link it to the condemnation of 'pleasures' and 'desires' in 4.1–3; cf. 5.5."[144] In this case, another set of implicatures would be in view:

4. People who indulge their heart egotistically pray to God.
5. People who indulge their heart promote conflicts.
6. People who indulge their heart enrich themselves by wicked means.

Therefore, the disambiguation of the verb leads toward two possible explicatures of the protasis: (1) "If any of us/you thinks to be religious/to

138. Allison, *James*, 358.

139. McKnight, *James*, 165.

140. McCartney, *James*, 128; Dan G. McCartney, "Self-Deception in James," *CTR* 8.2 (2011): 31–43.

141. Baker describes this person as the one who "has failed to embrace the word within, who has not cast the moral evil from his life, and who has not even heard the word properly." Baker, *Personal Speech-Ethics*, 96.

142. Johnson, *James*, 211. BDAG presents this use, and defines it as "enjoy oneself, live pleasurably." "ἀπατάω," BDAG 98. Allison points out that Muraoka's lexicon also includes that acceptation. Allison, *James*, 358. However, the *DGENT* does not include it, only the common "engañar, embaucar, extraviar." "ἀπατάω," *DGENT* 3: 743–4.

143. Johnson, *James*, 211. Also McKnight supports this option. McKnight, *James*, 165.

144. Allison, *James*, 358.

worship God correctly, yet do not control his/her speech but deceive his/her heart thinking he/she is worshipping God correctly";[145] (2) "If any of us/you thinks to be religious/to worship God correctly, yet do not control his/her speech while indulging his/her heart."[146] Consequently, it also points to different sets of implicatures. This last option sounds attractive if one thinks in terms of self-indulgence in 4:1–3 and 5:6. However, it rests on a very infrequent meaning of ἀπατέω.[147] The more frequent meaning "to deceive" is already salient in the discourse (1:6–7, 14, 16, 22). So, it is more probable that James intends option 1.

In any case, the worship of that person is worthless. The word μάταιος appears seventy-five times in the LXX. "The LXX links μάταιος to idol worship. So, it makes strong contrast with καθαρός, ἀμίαντος, and ἄσπιλος in the rest of the passage."[148] McCartney goes further and links James 1:26–27 with God's judgment against idolatrous religion in Jeremiah (2:5. 8:19. 10:15. 51:18 [28:18 LXX]).[149] There are other passages, however, that could be behind James's teaching.[150] His assertion is closer to Isaiah 10:13. The context of Isaiah 1:10–17 resounds as an echo behind James 1:26–27. In particular, Isaiah's exhortation also mentions the care for orphans and widows as a part of true worship (Isa 1:17). So, James's teaching is in the vein of OT concern regarding true/false worship, although here it is not alluding to any specific passage. Christian worship is worthless, futile, unless it is accompanied by speech control and the two other ingredients expressed in 1:27.

The second part of this pericope presents the correct form of worship of God. James describes religion in cultic terms of purity, pointing toward the object of worship, God as God and Father. As mentioned above, "pure," "undefiled," and "unstained" trigger in the readers/hearers cultic associations.[151] In 1:26, James presents two aspects of incorrect worship. Now, he presents two aspects of a correct adoration.

145. McKnight translates the sentence: "If persons think they are religious, and while thinking this do not bridle their tongue but instead choose to deceive their hearts, their religion is worthless." McKnight, *James*, 165.

146. McKnight translates the sentence: "If persons think they are religious, and while thinking this do not bridle their tongue but instead indulge their hearts, their religion is worthless." McKnight, *James*, 165.

147. Johnson quotes as evidence of this meaning Herm. Sim. 6.2.1; 6.4.4; 6.5.1; Herm. Man. 11.12; and Sir 14:16 and 30:23. Johnson, *James*, 211.

148. Allison, *James*, 359. See also Johnson, *James*, 211.

149. McCartney, *James*, 128.

150. Johnson lists other passages where ματαιός means "foolish" and "this foolishness is associated with idolatry": Wis 13:1; Esth 4:17; 3 Macc 6:11; Acts 14:15; Rom 1:21, 8:20; Eph 4:17. Johnson, *James*, 211.

151. Osborne points out that these two words have cultic associations "with 'pure' defining purity laws, and 'genuine' (or 'undefiled') defining those who are ritually clean and fit to approach God. Osborne, "James," 45.

> θρησκεία καθαρὰ καὶ ἀμίαντος παρὰ τῷ θεῷ καὶ πατρὶ αὕτη ἐστίν,
> ἐπισκέπτεσθαι ὀρφανοὺς καὶ χήρας ἐν τῇ θλίψει αὐτῶν,
> ἄσπιλον ἑαυτὸν τηρεῖν ἀπὸ τοῦ κόσμου

He uses this cultic language to explain that correct worship of God also includes two simultaneous actions: caring for orphans and widows and ethical purity.[152] Several scholars agree that James's presentation of God as "God and Father" emphasizes God's role as the protector of orphans and widows (Ps 68:5; Prov 15:25).[153] This connection between God as Father and the theme of orphans and widows could guide toward intertextual associations with passages such as Exodus 22:22–24; Deuteronomy 10:18; Psalms 68:5, 94, and 146; and Isaiah 1:17. If James intentionally wants his readers/hearers to make the connections, in RT terms, he is metarepresenting those texts via a loose interpretive resemblance.[154]

James describes this concern for orphans and widows as visiting them in their afflictions. At the level of explicature, the idea of ἐπισκέπτεσθαι is to visit in order to act in favor of the visited one (cf. Gen 21:1; Exod 3:16, 4:31; Luke 1:68, 78), in this case, to be closely involved in assisting the fatherless and widows in their needs.[155] As mentioned above, there are strong eschatological connections here. From the beginning of the letter there is an eschatological tone. In 1:2–4, refining faith by trials is a recurrent eschatological theme (cf. Isa 4:3–4; Mal 3:1–5; Zech 13:9).[156] In 1:9–11, there is an eschatological reversal of fortunes. In 1:12, there is a reward for those who remain steadfast in the midst of trials. The theme of salvation of the soul (1:21) and the macarism (1:25) point toward eschatological connections. Also, as mentioned above, eschatological passages like Malachi 3:1–5 could inform James's connection between a correct worship, righteousness, and the care for widows and orphans.

If the eschatological association with θλίψις is correct, then the calling of James is put in the context of the woes of the end of times. The urgency of

152. Jesus does something similar in Luke 11:37–41.

153. See, e.g., Hartin, *James*, 109; Laws, *James*, 89; McKnight, *James*, 169–70. Allison thinks that the precise connotation of "father" here is unclear. But the three alternatives for its presence he proposes are related to the presence of "orphans and widows." Allison, *James*, 361. For his part, Davids thinks that the phrase παρὰ τῷ θεῷ καὶ πατρί is probably a Septuagintalism meaning "in God's eye." Davids, *James*, 103. In James, God also is father of the lights (1:17), father of the human beings (3:9). The description of God as Father highlights his character as Creator, a creator who cares for his creation. We as his creatures must follow his example.

154. Hart and Hart phrase 1:27a as "If anyone takes care of orphans and widows who suffer hardship, *which is one of the things God has told us to do.*" Hart and Hart, *Analysis of James*, 57 (their emphasis). McKnight points out, "There is no reason to assign a source for James's concern: it is biblical, it is found in Jesus' ministry, and it is socio-economically present for the first messianic community." McKnight, *James*, 170.

155. As Allison points out, both ἐπισκέπτομαι and פקד "imply more than almsgiving." Allison, *James*, 362.

156. Penner, *The Epistle of James*, 187.

Christian involvement is greater.[157] Baker shows some implicatures: "[V]isiting orphans and widows exhibits love for them. It is faith in action. It presumes encouraging conversation, but also physical, financial, and any other assistance which will ease or remedy their plight."[158] In light of the rest of the letter, probably, it implies also legal assistance (2:6, 5:6). In any case, orphans and widows "stand for those most needing of help in James' world."[159] James is demanding active participation of his addressees in helping the needy.

The second action, which characterizes correct worship, is ἄσπιλον ἑαυτὸν τηρεῖν ἀπὸ τοῦ κόσμου. At the level of explicature, some tasks are necessary in order to understand the phrase. The pronoun refers to any person who worships God. The phrase ἄσπιλον ἑαυτὸν τηρεῖν ἀπό, with other similar constructions, "presumably reflects the Hebrew idiom, שמר + pronominal suffix + מן. "Guard against" might be as accurate a translation as the conventional "keep from"—"to guard yourself against the world, unspotted" (cf. 2 Pet 3:14).[160] The word "world," as in the rest of the epistle (2:5, 3:6, 4:4), refers to "the entire cultural value system or world order which is hostile toward what James frames as the divine value system."[161] As Baker puts it, "the person whose religion is pure and undefiled will indeed be involved in the world as the first aspect [to care for the orphans and widows] demands, but he will protect himself from allowing the evil corruption in the world to rub off on him."[162]

So, at the level of implicatures, keep oneself unstained from the world could imply to refuse to think or act immorally like those who do not obey God (Hart and Hart), to have correct moral attitude and action (Johnson), and to keep free from the evil influences in the surrounding culture, such as the desire to possess and gather (Davids).[163] In Lockett's words, "James ought not to be read as promoting sectarian separation from the world but only the specific separation from particular alien values embodied in the ambient culture."[164]

157. Martin, *James*, 53. McKnight thinks the opposite. He says that here "James is describing the socio-economic and emotional condition of the widows and orphans rather than the eschatological location of those sufferings." McKnight, *James*, 171. But this is not an either/or sentence. Both ideas could simultaneously be implied. It is precisely the eschatological environment of the exhortation that strengthens the requirement.

158. Baker, *Personal Speech-Ethics*, 98.

159. Allison, *James*, 363. Surprisingly, Davids does not include orphans and widows as examples of those who suffer in the letter of James. His concern is for the individual, but not for the responsibility of the community in helping those suffering the most. Peter H. Davids, "Why Do We Suffer? Suffering in James and Paul," in *Missions of James, Peter, and Paul*, ed. Bruce Chilton and Craig A. Evans, SupNovT 115 (Leiden: Brill, 2005), 435–66.

160. Other similar structures Allison presents are "διατηρήσατε οὖν ἑαυτοὺς... ἀπὸ παντὸς ἔργου πονηροῦ of T. Dan 6.8, the τηρήσῃς αὐτοὺς ἐκ of Jn 17.15, and the σε τηρήσω ἐκ of Rev 3:10." Allison, *James*, 365.

161. Lockett, "Unstained by the World," 58.

162. Baker, *Personal Speech-Ethics*, 98.

163. Davids, *James*, 103; Hart and Hart, *Analysis of James*, 58; Johnson, *James*, 213.

164. Lockett, "Unstained by the World," 74. See also Lockett, *Purity and Worldview*.

At a higher level of explicitness, it is possible to understand the illocutionary force of the pericope as an exhortation to have a correct worship before the God and Father. A global idea of this pericope might be this: "Let's have a correct worship before the one who is God and Father. As a matter of fact, if someone thinks he is religious but does not control his speech, and so deceives himself/herself, his/her religion is vain. Conversely, the pure and undefiled religion before our God and Father is to visit orphans and widows in their afflictions and keep oneself unstained by the world."

Some implicatures related to this exhortation in 1:26–27 are the following:

1. People who deceive their heart are double-minded.
2. People who deceive their heart fall into temptation.
3. People who deceive their heart just hear the word of God but do not practice it.
4. Widows and orphans live in the affliction of the end of times.
5. James exhorts us to visit orphans and widows in their affliction.
6. Someone who visits widows and orphans has a pure and undefiled worship before God the Father.
7. Someone who visits widows and orphans cares for them and provides for their needs.
8. The Scriptures teach us that we have to care for orphans and widows.
9. James exhorts us to do it because the Scriptures teach it.

Summary of How James Uses the OT in 1:26–27

This pericope does not openly allude to any specific OT passage. However, it is clear that James builds his instruction from the OT. Some echoes of passages like Malachi 3:1–5 can be detected. James seems to use interpretive resemblance of OT teachings regarding speech control, caring for orphans and widows, and ethical purity. If this perception is correct, James reinforces his teaching and his authority by using language that guides his readers/hearers to make general connections with the OT. In RT terms, James metarepresents the OT teaching by using loose interpretive resemblance. In this way, he builds his ethics of poverty and wealth by interpretively metarepresenting the OT.

Conclusions

The aim of this chapter was to study how James uses the OT in two passages where he deals with the issue of poverty and wealth. In order to study each text, a Relevance Theory approach is used. When examining potential allusions, the first four of Hays's criteria are used, in addition to the consideration of relevance function, as validation criteria. This chapter examines James 1:9–11 and 26–27.

James, from the beginning, sets his discourse in eschatological language. In 1:9–11, James emphasizes the reversal of fortunes for the poor and the rich. In order to do that, he builds his discourse with Isaianic language. He uses Isaiah 40:6–7. He evokes the text metarepresenting it metalinguistically. He uses several words of the text and adds some phrases. James's text is a loose resemblance of Isaiah 40:6–7. Furthermore, James uses Isaiah's context to strengthen his own discourse. He interpretively metarepresents Isaiah's text. That is, he takes the Isaianic text and uses it in his own discourse. He not only metalinguistically uses the OT text but also brings with it its implicatures. He recalls the ideas of vindication and punishment. At the level of explicature, he gives hope and warns his audience. He gives hope to the poor among the addressees, but he also warns those believers in better socioeconomic conditions, and gives a severe warning to rich believers. At the level of implicatures, he guides his addressees to derive eschatological teachings regarding reversal of fortunes and provides a new paradigm of honor and shame. His appeal to the OT strengthens his own discourse but also helps him to bring Isaiah's eschatological concepts into his own discourse via interpretive resemblance. This finding reinforces the thesis that James builds his ethics of poverty and wealth by interpretively metarepresenting the OT.

In 1:26–27, no clear allusions are detected. However, James's language is imbued with OT teaching. Echoes of the OT are discernible. With cultic language, James teaches that a true worship of God the Father includes at least three ingredients: controlled speech, care for orphans and widows, and ethical purity. The mention of orphans and widows is embedded in eschatological language. Words such as "Father," "visit," "orphans and widows," and "afflictions" may signal an intertextual link to several OT passages. If James wants his readers/hearers to make the connection, he is doing so through a loose interpretive resemblance of OT teaching. In this case, he reinforces his teaching and authority by using language that guides his addressees to make the general connections to the OT.

James's ethics of poverty and wealth is reflected in both explicatures and implicatures. At this point, at the level of explicatures the connections with the OT and the multiple illocutionary forces in his discourse are clear. The link with the OT also brings into James's discourse extra implicatures. James highlights the hope for the poor, and the Christian community's responsibility for the needy, in particular orphans and widows. Also, the implicatures confront the wealthy Christian with the severity of the eschatological reversal of fortunes and God's punishment of the wicked rich. In addition, the implicatures challenge the middle group of Christians by warning them about the foolishness of looking for the patronage of the ephemeral rich.

In these two passages, James lays the foundation of his teaching on poverty and wealth. In 1:9–11, he sets the eschatological reversal, reorients his addressees regarding the honor the humble have, and warns the community and in particular the wealthy regarding false and dangerous foundations of trust in riches. In 1:26–27, he closely relates God's worship and the care for the needy. The next chapter of this research shows how James builds his teaching on these ideas by interpretively metarepresenting the OT and Jesus's teachings.

Chapter 4

James 2:1–26

The previous chapter presented James's foundational ideas about poverty and wealth. James continues this theme in 2:1–26, openly criticizing his addressees' attitudes and actions against the poor. He builds his criticism on what he describes as a genuine faith in Jesus Christ. Daily life examples, rhetorical questions, diatribe, direct quotations, allusions, and biblical examples are the rhetorical repertoire of his discourse. Analysis in this chapter falls naturally into two main sections: 2:1–13 and 2:14–26. The study of James's use of the OT and the Jesus tradition is applied to each segment, and confirms that he built his ethics of poverty and wealth through an interpretive meta-representation of the OT and Jesus's teachings.

Methodology Applied to 2:1–13

James 2 is the most studied chapter in the epistle. Hundreds of books and articles present James's ideas from diverse angles. It is easy to become distracted by the myriad of interpretive issues, and to lose focus on what matters to this research: how James is using the OT in passages where he deals with poverty and wealth. In particular, it is a great temptation to engage in discussions on Paul's and James's views concerning the roles of works and faith, or whether the setting of 2:1–3 is a synagogue or a tribunal. All these issues are presented in footnotes when relevant.

As noted above, for the sake of clarity, 2:1–13 and 2:14–26 are here analyzed separately. OT passages are studied, the Jesus tradition is taken into account, and James's use of both are explored. In 2:1–13, the interpretive and metalinguistic use of the OT and the interpretive use of Jesus's words are combined to reinforce James's own discourse.

Elucidation of the Co-text

In Osborne's outline this text is the second subpoint, "Preferring the Wealthy in the Assembly," of his third major point, "Practical Christianity—Living Out the World" (1:19–2:26). For Johnson, the entire second chapter forms a unit under the heading "The Deeds of Faith." Davids concurs and titles his chapter 2 "Excellence of Poverty and Generosity."[1] Martin notes several parallels between 2:1–13 and 2:14–26.[2] The parallels between these segments of James 2 reinforce the idea of a unit. In our outline, 2:1–26 is a subset of 1:19–4:12. This segment, 2:1–13, is entitled "True faith does not discriminate against the poor."

In any case, themes present in 1:1–27 reappear here—in particular, the issue of poverty and wealth. As John Painter points out, "James 2:1–13 follows naturally after 1:26–27. Yet 2:5–6 also develops out of 1:9–11, which features the reversal of the fortunes of the rich and the poor because God has chosen the poor of this world to be heirs of the kingdom (2:5), a theme rooted in the Jesus tradition of Matt 5:3; Luke 6:20."[3] In Davids's structural diagram, the line of thought regarding poverty and wealth develops as follows: poverty excels over wealth (1:9–11). obedience requires generosity (1:22–25), and both poverty and generosity are excellent (2:1–26).[4] Therefore, it is possible to conclude that all these texts shed light on 2:1–13 (and on 2:14–26). In RT terms, the topic of poverty and wealth is salient in the comprehension process.

Scholars divide 2:1–13 in various ways.[5] Some see forms of diatribe here.[6] Even though there are elements of diatribe—in particular in 2:14–26—these do not constitute the main structuring principle of the segment.[7] Rhetorical analysis presents a more convincing structure.[8] In a rhetorical approach,

1. Grant R. Osborne, "James," in *James, 1–2 Peter, Jude, Revelation*, CBC 18 (Carol Stream, Ill.: Tyndale House, 2011), 16–7; Luke Timothy Johnson, *The Letter of James: A New Translation with Introduction and Commentary*, AB 37A (New Haven: Yale University Press, 1995), 11–6; Peter H. Davids, *The Epistle of James: A Commentary on the Greek Text*, NIGTC (Grand Rapids, Mich.: Eerdmans, 1982), 22–8.

2. Ralph P. Martin, *James*, WBC 48 (Waco, Tex.: Word Books, 1988), 78–9.

3. John Painter, "James," in *James and Jude*, ed. Mikeal C. Parsons and Charles H. Talbert, Paideia (Grand Rapids, Mich.: Baker, 2012), 89.

4. Davids, *James*, 28.

5. Osborne divides this "Preferring Wealthy in the Assembly" into three segments: 2:1–7, 8–11, and 12–13. Osborne, "James," 17. Hart and Hart split this section into two parts: 2:1–11, 12–13. They consider 2:1–11 as a hortatory paragraph, an appeal; and 2:12–13 as the motivational basis for that appeal. George Hart and Helen Hart, *A Semantic and Structural Analysis of James*, SSA (Dallas: SIL International, 2001), 59–72.

6. George Guthrie separates the section into two different pericopes, 2:1–11 and 2:12–13, subsumed under a broader segment 2:1–5:6. He considers 2:12–13 as a transitional passage. For him, 2:1–13 and 2:14–24 have the form of a diatribe. George H. Guthrie, "James," in *The Expositor's Bible Commentary: Hebrews-Revelation*, ed. Tremper Longman III and David E. Garland, EBC (Grand Rapids, Mich.: Zondervan, 2006), 209, 30. Taylor also follows this classification. Mark E. Taylor, *A Textlinguistic Investigation into the Discourse Structure of James*, LNTS 311 (New York: T&T Clark, 2006), 108.

7. Ben Witherington III, *Letters and Homilies for Jewish Christians: A Socio-Rhetorical Commentary on Hebrews, James, and Jude* (Downers Grove, Ill.: IVP Academic, 2007), 450.

8. Dale C. Allison, *A Critical and Exegetical Commentary on the Epistle of James*, ICC (New York: Bloomsbury, 2013), 374–5. Several scholars have seen Greco-Roman rhetorical structures here, dividing the segments with minor differences between them, but applying different names to each section. For example, Hartin presents theme (*propositio;* 2:1), reason (*ratio;* 2:2–4), proof (*rationis*

Table 4.1. Parallels between 2:1–13 and 2:14–26

My brothers... faith (2:1)	My brothers... faith (2:14)
The poor person in filthy clothes (2:2)	A brother or sister ill-clad and lacking in daily sustenance (2:15)
The poor... wealthy in faith (who) love God (2:5)	Faith... works [two terms used in association ten times in thirteen verses]
You are right (καλῶς ποιεῖτε) (2:8)	Excellent! (καλῶς ποιεῖς) (2:19)
The fine name by which you have been called (2:7)	God's friend (2:23)

2:1–13 is divided into three major subunits: an example of discrimination (2:1–7), discrimination as a violation of God's law (2:8–11), and God's retribution (2:12–13). In 2:12, an imperative controls the verse, λαλεῖτε. The conjunction γάρ connects 2:13 with 2:12 as the reason and parameter of God's judgment. So, 2:12–13 is the eschatological conclusion of the segment 2:1–13.

Description of the General Cognitive Environment

This pericope differs from the passages studied above. It includes explicit reference to the OT, and some probable allusions to and echoes of the OT. Therefore, the procedure applied here is slightly different. The description of the cognitive environment is focused on understanding the context in which the citations are present.

Scene in a Synagogue

In James 2:2–3, there is a synagogue scene. Among scholars, two possible settings are more frequently considered: a worship meeting or a judicial assembly.[9] Those who argue for a judicial scene rely on the legal language present in

confirmatio; 2:5–7), embellishment (*exornatio;* 2:8–11), and conclusion (*complexio;* 2:12–13). On his part, Wachob offers theme (2:1), reason (2:2–4), *probatio* (2:5–11), and conclusion (2:12–13). James argues from an example (2:5–7) and from judgment based on the written law (2:8–11). Watson has *propositio* (2:1), *ratio* (2:2–7), and *confirmatio* (2:8–13). Patrick J. Hartin, *James*, SP 14 (Collegeville, Minn.: Liturgical Press, 2003), 125–8; Wesley Hiram Wachob, *The Voice of Jesus in the Social Rhetoric of James*, SNTSMS 106 (Cambridge: Cambridge University Press, 2000), 63; Duane F. Watson, "James 2 in Light of Greco-Roman Schemes of Argumentation," *NTS* 39 (1993): 102–5. See also Cain Hope Felder, "Partiality and God's Law: An Exegesis of James 2:1–13," *JRT* 39.2 (1983): 51–69. It is hard to determine how influenced Jewish readers/hearers were by Greco-Roman rhetoric. In James's case, there is no clear Greco-Roman structure in the letter. Even though there are some discernible elements in the structure of some sections of the letter, the diversity of names and categories used in the analysis by those who see the presence of Greco-Roman rhetoric testify to this issue.

9. Allison presents six options and some supporters of each: A Christian (1) religious gathering, (2) building, or (3) court, or a Jewish (4) religious gathering, (5) building, or (6) court. Allison, *James*, 385–6.

the passage (κριταί, διακρίνομαι, ἕλκω εἰς κριτήρια, ἐλέγχω, παραβάτης, ἔνοχος, κρίνομαι, and κρίσις, echoes of Lev 19:15, and the explicit quotation of Lev 19:18b).[10] Even though this setting seems "quite viable and appealing," a worship setting is slightly better because "it is the more natural reading of the scenario."[11] As McKnight points out, "James clearly borrows Jewish language in 1:1 to refer to a messianic community. . . . Second, James knows the word 'church' as is seen in 5:14; it is reasonable to think he can use either term for the messianic community. Third, in James 2:2 James calls the synagogue 'your' *synagōgē*. That 'your' must refer to the messianic community."[12]

Several scholars have argued that a worship scene should be preferred.[13] In RT terms, several features of the context reinforce this view. The immediate context in James 1:26–27 points to a true worship scene. The word "group religion"/"religious" in 1:26–27 evokes a cultic setting. A pure religion implies not only adoration but also caring for the needy. At this point of the discourse, therefore, the worship setting is salient in the encyclopedic knowledge evoked by the word "synagogue." James refers to the place as "your synagogue" (2:2). Also, as Osborne points out, the word "synagogue" "was used as late as the second century alongside the house church as a Christian place of worship."[14] So, it is highly probable that in James's and his addressees' encyclopedic knowledge, ἐκκλησία and συναγωγή were interchangeable terms. In this context, then, there is a stronger connection with a worship meeting than with a judicial environment. In RT terms, the former is more relevant with less processing effort. That is, the processing effort invested in understanding James's example as a worship meeting is less than that in

10. Several scholars adopt the proposal of the synagogue as a Christian court: Roy B. Ward, "Partiality in the Assembly: James 2:2–4," *HTR* 62 (1969): 87–97; Craig L. Blomberg and Mariam J. Kamell, *James*, ZECNT 16 (Grand Rapids, Mich.: Zondervan, 2008), 108–11; Martin, *James*, 61; Davids, *James*, 108–9. Allison argues for a Jewish non-Christian court and points out that this forensic interpretation was known and had some popularity in "English-language commentaries of the seventeenth, eighteenth, and early nineteenth centuries" such as the works of Manton or Matthew Henry before Ward's publication. Allison, *James*, 386–7, 70–71.

11. Osborne, "James," 47.

12. Scot McKnight, *The Letter of James*, NICNT (Grand Rapids, Mich.: Eerdmans, 2011), 183. Sophie Laws gives examples of later use of the synagogue as a Christian place of meeting—Ebionites: Epiphanius, *Haer.* 30.18; Jerome, *Ep.* 112.13; Marcionites: MM's inscription from Lebaba; Christian gatherings: Herm. Mand. 11.9, 13, 14; Justin, *Dial.* 63.14. Sophie S. Laws, *A Commentary on the Epistle of James*, BNTC 16 (San Francisco: Harper & Row, 1980), 100. Witherington mentions ἐπισυναγωγή in Heb 10:25 as an example of Christian usage of the word. He also mentions *Didache* 16.2; Ign., *Pol.* 4:2. Witherington, *Letters and Homilies*, 454.

13. See, e.g., Martin Dibelius, *James: A Commentary on the Epistle of James* (Philadelphia: Fortress, 1976), 132–4; McKnight, *James*, 182–3; Osborne, "James," 46–7; François Vouga, *L'épître de saint Jacques*, CNT XIIIa (Geneva: Labor et Fides, 1984), 71. In relatively recent times, others have seen a judicial context. See, e.g., Allison, *James*, 385–8; Hartin, *James*, 131; Pedrito U. Maynard-Reid, *Poverty and Wealth in James* (repr., Eugene, Ore.: Wipf & Stock, 2004), 55; Ward, "Partiality in the Assembly," 87–97.

14. Osborne, "James," 47.

connecting it with a judicial setting, for more or less the same cognitive effects. In synthesis, by presenting a typical situation in a worship scene, James makes the criticism in 2:1–13 that instead of caring for and honoring the needy, his addressees are discriminating against them in favor of seeking the patronage of the rich.[15] These social aspects are discussed below.

Discrimination, Honor, Patronage

The scene in James 2:2–3 presents an example of προσωπολημψία. In this hypothetical (but sadly pretty common) case, two persons, apparently visitors, enter into the synagogue of the addressees.[16] James uses their appearance to describe one as a wealthy man, and the other as a poor man. The addressees guide the visitors in opposite directions. James criticizes the attitude behind this action. The attitude of offering the best seat is considered "silent flattery" (Plutarch, *Adul. amic.* 58B–D).[17] As Batten points out, "flattery was often associated with patronage during the Hellenistic and Roman periods, and one form of expressing it was to offer the best seat or the platform to the wealthy patron."[18] In the same vein, Kloppenborg points out: "The scene depicted in James 2:2–3—with its attention to seating arrangements and its deference to rank—would be recognized by James' addressees as a perfectly typical instance of the hierarchical social relationships produced by the practice of patronage."[19] For that reason, regarding the wealthy man described as having a golden ring and fine clothing, Kloppenborg concludes: "[T]he mention of the ring and the ἐσθῆτα λαμπρά—the term Polybios uses as an equivalent

15. At this point, Brosend's observation is worth mentioning: "[T]he emphasis is not on the type of gathering (worship, formal or informal adjudication of disputes, fellowship) but on the treatment of visitors no matter what the gathering." William F. Brosend II, *James and Jude*, NCBC (Cambridge: Cambridge University Press, 2004), 58. Commenting on this passage, Martin points out: "[I]t may well be that James also has the contents of 1:27 in mind. The subject of the 'poor' in the following verses surely includes the treatment of the orphan and widows." Martin, *James*, 60.

16. It is hard to decide, without much information about the addressees' setting, whether the synagogue refers to a Christian gathering or to a mixed group of Christian and non-Christian Jews. Scholars are divided. See the bibliography in the footnotes in Allison, *James*, 385–7. If James interchangeably uses congregation/synagogue, then, as McKnight argues, he is giving an example of discrimination in a messianic place of worship. McKnight, *James*, 183. In fact, 2:1 points out a Christian faith; James calls it "your synagogue" (2:2); those who see with favor the wealthy man and treat with disdain the poor are "you" (verbs in second person plural, 2:3); and James's accusation is against their attitude (2:4). Therefore, it seems more natural to understand the context as a Christian gathering.

17. Quoted also by Alicia J. Batten, *Friendship and Benefaction in James*, ESEC 15 (Dorset: Deo, 2010), 129. Kloppenborg clearly illustrates with Greco-Roman and Jewish examples (*Quomodo adulator* 58CD, Lucian's *Nigrinus* 21, *Gallus* 12, and a synagogue inscription) that "[t]he appearance of persons of rank in their finery, either in public space or in an assembly, activated behaviour broadly classed as 'flattery' and intimately associated with patron-client relations."–John S. Kloppenborg, "Patronage Avoidance in James," *HTS* 55 (1999): 766.

18. Batten, *Friendship and Benefaction in James*, 129.

19. Kloppenborg, "Patronage Avoidance in James," 767.

to the *toga candida* (10.5.1)—connotes the exhibiting of superior status. The description of the rich man is designed to underscore not just his wealth, but his rank."[20] This example and the arguments after it show James's deep concern for a genuine faith in Jesus. This genuine faith goes hand in hand with the honor and place the poor deserve in the Christian community. There are cultural issues behind distinctions between poor and rich that James criticizes at the level of implicatures.[21]

Identification of Possible OT Texts and Traditions Evoked

Two clear citations of the OT appear in 2:1–13. In 2:8, James uses Leviticus 19:18b with the introductory formula κατὰ τὴν γραφήν. A few verses later, in 2:11, he argues: ὁ γὰρ εἰπών . . . εἶπεν καί . . . , introducing Deuteronomy 5:17–18 (or Exod 20:13, 15). Apart from these explicit mentions of the OT, there are some possible allusions to the OT in the pericope. First, a study of Leviticus 19:18b is presented. Second, the use of the two commandments in 2:11 is analyzed. Later, allusions to the Jesus tradition and possible echoes are evaluated.

Leviticus 19:18b in James 2:8

The quotation in 2:8, ἀγαπήσεις τὸν πλησίον σου ὡς σεαυτόν, is equal to the text of Leviticus 19:18b (LXX), καὶ ἀγαπήσεις τὸν πλησίον σου ὡς σεαυτόν. James uses the text almost verbatim, save the omission of καί. In RT terms, this is a metalinguistic resemblance of Leviticus 19:18 (LXX). But James also uses it interpretively in his own discourse. He calls it νόμος βασιλικός.

Leviticus 19:18b in Its Context

The love command, "Love your neighbor as yourself," is part of the so-called holiness code (Lev 17–26). Chapters 18–20 of Leviticus form the core of this corpus.[22] Chapters 18 and 20 deal with sexual offenses and serve as a frame for chapter 19.[23] In this way, chapter 19 is the climax of the entire book.[24]

20. Ibid., 765. Some scholars think that the description of the wealthy man depicts a Roman equestrian. See, e.g., Laws, *James*, 98–9. But, as Johnson points out, "the broad contrast between rich and poor here does not demand such a literal identification of parties." Johnson, *James*, 221. See a good presentation of this idea and a critical evaluation in Manabu Tsuji, *Glaube zwischen Vollkommenheit und Verweltlichung: Eine Untersuchung zur literarischen Gestalt und zur inhaltlichen Kohärenz des Jakobusbriefes*, WUNT 2 93 (Tübingen: J. C. B. Mohr, 1997), 142.

21. Hartin sees similar countercultural implications of the text. Hartin, *James*, 147.

22. John E. Hartley, *Leviticus*, WBC 4 (Dallas: Word, 1992), 249.

23. M. F. Rooker, "The Best-Known Verse in Leviticus," *FM* 21.2 (2004): 4.

24. Mary Douglas proposes that chapters 18–20 have a "pedimental structure" where chapter 19 is the apex or climax. Through this literary arrangement, the theme of God's justice is explained. Mary Douglas, "Justice as the Cornerstone: An Interpretation of Leviticus 18–20," *Int* 53 (1999): 341–50. Milgrom calls this a "cardinal chapter," which has exerted influence "on later tradents." Jacob Milgrom, *Leviticus 17–22: A New Translation with Introduction and Commentary*, AB 3A (New York: Doubleday, 2000), 1602.

Even chapter 19 "may be characterized as a brief *torah* (instruction)," because it "includes a wide range of laws and commandments that are representatives of the basic teaching of the Torah."[25] Verses 2b–10 deal with religious commandments, vv. 11–18 deal with ethical duties, and vv. 19–37 deal with miscellaneous admonitions.[26] All of these laws have the purpose of "set[ting] the people of God on the road to holiness" (19:2).[27]

The nominal phrase אֲנִי יְהוָה, "I am YHWH," ends every subunit in 19:11–18.[28] In the LXX, each subunit ends with the sentence ἐγώ εἰμι κύριος ὁ θεὸς ὑμῶν, except the last one (19:17–18), which ends with the shorter sentence ἐγώ εἰμι κύριος. This feature, both in Hebrew and in Greek, is used literarily to organize the commandments and prohibitions into four groups or subunits: vv. 11–12, 13–14, 15–16, and 17–18.[29] It is also used theologically "[to mark] the divine authority with which the commandment is proclaimed."[30] George

25. Baruch A. Levine, *Leviticus: The Traditional Hebrew Text with the New JPS Translation*, JPSTC (Philadelphia: JPS, 1989), 124. Baruch J. Schwartz comments that in this chapter "[c]ommands pertain to virtually every area of Israelite life; there is no such thing as a command pertaining merely to relations between human beings . . . ; every commanded or prohibited action affects the sacred realm and is in the category of laws between God and human beings. . . . The ch expresses this by presenting an admixture of laws from every sphere." Baruch J. Schwartz, "Leviticus," in *The Jewish Study Bible*, ed. Adele Berlin, Marc Zvi Brettler, and Michael A. Fishbane (New York: JPS, 2004), 252.

26. Diverse ways to divide this chapter have been proposed. See more details in Milgrom, *Leviticus 17–22*, 1596–600.

27. Ibid., 1596. Joel Kaminsky highlights that "[t]his unusual mix of laws (e.g., ritual, moral, criminal)—unusual at least to our contemporary sensibilities—continues throughout the rest of Lev 19, fleshing out the complexity of the concept of holiness in the HB [Holiness Book] stressed in the chapter's opening (Lev 19:2)." Joel S. Kaminsky, "Loving One's (Israelite) Neighbor: Election and Commandment in Leviticus 19," *Int* 62 (2008): 125. Many scholars have noticed the parallel between the laws mentioned here and the Ten Commandments. At least the first, second, fourth, and fifth commandments are clearly present. See the discussion in Rooker, "The Best-Known Verse in Leviticus," 5–6; Milgrom, *Leviticus 17–22*, 1600–2; Hartley, *Leviticus*, 310.

28. Erhard S. Gestenberger points out that this formula of self-introduction (אֲנִי יְהוָה or אֲנִי יְהוָה אֱלֹהֵיכֶם) is used here "more frequently than elsewhere as an organizational device." Erhard Gerstenberger, *Leviticus: A Commentary*, OTL, 1st American ed. (Louisville: Westminister John Knox Press, 1996), 261. It introduces and ends the chapter (vv. 2 and 37); it also appears in vv. 3, 4, 10, 12, 14, 16, 18, 25, 28, 30, 31, 32, 34, and 36. It appears eight times as "I am the Lord" and eight times as "I am the Lord your God." Regarding the use of this literary device, Franziska Bark comments that "Moses as mediator hardly surfaces in the flux of chapters 18–21 and *ani adonai, ani adonai eloheikhem* turns into a counterpoint whose rhythmic presence come across forcefully." Franziska Bark, "'Listen Your Way in with Your Mouth': A Reading of Leviticus," *Judaism* 48 (1999): 201.

29. Some scholars include here also vv. 9–10; see Hartley, *Leviticus*, 307; Gerstenberger, *Leviticus*, 261. Nevertheless, this unit ends with the longer אֲנִי יְהוָה אֱלֹהֵיכֶם. The LXX consistently has the phrase ἐγώ εἰμι κύριος ὁ θεὸς ὑμῶν in vv. 10, 12, 14 and 16; but v. 18 ends with the shorter phrase ἐγώ εἰμι κύριος. Milgrom, however, divides this section into four thematic subunits: ethical duties or deeds (vv. 11–13), exploitation of the helpless (v. 14), injustice and indifference (vv. 15–16), and reproof and love (vv. 17–18).

30. G. Keerankeri, *The Love Commandment in Mark: An Exegetico-Theological Study of Mk 12,28–34*, AnBib 150 (Rome: Editrice Pontificio Istituto Biblico, 2003), 102. Carson points out

Keerankeri correctly points out that "[t]he section [of 19:11–18] has a predominant social focus in its understanding of holiness which brings to a climax the general social preoccupation that defines the laws in Ch 19, as compared to the rest of the book."[31] These are commandments and prohibitions against theft and deceit (vv. 11–12), against oppression of others and abuse of the handicapped and for fear of God (vv. 13–14), against injustice and slander and for just judgment (vv. 15–16), and against hate and taking vengeance and for loving one's neighbor (vv. 17–18).[32]

The love command forms part of the last and climactic subunit in 19:11–18. This final subunit (vv. 17–18) consists of four prohibitions and two positive commandments:

17a	לֹא־תִשְׂנָא אֶת־אָחִיךָ בִּלְבָבֶךָ	οὐ μισήσεις τὸν ἀδελφόν σου τῇ διανοίᾳ σου,
17b	חוֹכֵחַ תּוֹכִיחַ אֶת־עֲמִיתֶךָ	ἐλεγμῷ ἐλέγξεις τὸν πλησίον σου
17c	וְלֹא־תִשָּׂא עָלָיו חֵטְא׃	καὶ οὐ λήμψῃ δι᾽ αὐτὸν ἁμαρτίαν.
18a	לֹא־תִקֹּם וְלֹא־תִטֹּר אֶת־בְּנֵי עַמֶּךָ	καὶ οὐκ ἐκδικᾶταί σου ἡ χείρ, καὶ οὐ μηνιεῖς τοῖς υἱοῖς τοῦ λαοῦ σου
18b	וְאָהַבְתָּ לְרֵעֲךָ כָּמוֹךָ	καὶ ἀγαπήσεις τὸν πλησίον σου ὡς σεαυτόν,
18c	אֲנִי יהוה׃	ἐγώ εἰμι κύριος.

You shall not hate your brother in your heart. Reprove your kinsman; and/but incur no guilt because of him. You shall not take vengeance or bear a grudge against your countrymen. Love your neighbor as yourself. I am the Lord. (from the MT)

You shall not hate your brother in your mind/with your thoughts. Strongly reprove your neighbor and/but incur no guilt because of him. Your hand shall not take vengeance and you shall not bear a grudge against your countrymen. Love your neighbor as yourself. I am the Lord. (from the LXX)

Baruch Schwartz points out that traditional interpretation tends to treat each phrase separately. He proposes an integrated translation where v. 18 is an explanation of v. 17: "Do not hate your kinsfolk in your heart, rather, reprove your kinsman so as to incur no guilt because of him. In other words: Do not take vengeance or bear a grudge against your countrymen, rather, love your

---

that "the theological function establishes that the ultimate ground of all of these commandments is God himself—not (in the first instance) the utilitarian nature of each commandment or its social benefits, but God himself." D. A. Carson, "James," in *Commentary on the New Testament Use of the Old Testament*, ed. G. K. Beale and D. A. Carson (Grand Rapids, Mich.: Baker, 2007), 999.

31. Keerankeri, *The Love Commandment in Mark*, 46.

32. Hartley, *Leviticus*, 308.

fellow as yourself."[33] Other scholars, however, also see this subunit—and particularly the love command—as the climax of the entire unit.[34]

Parallelism between lines in vv. 17–18 has been noted. Jacob Milgrom presents a parallelism of prohibition (17a/18a), remedy (17b/18b), and rationale (17c/18c).[35] Others see a parallelism between the negative (17a/18a) and the positive commands (17b+c/18b).[36] In any case, love is contrasted with an inner wrong attitude or hate toward a fellow.[37] Also, reproof is a way to show love to a fellow.[38]

Following the negative commands, God gives them a positive command: וְאָהַבְתָּ לְרֵעֲךָ כָּמוֹךָ (MT), καὶ ἀγαπήσεις τὸν πλησίον σου ὡς σεαυτόν (LXX), "Love your neighbor as yourself." At the level of explicature, some decisions are required. The connective וְ/καί is adversative, contrasting the command to love not only with the two prohibitions in v. 18, but also with the prohibition in v. 17, and conceptually with all the prohibitions in the unit (19:11–18).[39] אהב appears 218 times in the OT. Its primary meaning is "to love."[40] Considering לְ as indicating the *dativus commodi*, Abraham Malamat argues that in this context אָהֵב לְ has the idea of "[to] be of use to, be beneficial to, assist."[41] Nevertheless, the preposition seems to mark the direct object.[42] Hence, the sense of "to love" does not change because of the presence of לְ.[43] In the

33. Schwartz, "Leviticus," 254. Levine thinks something similar. He says that "the context suggests the interpretation that an individual should not allow ill feelings to fester; rather, he should confront his kinsman and admonish him directly, in this way avoiding grudges and vengeance that breed hatred." He adds: "Moreover, a proper attitude promotes love for one's neighbor." Levine, *Leviticus*, 129. See also Milgrom, *Leviticus 17–22*, 1650–51; Hans-Peter Mathys, *Liebe deinen Nächsten wie dich selbst: Untersuchungen zum alttestamentlichen Gebot der Nächstenliebe (Lev 19,18)*, OBO 71 (Göttingen: Vandenhoeck & Ruprecht, 1986), 2–3.

34. Gerstenberger, for example, points out that vv. 17–18 "are the crowning conclusion to everything that has been said about the welfare of one's fellow human beings within the community." For that reason, rather than offering "norms of action, they preach a certain disposition, one ideally characterized not by any deep-seated, deadly hatred (v. 17a), but rather by 'love' or solidarity (v. 18ab)." Gerstenberger, *Leviticus*, 270.

35. Milgrom, *Leviticus 17–22*, 1646.

36. Richard A. Allbee, "Asymmetrical Continuity of Love and Law between the Old and New Testaments: Explicating the Implicit Side of a Hermeneutical Bridge, Leviticus 19:11–18," *JSOT* 31 (2006): 162. This parallelism seems to be behind the translation of Schwartz. See above.

37. Milgrom, *Leviticus 17–22*, 1651.

38. Allbee, "Leviticus 19:11–18," 162.

39. Mathys, *Liebe deinen Nächsten wie dich selbst*, 2, 57–81.

40. "אָהֵב," BDB 12.

41. Abraham Malamat, "'Love Your Neighbor as Yourself': What It Really Means," *BAR* 16.4 (1990): 51. For other scholars who support this understanding of the construction אהב לְ, see Hartley, *Leviticus*, 318; Reinhard Neudecker, "'And You Shall Love Your Neighbor as Yourself—I Am the Lord' (Lev 19:18) in Jewish Interpretation," *Bib* 73 (1992): 503–4.

42. This is a lamed of interest, which "marks the person for or against whom an action is directed." Bruce K. Waltke and Michael Patrick O'Connor, *An Introduction to Biblical Hebrew Syntax* (Winona Lake, Ind.: Eisenbrauns, 1990), 207.

43. Levine, *Leviticus*, 130. Mathys quotes 2 Chr 19:2 as an example of the use of לְ as marker of direct object with the same verb. Mathys, *Liebe deinen Nächsten wie dich selbst*, 5.

case of the LXX, ἀγαπάω appears 283 times, almost always with the sense of "to love."[44] Here, as frequently in the LXX, the future tense is used to convey command (Lev 19:1–18; cf. Exod 20:1–17; Deut 5:6–21). The context helps to understand the nuance of "to love." Here, it is more than an emotion or an attitude; it implies deeds.[45] If the prohibitions and commandments in 19:11–18 show what love means in this context, then John Makujina is right when he says: "The love that is commanded covers two areas. The first is more tangible in that it entails caring for the physical and material well-being of another. The second concerns the emotional welfare of others by instructing the Israelite to care for his neighbor's reputation, honor, dignity and happiness."[46]

The recipient of the love is רֵעֲךָ, τὸν πλησίον σου, "your neighbor." In the context, there are several words that help to understand who the neighbor is: בַּעֲמִיתוֹ/τὸν πλησίον (vv. 11–12), רֵעֲךָ/τὸν πλησίον (vv. 13–14), עֲמִיתֶךָ/τὸν πλησίον σου, בְּעַמֶּיךָ/τῷ ἔθνει σου, רֵעֶךָ/τὸν πλησίον σου (vv. 15–16), אָחִיךָ/τὸν ἀδελφόν σου, עֲמִיתֶךָ/τὸν πλησίον σου, בְּנֵי עַמֶּךָ/τοῖς υἱοῖς τοῦ λαοῦ σου, רֵעֲךָ/τὸν πλησίον σου (vv. 17–18). In the LXX, πλησίος is used for the translation of several of the Hebrew words. Milgrom says that all of these terms are nearly synonymous in describing the Israelite.[47] The command to love, הַגֵּר, the resident non-Israelite in 19:34 implies that רֵעַ, πλησίος, here means "fellow Israelite."[48] If v. 18 included the "resident non-Israelite," it is unlikely that the command in 19:34 would be necessary. In any case, these two nouns in 19:17 and 34 indicate the extension of the mandate. The love commandment is not limited to the neighbor; it also includes the foreigner in the land. In general terms, therefore, "neighbor" in this section describes those one comes in contact with as those residing nearby.[49]

The modifier כָּמוֹךָ, ὡς σεαυτόν, "as yourself," has been interpreted in at least two ways. The most common interpretation is to consider it an

44. "ἀγαπάω," LEH, 2.

45. Milgrom points out that "[t]his is especially true in Deuteronomy, which speaks of covenantal love. The *gēr* is 'loved' by providing him with food and shelter (Deut 10:18–19). God is 'loved' by observing his commandments (Deut 11:1 . . .), and God, in turn, 'loves' Israel by subduing its enemies (Deut 7:8. . .)." Milgrom, *Leviticus 17–22*, 1653.

46. J. Makujina, "The Second Greatest Commandment and Self-Esteem," *MSJ* 8 (1997): 214. The command, at least, as Allbee points out, "minimally precludes doing any of the things prohibited in Lev 19:11–18 to them [neighbors] or to their detriment, which is the import of this individual law. . . and the *common* concern for all of them." Allbee, "Leviticus 19:11–18," 164 (his emphasis). Richard Bauckham comments that "at least in the case of verses 9–18 it is in fact very easy to read the love commandment as the summary of these various commandments." Richard Bauckham, *James: Wisdom of James, Disciple of Jesus the Sage* (London: Routledge, 1999), 144.

47. Milgrom, *Leviticus 17–22*, 1655.

48. Ibid., 1654; Mathys, *Liebe deinen Nächsten wie dich selbst*, 38–9.

49. Allbee, "Leviticus 19:11–18," 164 n. 109.

adverbial modifier of the verb.[50] The LXX follows this understanding of the phrase. Milgrom translates the command: "Love (the good) *for* your fellow as you (love the good for) yourself."[51] Others understand the command as "Love your neighbor as you love yourself."[52] On the other hand, the modifier can be considered adjectival. In this case, the phrase is in apposition to the noun and is understood as "who is like you."[53] In this sense, the command is "Love your neighbor who is like you." As will be shown in the next section, both interpretations have support in Judaism. The difference in interpretation depends on where the emphasis falls. In the first case, the emphasis is on the command—to love. In the second case, the emphasis is on the motive of such an action—because [your neighbor] is like you.[54] Given the fact that the LXX understands the phrase as adverbial and that James uses this text in his letter, the first interpretation is preferred. So, a person should show love and care for the other in the same way he/she cares for him/herself.

The love command is the climax of this section. The context helps one to understand what love means. It is more than a feeling; it implies concrete actions. The object of that love is mainly the fellow Israelite, but includes the foreigner who lives among them. The modifier "asyourself" may indicate how to love or the motivation of that love.

Some implicatures derived from this command and strongly implicated by the context might be the following:

1. People who love their neighbor provide food for the needy.
2. People who love their neighbor speak truth with him/her.
3. People who love their neighbor pay their wages to him/her.
4. People who love their neighbor care for the disabled.
5. People who love their neighbor act with justice in the tribunal.
6. People who love their neighbor care for the life of him/her.
7. People who love their neighbor do not act with vengeance against him/her.

Leviticus 19:18b in Second Temple Judaism

The love command is widely attested in Second Temple literature.[55] Different theologies underlie "its various interpretations. Ancient Jewish theology employed many different arguments to support the notion of loving one's

50. Milgrom, *Leviticus 17–22*, 1655; Mathys, *Liebe deinen Nächsten wie dich selbst*, 6–9; Keerankeri, *The Love Commandment in Mark*, 52–3.

51. Milgrom, *Leviticus 17–22*, 1655.

52. Neudecker, "You Shall Love Your Neighbor as Yourself," 505.

53. Ibid.; Milgrom, *Leviticus 17–22*, 1655.

54. K. Berthelot convincingly argues for the second. K. Berthelot, *L' 'humanité de l'autre homme' dans la pensée juive ancienne*, JSJSup 87 (Leiden: Brill, 2004), 241.

55. This section follows mainly the examples of S. Ruzer, "From 'Love your Neighbor' to 'Love your Enemy': Trajectories in Early Jewish Exegesis," *RB* 109 (2002): 376–89; G. S. Oegema,

neighbor; examples include *Imitatio Dei*, striving to attain holiness, and loving one's fellow human as an image of God."[56]

Ben Sirach (around 185 B.C.) uses Leviticus 19:17–18 several times. He seems to understand כָּמוֹךָ as "one who is like you." For example, in 7:21, he says: "Let a wise servant be dear to you as your own self; refuse him not his freedom" (NAB); in 31:15: "Recognize that your neighbor feels as you do, and keep in mind your own dislikes" (NAB). See also 27:1–28:7.[57] This interpretation is present also in Jubilees 36:4: "And among yourselves, my sons, be loving of your brothers as a man loves himself, with each man seeking for his brother what is good for him, and acting together on the earth, and loving each other as themselves."[58]

Other Jewish groups seems to understand כָּמוֹךָ adverbially. For example, Testament of Gad 6:1 says: "Now, my children, each of you love his brother. Drive hatred out of your hearts. Love one another in deed and word and inward thoughts."[59] (Cf. T. Gad 4:1–2; T. Zeb. 5:1, 8:5; T. Jos. 17:1–2; T. Iss. 7:6–7; T. Sim. 4:7; T. Reub. 6:9.) Other similar interpretations are a variation of the Golden Rule. For example, Tobit 4:15 says: "And what you hate, do not do to anyone. Do not drink wine to excess or let drunkenness go with you on your way" (NRSV; cf. Tg. Yer. I on Lev 19:18b; Tg. Ps.-J. on Lev 19:18b).

Who is the neighbor? There are different answers from the literature of this period. Some groups understand "neighbor" as any fellow Israelite or proselyte. For example, Sipra Qedoshim 4 comments on Leviticus 19:18a: "'You shall not take vengeance or bear a grudge against the children of your people' (Lev 19,18a); you may take vengeance and bear a grudge against others."[60] Sipra Qedoshim 8 includes proselyte in the love command. On the other hand, the Damascus Document presents the concept of neighbor in a very restrictive way. For example, CD 9:2–5 says: "And concerning the saying: *You shall not take vengeance on the children of your people, nor bear any rancor against them* (Lev 19:18), if any other member of the Covenant accuses his

---

Für Israel und die Völker: Studien zum alttestamentlich-jüdischen Hintergrund der paulinischen Theologie, NovTSup 95 (Leiden: Brill, 1999), 255–64.

Regarding the use of the love command in Second Temple literature, Armin Lange and Matthias Weigold mention CD A 9:2; 4QDa (4Q269) 8.ii.10; 4QDe (4Q270) 6.iii.16–17; CD A 6:20–21; 4QDd (4Q269) 4.ii.2; Sir 13:15 (ms A); Jub. 7:20; Let. Aris. 228; T. Iss. 5:2; T. Gad 4:2; and T. Benj. 3:3–4. Armin Lange and Matthias Weigold, eds., *Biblical Quotations and Allusions in Second Temple Jewish Literature*, JAJ (Göttingen: Vandenhoeck & Ruprecht, 2011), 84.

56. G. S. Oegema, "'Love Your Neighbor as Yourself': Jesuanic or Mosaic?," *BN* 116 (2003): 79.

57. T. Söding, "Nächstenliebe bei Jesus Sirach: Eine Notiz zur weisheitlichen Ethik," *BZ* 42 (1998): 239–47.

58. James H. Charlesworth, *The Old Testament Pseudepigrapha*, vol. 2 (New York: Yale University Press, 1985), 124.

59. James H. Charlesworth, *The Old Testament Pseudepigrapha*, vol. 1 (New York: Yale University Press, 1983), 816.

60. Neudecker, "You Shall Love Your Neighbor as Yourself," 500.

companion (neighbor) without first rebuking him before witnesses . . . he is one that takes vengeance and bears rancor, although it is expressly written, He (God) takes vengeance upon his adversaries and bears rancor against his enemies (Nah 1:2)."[61]

Ben Zion Wacholder observes that throughout this section "CD is careful to emphasise who is subject to, and protected by, these regulations. In harmony with Lev 19:16–18, which this section is exegeting, CD makes clear by the repetition of exclusive terms like 'your people' (9:2), 'enterers of the covenant' (9:2–3), and neighbour (9:3–8), that Israelites, i.e. those who are community members, are not to be victims of revenge, but are to be loved. However, in contrast to Israel, revenge seems quite legitimate when taken against the enemies of God."[62]

The same line of thought is observed in 1QS I. 6:9–11: "all those who have freely devoted themselves to the observance of God's precepts, that they may love all the sons of light, each according to his lot in God's design, and hate all the sons of darkness, each according to his guilt in God's vengeance."[63] So, in synthesis, there is a tendency in some groups to understand the concept of neighbor in very restrictive ways as a member of their own community, even though a few have a broader understanding of the concept of neighbor that includes proselyte. Jesus, and later James, will broaden that concept further.

There is also a tendency to combine two love commandments, those of Deuteronomy 6:5 and Leviticus 19:18b (Jub. 7:20, 36:4–7; T. Ben. 4:3; T. Dan 5:3; T. Iss. 5:2, 7:6; T. Zeb. 5:1). For example, Testament of Issachar 5:2: "love the Lord and your neighbor; be compassionate toward poverty and sickness."[64] In this sense, in the Testaments of the Twelve Patriarchs, the two commandments are seen as so deeply interrelated that whoever loves God loves also people, and vice versa.[65] Furthermore, there is a tendency to see the love command as a summary of the entire Law. A saying attributed to Hillel (110 B.C–A.D. 10) is frequently quoted: "Whatever is hateful to you, do it not unto your fellow man. This is the essence of the Torah, while the

61. Géza Vermès, *The Complete Dead Sea Scrolls in English*, rev. ed., PengC (London: Penguin, 2004), 139–40 (his emphasis).

62. Ben Zion Wacholder, "Rules of Testimony in Qumranic Jurisprudence: CD9 and 11Q Torah 64," *JJS* 40 (1989): 168.

63. Ruzer, "Trajectories in Early Jewish Exegesis," 380 n. 32. There is no clear evidence in Second Temple literature, which supports an explicit love for enemies. Ruzer, "Trajectories in Early Jewish Exegesis," 387–9; Hans Dieter Betz, *The Sermon on the Mount: A Commentary on the Sermon on the Mount, Including the Sermon on the Plain (Matthew 5:3–7:27 and Luke 6:20–49)*, Hermeneia (Minneapolis: Fortress, 1995), 309–11. William Klassen argues for the presence of the command to love enemies. He, however, builds his argument by focusing on the theme of vengeance rather than in quotations of loving the enemy. William Klassen, *Love of Enemies: The Way to Peace*, OBT 15 (Philadelphia: Fortress, 1984), 43–71.

64. Charlesworth, *OTP*, 1:803.

65. Oegema, *Für Israel und die Völker*, 259.

rest is commentary thereof; go and learn it" (b. Šabb 31a). Also commenting on Leviticus 19:18b, Rabbi Aqiba (A.D. 50–135) calls this כלל גדול בתורה, "a central principle in the Torah" (Sipra Qedoshim 4:12). Jesus also collates both love commandments. Later also, in James, both commandments are present.

Throughout the Second Temple period, different developments in the interpretation of the love command can be noticed. The main differences are in distinguishing who the neighbor is. For some groups the concept is understood very narrowly. Other people see the concept more universally. There is also a tendency to combine Deuteronomy 6:5 with Leviticus 19:8b, the two love commandments, and to present them as the summary of the Torah. The next section shows that Jesus redefines the concept of neighbor and reaffirms the centrality of the two love commandments.

Leviticus 19:18b in the Synoptic Gospels

The love command appears explicitly five times in the Synoptic Gospels. Four times, Jesus quotes it (Matt 5:43, 19:19, 22:39; Mark 12:31).[66] In Luke 10:27, a lawyer cites the love command. The love command is quoted three times in Matthew's Gospel (Matt 5:43, 19:19, and 22:39). The three times, Jesus is the one who uses the passage.[67] The first time is in the Sermon on the Mount. It is part of the last of six "antitheses" directed against the scribes' and Pharisees' interpretation of the Torah.[68] This pericope consists

66. For more details about Jesus's use of Scriptures, see Richard B. Hays, *Reading Backwards: Figural Christology and the Fourfold Gospel Witness* (Waco: Baylor University Press, 2014); Steve Moyise, *Jesus and Scripture: Studying the New Testament Use of the Old Testament* (Grand Rapids, Mich.: Baker, 2010); Emerson B. Powery, *Jesus Reads Scripture: The Function of Jesus' Use of Scripture in the Synoptic Gospels*, BI 63 (Leiden: Brill, 2003).

67. Regarding the authenticity of the quotations, see Arland J. Hultgren, "Double Commandment of Love in Mt 22:34–40: Its Sources and Compositions," *CBQ* 36 (1974): 73–8; William Klassen, "The Authenticity of the Command: 'Love Your Enemies,'" in *Authenticating the Words of Jesus* (Leiden: Brill, 1999), 385–407; Reginald H. Fuller, "Double Commandment of Love: Test Case for the Criteria of Authenticity," in *Essays on the Love Commandment*, ed. Luise Schottroff (Philadelphia: Fortress, 1978), 41–56.

68. Many scholars have seen these antitheses as an annulment of the Torah. Nevertheless, there are also many scholars who argue that these antitheses are a confrontation with traditional Pharisaic interpretation. For bibliography in this regard, see Matthias Konradt, "The Love Command in Matthew, James, and the Didache," in *Matthew, James, and Didache: Three Related Documents in Their Jewish and Christian Settings*, ed. Huub van de Sandt and Jürgen K. Zangenberg, SBLSymS 45 (Atlanta: Society of Biblical Literature, 2008), 272 nn. 4 and 5; Brice L. Martin, "Matthew on Christ and the Law," *TS* 44 (1983): 56 n. 13. Cheung points out that "[t]he arrangement of these 'antitheses' suggests that the last 'antithesis' is not only a final example of the greater righteousness demanded of the disciples, but the five culminate in the last 'antithesis' that forms the climax of the section with the underlying principle of them all. . . . Lev 19:18 thus plays a significant part in Mt. 5:17–18 in two ways: as a separated commandment in the last 'antithesis' . . . and as the climax of a series of commandments that functions as a hermeneutic principle for the choice and interpretation of the individual commandments."

of a thesis (v. 43), an antithesis (vv. 44–45), a reason (vv. 46–47), and a conclusion (v. 48). As in the other "antitheses," Jesus "begins with the refutation of the inadequate interpretation introduced by the reference to the chain of tradition."[69] He says: ἠκούσατε ὅτι ἐρρέθη· ἀγαπήσεις τὸν πλησίον σου καὶ μισήσεις τὸν ἐχθρόν σου (Matt 5:43). The first part of the quotation corresponds to Leviticus 19:8b. The last part, ὡς σεαυτόν, is omitted. Donald Hagner argues that these words "are probably omitted here in order to form a more exact parallel with the second member, μισήσεις τὸν ἐχθρόν σου, 'you shall hate your enemy.'"[70] The second half of the saying, "and you shall hate your enemy," is not part of Leviticus 19:18 nor of any other OT passage. Blomberg points out that it is possible that Jesus is summarizing "a very natural inference that could be drawn from the original meaning of various OT passages."[71] In any case, this seems to have been the interpretation of some groups in the Second Temple period.[72]

In the antithesis (vv. 44–45), Jesus amplifies the nuance of πλησίον by saying ἀγαπᾶτε τοὺς ἐχθροὺς ὑμῶν καὶ προσεύχεσθε ὑπὲρ τῶν διωκόντων ὑμᾶς (5:44). The reason is that in this way his followers will be distinguished from the others (5:46–47). The *imitatio Dei* has to be the aim of Jesus's followers.[73] As the disciples love their enemies and pray for those who persecute them, they become children of God (5:45) and perfect, τέλειοι, like God (5:48). This *imitatio Dei* is in the context of teaching related to the kingdom of God and its eschatological inauguration.[74]

For Jesus, love is more than feelings. It includes deeds. In the parallel text of Luke 6:27–36, although the love command is not mentioned, Jesus exemplifies what it means to "love your enemies."[75] He exhorts his disciples to do

---

Luke L. Cheung, *The Genre, Composition, and Hermeneutics of the Epistle of James* (Eugene, Ore.: Wipf & Stock, 2006), 112.

69. Betz, *The Sermon on the Mount*, 301. The parallel passage in Luke 6:27–36 lacks the love command, although it is clearly implied in it.

70. Donald A. Hagner, *Matthew 1–13*, WBC 33a (Dallas: Word, 1993), 134.

71. Craig L. Blomberg, "Matthew," in *Commentary on the New Testament Use of the Old Testament*, ed. G. K. Beale and D. A. Carson (Grand Rapids, Mich.: Baker, 2007), 27. Luz affirms that the omission is for rhetorical reasons. Ulrich Luz, *Matthew 8–20: A Commentary*, Hermeneia (Minneapolis: Augsburg, 1989). Betz adds: "[I]f one understands the love-command in a particularistic or popular-ethical way, hatred of the enemy will follow in practice." Betz, *The Sermon on the Mount*, 301.

72. See above, CD 9:2–5.

73. Oegema, *Für Israel und die Völker*, 268.

74. The phrase "kingdom of heaven" appears many times in the sermon (5:3, 10, 19; 6:10, 33; 7:21). Themes such as entering into the kingdom, persecution for Jesus's sake, and rewards illustrate the eschatological tone of the sermon.

75. There has been much debate around the concept of enemy here. In the context, personal and general enemies such as Jewish religious leadership, the Roman Empire, and also local enemies seem to be implied. Some scholars see enemies in general terms as those hostile toward the disciples. See, e.g., Dale C. Allison, Jr., and W. D. Davies, *Introduction and Commentary on Matthew 1–7*, vol. 1 of *A Critical and Exegetical Commentary on the Gospel according to*

good (6:27), to bless instead of curse (2:28), to pray, to offer the other cheek (6:29), and so on. Furthermore, although Jesus's "redefinition" of neighbor includes enemies, it is not completely new;[76] "the Matthean Jesus radicalizes the love command by claiming that loving care for the well-being of others is entirely independent of how the other acts toward oneself."[77] In the Beatitudes, Jesus blesses those who are peacemakers, for they will be called children of God (5:9). Also, he blesses those who are persecuted for righteousness' sake, for theirs is the kingdom of heaven (5:10). Similarly, to love enemies is an act of peace, and is characteristic of the people of the kingdom of God.

Jesus quotes Leviticus 19:18b again in Matthew 19:19. This pericope (19:16–22) is in the context of narratives set in Judea (19:1–20:16), just before Jesus's ascent to Jerusalem (20:17).[78] A major theme in this section of the Gospel is regarding the following of Jesus in light of the kingdom of God (19:12, 14, 20:1). For example, Jesus teaching his disciples about the cost of discipleship (19:23–20:16) follows the dialogue with a young rich man (19:16–22). A young man asks Jesus what he must do in order to have eternal life (19:16).

Saint Matthew, ICC (Edinburgh: T&T Clark, 2004), 551; Craig L. Blomberg, *Matthew*, NAC 22 (Nashville: Broadman & Holman, 1992), 114–5; Leon Morris, *The Gospel according to Matthew*, PNTC (Grand Rapids, Mich.: Eerdmans, 1992), 130; John Nolland, *The Gospel of Matthew: A Commentary on the Greek Text*, NIGTC (Grand Rapids, Mich.: Eerdmans, 2005), 264; Thomas W. Ogletree, "The Essential Unity of the Love Commands: Moving beyond Paradox," *JRE* 35 (2007): 695–700; Grant R. Osborne, *Matthew*, ZECNT 1 (Grand Rapids, Mich.: Zondervan, 2010), 212; John Piper, *"Love Your Enemies": Jesus' Love Command in the Synoptic Gospels and the Early Christian Paraenesis* (Grand Rapids, Mich.: Baker, 1991).

Others see more specifically an outsider hostile to God's people, because they are Christ's disciples; e.g., R. T. France, *Matthew: An Introduction and Commentary*, TNTC 1 (Downers Grove, Ill.: InterVarsity Press, 1985), 133; Robert H. Gundry, *Commentary on the New Testament* (Grand Rapids, Mich.: Baker, 2010), Loc. 2417 of 56468. Some scholars see not only outsiders but also disciples who hate, curse, and abuse them; e.g., Warren Carter, "Love Your Enemies," *WW* 28 (2008): 16. Others see personal, political. and national enemies; e.g., Craig S. Keener, *A Commentary on the Gospel of Matthew* (Grand Rapids, Mich.: Eerdmans, 1999), 202–3; Marius Reiser, "Love of Enemies in the Context of Antiquity," *NTS* 47 (2001): 425. Finally, some scholars see an even more specific enemy, such as the Romans and their collaborators; e.g., Oscar Jacob Frank Seitz, "Love Your Enemies: The Historical Setting of Matthew 5:43f, Luke 6:27f," *NTS* 16 (1969): 43–52. Milavec sees the enemies as the disciples' own families. Aaron Milavec, "The Social Setting of 'Turning the Other Cheek' and 'Loving One's Enemies' in Light of the Didache," *BTB* 25 (1995): 131–43. Horsley proposes the enemies are local adversaries in small villages where Christians live. Richard A. Horsley, "Ethics and Exegesis: 'Love Your Enemies' and the Doctrine of Nonviolence," in *Love of Enemy and Nonretaliation in the New Testament*, ed. Willard M. Swartley, SPS (Louisville: Westminster/John Knox, 1992), 72–101.

76. See, e.g., the historical background given by Piper, *Love Your Enemies*, 19–48. Betz says: "Jesus' demand in the SM [the Sermon on the Mount] has precedent or preparation in the history of ideas, although it did represent a new step at that time." Betz, *The Sermon on the Mount*, 311.

77. Konradt, "The Love Command," 273.

78. Matthew's version of this pericope has the love command. Its parallels in Mark 10:17–30 and Luke 18:18–30 do not have it.

Jesus answers him by saying that he has to keep the commandments (19:17).[79] After that, he gives a list of five of the Ten Commandments[80] and ends with ἀγαπήσεις τὸν πλησίον σου ὡς σεαυτόν (19:18). The young man argues that he has kept all of these commandments. Jesus then adds: εἰ θέλεις τέλειος εἶναι, ὕπαγε πώλησόν σου τὰ ὑπάρχοντα καὶ δὸς [τοῖς] πτωχοῖς, καὶ ἕξεις θησαυρὸν ἐν οὐρανοῖς, καὶ δεῦρο ἀκολούθει μοι (19:21). The young man, however, decides not to renounce his riches (19:22; cf. 6:19–24).

At first sight, this quotation of the love command seems to be just one more in the list. This is, however, the second occasion in Matthew where Jesus speaks about the love command. In this passage, two things relate this pericope to Matthew 5:43–48: the love command and the concept τέλειος (important also for James). On one hand, the use of the love command has to be understood in light of the other occurrences of it in the Gospel. Here, the love command is related to other commands "that lead to eternal life"[81] and to supporting the poor. On the other hand, the adjective τέλειος appears only three times in Matthew, here and two times in 5:48. Regarding these two connections between both passages, Luz comments that three points are important for Matthew:

> 1. There is doubtless a qualitative element in perfection that is intimated in both texts by love.... For the young man to give up his possessions as he was challenged to do was a radical expression of the love command that for Jesus knows no boundary... perfection is love. 2. But there is also a quantitative element in perfection. To become perfect is to go beyond what is normal and customary.... Jesus gives him a commandment that makes love concrete and radical... perfection is... complete obedience. 3. Finally, perfection is a matter of complete attachment to Jesus that is expressed in our text with the call "follow me"... perfection is a matter of following Jesus.[82]

As Cheung points out, "it is in obedience to Jesus's interpretation of the Torah, centred in the love command, that one can be perfect."[83]

79. In this pericope, "to have eternal life" is τὸ ἀγαθόν (19:17). See D. A. Carson, "Matthew," in *Matthew, Mark, and Luke*, EBC 8 (Grand Rapids, Mich.: Zondervan, 1984), 422. For a comparison with Mark 10:17–30, see Nolland, *Matthew*, 788–94.

80. The text of these commandments follows the LXX. The commandments are the sixth, seventh, eighth, ninth, and fifth. All are part of the "second table" of the commandments and relate to relationships between people. France comments that "[t]he selection of these five from among the ten is probably because they all concern observable behavior toward other people rather than the more 'inward' focus of the first four commandments." R. T. France, *The Gospel of Matthew*, NICNT (Grand Rapids, Mich.: Eerdmans, 2007), 734.

81. Emerson B. Powery, "Under the Gaze of the Empire: Who Is My Neighbor?," *Int* 62 (2008): 138.

82. Luz, *Matthew 8–20*, 513–4. Konradt argues that Matthew inserts this command "because he wants to present the demand to charitable use of one's possessions... as an application of the Old Testament love command." Konradt, "The Love Command," 273.

83. Cheung, *Epistle of James*, 107.

The third and final occasion in which the love command is mentioned in Matthew is in 22:22. Although the context and purpose of Mark 12:28–31 is slightly different from those of this pericope (Matt 22:28–34), the use of Leviticus 19:18b is the same.[84] A lawyer (νομικός in Matthew, γραμματεύς in Mark) asks Jesus for the greatest commandment (12:28). Jesus answers by quoting Deuteronomy 6:5, "ἀγαπήσεις κύριον τὸν θεόν σου ἐν ὅλῃ τῇ καρδίᾳ σου καὶ ἐν ὅλῃ τῇ ψυχῇ σου καὶ ἐν ὅλῃ τῇ διανοίᾳ σου."[85] Jesus refers to this as the greatest and first commandment. Then, possibly using the Jewish technique of *gezarah shewah*,[86] he adds "the second is like it" and quotes the love command (Matt 22:39). He concludes by saying that upon these two commands depends all the law and the prophets (Matt 22:40). As Hagner says, "[t]he twofold commandment as set forth in this passage may appropriately be thought of as nothing less than a 'hermeneutic program' for the understanding and application of the law and the prophets."[87] In the Markan version, Jesus says that there is no other commandment greater than these (Mark 12:31). Furthermore, the scribe paraphrases Jesus's answer by commenting that these two commands are greater than all burn offerings and sacrifices (Mark 12:32–33).[88] Finally, seeing the wisdom of the scribe's answer, Jesus tells him: οὐ μακρὰν εἶ ἀπὸ τῆς βασιλείας τοῦ θεοῦ (Mark 12:34).

In this pericope, loving God and loving the neighbor summarize "all the law and the prophets."[89] The phrase "the law and the prophets" appears four times in Matthew (5:17, 7:12, 11:13, and 22:40). Each time, Oscar Brooks says, "'law and prophets' are used together, it is in a context where Jesus projected his awareness that his teaching and ministry are a new departure."[90] A progression in Matthew's argument can be observed. In 7:12, the Golden Rule "is the law and the prophets." In 19:16–22, the love command is listed with other commands from the Decalogue. Now, Jesus summarizes all of those commands with the love command—i.e., "the social commandments from the Decalogue unfold the love command."[91] Also, the two love commands

84. For parallels and differences with Mark 12:28–34, see Nolland, *Matthew*, 909–13; Hultgren, "Double Commandment," 373–8. For example, in Matthew, the pericope has a polemic tone and is inserted in a sequence of confrontation with the Pharisees and Sadducees, whereas in Mark it is more of a cordial dialogue. For the Markan pericope form, see Keerankeri, *The Love Commandment in Mark*, 71–4.

85. The Mark version is longer and includes the Shema' (Deut 6:4).

86. Keener, *Matthew*, 531.

87. Donald A. Hagner, *Matthew 14–28*, WBC 33b (Dallas: Word, 1995), 648.

88. This affirmation echoes passages such as 1 Sam 15:22, Hos 6:6, and Mic 6:6–8, all passages from the Prophets.

89. Jesus is not alone in summarizing the entire law in these two commands, as is pointed out above (see pages 127–30 above).

90. Oscar S. Brooks, "The Function of the Double Love Command in Matthew 22:34–40," *AUSS* 36 (1998): 20.

91. Konradt, "The Love Command," 278.

determine how one should interpret and apply the others. Both commands have hermeneutical priority over the others, but they do not cancel them.[92]

Luke presents the love command once in 10:27. The pericope (10:25–37) is similar to Matthew 22:34–40 and Mark 12:28–31, but it differs significantly from them.[93] This pericope is located amid the narratives of Jesus's journey toward Jerusalem, after the sending of the seventy (two?) (10:1–20) and Jesus's jubilation about the eschatological time of fulfillment that his disciples are living in (10:21–24). Structurally, it consists of (1) the reason for the lawyer's question (10:25a, 29a), (2) the lawyer's question (10:25b, 29b), (3) Jesus's counter question (10:26, 30–36), (4) the lawyer's answer (10:27, 37a), and (5) Jesus's concluding challenge (10:28, 37b).[94]

The lawyer asks Jesus what he must do to inherit eternal life. Jesus responds with two counterquestions asking the lawyer what he reads in the law. The lawyer's answer includes both Deuteronomy 6:5 and Leviticus 19:18b. Jesus says to him: "You have answered correctly, do this and you will live" (10:28). The lawyer sees the implications of Jesus challenge and asks again: "Who is my neighbor?" (10:29). Jesus then tells the parable of the Good Samaritan (10:30–35). Then, Jesus asks a key question: τίς τούτων τῶν τριῶν πλησίον δοκεῖ σοι γεγονέναι τοῦ ἐμπεσόντος εἰς τοὺς λῃστάς (10:36). The lawyer answers: ὁ ποιήσας τὸ ἔλεος μετ' αὐτοῦ (10:37a). The dialogue "focuses on the definition of one's neighbor."[95] Jesus then shifts the focus from "who is my neighbor" to "whom will I be a neighbor to." The characters in the parable show that for Jesus the concept of neighbor goes beyond national or racial boundaries. One becomes a neighbor to whoever is in need when one shows mercy and love to him or her.

In summary, Jesus expands the meaning of the love command of Leviticus 19:18b. With respect to Second Temple literature, Jesus is in line with those who universalize the concept of neighbor. He also collates the love commandments, and presents them as the summary of the Torah. He has, however, his own distinct emphases. Jesus expands the concept of neighbor

92. Cheung, *Epistle of James*, 109.

93. David Pao and Eckhard Schnabel point out the three main differences between the Lukan pericope and that of Matthew/Mark: "First, unlike Luke, who places this dialogue earlier in Jesus' ministry, Mark and Matthew place this passage in the final days of Jesus' earthly ministry. Second, the question that Jesus is addressing in Mark and Matthew centers on the 'greatest command' while the way to inherit eternal life is the topic in Luke. Third, Jesus is the one citing the OT in Mark and Matthew, while the lawyer cites the two OT texts in Luke. Finally, the parable of the Good Samaritan, which follows in Luke, is missing in Mark and Matthew." David W. Pao and Eckhard J. Schnabel, "Luke," in *Commentary on the New Testament Use of the Old Testament*, ed. G. K. Beale and D. A. Carson (Grand Rapids, Mich.: Baker, 2007), 319. For the historicity of this pericope, see Darrel L. Bock, *9:51–24:53*, vol. 2 of *Luke*, BECNT (Grand Rapids, Mich.: Baker, 1996), 1018–21.

94. John Nolland, *Luke 9:21–18:34*, WBC 35b (Dallas: Word, 1993), 580; Bock, *9:51–24:53*, 1021.

95. Pao and Schnabel, "Luke," 319.

by explicitly including enemies as among those one should love. Also, he calls for a reorientation regarding the theme of neighbor. Rather than asking who one's neighbor is, Christians have to become neighbors to those in need, especially the poor (Matt 19:21; Luke 10:30–37). Additionally, he eschatologically relates the love command to the kingdom of God. Love is an act of peace and a characteristic of the people of the kingdom of God. To obey the love command is more than an *imitatio Dei*, it is also an *imitatio Christi* that leads believers to perfection (Matt 5:48, 19:21). It is an invitation to follow him, where love and perfection meet. Jesus gives hermeneutical priority to the love commands (to love God and the neighbor), because all the law and the prophets "hang" on them.

With this in mind, it is possible that some other implicatures could be derived from Jesus's teaching:

1. People who love their neighbor show themselves to him/her as neighbor in order to help him/her.
2. People who love their neighbor are perfect before God.
3. People who love their neighbor imitate Christ.
4. People who love God and their neighbor fulfill the Law and the Prophets.

Given the close relation between Matthean traditions and James, it is highly probable that some of these traditions about Jesus's use of Leviticus 19:18b are present in the encyclopedic knowledge shared by James and his addressees.

Leviticus 19:18b in James 2:8

At the beginning of the second section (2:8–13) of this pericope, James presents his biblical argument. He points out: εἰ μέντοι νόμον τελεῖτε βασιλικὸν κατὰ τὴν γραφήν· ἀγαπήσεις τὸν πλησίον σου ὡς σεαυτόν, καλῶς ποιεῖτε (2:8). He presents two conditional structures in parallel (2:8–9). The first one begins with εἰ μέντοι, the second with εἰ δέ. For some scholars, μέντοι has an adversative sense here as in its other seven occurrences in the NT (John 4:27, 7:13, 12:42, 20:5, 21:4; 2 Tim. 2:19; Jude 8),[96] with a hint of irony.[97] With this sense, it would introduce a contrast to 2:6. However, the clause in 2:6 is relatively removed from 2:8. Instead, the strong contrast μέντοι . . . δέ (2:8–9) points toward an intensive use of μέντοι.[98] The intensive sense fits slightly

96. Douglas J. Moo, *The Letter of James*, PNTC (Grand Rapids, Mich.: Eerdmans, 2000), 110.

97. Blomberg and Kamell, *James*, 115–6; Davids, *James*, 114; Joseph B. Mayor, *The Epistle of St. James: The Greek Text with Introduction, Notes, and Comments*, 2nd ed. (London: Macmillan, 1897), 86; Painter, "James," 95.

98. Johnson, *James*, 230.

better in this context than the adversative.[99] In this paragraph, James continues his challenge to believers rather than drawing a contrast with the wealthy.[100] The contrast μέντοι . . . δέ reinforces James's rhetoric. In RT terms, the use of μέντοι constrains the derivation of implicatures. In this case, James shows that although his addressees want to fulfill the royal law, their discrimination against the poor is an evidence of their infringement of it.

Regarding the use of the love command here, several observations stand out. First of all, the phrase κατὰ τὴν γραφήν presents a relationship between the written law and the "royal law."[101] Hence, the law under consideration is in some way related to Mosaic law. In fact, discrimination, adultery, and murder are all violations of Mosaic law. Second, the law is also called βασιλικόν. Carson points out that "*basilikos* means 'pertaining to the king' or 'belonging to the king,' 'royal' in that sense."[102] In v. 5, the poor are called κληρονόμους τῆς βασιλείας (cf. Luke 6:20). So, the law is related to the kingdom with God as its king. Third, the love command sums up the law. Finally, love is related to mercy (2:13). All of these issues revolving around James's use of the love command suggest that he is using the Jesus tradition.[103]

There are some important connections between James and the Jesus tradition in the use of the love command. First, in both, the love command "functions as a summarizing statement of God's social will."[104] Second,

99. Allison, *James*, 401; Johnson, *James*, 230; Martin, *James*, 67; Dan G. McCartney, *James*, BECNT (Grand Rapids, Mich.: Baker, 2009), 147–8; McKnight, *James*, 203–5 and n. 124; Moo, *James*, 110; Osborne, "James," 52.

100. Osborne, "James," 52.

101. Pierre Keith, "La citation de Lv 19,18B en Jc 2,1–13," in *The Catholic Epistles and the Tradition*, ed. J. Schlosser (Leuven: Leuven University Press, 2004), 242.

102. Carson, "James," 1000.

103. There are many connections between James's letter and the synoptic tradition. Regarding James's use of Lev 19, Bauckham says: "What emerges as distinctively Christian in James' use of Leviticus 19 is that he reads some specific commandments in light of the teachings of Jesus." He mentions these parallels: Jas 4:11//Matt 7:1, Luke 6:37; Jas 5:9//Matt 7:1–2, Luke 6:37; and Jas 5:12//Matt 5:33–37. Bauckham, *James*, 145. See also the detailed list of parallels in David H. Edgar, *Has God Not Chosen the Poor? The Social Setting of the Epistle of James*, JSNTSup 206 (Sheffield: Sheffield Academic, 2001), 76–94. Also see David H. Edgar, "The Use of the Love-Command and the Shema' in the Epistle of James," *PIBA* 23 (2000): 9–22; Patrick J. Hartin, "James and the Jesus Tradition: Some Theological Reflections and Implications," in *Catholic Epistles and Apostolic Tradition*, ed. Karl-Wilhelm Niebuhr and Robert W. Wall (Waco: Baylor University Press, 2009), 55–70; Virgil V. Porter, Jr., "The Use of the Sermon on the Mount in the Epistle of James" (Ph.D. diss., Dallas Theological Seminary, 2003); Wesley Hiram Wachob and Luke Timothy Johnson, "The Sayings of Jesus in the Letter of James," in *Authenticating the Words of Jesus*, ed. Bruce D. Chilton and C. F. Evans (Boston: Brill, 2002), 431–50.

104. Konradt, "The Love Command," 281. Similarly to Paul, James uses the love command without an explicit link with the greatest command. Paul uses Lev 19:18b in Rom 13:9 and Gal 5:14. In both passages he uses it as a summary of the Law. For more details see, e.g., Michael Thompson, *Clothed with Christ: The Example and Teaching of Jesus in Romans 12:1–15:13*, JSNTSup 59 (Sheffield: JSOT, 1991), 121–40; Harm W. Hollander, "The Words of Jesus: From Oral Traditions to Written Record in Paul and Q," *NovT* 42 (2000): 340–57.

in James and in the Jesus tradition, the problem of wealth is linked with the nonfulfillment of the love command (cf. Matt 19:16–22). Third, in both, love is related to mercy (cf. Luke 10:30–37). Fourth, in both, the love command is present in an eschatological context. "In Matthew, the love command is set in the context of the new era with the coming of Christ, fulfilling the Torah."[105] Here, the obedience to the love command is portrayed in light of an imminent judgment (2:12).[106]

Based on these connections, some inferences can be made as implicatures. First, many scholars conclude that the "royal law" here means "the Torah fulfilled and expanded by Christ."[107] If this is correct, then James is following Jesus in his use of the love command but also expanding it by including Jesus's teachings as law. Besides the connections mentioned above between Jesus's and James's use of Leviticus 19:18b, the parallels between James and Matthew strengthen the case for James's use of the Jesus tradition. In Matthew 19, Jesus closely relates Leviticus 19:18b (Matt 19:19) with the kingdom of heaven (19:23) and kingdom of God (19:24), and His throne as king (19:28). In James, the love command is described as royal law (Jas 2:8). James alludes to Jesus's words in James 2:5. These words speak about the poor being heirs of the kingdom. Thus, it is highly likely that James considers the royal law as the Torah interpreted by Jesus and also includes Jesus's teachings as law.

A second inference made from the connection of James and the Jesus tradition is that the love command is to be expressed concretely, in this case by not discriminating against the poor in favor of the rich (cf. Lev 19:15). It is expressed also by showing oneself as a neighbor to the needy (Jas 1:27, 2:14–16; cf. Luke 10:30–33),[108] and dealing fairly with laborers (5:1–6; cf. Lev 19:13).

The Commandments in James 2:11

In order to strengthen his argument, James quotes two commandments from the second part of the Decalogue. He introduces them by emphasizing the lawgiver: the one who said . . . also said (Jas 2:11; cf. 4:11–12). James assumes his audience is familiar with the tradition of God giving the law at Sinai (Exod 20:1). At the level of explicature, this information, part of the encyclopedic knowledge shared by James and his addressees, is used for referent

105. Cheung, *Epistle of James*, 119.

106. The idea of an imminent judgment is present throughout the letter: the reversal of fortunes (1:9–11), the crown of life (1:12), the near coming of the Lord (5:8), and the clearest assertion of this imminence, "the judge is standing at the gates" (5:9).

107. Blomberg and Kamell, *James*, 116; Davids, *James*, 114; Johnson, *James*, 230; Moo, *James*, 112. For other views, see the wide bibliography in the analysis of Allison, *James*, 403–5. Contra Matt A. Jackson-McCabe, *Logos & Law in the Letter of James: The Law of Nature, the Law of Moses, & the Law of Freedom*, SupNovT (Leiden: Brill, 2001), 153–4.

108. Contra Victor Paul Furnish, *The Love Command in the New Testament* (Nashville: Abingdon, 1972), 182.

assignment. Otherwise, the referent of the participle ὁ εἰπών (2:11) "is an enigma."[109] James uses the aorist subjunctive in the prohibitions instead of the future indicative of the LXX. The textual variants in this verse testify to the intent to harmonize James's text with the LXX.[110] He follows the same order as the LXX (as Luke 18:20; Rom 3:19) over against the MT (cf. Mark 10:19). In any case, this order at the end of the day may not be important for the sake of the discourse because, as Allison points out, James could be paraphrasing the commandments. In that case, "the order means little or nothing."[111]

The Ten Commandments have a special place in Second Temple literature. They summarize all the law (Philo, *Decal.* 19–20; Tg. Ps.-J. Exod 24:12; Cant. Rab. 14:2). It is common in Second Temple literature to associate Leviticus 19:18b with the second part of the Ten Words. Philo, in *De decalogo* 110, calls φιλανθρώποι those who keep the second five commandments of the Decalogue.[112] Also Jesus summarizes the whole law and the prophets in the Shema' and Leviticus 19:18b in Matthew 22:37–40. Thus, it is not surprising that James illustrates his case with two commandments after pointing to Leviticus 19:18b as the "royal law" (2:8).

There is no agreement among scholars about whether James is alluding to any specific problem of his addressees,[113] or whether he mentions two of

109. Allison, *James*, 52. Although this fact by itself does not prove the ethnic origin of the addressees, it contributes to understanding James's addressees as mainly a Jewish-Christian community.

110. Johnson, *James*, 233.

111. Allison, *James*, 415. Cf. Jer 7:8–9; Hos 4:1–2.

112. Allison also mentions rabbinic tradition: Sifra 200 on Lev 19:18; t. Soṭah 9.11; y. Ned. 41c (9.4); Gen. Rab. 24.7. Ibid., 407.

113. Ralph Martin links these accusations with the Jewish revolt in the 60s. He assumes James is evoking a literal case of murder. However, his reconstruction of the historical setting is unlikely. The same problem appears in his interpretation of Jas 4:1–3. Martin, *James*, 70. Other scholars associate a metaphorical understanding of murder with discrimination. As a result, discrimination is a subset of murder, a type of "murder." McKnight, *James*, 216–8; Osborne, "James," 54–5. Davids thinks that James chooses these two commandments because murder is frequently associated with discrimination against the poor, and gives some examples (Jer 7:6, 22:3; Sir 34:26; T. Gad 4:6–7; 1 John 3:15; Amos 8:4). Davids, *James*, 117. None of these examples, though, deals specifically with discrimination but with oppression. Moo thinks that as anger equals murder in Jesus's teaching (Matt 5:21–22), in the same way, it would be possible that favoritism is a type of murder in James. He recognizes, however, that James's text does not provide the evidence to support this idea. Moo, *James*, 115. On his part, McKnight thinks James uses the concept of murder as a clear problem of the addressees, and interprets the concept metaphorically. McKnight, *James*, 217. He is right in pointing out that James seems to metaphorically use murder in 4:1–3, associated with envy, greed. However, he also metaphorically uses the idea of adultery as friendship with the world (4:4). For Hartin, both metaphorical ideas of murder and adultery "embrace actions that discriminate against the poor." Hartin, *James*, 137. The metaphorical use of murder in 4:1–3 does not prove that murder equals discrimination in 2:11. Also, it is possible that murder in 5:6 is literal. So, when using murder in 2:11, he could be thinking of that example. In any case, it is not necessary to associate murder with any specific problem in

the Ten Commandments to illustrate his point presented in 2:10. Carson says James quotes these two commandments "to demonstrate the indivisible unity of the law."[114] For Maynard-Reid, James "links such partiality with such sins as murder and adultery... as indication of how heinous the crime of discrimination against the poor is to James."[115] James seems to use these two commandments influenced by the Jesus tradition. In this way, he puts discrimination against the poor at the same level of severity.

Some possible implicated conclusions derived from the explicature and the context might be the following:

1. If you [any one of the addressees] do not commit adultery but you commit murder you become transgressor of the [royal] law.
2. In the same way, people who commit discrimination against the poor are transgressors of the royal law.
3. People who commit discrimination against the poor contradict their faith in the glorious Lord Jesus Christ.

Other possible implicatures relate to the type of sin mentioned:

4. Discrimination is as heinous as adultery or murder.

Possible Allusions and Echoes of Scripture in James 2:1–13

Many scholars identify other OT texts in this pericope.[116] In the report of the SBL group, Anthony Hanson concludes: "James 2.1–13 seems to be based on Lev. 9.11–18: the themes of blaspheming the Name, showing partiality to the rich and powerful, and loving one's neighbour as oneself are all in common."[117] Johnson argues the presence of Leviticus 19 behind the letter. In particular, he points out Leviticus 19:15 behind 2:1, 9.[118] McCartney also

order to understand James's rhetoric. The point James makes in 2:10–11 is that committing discrimination against the poor (a sin not included in the Ten Commandments) is a violation of the royal law, as are murder or adultery (both included in the Ten Commandments). Allison, *James*, 416; Dibelius, *James*, 147; Guthrie, "James," 236; Laws, *James*, 114–5; William Varner, *The Book of James: A New Perspective; A Linguistic Commentary Applying Discourse Analysis* (Woodlands, Tex.: Kress Biblical Resources, 2010), 101. So, it is as heinous as those other two. It is more probable that James uses these two commandments influenced by tradition. Jesus uses the same two (Matt 5:21–30); also Paul mentions both related to Lev 19:18 (Ro13:9). For James, discrimination is a type of dishonor, disrespect (2:6), not anger, envy, or greed.

114. Carson, "James," 1002.

115. Maynard-Reid, *Poverty and Wealth*, 66.

116. In this case the evaluation of accessibility of the cognitive environment is made with each potential allusion or echo.

117. Anthony T. Hanson, "Seminar Report: Report on Working Group on 'The Use of the Old Testament in the Epistle of James,' Tübingen, 1977; Châtenay-M, 1978," *NTS* 25 (1979): 526–7.

118. Luke Timothy Johnson, "The Use of Leviticus 19 in the Letter of James," *JBL* 101 (1982): 399.

Table 4.2. Comparison of Leviticus 19:15 and James 2:1, 9

Lev 19:15 (LXX)[a]	Jas 2:1	Jas 2:9
οὐ ποιήσετε ἄδικον ἐν κρίσει· οὐ **λήμψῃ πρόσωπον** πτωχοῦ οὐδὲ θαυμάσεις πρόσωπον δυνάστου· ἐν δικαιοσύνῃ κρινεῖς τὸν πλησίον σου.	ἀδελφοί μου, μὴ ἐν **προσωπολημψίαις** ἔχετε τὴν πίστιν τοῦ κυρίου ἡμῶν Ἰησοῦ Χριστοῦ τῆς δόξης.	εἰ δὲ **προσωπολημπτεῖτε**, ἁμαρτίαν ἐργάζεσθε ἐλεγχόμενοι ὑπὸ τοῦ νόμου ὡς παραβάται.

[a]John William Wevers, ed., *Leviticus, Vetus Testamentum Graecum*, Auctoritate Academiae Scientiarum Gottingensis editum (Göttingen: Vandenhoeck & Ruprecht, 1986), 213.

sees echoes of Leviticus 19:10 in 2:1–6.[119] In this last case, the nexus with Leviticus 19:10 is tenuous. The only connection between Leviticus 19:10 and James 2:1–6 is the theme of poverty. On the other hand, the text of Leviticus 19:15 has stronger links than Leviticus 19:10. However, the context in James seems slightly different from Leviticus 19:15. This last text presumes a legal setting (Lev 19:15a). In Leviticus 19:15b (LXX), the exhortation οὐ λήμψῃ πρόσωπον πτωχοῦ points in the opposite direction to the example presented in James 2:1. Leviticus 19:15 prohibits favoritism toward the poor or deference to the great in court. Conversely, James argues against προσωπολημψία toward the rich in any circumstance. The example James gives illustrates discrimination against the poor in favor of the rich in a worship meeting. Honor and shame are central in this case of discrimination (2:6), not favoritism of judges.

Even though Leviticus 19:15 differs slightly from James's example, many scholars see Leviticus 19:15 behind these verses.[120] Following Hays's criteria of validity—(1) availability, (2) volume, (3) recurrence, and (4) thematic coherence—at least an echo may be discerned. Regarding the criterion of availability, Leviticus is well attested in the first century. In fact, James quotes Leviticus 19:18b a few verses later.[121] So, it is highly probable that the passage was available to James and his addressees. Regarding volume, namely, the number of similarities in words or phrases between the NT text and its potential OT source, in James 2:1 and 9 there are related words, but not an exact correspondence with Leviticus 19:15. In 2:1 the noun προσωπολημψία and in 2:9 the verb προσωπολημπτέω are close to the phrase λαμβάνω πρόσωπον in Leviticus 19:15, as table 4.2 shows.

119. McCartney, *James*, 44.

120. E.g., Allison, *James*, 381; Hubert Frankemölle, *Der Brief des Jakobus, Kapitel 2–5*, GTB 518 (Gütersloh: Echter, 1994), 373; Laws, *James*, 93; Mayor, *St. James*, 78; McKnight, *James*, 176; Franz Mussner, *Der Jakobusbrief*, 3rd expanded ed. (Freiburg: Herder, 1975), 115; Wiard Popkes, *Der Brief des Jakobus*, THKNT 14 (Leipzig: Evangelische Verlagsanstalt, 2001), 158–76.

121. Allison mentions that t. Sanh. 6.2 cites it and Sipra Lev 200 comments on it. Allison, *James*, 381.

The third criterion, recurrence, is the number of times a text is quoted within the same author or in the NT. In this case, as Johnson shows, Leviticus 19 seems to be behind the letter of James, even though there is not one instance of explicit quotation of Leviticus 19:15 in the whole NT. Finally, regarding the fourth criterion, global coherence, Allison argues: "Jas 2:1–7 and LXX Lev 19:15 are of the same intent insofar as they prohibit discrimination against the poor."[122] This coherence would be greater if a judicial setting were certain.

This echo of Leviticus 19:15 could guide the readers who make the connections toward extra implicatures:

1. What is true about discrimination in the tribunal it is true in any circumstance.
2. Anyone who shows favoritism toward the rich against the poor is a sinner.
3. Anyone who shows favoritism toward the rich against the poor is guilty under the royal law.

Nevertheless, it is not clear whether James wants his addressees to make the connections. In RT terms, in this case, the addressees could derive almost the same implicatures with a similar processing effort by making the connection with Leviticus 19:15 as by not making it. The readers/hearers could derive implicatures 1 and 2 without making the connection with Leviticus 19:15 (cf. Job 34:19).[123] In fact, as McCartney rightly points out, James seems to make use of Leviticus 19 via Jesus's teaching and not directly from the OT.[124]

Therefore, in summary, in an analysis using Hays's criteria, an echo of Leviticus 19:15 (LXX) is discernible. However, it is not clear whether James is evoking it from the OT or from the Jesus tradition. The criterion of relevance makes this connection more tenuous. The cognitive benefits are

122. Allison, *James*, 381.

123. In Felder's view, "there is evidence that James's thoughts in 2:4 reflect a general familiarity with the standing which "impartiality" had as part of the Jewish legal tradition rather than a direct reference to any biblical text." Felder, "Partiality and God's Law," 54.

124. McCartney says: "Since James quotes Lev. 19:18, it is hard to argue that James was unaware of the significance of Lev. 19 for his own ethical admonitions. On the other hand, it might be nearer the mark to say, with Bauckham . . . that James as a disciple of Jesus is adapting the ethical teaching of Jesus, for whom Lev. 19 seems to play a determinative role. Much of this is also found in the Sermon on the Mount (Matt. 5–7) and/or the parallel Sermon on the Plain in Luke 6. Further, the reflections of Lev. 19 found in James sometimes have the character of their form and content in Jesus's sermon more than in Lev. 19 itself. Note especially how the warning in Lev. 19:12 against swearing falsely is reflected in James 5:12, not directly, as it is in Lev. 19, but in the intensified and generalized form found in Jesus's teaching recorded in Matt. 5:34–37. In fact, none of the allusions to Lev. 19 in James is without some parallel in Jesus's teaching recorded in the Gospels." McCartney, *James*, 45.

similar whether making the connection with Leviticus 19:15 (LXX) or not, although making the connection requires greater processing effort.

Another possible echo is behind the phrase τοῖς ἀγαπῶσιν αὐτόν (Jas 2:5). This phrase seems to echo Deuteronomy 6:5. Its nearness to the explicit mention of Leviticus 19:18b in James 2:8 strengthens this possibility (cf. Matt 22:37–39).[125] Without a doubt, the Supreme Commandment, the Shema', is part of the encyclopedic knowledge shared by James and his addressees. This phrase seems to be a loose interpretive resemblance of the Supreme Commandment. As Allison points out, "[g]iven the pertinent Jewish and Christian texts, it is not unexpected that James would associate the imperative to love God with the imperative to love neighbor."[126] James is close to Jesus's association of the two greatest commandments with the kingdom of God (Mark 12:29–34). If James intentionally follows Jesus's teachings here in this regard, then it is possible that James wants his readers/hearers to make the same connections. A possible implicature of this sentence might be the following:

1. People who love God also express their love to their neighbor by not discriminating against him/her, nor seeking patronage.

Some scholars see vaguer connections to different passages. But it is not clear whether James intends his readers/hearers to make those associations. One of the principal problems with these proposals is that they tend to reflect positions that other scholars do not seem to endorse. For example, Bauckham sees in the expression "the Jesus Christ, the Lord of glory" in 2:1 a Christological exegesis of Psalm 24.[127] He also sees the phrases "the implanted word" in 1:25 and "the law of freedom" in 2:12 as reflections of James's exegesis of Jeremiah 31:31–34 (Jer 38 [LXX]), the new covenant of Jeremiah.[128] However, it is noticeable that in her well-respected article, Kamell exhaustively explores Jeremiah 31 in James 1:25 but does not consider 2:12 as pertinent for her analysis.[129] This shows that even though the connection with Jeremiah 31 is clear in 1:25, it is not so in 2:12. On his part, when commenting on 2:3, Pierre Keith thinks the phrase ὑπό τὸ ὑποπόδιόν μου is an allusion to Psalm 109:1 (LXX), which at the same time leads toward a possible

125. Allison, *James*, 408; Cheung, *Epistle of James*, 99–121; Frankemölle, *Der Brief des Jakobus*, 404–5; Jackson-McCabe, *Logos & Law*, 174–6; Johnson, *James*, 235; Mark E. Taylor and G. H. Guthrie, "The Structure of James," *CBQ* 68 (2006): 112–3.

126. Allison, *James*, 408. Allison mentions T. Iss. 5:1–2; T. Dan 5:3; T. Jos. 11:1; Philo, *Decal.* 108–11; Mark 12:29–34; Luke 10:27; Did. 1:12; Sib. Or. 8:48–82.

127. Bauckham, *James*, 139.

128. Ibid., 141.

129. Mariam J. Kamell, "Incarnating Jeremiah's Promised New Covenant in the 'Law' of James," *EvQ* 83 (2011): 19–28. The same is true in Jason A. Whitlark, "Εμφυτος Λόγος: A New Covenant Motif in the Letter of James," *HBT* 32 (2010): 144–65.

reference to an eschatological judgment.[130] Again, although there is a mention of a judgment in 2:13, the connection with "footstool" seems more circumstantial in the example (2:2–3) than eschatologically intentional.

Words of Jesus Alluded to in James 2:1–13

There is wide agreement that James evokes some of Jesus's sayings, in particular the Matthean Beatitudes.[131] Kloppenborg strongly argues for James's familiarity with Q 6:29 (Matt 5:39–40//Luke 6:29) and Q 12:58–59 (Matt 5:25–26//Luke 12:58–59).[132] He also makes the case that James 2:5 is an allusion to Q 6:20 (Matt 5:3//Luke 6:20) via *aemulatio* and that 2:7 is close to Q 6:22 (Matt 5:11//Luke 6:22). In this way, James would be aware not just of Q 6:20 but also of its literary context Q 6:20–29 (Matt 5:3–12, 38–40//Luke 6:20–23, 27–29; Luke 6:24–26).[133] However, the clearest relationship between James and the Beatitudes is with Q 6:20. Wachob makes a strong case for the presence of Q 6:20b in James 2:5, "Blessed are you who are the poor, for yours is the kingdom of God" (ESV); although James uses it for his own purposes.[134] It is hard to know, though, if James is metarepresenting the words of Jesus via a combination of a metalinguistic and interpretive resemblance or just through interpretive resemblance. This is because James seems to be familiar with Jesus's oral tradition or preliminary forms of Q.[135] In any case, it is clear that James evokes Jesus's words. It is highly probable these words form part of the encyclopedic knowledge shared by James and his addressees. In that sense, at least, an interpretive resemblance is in view. In other words, James wants his readers/hearers to make the connections with Jesus's teachings even though the phrases are not the exact words. In that way, James reinforces his case by appealing to Jesus's teaching and authority.

At this point, in this long section, several explicit OT quotations are studied. James uses a combination of metalinguistic and interpretive resemblance of Leviticus 19:18b in 2:8. Therefore, it is highly probable that some of the implicatures detected in the OT text are present in James's use of it:

130. Keith, "Lv 19,18b en Jc 2,1–13," 229.

131. For an exhaustive list of passages, see Patrick J. Hartin, *James and the Q Sayings of Jesus*, JSNTSup 47 (Sheffield: JSOT, 1991), 75–94; Wachob and Johnson, "The Sayings of Jesus," 431–50; Edgar, *Has God Not Chosen the Poor?*, 75–94.

132. Here, Q refers to the material common to Matthew and Luke. The references follow the chapter and verse in Luke. This research does not follow any particular theory of Q.

133. John S. Kloppenborg, "The Reception of the Jesus Traditions in James," in *The Catholic Epistles and the Tradition*, ed. J. Schlosser, BETL 176 (Leuven: Leuven University Press, 2004), 136–42.

134. Wachob, *The Voice of Jesus*, 138–51. See also Hartin, *James and the Q Sayings of Jesus*, 242–3.

135. As an example of this tension, even though Allison recognizes that the scholarly consensus is that "James did not know any of the extant written gospels. He was rather familiar with oral tradition, with written Q, or with a developing form of Q allied to Matthean tradition." So, he concludes: "[I]t is not so clear why we should decline to see a literary relationship." Allison, *James*, 59, 61.

1. People who love their neighbor provide food for the needy.
2. People who love their neighbor speak truth with him/her.
3. People who love their neighbor pay their wages to him/her.
4. People who love their neighbor care for the disabled.
5. People who love their neighbor act with justice in the tribunal.
6. People who love their neighbor care for the life of him/her.
7. People who love their neighbor do not act with vengeance against him/her.

It is argued that James follows Jesus's interpretation of Leviticus 19:18b in his use of this text in James 2:8. If this is correct, then many of the implicatures detected in Jesus's use of the love command are present in James's text too:

1. People who love their neighbor show themselves to him/her as neighbor in order to help him/her.
2. People who love their neighbor are perfect before God.
3. People who love their neighbor imitate Christ.
4. People who love God and their neighbor fulfill the Law and the Prophets.

James also explicitly uses a combination of metalinguistic and interpretive resemblance of two of the Ten Commandments in 2:11. Some implicatures derived from his use are the following:

1. People who commit discrimination against the poor are transgressors of the royal law.
2. People who commit discrimination against the poor contradict their faith in the glorious Lord Jesus Christ.
3. Discrimination is as heinous as adultery or murder.

Furthermore, some allusions and echoes are detected. It is argued that an echo of Deuteronomy 6:5 is present in James 2:5 and a tenuous echo of Leviticus 19:15 is detected in 2:1, 9. A possible implicature there might be the following:

1. People who love God also express their love to their neighbor by not discriminating against him/her, nor seeking patronage.

Finally, some allusions to the Jesus tradition are present. The most probable is the tradition behind Luke 6:20b reflected in James 2:5. James uses an interpretive metarepresentation of the Jesus tradition. A couple of possible implicatures might be the following:

1. Jesus taught the poor are blessed because God chose them.
2. We have to honor the poor because Jesus taught us to do so.

Interpretation of the Text in James

James points out a critical problem in the conduct of his addressees, "my brothers" (2:1). God is their benefactor (1:16–18). However, they look for patronage by giving preferential treatment to the wealthy. In doing so, they discriminate against the poor. As a result, they have experienced a faith that is far from worshipping God with a pure and undefiled religion. Instead of visiting orphans and widows in their afflictions, they are dishonoring the poor. Therefore, James exhorts them to have a faith in the glorious Lord Jesus Christ without discriminations (2:1).[136] In order to support his thesis, he presents an example of the problem (2:2–4). Furthermore, he supports his admonition with three rhetorical questions that highlight the inconsistency of his addressees' conduct (2:5–7). Finally, he grounds his exhortation with biblical (2:8–12) and eschatological arguments (2:13).

James builds the first stage of his argument (2:1–4) in two steps. First, in the protasis he presents the hypothetical example (2:2–3). Later, in the apodosis, he uses two rhetorical questions that require an affirmative answer in order to point out the actual problem (2:4). With a paronomasia, he plays with the sounds of the words διεκρίθητε/κρίται. At a higher level of explicitness, the illocutionary force of both questions is accusation.[137]

The example presents a hypothetical but real case of discrimination and patronage. James describes a worship-meeting scene. Two visitors enter into

136. The genitive catena τὴν πίστιν τοῦ κυρίου ἡμῶν Ἰησοῦ Χριστοῦ τῆς δόξης, in 2:1, is awkward. There have been different proposals to solve it. Allison summarizes ten different options citing their respective supporters: (1) δόξης goes with προσωπολημψίαις, "partiality arising from opinion," (2) δόξης goes with πίστιν, "faith in the glory of our Lord Jesus Christ," (3) assuming hyperbaton or adding τοῦ κυριοῦ to the final clause, as KJV, "the faith of our Lord Jesus Christ, the Lord of Glory," (4) "glory" in apposition to "Jesus Christ," "faith in the Lord Jesus Christ, the Glory," (5) inserting a comma after ἡμῶν, "our Lord, Jesus Christ of glory," (6) considering δόξης a qualitative genitive, "our glorious Lord Jesus Christ," (7) repeating ἡμῶν or moving it to the end of the clause, "our Lord Jesus Christ, our glory," (8) interpreting the sentence: "Have not the faith of our Lord Jesus Christ with regards to honourable appearances," (9) δόξης as a discourse marker, "my dear brothers and sisters, here is my proposition (to be discussed according to honour): show not partiality as you possess the faith of our Lord Jesus Christ," and (10) "Do not find in προσωποληψίαις reliable evidence of the glory that accords with our Lord Jesus Christ." However, he endorses none of them. He goes with Major and proposes to remove ἡμῶν Ἰησοῦ Χριστοῦ. Allison, *James*, 382–4. The widest accepted solution, nevertheless, is to consider δόξης a qualitative genitive, and to understand the phrase "our glorious Lord Jesus Christ" (almost all the Spanish versions follow this; the exception is Biblia de Jerusalén Latinoamericana, which translates "nuestro glorificado Señor Jesucristo" [our glorified Lord Jesus Christ]). See, e.g., Davids, *James*, 106–7; Dibelius, *James*, 128; Guthrie, "James," 231; Johnson, *James*, 220–1; Simon J. Kistemaker, *Exposition of James and the Epistles of John*, BNTC (Grand Rapids, Mich.: Baker, 1986), 71–2; René Krüger, *Pobres y ricos en la epístola de Santiago: El desafío de un cristianismo profético* (Buenos Aires: Lumen, 2005), 201–2; Martin, *James*, 60; McCartney, *James*, 136–7; Popkes, *Der Brief des Jakobus*, 159; Vouga, *L'épître de saint Jacques*, 71; Wachob, *The Voice of Jesus*, 68–9.

137. McKnight, *James*, 188.

the gathering. James describes their appearance in order to highlight the contrasting attitudes of his addressees based on external judgments. All eyes are on the wealthy man (2:3), and their words seem to imply silent flattery. By contrast, they dishonor the poor man in their treatment of him. In 2:4, James moves from the example to the real problem through a double rhetorical question. He points out that his addresseesare bad judges with evil thoughts when judging appearance (2:4).

The first question points to the external problem: οὐ διεκρίθητε ἐν ἑαυτοῖς; At the level of explicature, the verb διακρίνω could mean "to be uncertain, doubt, waver," as in 1:6,[138] or "to make distinctions, separate, discriminate" (cf. Acts 15:9).[139] Here, the context of the protasis points toward "making distinctions between rich and poor." Even though some scholars think the ambiguity of the term is intentional here, implying both senses, the latter meaning is the more probable, or at least more predominant.[140] The passive form διεκρίθητε should be understood with the force of a middle voice.[141] The prepositional phrase ἐν ἑαυτοῖς probably means "among yourselves," not "inside of yourselves."[142] Thus, using an illustrative example and a rhetorical question, James criticizes his audience for recurrent acts of discrimination against the poor in their own community (note the plural προσωλημψίαις in 2:1).[143]

The second question signals the inner problem: καὶ ἐγένεσθε κριταὶ διαλογισμῶν πονηρῶν; By expressing discrimination against the poor, they reveal a problem in their heart. They become judges with evil thoughts. The Semitism κριταὶ διαλογισμῶν πονηρῶν expresses the quality of these judges (cf. 1:25, 2:1; Luke 18:6). Διαλογισμός in this case is "the content of reasoning or conclusion reached through use of reason, thought, opinion, reasoning, design."[144] As Johnson points out, this noun has a negative connotation throughout the NT (Matt 15:19; Mark 7:21; Luke 5:22, 6:8, 9:46–47, 24:38;

138. "διακρίνω," BDAG 231; Martin, *James*, 63; Mayor, *St. James*, 85.

139. Davids, *James*, 110; Dibelius, *James*, 136; Laws, *James*, 102.

140. Johnson sees a rich ambiguity. Johnson, *James*, 223. Osborne arrives at a similar conclusion. For him, an inner and an outer attitude are present in this verb, so the "double-minded" heart toward God (1:6–8) results in divisive conduct in the church. Osborne, "James," 49. For Moo, although the idea of discrimination fits well here, the concept of "doubt, waver" is better, because this is the meaning in 1:6, and it is the more common meaning in the NT. In this sense, discrimination is another manifestation of wavering. However, as Moo notices, the illustration (2:2–3) makes the meaning "to discriminate" so natural here that he admits: "[T]his conclusion was obvious on the face of the matter." Moo, *James*, 104. Also, the meaning of the adjective ἀδιάκριτος in 3:17, "without discrimination," seems to reinforce the idea of discrimination here. Allison, *James*, 393, 583–4. Those who have God's wisdom do not act as they do. God's wisdom does not discriminate. Therefore, the meaning "to discriminate" is preferred.

141. Allison, *James*, 393; Dibelius, *James*, 136; Laws, *James*, 102.

142. Allison, *James*, 394.

143. In this case, both verbs in the aorist, διεκρίθητε and εγένεσθε, depict the complete situation without specifying the duration of the action.

144. "διαλογισμός," BDAG 232.

Rom 1:21, 14:1; 1 Cor 3:20; Phil 2:14; 1 Tim 2:8).[145] Therefore James accuses his audience of discriminating against the poor when looking for the patronage of the rich. As McKnight points out, "[w]hat James has in mind with 'evil thoughts,' then, is corrupt mental processes. Besides severing the unity of the messianic community, such processes include at least (1) usurping the place of God (4:11–12), (2) using worldly standards that roots honor in wealth and status (2:2–3), and (3) corrupting the mind of Christians to render judgment on God's will for the community."[146]

These attitudes are incongruent with their faith in the glorious Lord Jesus Christ. With this example and the rhetorical questions James confronts his readers and leads them toward a change of mind via implicatures. The following are a couple of strongly communicated implicatures:

1. Believers should not discriminate among themselves.
2. People who discriminate against the poor have evil thoughts and wrongly judge them.

In next stage of his argument, James reinforces his thesis with Jesus's teaching and the OT (2:5–8). With great kindness he indicates the contradiction of their attitude through three rhetorical questions. In this regard, Painter says: "[T]he rhetoric of questions can be almost as directive as the use of imperative, though psychologically it may be more persuasive."[147] His address of them as "my beloved brothers" reflects his kindness and closeness (2:5, cf. 1:2, 16, 19; 2:1, 14; 3:1, 12; 4:12; 5:7, 10, 12, 19). The first question appeals to Jesus's teachings. James reminds them that God has chosen the poor in the eyes of the world to be heirs of the kingdom (an allusion to the tradition behind Luke 6:20b). God promised this kingdom to those who love him (an echo of Deut 6:5). These implicatures are strongly communicated in the first rhetorical question:

1. The poor by the world's standards are really rich in faith by God's standards.
2. Christians should not discriminate against the poor because God chose them as heirs of his kingdom, as Jesus taught us.
3. Christians should not discriminate against the poor because they are rich in God's eyes.
4. God makes heirs of his kingdom all those who love him, including the poor.

Instead of aligning with Jesus's perspective, with their attitude of discrimination against the poor, they dishonor the poor and disobey Jesus.

145. Johnson, *James*, 224.
146. McKnight, *James*, 190.
147. Painter, "James," 93.

Instead of honoring those whom God honors, they are looking for patrons in the wrong place. The second and third rhetorical questions make this clear. The addressees seem to be looking for the patronage of the wealthy represented by the rich in 2:2–4. For that reason, throughout these rhetorical questions, James makes patent the contradiction of his addressees' attitude. The wealthy oppress the community and drag some of them into courts (2:6). Furthermore, the rich blaspheme the good name that is invoked upon them (2:7). These questions implicitly communicate, via implicatures, James's opinion and teaching regarding patronage and the correct treatment Christians should show to the poor. This attitude and action revolve around what James understands as having a genuine and consistent faith in the glorious Lord Jesus Christ (2:1). Consider this sequence of premises that leads toward those implied conclusions:

1. James says: But you have dishonored the poor. Are not the rich the ones who are oppressing you and those who drag you into court?
2. Discrimination against the poor is sinful.
3. People who discriminate against the poor dishonor them.
4. People who oppress others and drag them into court are not doing God's will.
5. To look for the favor/patronage of that type of people is not wise.

The following are some of the implicated conclusions strongly communicated in these last two rhetorical questions and James's argument from 2:1–5:

1. Christians should not do what the rich do to them.
2. Christians dishonor the poor when looking for patronage of the rich.
3. Christians dishonor the poor when mistreating them and ignoring them.
4. The rich dishonor and mistreat the addressees by dragging them into court and blaspheming the good name.
5. Christians should not discriminate against the poor by looking for patronage of the rich.
6. Christians should look for God's benefaction.
7. Christians should honor the poor by caring for them and giving them just treatment.

It is possible to see other implicatures that are more weakly communicated. For example:

8. "The rich of this world are not inclined to be rich in faith or to be citizens of the kingdom of God."[148]

148. Ibid., 94.

James goes a step further in his argument. He demonstrates the inconsistency of having faith in the glorious Lord Jesus Christ and discriminating against the poor (2:1–7). Next, James argues that discrimination is a clear violation of the royal law (2:8–11). James assumes his readers/hearers know this law, but do not realize their attitude is a violation of it. So, using the principle of the wholeness of the law, he points out that discrimination is as severe a transgression of God's word as adultery or murder (2:8–11). His addressees must always speak and act consciously of God's evaluation (2:12). God's evaluation is under the law that gives freedom. This law has already been implanted in believers' hearts (1:19–25). So, they must act with mercy in light of eschatological judgment (2:13). As Osborne points out, "our mercy must 'conquer' our evil disposition toward prejudice. If we 'have been merciful' to others, 'God will be merciful when he judges' us."[149]

This segment closes James's argument. His use of the OT not only strengthens his argument but also enriches his ethics of poverty and wealth. At this point, some implicatures strongly communicated with these arguments are the following:

1. Christians live under the royal law, as Jesus taught us.
2. The one who fulfills the love command obeys the royal law.
3. "Loving your neighbor as yourself means treating others' concerns as important as you own."
4. "Loving our neighbors as ourselves means treating others' needs as needs we have in common as neighbors—and so caring for others' needs in unison."[150]
5. Loving your neighbor involves good treatment of the poor.
6. The one who discriminates against the poor violates the love command.
7. Discrimination is as heinous as adultery or murder.[151]

149. Osborne, "James," 57.

150. Implicatures 3 and 4 come from George M. Stulac, *James*, IVPNTC 16 (Downers Grove, Ill.: InterVarsity Press, 1993), 102–3.

151. Some scholars disagree with this implicature. However, those who have personally experienced humiliation and the deep denigration of discrimination agree with this assertion. There could be a perception that some sins are more socially scandalous than others. However, the point of James here is that the practice of discrimination inside of the community is a serious offense against God and the poor. The examples of murder and adultery reinforce the severity of this sin. Both sins were castigated with capital punishment (Exod 21:9; Lev 20:10). James puts discrimination on the same level of severity as murder or adultery. See, e.g., Salomon Andria, "James," in *Africa Bible Commentary*, ed. Tokunboh Adeyemo (Grand Rapids, Mich.: Zondervan, 2006), 1512; Arthur James, "James," in *South Asia Bible Commentary*, ed. Brian C. Wintle (Rajasthan, India: Open Door, 2015), 1733; Krüger, *Pobres y ricos en la epístola de Santiago*, 232; Elsa Tamez, *No discriminen a los pobres: Lectura latinoamericana de la carta de Santiago* (Estella: Verbo Divino, 2008), 63.

8. The one who discriminates against the poor sins against God, the Lawgiver.
9. A worshipper of Christ does not only speak but also acts consistently with the love command.
10. God will judge Christians with the law of freedom, so they should act accordingly.
11. God will show mercy to those who show mercy to the poor.

Summary of How James Uses the OT in 2:1–13

For the first time in this analysis, James uses direct quotations. He metalinguistically metarepresents the OT. That is, he uses the words from the LXX. The form of his OT quotation resembles both Leviticus 19:18b and Deuteronomy 5:17–18 (or Exod 20:13, 15). But at the same time, he interpretively uses these passages. He implies that discrimination is a transgression of the love command. This violation is as severe as adultery or murder, the other two metalinguistic quotations. In these last two quotations, he emphasizes the Lawgiver, so discrimination is a direct offense against Him. In particular, his use of Leviticus 19:18b brings into his own discourse several implicatures that contribute directly to his ethics of poverty and wealth. James seems to apply to Leviticus 19:18b something similar to Hillel's third rule, *Binyan 'ab mikkathub 'ekhad*, where the love command is the rule for evaluating discrimination against the poor. He also seems to use Hillel's fifth rule, *Kelal upherat*, by summing up the royal law in this love command. This use of the OT in this passage confirms that James builds his ethics of poverty and wealth by interpretively metarepresenting the OT.

As in the case of 1:26–27, James uses language that guides his readers/hearers to make connections not only with the OT but also with Jesus's words. He does an interpretive resemblance of Deuteronomy 6:5, Leviticus 19:5, Jesus's teaching reflected in Luke 6:20b, and Jesus's use of the love command. In doing so, he strengthens his argument concerning discrimination against the poor.[152] Therefore, James not only interpretively metarepresents the OT but also uses Jesus's teaching. In this way he builds his ethics of poverty and wealth.

Although in this section James mainly addresses the financial middle group of the community, poor Christians in the group would read this section as

152. Carson argues that "James presupposes a profoundly Christian understanding of the law." First, the verb τελέω has the same meaning here as in Luke 2:39 and Rom 2:27. Second, James uses βασιλικός in the sense of "pertaining to the king." Third, the phrase "royal law" does not refer to the specific love commandment but rather to some larger corpus. Fourth, the concatenation of "royal" with "kingdom" (2:5) strongly suggests that what James has in mind is the law that belongs to the kingdom of God. Thus he concludes, "'royal law,' like 'the perfect law that gives freedom' (1:25), is James's way of referring to the demands of God mediated through Jesus." Carson, "James," 999–1000.

vindictive, with hope and consolation. Conversely, wealthy Christians would read it as a warning about where they are putting their trust and what they are looking for in the assembly meetings.

Methodology Applied to 2:14–26

James 2:14–26 is well known in debates about justification, and in discussions of the relationship between Paul's writings and James. James uses Genesis 15:6 (LXX) to support his argument that one cannot have faith without deeds. Also he evokes the Aqedah and Rahab narrative. The passage is a continuation of his argument on genuine faith in the glorious Lord Jesus Christ, and the pure and undefiled religion before God (1:26–27). The text is studied here with a main focus on how James uses the OT. He uses the OT interpretively in order to strengthen his own discourse.

Elucidation of the Co-text

There are several threads that link 2:14–26 to 2:1–13 and earlier parts of James's discourse.[153] In 1:2–4, James encourages his addressees to support trials because these permit them to strengthen their faith. In 1:5–8, he encourages them to ask for wisdom, but with faith, without doubting. In 2:1, James exhorts his addressees to have a faith in Jesus without discrimination against the poor. Now, in 2:14–26, he expands the topic of faith and explains to them what he means by faith.[154] Other connections with other parts of James's discourse revolve around "doing." In 1:22–25, James exhorts his addressees to be ποιηταὶ λόγου and not just ἀκροαταί. In 2:12, he exhorts them to speak and do as those who are about to be judged by God under the law of freedom. Then he expands the concepts of speaking and doing. Again, care for the poor (2:14–17) recalls the pure and undefiled religion in 1:26–27. Furthermore, the theme of mercy in 2:13 is a strong pivot between the two sections. As William Dyrness shows, discrimination is lack of the mercy God expects from His people (2:1–12). In contrast, the works James presents in 2:14–26 are equivalent to the "doing of mercy," in particular in 2:14–17. Also James presents Rahab as an example of showing mercy through hospitality.[155]

The quotation and allusions are part of the pericope 2:14–26. This pericope is part of the major section "The daily Christian life should reflect the

153. See, e.g., Martin, *James*, 78–9; Taylor, *Discourse Structure of James*, 92.

154. Painter points out: "The theme of 2:14–26 follows naturally from 2:1–13 in that the argument moves from not discriminating against the poor in favor of the rich (2:1–13) to a positive concern for and care of those who are poor and needy (2:14–26). Painter, "James," 101. See also Watson, "James 2," 108.

155. William Dyrness, "Mercy Triumphs over Justice: James 2:13 and the Theology of Faith and Works," *Them* 6.3 (1981): 11–6.

presence of the implanted word" (1:19–4:12). As our outline above shows,[156] it is the second subdivision of "true faith: no discrimination but deeds" (2:1–26). Several outlines have been proposed for 2:14–26.[157] Allison's outline presents a detailed analysis that allows the presence of the OT to be more easily seen.[158]

- I. Introduction of subject via two questions (14)
  - A. Question 1: What good is faith without deeds? (14a)
  - B. Question 2: Can faith alone save? (14b)
- II. Introductory illustration (Question 3, 15–16)
  - A. Depiction of unfortunates: "If a brother or sister. . ." (15)
  - B. Response to unfortunates: "And you say. . ." (16a)
  - C. What good is it? (16b)
- III. Inference to statement of thesis: Faith without deeds is dead (17)
- IV. Objection to thesis: One can have faith, another deeds (18a)
- V. Response to objection: One cannot have faith without deeds (18b–25)
  - A. Retort I: Deeds demonstrate faith (18b)
  - B. Retort II: The inadequacy of simple belief (19)
  - C. Retort III through two illustrations (20–25)
    - 1. Introductory question: "Do you want to know. . . ?" (20)
    - 2. The example of Abraham (21–24)
      - a. Question about Gen 22: "Was not Abraham. . . ?" (21)
      - b. The working together of faith and deeds (22)
      - c. Scriptural support and clarification (23)
      - d. Conclusion about Abraham: "You see that. . ." (24)
    - 3. The example of Rahab (25)
- VI. Conclusion: Restatement of thesis (26)
  - A. Similitude (26a)
  - B. Assertion (26b)

In Allison's outline, James alludes to and quotes the OT in point V. Our outline shows that James develops his argument in three stages. Verses 14–16 form an inclusio with the question τί τὸ ὄφελος. The expression οὕτως καί closes this paragraph in v. 17, with the presentation of his thesis: Faith without deeds is dead. This segment emphasizes that true faith is sensitive to the needy (2:14–17). Verses 18–19 have a type of diatribe that deals with an objection to the thesis presented in vv. 14–17. James emphasizes that true faith includes deeds (2:18–19). Finally, in vv. 20–26, James presents two OT

156. See pages 75–76.

157. Blomberg and Kamell, *James*, 128; Hart and Hart, *Analysis of James*, 73–9; Moo, *James*, 119; Watson, "James 2," 118.

158. Allison, *James*, 442. Clearly, there are other outlines of this pericope. This outline, however, makes more evident the presence of the OT. For other ways of seeing the passage, see, e.g., McKnight, *James*, 50–5; Taylor, *Discourse Structure of James*, 98–120.

examples that reinforce his thesis. James quotes or alludes to the OT in the second and third segments.

Description of the General Cognitive Environment

In this section, there is no need to evaluate competing aspects of the cognitive environment. The Shema' is clearly alluded to in 2:19, Abraham's and Rahab's stories are well known, and there is a clear quotation of Genesis 15:6 in 2:23. So, following the procedure for 2:1–13, here a description of one aspect of the cognitive environment that sheds light on the text is presented: the issue of extreme poverty.

Extreme Poverty

As shown above, people below the subsistence level represented around 28% of the population in urban areas of the Roman Empire. In rural areas, the situation was even worse. James 5:1–5 considers the situation of daily laborers in particular. But widows and orphans were in danger of starving. As mentioned in the analysis of 1:26–27, all widows and orphans were part of the expendable class. The image of a brother or sister lacking daily food and clothing to the point of nakedness depicts a scene of extreme poverty (2:15). The situation pushed the extremely poor to beg, which exposed their shame more patently. They were outside of the patronage system, because they had nothing to give back.[159] James describes their vulnerability with eschatological language; he calls it "afflictions" (1:27). Thus in 2:15–16 not only is lack of food and clothing considered, but also honor and shame.

Identification of Possible OT Texts and Traditions Evoked

In this segment, James clearly alludes to the Shema' (2:19), the Aqedah (2:21), and Rahab's narrative (2:25). In 2:23, James's argument combines the Aqedah with the quotation of Genesis 15:6 (LXX). In the following, each allusion and the quotation are studied in order to understand James's use of them.

The Shema' in James 2:19

In his argument against the idea that a believer can have faith without deeds, James contends that a simple assertion of God's oneness is comparable to

159. See a good discussion of the implication of the inequalities of this patronage system and the vulnerability of the extremely poor in Alicia J. Batten, "God in the Letter of James: Patron or Benefactor?," *NTS* 50 (2004): 257–72; Batten, *Friendship and Benefaction in James*; David A. deSilva, *Honor, Patronage, Kinship, and Purity: Unlocking New Testament Culture* (Downers Grove, Ill.: InterVarsity Press, 2000), 94–119; Hartin, *James*, 143–8; Helen Rhee, *Loving the Poor, Saving the Rich: Wealth, Poverty, and Early Christian Formation* (Grand Rapids, Mich.: Baker, 2012), locs. 823–1120 of 9742; Nancy J. Vyhmeister, "The Rich Man in James 2: Does Ancient Patronage Illumine the Text?," *AUSS* 33 (1995): 265–83.

what demons could say. This assertion is central in Jewish and Christian faith. It is a clear allusion to Deuteronomy 6:4: "The Lord our God, the Lord is one." Its recitation is well attested. It is probable that "already by the first century, Deut 6:4–9 + 11:13–21 + Num 15:37–41 was recited at sunrise and sunset" (cf. m. Ber. 1–4; m. Tamid 5.1; b. Ber. 21b, 47b; 3 En. 15b.3; Philo, *Spec.* 4.141; *Opif.* 171; Josephus, *Ant.* 4.212).[160] In the NT, the Shema' is quoted or evoked several times (Mark 12:29–32; Rom 3:30; 1 Cor 8:4; Eph 4:6; 1 Tim 2:5; and maybe John 10:30, 17:3). So, the passage in all certainty was part of James's and his addressees' shared encyclopedic knowledge. In fact, it is a Jewish and Christian fundamental creedal.[161] In RT terms, James uses Deuteronomy 6:4 metalinguistically. That is, there is a loose resemblance in form: εἷς ἐστιν ὁ θεός. LXX reads: ἄκουε, Ἰσραήλ· κύριος ὁ θεὸς ἡμῶν κύριος εἷς ἐστιν. James also uses it interpretively. He does not explain the verse. Instead he uses it to highlight his point in the discourse.[162] Some implicated premises seem to be the following:

1. The Shema' is a central statement of faith for both Jews and Christians.[163]
2. People who believe in God publicly confess the Shema'.

But James ironically argues that a simple assertion of the Shema' without a working faith is less than demons' actions.[164] James points out that demons also believe that, but unlike the person James addresses they also shudder. At a higher level of explicitness, the assertion seems to be this:

1. [with irony] You believe that God is one. You do well [to believe so]. [However, this is not enough. As a matter of fact] also the demons believe [that God is one] and shudder [in God's presence].

So, James strongly implies the following:

160. Allison, *James*, 474 and n. 267. See also Donald Verseput, "James 1:17 and the Jewish Morning Prayers," *NovT* 39 (1997): 179–88. For apotropaic use and monotheism in Second Temple literature, see Armin Lange, "The Shema Israel in Second Temple Judaism," *JAJ* 1 (2010): 207–14.

161. McKnight, *James*, 240–2.

162. As McCartney says, "[T]he specific doctrine in question is not the main issue; rather, it is that bare knowledge of theological truth is something that even demons share, but it hardly benefits them." McCartney, *James*, 160.

163. Contra Allison, *James*, 474. McKnight, on his part, makes the case that James presents a triple Jesus creed: God is one (Deut 6:4–5; Jas 2:18), love God (Deut 6:4–5; Jas 1:12, 2:5), and love others (Lev 19:18; Jas 2:8). McKnight, *James*, 241.

164. In this regard, Verseput points out: "The obvious deficiency of the belief which is shared by the demons arises neither from the specific object of faith nor from a contrast between mere cognitive assent and a personal trust in God, but solely from its existence apart from deeds." Verseput, "James 1:17," 187.

2. A person who confesses the Shema' with a faith that has no deeds does not have a real faith.
3. That kind of faith is less than what demons can "confess."[165]

The Abraham Narrative in James 2:21–24

James is arguing from 2:14–20 that one cannot have faith without deeds. In particular, he emphasizes merciful deeds. A person who has a true faith shows compassion and helps the needy (2:15–16). James points out that faith without deeds is dead (2:17, 26). In 2:20, he challenges his imaginary interlocutor with a restatement of his thesis, faith without deeds is fruitless, useless. He plays with the words of the same root, ἔργων/ἀργή, in order to emphasize that "faith that lacks works does not work! . . . [I]t is entirely ineffective to save."[166] As a result, in 2:14, James strongly implies that this type of faith cannot save. He understands salvation as the entire eschatological process "that begins with initial faith in Christ and climaxes in heavenly glorification."[167] In 2:20, he implies that true faith produces deeds; it is fruitful. In contrast, faith without deeds is mere intellectual recognition but not true faith at all (2:19). In order to prove his point he introduces the story of two emblematic believers: Abraham (2:21–24) and Rahab (2:25).

In the case of Abraham, James evokes the Aqedah (2:21) and introduces Genesis 15:6 (LXX) with a formula of fulfillment in order to justify his thesis.[168] In both cases, James assumes his addressees know Abraham's story. The citation differs slightly from the LXX, καὶ ἐπίστευσεν Ἀβρὰμ τῷ θεῷ, καὶ ἐλογίσθη αὐτῷ εἰς δικαιοσύνην. James reads: ἐπίστευσεν δὲ Ἀβραὰμ τῷ θεῷ, καὶ ἐλογίσθη αὐτῷ εἰς δικαιοσύνην. Philo, in *Leg.* 3.81, has the same text as James.

Genesis 15:6 in the OT Context

The Abraham narrative begins in Genesis 11:27 with Terah's generations. In 12:1–3, God calls and blesses Abram. In Genesis 13, God promises Abram land and numerous offspring (14:14–18). In Genesis 14, after fighting against and defeating Chedorlaomer, Melchizedek blesses him (14:19–20). After these things, God appears again to Abram in a vision and talks with him (15:1–5). God promises to reward him (15:1). Abram asks God for an offspring (15:3). God tells him that he will have as numerous offspring from his own loins as the stars (15:3–5). In that context, the LXX reads: καὶ ἐπίστευσεν Ἀβρὰμ τῷ θεῷ, καὶ ἐλογίσθη αὐτῷ εἰς δικαιοσύνην (Gen 15:6). The MT reads: וְהֶאֱמִן בַּיהוה וַיַּחְשְׁבֶהָ לּוֹ צְדָקָה. The LXX places a major emphasis on Abram's

165. As McKnight puts it, "they are worse than demons! Demons shudder in the presence of God, but the workless messianists are seemingly oblivious to the superficiality of their faith and the doom they face if they do not turn from their callousness. McKnight, *James*, 242.

166. Blomberg and Kamell, *James*, 136.

167. Ibid., 129. In James, the verb σώζω appears three times (1:21, 2:14, 5:20).

168. Carson, "James," 1003.

faith. First, it contains Abram as the explicit subject in the first sentence. In the Hebrew, the subject is implicit. Furthermore, in the second sentence, the LXX uses the passive voice, ἐλογίσθη, instead of the active voice of the MT, וַיַּחְשְׁבֶהָ. In the Hebrew the implicit subject of the verb וַיַּחְשְׁבֶהָ is God. In Greek, the implicit subject of the verb in the passive voice is Abram's act of believing. In this way, the LXX places greater emphasis on Abraham's faith. In any case, in Greek, the divine passive is clear. The explicature of the verse in the MT is then the following:

1. And he [Abraham] put his faith in Yahweh, and he [Yahweh] reckoned it to him [Abraham] as righteousness.[169]

The LXX is slightly different:

2. And Abram put his faith in God, and [his act of believing in God] was reckoned to him [by God] as righteousness.

In order to understand the assertion, it is necessary to define the concepts "put his faith in," "reckoned," and "righteousness." In the context, Abram trusts in God's words regarding his future offspring. The waw + perfect construction, וְהֶאֱמִן, emphasizes Abram's continuous faith.[170] The hiphil form of the verb plus בְּ. "involves accepting what someone says as true," but also "it has the added sense of acting in response to what is heard with trust or obedience."[171] Benjamin Schliesser explains that this attitude "does not consist in his full understanding [*sic*] the ways of Yahweh ... but in his full surrender to the assurance that came towards him on God's initiative."[172] This faith began to be manifested in deeds in his departure from Ur (12:4;

169. Given the ambiguity produced by the absence of explicit subject and the referent of the pronoun in the prepositional phrase לוֹ, in Jewish circles few scholars have argued that the subject and indirect object of "reckoned" is just the opposite, as here: Abraham reckoned to God as righteousness. See, e.g., Daniel A. Klein, "Who Counted Righteousness to Whom? Two Clashing Views by Shadal on Genesis 15:6," JBQ 36 (2008): 28–32. See a good evaluation and criticism of this view in R. W. L. Moberly, "Abraham's Righteousness (Genesis 15:6)," in *Studies in the Pentateuch*, ed. John A. Emerton, VTSup 41 (Leiden: Brill, 1990), 105–8; Manfred Oeming, "Der Glaube Abrahams: Zur Rezeptionsgeschichte von Gen 15,6 in der Zeit des zweiten Tempels," *ZAW* 110 (1998): 19–21.

170. Moberly, "Abraham's Righteousness," 105; Max Rogland, "Abram's Persistent Faith: Hebrew Verb Semantics in Genesis 15:6," *WTJ* 70 (2008): 239–44; Gordon J. Wenham, *Genesis 1–15*, WBC 1 (Dallas: Word, 2002), 329. As Moberly points out, "[t]he most natural meaning of this is that Abraham's faith in Yahweh was his constant response, and therefore the reference in Gen. xv 6 constitutes one particular example which represents and summarizes a regular occurrence." Moberly, "Abraham's Righteousness," 105.

171. R. W. L. Moberly, "אָמַן," *NIDOTTE* 1:431.

172. Benjamin Schliesser, *Abraham's Faith in Romans 4: Paul's Concept of Faith in Light of the History of Reception of Genesis 15:6*, WUNT 2 224 (Tübingen: Mohr Siebeck, 2007), 138.

cf. Heb 11:8). However, as Gordon Wenham says, "[i]t is in crisis situations that faith or the lack of it is revealed, and therefore commented on, e.g., Isa 7:9; Jon 3:5; Ps 78:22, 32."[173] In this case, after the crisis of the kings in Genesis 14, Abram sees more patently the need of an offspring. After God's words, Abram trusts again in God's promise. As a result, God credited it to him as righteousness. Immediately after these words, God makes the covenant with Abram (15:7–21).

The phrase וַיַּחְשְׁבֶהָ לּוֹ צְדָקָה is crucial. The verb חשב with לְ has the idea of reckoning something to someone; in this case, צְדָקָה. God evaluates Abram's faith and reckons it to him as righteousness. In Genesis 15:6 and Psalm 106:31, R. W. L. Moberly suggests that צְדָקָה "as right human behavior merges with ṣᵉdāqâ as divine blessing."[174] He concludes: "The statement that Yahweh 'reckoned righteousness' indicates both the divine recognition of the true quality of the behaviour of Abraham and Phinehas and the affirmative response which brought lasting blessing. . . . In each case there was an outstanding example of human faithfulness to Yahweh, to which Yahweh had responded in a way that was of enduring benefit to Israel."[175]

Or, as John Walton indicates, "[b]ecause Abram takes God at his word, God credits him with a legacy on the basis of the 'rightness' of this faith. He accomplishes this by formally establishing the covenant with him. Recognized righteousness becomes the basis for blessing."[176] K. A. Matthews points out regarding this righteousness: "But the righteousness that Abram receives is not due to conformity to a covenant standard. Rather, this righteousness is extrinsic to Abram and is solely bequeathed by God's gracious declaration."[177]

In conclusion, Abram believed in God since his calling from Ur. He trusted in God and showed his belief through his obedience. The climax of this trust is his total confidence in God's promise of an offspring. God reckoned this legitimate faith as righteousness. As a result, he blessed Abram with a covenant and an offspring.

Genesis 15:6 in the OT and Second Temple Literature

The text of Genesis 15:6 is mentioned or alluded to in the OT or in Second Temple literature. The faithfulness of Abraham and the connection between the Aqedah and Genesis 15:6 are highlighted. This faithfulness is central in Nehemiah 9:7–8. In Sirach 44:20–21, Abraham keeps the law even before

173. Wenham, *Genesis 1–15*, 329. Schliesser points out: "The totality of his [Abraham's] outer conduct and his inner life, his doing and being, is embraced by faith." Schliesser, *Abraham's Faith in Romans 4*, 139.

174. Moberly, "Abraham's Righteousness," 125.

175. Ibid., 126.

176. John H. Walton, *Genesis*, NIVAC (Grand Rapids, Mich.: Zondervan, 2001), 422.

177. K. A. Matthews, *Genesis 11:27–50:26*, NAC 1B (Nashville: Broadman & Holman, 2005), 168.

Sinai. He proved faithful when tested. For this faithfulness, God blesses him. In 1 Maccabees 2:52, Abraham's faithfulness when tested is stressed. Mattathias exhorts his readers through a rhetorical question: "Was not Abraham found faithful when tested, and it was reckoned to him as righteousness?" (1 Macc 2:52 NRSV) The book of Jubilees shows the same emphasis on Abraham's faithfulness (14:6, 17:16–18, 18:16). The climax of that faithfulness is Isaac's sacrifice. Philo mentions or alludes to the text several times (*Abr.* 262; *Deus* 1–4; *Leg.* 3.81; *Heir* 90; *Virt.* 216). In particular, in *Deus* 1–4 he puts together Genesis 22 and Genesis 15:6.[178] Manfred Oeming finds in this literature a close connection between "faith" and "willingness to sacrifice."[179]

The Aqedah in Second Temple Literature

As noted above, Genesis 15:6 is closely related to the Aqedah in Second Temple literature. Understanding the role of the Aqedah in this literature sheds light on how James uses those verses together. Jason Ripley presents a good summary of different aspects highlighted in the literature during this period: cultic concerns, angelic opposition, the morality of the episode, the faithfulness of father and son, and application to Jewish-Gentile relations.[180] As Ripley rightly points out, "the cultic concerns dominate many interpretive expansions."[181]

The principal sources are Jubilees, Philo, Josephus, and 4 Maccabees. Jubilees 17:15–18:19 presents a version of the Aqedah. In it, an evil spirit, Mastema, plots to test Abraham (Jub. 17:15–18). Emulating Job 1, Mastema incites God to prove Abraham's faith by offering Isaac as a burnt offering (Jub. 17:16; cf. LAB 32.1). God is aware of Abraham's faith because he has already tested him with his land, famine, wealth of kings, his wife, circumcision, Ishmael, and Hagar (Jub. 17:17). In Jubilees 18:1–2, God gives instructions to Abraham.

178. Not much is found in Qumran. A similar language appears in 4Q398 14–17 II.7, "And it will be reckoned to you as righteousness." Allison sees here an allusion to Gen 15:6. Allison, *James*, 493. Oeming sees in 4Q225 2 i:8, a paraphrase of Gen 15:6, but it is incomplete. Oeming, "Der Glaube Abrahams," 27–30. One important contribution of this fragment is that 4Q225 supports the passive form found in LXX. It reads: ותׄחׄשב לו צדקה. See the discussion in Joseph A. Fitzmyer, "The Interpretation of Genesis 15:6: Abraham's Faith and Righteousness in a Qumran Text," in *Emmanuel: Studies in the Hebrew Bible, Septuagint, and Dead Sea Scrolls in Honor of Emmanuel Tov*, ed. Shalom M. Paul et al. (Leiden: Brill, 2003), 265–7.

179. Oeming, "Der Glaube Abrahams," 30. For more details and similar conclusions, see Schliesser, *Abraham's Faith in Romans 4*, 4.

180. Jason J. Ripley, "Aqedah," *EDEJ* 354–6.

181. Ibid., 354. This is contrary to Eberhart's opinion that the secularized metaphorical meaning of sacrifice is what predominates. Christian Eberhart, "The Term 'Sacrifice' and the Problem of Theological Abstractions: A Study of the Reception History of Genesis 22:1–19," in *Multivalence of Biblical Texts and Theological Meanings*, ed. Christine Helmer and Charlene T. Higbe, SBLSymS 37 (Atlanta: Society of Biblical Literature, 2006), 59. For other studies, see, e.g., Robin M. Jensen, "The Offering of Isaac in Jewish and Christian Tradition: Image and Text," *BibInt* 2 (1994): 85–110; Ediberto López, "Relecturas de Génesis 22: El temprano judaísmo y el cristianismo primitivo y el sacrificio de Isaac," *RIBLA* 40 (2001): 62–83.

Abraham goes with Isaac to the appointed place (Jub. 17:3–8). At the point of Isaac's sacrifice, in the presence of Mastema, God instructs the angel of the presence to stop Abraham and to provide the ram for the sacrifice. Abraham's faith is vindicated and Mastema is shamed (Jub. 18:3–16). Later, after Sarah is dead and buried, in the tenth test of Abraham, the patriarch is again found faithful (Jub. 19:8; cf. m. 'Abot 5:3). Abraham believed God, and it was counted for him as righteousness in Mamre (Jub. 14:6). However, his faith is highlighted throughout his different tests even before this encounter with God in Mamre (cf. Jub. 13:28–29, 17:17). In the same vein, 1 Maccabees 2:51–52 connects Genesis 15:6 with tests: "Was not Abraham found faithful when tested, and it was reckoned to him as righteousness?"

Philo presents the Aqedah in several ways in his writings. In some of them, Isaac is sacrificed (*Leg.* 3.209; *Migr.* 140; in 4 Macc 7:13, 13:10–13, and 15:23–28 Isaac is an example of faithfulness in the midst of tortures). In others, he survives (*Fug.* 24.132; *Somn.* 1.34.194–95; *Abr.* 177). In his *On the Life of Abraham*, Philo presents the event (*Abr.* 167–205). Abraham and Isaac are models of obedience and deep love (*Abr.* 168–70; cf. also *Deus* 4; LAB 18.4–5).[182] Abraham's faith is highlighted (*Abr.* 175; cf. *Somn.* 1.194) and presented as a model for priestly ministry (*Abr.* 198; cf. 4Q225). Philo understands Isaac's sacrifice as an example of happiness and rejoicing of a wise man before God (*Abr.* 201). In his *On the Migration of Abraham*, Philo allegorizes the story and compares the mind with Abraham (*Migr.* 139–40). In his *On Flights and Findings*, he reflects on the ram provided for the sacrifice (*Fug.* 132–36).

In other texts, Isaac is actively involved in the process. In his depiction of the Aqedah (*Ant.* 222–36), Josephus highlights both Abraham's and Isaac's obedience (*Ant.* 1.231). For him, Isaac was twenty-five years old, the priestly age.[183] He helps his father to build the altar (*Ant.* 1.227) and is actively involved in the sacrifice (*Ant.* 1.232). Judith 8:26–27 presents the event as a test for Isaac.

In summary, in Second Temple literature, the Aqedah is the example par excellence of Abraham's faithfulness and obedience. His love and obedience are under test. He proved his faith in God, and is crowned with blessings. Isaac, his son, is also praised for his willingness and obedience. With reason, 1 Maccabees 2:52 highlights Genesis 15:6 fulfilled when Abraham is tested. James follows a similar pattern of thought in his argument on faith and works.

Genesis 15:6 and the Aqedah in James 2:23

James argues that a true faith in the Lord Jesus Christ should be without discrimination against the poor (2:1). Discrimination is a transgression of the

182. In LAB 32.3 Isaac is willing to be offered as a sacrifice, as an example to future generations; cf. 4 Macc 13:12, 16:20.

183. Ripley, *EDEJ* 356.

royal law (2:8–9). Instead, believers must show a true faith by their merciful deeds toward the needy (2:14–16). If one does not show deeds, his faith is dead (2:17). A true faith is a "working faith." In his diatribe (2:18–26), he insists that one cannot have faith without deeds (2:20). In order to demonstrate his statement, he offers two biblical examples: Abraham and Rahab. Abraham's faith was constantly accompanied by deeds. The emblematic case is the Aqedah (Gen 22:1–19).

In 2:21–22, James presents the example of Abraham. He calls him "our father." He argues through a rhetorical question that God justified Abraham in the Aqedah (2:21). "God declared Abraham righteous because of his faithful obedience (a verdict which anticipates the eschatological verdict)."[184] The mention of this event is significant, because in Jewish literature, as shown above, the binding of Isaac is considered the maximum test of Abraham's faith (Philo, *Abr.* 167; Jub. 17:17–18, 19:2–8; cf. m. 'Abot 5:3).[185] James assumes his readers/hearers know the story. Here, in RT terms, James interpretively metarepresents Genesis 22. It is a loose representation of Genesis 22. His readers/hearers make the connection with the whole story. The point of James is that Abraham's faith was acting along with his deeds, and they completed his faith in the Aqedah (2:22). In this context, James says, "and the Scripture was fulfilled" and quotes Genesis 15:6 (LXX).[186] In 2:24, he emphasizes his thesis that a person is justified by faith and deeds, and not by faith alone.

The quotation is introduced by the fulfillment formula καὶ ἐπληρώθη ἡ γραφὴ ἡ λέγουσα (2:23a; cf. Matt 26:54, 56; Mark 14:49; Luke 4:21; John 13:18; 17:12; 19:24, 36; Acts 1:16). The sense of ἐπληρώθη is not clear.[187] The first

184. Allison, *James*, 483; Blomberg and Kamell, *James*, 136; McKnight, *James*, 246–7; Moo, *James*, 134–5. As Allison points out, many scholars see the verb as demonstrative instead of declarative. Their interpretation is that Abraham's works "showed him to be righteous in truth." See, e.g., Davids, *James*, 127–8; Hartin, *James*, 154; Johnson, *James*, 242; Mariam J. Kamell, "The Soteriology of James in Light of Earlier Jewish Wisdom Literature and the Gospel of Matthew" (Ph.D. diss., University of Saint Andrews, 2010), 181. Osborne is right in asserting that James uses both senses here: ethical rightness and vindication in the judgment. Osborne, "James," 62. The bibliography grows exponentially if the discussion on Paul's use of the word group is included. See, e.g., Todd C. Penner, "The Epistle of James in Current Research," *CurBS* 7 (1999): 257–308; Wiard Popkes, "Two Interpretations of 'Justification' in the New Testament Reflections on Galatians 2:15–21 and James 2:21–25," *ST* 59 (2005): 129–46.

185. For more details on the Aqedah traditions, see Ripley, *EDEJ* 355–8.

186. Paul also quotes this verse in Rom 4:3 and Gal 3:6, but the present work is focused on how James uses the OT, not in a comparison between the two authors. The bibliography on this topic is as vast as the stars in the sky. Paul focuses on how Gentiles come to believe apart from the works of the law, in particular regarding circumcision. See, e.g., the book and its extensive bibliography; Schliesser, *Abraham's Faith in Romans 4*.

187. Allison presents a list of six different ways scholars have understood it. Allison, *James*, 490–1. Davids and Martin think this is not a fulfillment formula but that James uses it "to show that this OT verse... is confirmation of what James has been saying." Davids, *James*, 129; Martin, *James*, 93.

phrase of the quotation, ἐπίστευσεν δὲ Ἀβραὰμ τῷ θεῷ, maybe sheds some light.[188] As mentioned above, the Hebrew וְהֶאֱמִן emphasizes Abraham's continuous faith, his trust in God's word. In James's argument, faith and deeds are always tied together. So, the Aqedah was one later example of what God observed in Abraham since calling him from Ur (Gen 12:1–5; cf. the imperfect tense συνήργει in 2:22). It was not any simple example; it was the supreme life of obedience and faith. His interpretation is in line with what one observes in Second Temple literature. Maybe, in that sense, Moo's proposal sounds appropriate: "Abraham's faith, in its relationship to righteousness, found its ultimate significance and meaning in Abraham's life of obedience."[189] In this way, the Scripture of Gen 15:6 is fulfilled in the Aqedah.

In RT terms, James metarepresents Genesis 15:6 in a combination of metalinguistic and interpretive resemblance. He uses almost every word of Genesis 15:6 (LXX). This is a metalinguistic use of Genesis 15:6. However, he connects the quotation with the Aqedah and interprets it in light of that event. This is interpretive resemblance. He intimately links faith and deeds. This type of faith, it is James's point, God reckoned as righteousness. Righteousness here, as Blomberg and Kamell point out, is closer in meaning to the OT concept of חֶסֶד, "covenant faithfulness."[190]

James also says that Abraham "was called a/the friend of God" (2:23).[191] This title is well known in Second Temple literature (Philo, *Sobr.* 56; *Abr.* 89, 273; T. Abr. (A) 1:6; 2:3, 6; Jub. 19:9; 4 Ezra 3:14).[192] This literature probably derives its use from passages such as 2 Chronicles 20:7 or Isaiah 41:8. The LXX translates the verb אהב in both cases with forms of ἀγαπάω (ἠγαπημένῳ σου; ὃν ἠγάπησα). Also, Johnson sees some influence of Greco-Roman moral discourse in this "pregnant expression," which stresses "the essential equality and unity of friends."[193] In view of friend of God/friend of the world in James 4:4, Osborne rightly concludes: "Abraham's faith-exhibited-in-deeds gave him a deep, intimate relationship with God, while those who claim faith but deny it with their worthless worklessness are in reality friends with the world and thereby enemies of God."[194]

188. Here, the aorist depicts perfective aspect. It presents the action of believing without focusing on its internal development or duration. Stanley E. Porter, *Verbal Aspect in the Greek of the New Testament: With Reference to Tense and Mood* (New York: P. Lang, 1989).

189. Moo, *James*, 138.

190. Blomberg and Kamell, *James*, 138.

191. The clause καὶ φίλος θεοῦ ἐκλήθη could modify the verb ἐπληρώθη, or more probably it is a parallel sentence that is part of the content of the ὅτι clause in 2:22, or it could even be considered a separate statement. See Allison, *James*, 494. The passive voice of ἐκλήθη is very probably a divine passive, given the parallel with the quotation of Gen 15:6, contra McKnight, who considers it impersonal. McKnight, *James*, 254 n. 125.

192. See the exhaustive list in Allison, *James*, 494 n. 3.

193. Johnson, *James*, 243–4.

194. Osborne, "James," 64.

Bauckham points out that Abraham and Rahab are παραδείγματα, examples or models worthy of imitation.[195] In RT terms, this literary form permits the writer to communicate more at the level of implicature. But, as in the case of metaphors, conclusions are weakly implicated. The hearer/reader "is given a greater share of the responsibility for the interpretation."[196] Most of the implicated premises come from the shared encyclopedic knowledge between James and his addressees.[197] In this case, there is a clear contrast between Abraham and Rahab, as is discussed below. Abraham is a well-known example of faith, wealth, charity, and hospitality. As Kamell points out, "Abraham regarded his wealth, even his prized son, as a gift from God, and so for James he functions not merely as an example of hospitality and caring for the poor but as the correct model of a wealthy person's necessary humility before God, the model who stands in opposition not merely to the rich young man from the Gospels [the young rich in Mark 10:17–23 and par.] but also to the wealthy person in 2:2 or 5:1–6."[198]

He is presented as "our father" and "friend of God." His closeness to the readers is an invitation to imitate him. So, some of the implicatures of the passage strongly implicated might be the following:

1. Abraham has a working faith that shows merciful deeds.
2. He is the greatest example of faith that shows obedience.
3. Any believer must follow his example.

195. Job, Elijah, and the prophets also appear in James as examples. Bauckham, *James*, 56. See also Kurt A. Richardson, "Job as Exemplar in the Epistle of James," in *Hearing the Old Testament in the New Testament*, ed. Stanley E. Porter (Grand Rapids, Mich.: Eerdmans, 2006), 213–29.

196. Diane Blakemore, *Understanding Utterances: An Introduction to Pragmatics*, BTL 6 (Oxford: Blackwell, 1992), 164. See also Robyn Carston, "Lexical Pragmatics, AdCoc Concepts, and Metaphor: From a Relevance Theory Perspective," *IJL* 22 (2010): 153–80; Robyn Carston, "XIII—Metaphor: Ad Hoc Concepts, Literal Meaning, and Mental Images," *PAS* 110 (2010): 295–321; Manuel Hernández Iglesias, "*Ad Hoc* Concepts and Metaphor," in *Explicit Communication: Robyn Carston's Pragmatics*, ed. Belén Soria and Esther Romero, PSPLC (Basingstoke, England: Palgrave Macmillan, 2010), 173–82; Adrian Pilkington, "Metaphor Comprehension: Some Questions for Current Accounts in Relevance Theory," in *Explicit Communication: Robyn Carston's Pragmatics*, ed. Belén Soria and Esther Romero, PSPLC (Basingstoke, England: Palgrave Macmillan, 2010), 156–72; Markus Tendahl and Raymond W. Gibbs, Jr., "Complementary Perspectives on Metaphor: Cognitive Linguistics and Relevance Theory," *JPrag* 40 (2008): 1823–64.

197. Ong points out in this regard: "Citing examples has a similar effect to quoting because it recalls the words and actions of those cited, so that one's reading of the textual situation is influenced by one's knowledge and opinion of the models cited." Later, he adds: "Unlike ordinary metaphors which basically say 'the tenor is the vehicle,' these examples say 'what if the tenor is the vehicle?' e.g. 'what if you were Abraham?' By recalling what Abraham did, the addressee can fill in the ethical gap of how to behave in his present situation." Siow-Heng Ong, *A Strategy for a Metaphorical Reading of the Epistle of James* (Lanham, Md.: University Press of America, 1996), 126–7, 42.

198. Mariam J. Kamell, "The Economics of Humility: The Rich and the Humble in James," in *Engaging Economics: New Testament Scenarios and Early Christian Reception*, ed. Bruce W. Longenecker and Kelly D. Liebengood (Grand Rapids, Mich.: Eerdmans, 2009), 174.

4. As Abraham obeyed God's word, the believer should love his/her brothers and sisters in need.
5. A person who has a real faith in God and in the glorious Lord Jesus Christ shows it through his/her deeds.
6. A person with this type of faith shows deeds even in the most critical situations, as Abraham was obedient to God in the Aqedah.
7. A person with a real faith is a friend of God [this will be clearer in 4:4].
8. A person with a real faith cares for the poor and does not discriminate against them.

The Rahab Narrative in James 2:25

In 2:20, James emphasizes his case that one cannot have faith without deeds. In order to support his argument, he presents the Abraham narrative (2:21–24). Now, he uses another biblical example to support his thesis, the Rahab narrative. In this case, he does not quote a direct verse, but evokes the story by mentioning the main lines of it. He presents the main characters, Rahab and the spies, οἱ ἀγγέλοι.[199] In RT terms, he interpretively metarepresents Joshua 2:1–22. It is a loose resemblance of the text.

Although James 2 and Hebrews 11 mention Rahab as an example, there are few mentions of her in Second Temple literature. Josephus, in *Antiquitates judaicae* 5.2–15, narrates Rahab's story. He presents her as an innkeeper who helps the two spies (*Ant.* 5.8). Josephus does not mention Rahab's faith, but her instinct of preservation (*Ant.* 5.12–13). In his recounting, later Joshua rescued her and her family, gave her land, and held her in great esteem (*Ant.* 5.30).[200] In LAB 20.6, the conquest of Jericho is mentioned with no allusion to Rahab's episode. Later rabbinic literature mentions her as an example of faith of a classic proselyte (Midr. Sipre Zutta Num 10.29; Midr. Pesiq. Rab Kah. 13.4; Midr. Mek. R. Ismael Exod 18.1), or even as a prophetess of God (Ruth Rab. 2.1).[201] Some rabbinic traditions also put together the Aqedah and Rahab's story as examples for Israel's benefit (Gen. Rab. 22.4). However, as is often the case with rabbinic literature, it is not clear whether or not these traditions extend back to the first century.

199. Wall thinks the use of ἀγγέλοι recalls the story in Num 13:1 (LXX), where the spies are sent out as God's messengers. James would be familiar with that story. Robert W. Wall, *Community of the Wise: The Letter of James*, NTC (Valley Forge, Pa.: Trinity, 1997), 152–3.

200. Swart presents a brief analysis of this story in Josephus. Gerhard Swart, "Rahab and Esther in Josephus: A Comparative Analysis," in *Biblical Figures in Deuterocanonical and Cognate Literature*, ed. Ulrike Mittmann-Richert and Hermann Lichtenberger, DCL (Berlin: de Gruyter, 2009), 471–86.

201. See the analysis of these and other examples in Martinus Adrianus Beek, "Rahab in the Light of Jewish Exegesis," in *Von Kanaan bis Kerala: Fest, Prof Mag Dr J O M van der Pleog zur Vollendung des siebzigsten Lebensjahres am 4, juli 1979*, ed. W. C. Delsman, J. R. T. M. Peters, and J. T. Nelis, AOAT 211 (Kevelaer: Butzon und Bercker, 1982), 37–44; Frédéric Manns, "Luc 7,47 et les traditions juives sur Rahab," *RSR* 61 (1987): 1–16.

In Joshua 2:1–22, Rahab is presented as a reliable believer in God, and well informed.[202] Both the spies and the royal emissaries trust her (2:1–7). In 2:9, she expresses her faith: "I know that Yahweh has given you the land" (2:9a), "for Yahweh your God, he is God in the heavens above and on the earth beneath" (2:11b). She is aware of God's victories beyond Jericho's borders (2:9–10). So, she acts according to that faith by receiving the spies and protecting them.

James assumes his addressees know the story line. Through a rhetorical question that requires a positive answer, he points out that like Abraham, ὁμοίως δέ (2:25), Rahab the prostitute was justified by God ἐξ ἔργων. The deeds are alluded to in the adverbial phrases ὑποδεξαμένη τοὺς ἀγγέλους καὶ ἑτέρᾳ ὁδῷ ἐκβαλοῦσα.[203] In Hebrews 11:31, Rahab's faith is highlighted, πίστει Ῥαὰβ ἡ πόρνη οὐ συναπώλετο τοῖς ἀπειθήσασιν δεξαμένη τοὺς κατασκόπους μετ'εἰρήνης. Nevertheless, here James lets her faith be implicit.[204] In that way, James stresses his point that one cannot have faith without deeds.[205]

Why does James include this story in his argument? As Johnson shows, in rabbinic literature, Rahab "was celebrated as a proselyte and as a model of hospitality" (b. Meg. 14b–15a; Mekilta on Exod par. Jith. Ama. 18:1; Exod. Rab. 27:4; Num. Rab. 3:2, 8:9, 16:1; Deut. Rab. 2:26–27; Ruth Rab. 2:1; Song Rab. I, 3, 3; I, 15, 2; IV, 1, 2; VI, 2, 3; Eccl. Rab. V, 6, 1; V, 11, 1; VIII, 10, 1).[206] However, as Allison notes, she is absent from intertestamental literature, even from Qumran or Philo.[207] The exception is Josephus, *Antiquitates judaicae* 5:5–30. He mentions her, but as innkeeper not as a prostitute. Allison presents a long list of fifteen different answers to that question.[208] However, Wall's words seem appropriate: "There is remarkable consistency in this history of Rahab criticism within Judaism and early Christianity: she represents the least, the last, and the lost among us all, whose newly found devotion bears witness to the hospitable God who seeks and finds the outsider to save."[209]

202. David Marcus, "Prolepsis in the Story of Rahab and the Spies (Joshua 2)," in *Bringing the Hidden to Light: Essays in Honor of Stephen A. Geller*, ed. Kathryn F. Kravitz and Diane M. Sharon (Winona Lake, Ind.: Eisenbrauns, 2007), 152.

203. Blomberg and Kamell consider the adverbial participles instrumental. Blomberg and Kamell, *James*, 140.

204. Also, for the close relationship between James and Matthew, it is probable that Rahab appearing in the lineage of Jesus (Matt 1:5) is part of the encyclopedic knowledge shared by James and his addressees.

205. Blomberg and Kamell consider that "Abraham and Rahab . . . form a merismus, so that everyone in between them is included as needing to exhibit transformed living in order to demonstrate the genuineness of faith." Blomberg and Kamell, *James*, 140.

206. Johnson, *James*, 245.

207. Allison, *James*, 500. See also Anthony T. Hanson, "Rahab the Harlot in Early Christian Tradition," *JSNT* 1 (1978): 53–60.

208. Allison, *James*, 502–4.

209. Robert W. Wall, "The Intertextuality of Scripture: The Example of Rahab (James 2:25)," in *Bible at Qumran: Text, Shape, and Interpretation*, ed. Peter W. Flint, SDSSRL (Grand Rapids, Mich.: Eerdmans, 2001), 230.

James's addressees probably call up several implied assumptions triggered by the idea of πορνή. In the first century, prostitution was strongly associated with oppression and poverty,[210] as it still is in many countries. As Lynn Cohick points out, "for the most part prostitutes had little say in the sexual encounter, for most prostitutes were slaves or were pimped by men who had legal control over them, such as fathers or husbands. Thus they were viewed primarily as economic tools used for profit by owners, human tools in the same sense as slaves."[211]

In this case, James uses the contrast between Abraham and Rahab, the patriarch and the prostitute, for his argument.[212] Both of them have working faith. God justifies both of them because they show their faith through deeds. James signals in 2:5 that God has chosen the poor to be rich in faith and heirs of his kingdom. Rahab the prostitute is an example of those poor who are rich in faith. In 2:2–3, James criticizes discrimination against the poor. Here, he presents Rahab as an example of hospitality and faith, just the opposite of the story in 2:2–3.[213] Therefore, some implicatures of Rahab example might be the following:

1. God also loves Rahab the prostitute.
2. Rahab was a poor person who also showed a true faith by her hospitality to the needy.
3. Any believer should show his/her faith by caring for the needy.
4. The humble brother or sister should show his/her faith by helping others.
5. It is hospitality not discrimination that should prevail in the Christian community.

Interpretation of the Text in James

James highlights faith from the beginning of his letter. In 1:2–8, he shows how trials strengthen the faith of the community. Trials are vehicles for maturity. Also, faith is fundamental in asking God for wisdom. Lack of faith is evidence

210. See J. Massynbaerde Ford, "Bookshelf on Prostitution," *BTB* 23.3 (1993): 128–34.

211. Lynn H. Cohick, *Women in the World of the Earliest Christians: Illuminating Ancient Ways of Life* (Grand Rapids, Mich.: Baker, 2009), 282.

212. Blomberg and Kamell emphasize these contrasts: "Rahab differs in almost every way from Abraham. Whereas Abraham was a wealthy, moral male, the father of the Jewish nation, and a major figure in his society, Rahab was probably poor, definitely immoral, a female, an outcast of the Canaanite nation, and a minor figure in her society." Blomberg and Kamell, *James*, 140. In this regard, Wall points out: "[T]he creative handling of the Rahab tradition in James 2:25 amplifies the point under consideration, not only by what is said but what is left unsaid about her biblical story." Wall, "The Example of Rahab," 229.

213. Pedrito U. Maynard-Reid, *James: True Religion in Suffering*, ALBA (Boise: Pacific, 1996), 122.

of double-mindedness and instability (1:5–8). Faith is linked with eschatological hope in God's word (1:9–12). A correct religious life before God is to care for the needy, in particular orphans and widows, and keep oneself unstained by the world (1:26–27). In this big picture, James sees a problem of incongruence between what his addressees say and what they do regarding the practice of their faith. The problem revolves around their treatment of the poor and their seeking the patronage of the wealthy. In 2:1–13, James shows the incongruence between their conduct and their faith in the glorious Lord Jesus Christ. He confronts them with a hypothetical but real case of discrimination against the poor and looking for patronage. He argues from Jesus's words and his interpretation of the law, and shows the real treatment the rich give to the members of the church (2:5–7). He emphasizes that discrimination is lack of mercy, a clear violation of God's royal law (2:8–11). God will judge their attitude and actions against the poor (2:12–13). Their faith is incongruent. Comparing 2:1–13 and 2:14–26, George Guthrie points out: "In general, both passages address the problem of a professed faith characterized by inattention to the poor... but that inattention is shown in vv. 14–26 to have a deeper, sinister cause—an inadequate understanding of faith's implications."[214]

Now, in 2:14–26, James presents his understanding of what he means by faith. Faith, for James, is an acting/working faith. It is to "believe in and follow Jesus."[215] This type of faith, James argues, always is accompanied by deeds. There is no option; a faith that does not produce deeds is not a salvific faith (2:14). When James talks about deeds, he focuses on merciful deeds toward the needy. In 2:15–16, he presents an example from daily life.[216] He presents a poor brother or sister. They are from the bottom of the ES_7 level in Longenecker's scale. They lack essential clothes and food. They lack honor,[217] although God has given them a high position (1:9), they were chosen by God, and are heirs of his kingdom (2:5). They have less than the poor person with filthy clothing who visits their synagogue (2:2). They γυμνοὶ ὑπάρχουσιν καὶ λειπόμενοι εἰσιν τῆς ἐφημέρου τροφῆς.

They are part of the community. Their situation is patent. They do not need to ask anything; their despair is obvious. But, the community, instead of "visiting" them (1:27), gives them only good words. This contrasts with 2:12, "so speak and so act as those who are to be judged under the law of liberty"

214. Guthrie, "James," 237.

215. Osborne, "James," 58.

216. Speaking on the nature of the example, Moo comments: "[T]he fact that James again chooses an example of mistreatment of the poor in the Christian community makes clear that the illustration represents a pattern of behavior that is all too typical for James's readers." Moo, *James*, 124.

217. Brosend says: "Recalling what was discussed in 2:1–13 about honor and shame, we are reminded that while 'bodily needs' were presented for attention, more was at stake than a meal and a coat. Responding to these needs gives the community an opportunity to restore a person or persons to honor." Brosend, *James and Jude*, 77.

(ESV). They speak but do not act accordingly (2:16). This example assumes the addressees have "the means or access to the means from the community to relieve the want."[218] Ironically, in the example, the person from the community detects the problem, but instead of helping them, he says a blessing, "go in peace" and "be warmed and filled" (2:16).[219] The community offers kind words but does nothing. They do not show themselves as neighbors of the needy, as Jesus taught. With this passivity, they violate the love command. The expression "go in peace" is a well-attested expression of desire for God to give his peace to that person (Judg 6:23, 18:6, 19:20; 1 Sam 20:22, 29:27; Mark 5:34; Luke 7:50, 8:48, 24:36; John 20:19; Eph 6:23). The next two wishes, be warmed and filled, are evidence that the community detects the problem but decides to do nothing to solve it. Johnson sees here also a failure to control the tongue and feed orphans and widows that evidences an empty religion (1:26–27).[220] The imperatives θερμαίνεσθε καὶ χορτάζεσθε could be middle or passive voice.[221] If middle voice is intended, the irony could highlight the insensitiveness of those who have the means to solve the situation but do nothing. "The insult of the person merely becomes even more outrageous."[222] If the passive voice is intended, the irony could highlight the idea they have that God could solve the problem by other means but not through them. In any case, the point is clear: they express a faith that is not accompanied by deeds, a faith that cannot save (2:14). They reckon that God gives peace, clothing, and food, but deny their role to visit the poor in their afflictions. This example seems to echo Jesus's teaching in Matthew 25:31–46. [223] There are people who claim to believe in God but do nothing to alleviate the situation of the needy. For that reason, James asks again: τί τὸ ὄφελος; (2:14, 16). From this example, he reformulates his point: a faith that does not act not only does not save (2:14), but also is dead in itself (2:17).

Anticipating a potential objection to his teaching, James uses a diatribe to prove his point again (2:18–25).[224] He insists that deeds show a true faith. One

218. Ibid.

219. Many scholars detect irony and even cruelty behind those pious words. See, e.g., Allison, *James*, 466; Hartin, *James*, 150; Laws, *James*, 121; McKnight, *James*, 231.

220. Johnson, *James*, 239.

221. For the passive voice, see Laws, *James*, 121; Mayor, *St. James*, 97–8; McKnight, *James*, 231. For the middle voice, see Martin, *James*, 85; Osborne, "James," 122; Popkes, *Der Brief des Jakobus*, 194.

222. Blomberg and Kamell, *James*, 131.

223. The hypothetical case in 2:15–16 seems to echo Matt 25:31–46. In any case, James's illustration is in the same vein of Jesus's teaching. In Jesus's teaching, those who do not show mercy are condemned, and those who care for the needy inherit the kingdom (but cf. Tob 4:16 with a similar exhortation to give food and clothing to the needy). See, e.g., Hartin, *James*, 150. If the connection is intentional, in that case, James is interpretively metarepresenting Jesus's teaching. Through this link, James would reinforce his confrontation by highlighting the eschatological judgment of those who do nothing to alleviate the afflictions of the needy.

224. Scholars agree that the teaching of the diatribe is clear, although the analysis of the components of the dialogue is complex and unclear. Allison presents a summary of twelve

cannot have a true faith without deeds. James with irony shows that a public confession of the Shema' per se does not prove anything. Even demons "believe" that and shudder before God's presence (2:20).

In order to complement his diatribe, for the fourth time, James reformulates his point through a rhetorical question (2:20). With a wordplay, ἔργα/ἀργή, he asks: Do you want to know that faith without works doesn't work, is useless, ἀργή? It is strongly implicated in the discourse that the person who thinks that it is possible to have faith without deeds is ἄνθρωπος κενός (2:20). At this point, James says that a faith without deeds does not save, is dead, is similar to what a demon could affirm, which is barren and unproductive. This faith seems to be unproductive in at least two ways. First, a person with that type of faith will experience condemnation in the eschatological judgment, what James calls humiliation (1:10). Second, that type of faith does not contribute to a better community, to one with fewer afflictions (cf. 5:13–18 and the role of faith in the community's healing). James adds two biblical examples to reinforce his thesis.[225] In that way, he guides his addressees to follow correct examples of his teaching: Abraham and Rahab.

First, James uses Abraham's example to show a lifelong obedient faith. Through a rhetorical question, James evokes the Aqedah (2:21) to show how God recognizes Abraham's righteousness. It is precisely this event that serves as the greatest example of obedient faith. What Abraham shows throughout his life, his trust in God, is highlighted in the binding of Isaac. Abraham had believed in God, trusted in him since his calling from Ur. He showed the same faith/trust in God in Genesis 15:1–6. As a result, God reckoned that faith as righteousness (Gen 15:6), and made a covenant with him and his descendants (Gen 15:7–21). Several years later, Abraham showed a more mature faith. That is the point in James 2:22 (and in 1:2–4 too). Abraham's deeds were an integral manifestation of his faith. His faith matured through his deeds: ἡ πίστις συνήργει τοῖς ἔργοις αὐτοῦ καὶ ἐκ τῶν ἔργων ἡ πίστις ἐτελειώθη.[226] For that reason, in James's eyes, the Aqedah is a fulfillment of God's word (2:23). As Allison points out, "faith is not a static given (cf. 2 Thess 1.3), and it becomes fully what it should be through trial, when it exercises itself and overcomes the obstacles that face it."[227] He uses Genesis 15:6 (LXX) to reinforce his claim that faith and deeds work together; they are inseparable. Also Abraham was called a friend of God. Later, James will call his audience

different proposals. After that, he concludes: "Not one of these explanations satisfies, and this commentator is unable to offer anything better in their place.... If every interpretation seems dubious, it is better to defend none." What is clear is that there is a dialogue with an interlocutor. The main point, however, is clear, that "although faith and deeds can be conceptually distinguished, they cannot be separated in real life." Allison, *James*, 468–71.

225. Carson seems to think that these examples are unnecessary for the argument. When explaining Gen 15:6 in Jas 2:23, he asks: "Is biblical evidence for this thesis required?" Carson, "James," 794.

226. Ibid., 1004; Moo, *James*, 137.

227. Allison, *James*, 488.

"adulteresses" because with their actions and attitudes they are becoming friends of the world (4:4). A friend of God is someone like Abraham. In 2:24, James generalizes what he says about Abraham. God justifies any person by his deeds (which are an integral part of his faith) and not from faith alone (a faith separated from deeds: 2:14, 18–19).

A final example reinforces the point but widens the implications. Rahab is an example of hospitality. James presents her as Rahab the prostitute. Again, through a rhetorical question, he emphasizes her deeds of mercy with the messengers. God justified her also by her deeds (which are intimately related to her faith) (2:25; cf. 2:21). She entertained the messengers even at the cost of her life. Also, she sent them by another route, in order to avoid the royal army of Jericho. These deeds, as in Abraham's case, are shown in a key moment of trial. Faith and deeds are profoundly related to one another. Rahab is an example of hospitality and care for the needy, even in risky situations. Contrary to the addressees' attitude of discrimination (2:2–4) and disregard for the needs of the extreme poor of their own community (2:15–16), Rahab showed compassion, mercy, and hospitality because of a true faith.

James closes his argument by reinforcing his teaching through a similitude and an assertion. In 2:26, he says: "As the body apart from the spirit is dead, so also faith without deeds is dead." Elsa Tamez deduces: "Faith here relates to the body, and works to the spirit. Works give life to faith. In the same way, solidarity with the poor gives life to the needy bodies of them (v. 17)."[228]

Summary of How James Uses the OT in 2:14–26

James uses the OT in various ways in this section. He is more explicit in his appeal. James alludes metalinguistically to Deuteronomy 6:4 in 2:19. Both passages have several words in common. His allusion is a loose resemblance of Deuteronomy 6:4 (LXX). But he also metarepresents Deuteronomy 6:4 interpretively. He uses the allusion in 2:19 to highlight the contradiction of pretending to have faith without deeds.

James also evokes Abraham and Rahab traditions. He interpretively metarepresents Genesis 22. The phrase ἀνενέγκας Ἰσαὰκ τὸν υἱὸν αὐτοῦ ἐπὶ τὸ θυσιαστήριον is a loose resemblance of the entire chapter. Following a fulfillment language, he links Genesis 15:6 (LXX) with the Aqedah. He metalinguistically metarepresents Genesis 15:6 (LXX). Few words differ from LXX. At the same time, he uses the quotation in his discourse of fulfillment. He interpretively metarepresents the text. Finally, he also evokes Rahab tradition. He interpretively metarepresents Joshua 2:1–21. His mention of it is a loose resemblance of the entire story. He uses it to reinforce his argument that one cannot have faith without deeds.

228. Tamez, *No discriminen a los pobres*, 72.

Both narratives also are exemplars of a correct expression of faith. James uses the stories to provide his addressees with examples. He communicates his teachings via implicatures. Some of the teachings are strongly communicated (as examples 1–8 illustrate). These narratives are concrete examples of an adequate understanding of faith's implication. Abraham is an example of obedient faith; Rahab is an example of hospitality. Other teachings are weakly implicated (as examples 1–13 illustrate). Here James shares responsibility with his addressees to derive teaching from the the biblical exemplars. For example, Rahab is a poor woman who helps others in need. She takes the initiative in providing what is required. Thus James could imply to his poor addressees that they should imitate that attitude. Again, this section shows that James is building his ethics of poverty and wealth by interpretively metarepresenting the OT.

Conclusions

At this point, through RT, one can see with greater clarity how James builds his ethics of poverty and wealth mainly from what is implicit in the text. Rhetorical questions and examples permit James to influence and lead his addressees toward a correct attitude to and concept of the poor and the needy in a broader way than the explicit language of assertions. As this chapter makes clear, James builds his teaching from the OT and the Jesus tradition. His use of these traditions permits him to strengthen his discourse in several ways. James builds his ethics of poverty and wealth by interpretively metarepresenting the OT and Jesus's teachings.

In 2:1–13, James metalinguistically metarepresents three OT passages: Leviticus 19:18b (LXX) and Deuteronomy 5:17 and 18 (LXX) (or Exod 20:13, 15 [LXX]). The three are literal resemblances of the OT. That is, the text James uses is equal to the text in the LXX. At the same time, he uses the texts interpretively. In particular, James seems to interpret Leviticus 19:18b, the love commandment, through Jesus's teaching and use of it. In fact, in 2:5, James interpretively metarepresents Jesus's words reflected in Luke 6:20. James alludes to other texts. In the same verse, he evokes Deuteronomy 6:5. It is provable that he also metarepresents Leviticus 19:15. However, in RT terms, his addressees could obtain almost the same cognitive effects with less processing effort. In other words, even though the analysis of Leviticus 19:15 in James 2:1–13 meets Hays's four criteria, from the study of the criteria of relevance, it is hard to determine whether or not James wants his readers/hearers to make the connection with that passage, because the processing effort invested in making the connection with the OT text is not compensated by extra cognitive benefits.

James uses all these texts to support his criticism. He points out the incongruence between a faith in Jesus Christ and discrimination against the poor.

In looking for patronage, his addressees are not only not taking into account his warning regarding wealth, but also dishonoring the poor. Discrimination against the poor is as heinous as adultery or murder. Clearly, in this section, his metarepresentations strengthen his argument and his authority, because his thoughts are not only his own reflections but rest on the OT and on Jesus's teachings. This is how he builds his ethics of poverty and wealth. He does it by interpretively metarepresenting the OT and Jesus's teaching.

James's use of the example in the synagogue, rhetorical questions, and the OT and the Jesus tradition in this section permit him to build his ethics of poverty and wealth via implicatures. Instead of just saying, "Do not have a faith in our glorious Lord Jesus Christ with discrimination," he guides his addressees to contrast their attitude toward the poor and the rich with Jesus's teachings and the love command interpreted by him. This exercise shows them what James understands by genuine faith, the place the honor of the poor should have, the different facets the love command implies, and how severe discrimination is.

In 2:13–26, James is more explicit in his appeal to the OT. He metalinguistically metarepresents two texts: Deuteronomy 6:4 (LXX) in 2:20, and Genesis 15:6 (LXX) in 2:23. In the case of Deuteronomy 6:4, it is a loose resemblance of the OT. In the case of Genesis 15:6, it is a literal representation of the text. In both cases, he uses the OT interpretively. He evokes the first text in the diatribe to highlight that an affirmation of a central assertion of Judaism and Christianity is useless if it is not expressed from a faith that works; it is worse than demons' "faith." In the second case, James uses the text with a fulfillment formula to show that the binding of Isaac is a fulfillment of that text.

In this section, James uses interpretive resemblance of two biblical stories: the Aqedah and the Rahab narrative. Both cases are loose resemblances of the OT. James uses these texts to reinforce his thesis that one cannot have faith without deeds. Faith without deeds is useless, barren (2:20), faith and deeds work together, and faith matures by deeds (2:21), a person is justified by faith and deeds (2:24), and faith without deeds is dead (2:26). At the same time, the use of biblical stories permits him to teach his addressees via implicatures. Both stories are examples of "working" faith. Abraham is an example of obedient faith, Rahab of hospitality. But these stories also permit James to exploit weak implicatures. In this way, he guides his addressees to imitate these biblical models, sharing with them the responsibility of deriving conclusions. He introduces both examples with rhetorical questions. At a higher level of explicitness, James uses the illocutionary force of these questions to strongly guide his addressees to agree with him. He does the same in 2:4, 5, 6, 7, and 14.

In this section, James continues building his ethics of poverty and wealth via implicatures. The example of the poor brother and sister and both OT narratives help James to deepen his concept of true faith, the close relationship between faith and merciful deeds, concrete expressions of the love commandment, and so on. These passages confirm that James builds his ethics of poverty and wealth by interpretively metarepresenting the OT and Jesus's teaching.

In summary, the RT analysis used here helps to discern the presence of allusions. But it also helps to detect how James uses OT texts in his discourse. It permits, for example, the analysis of the illocutionary force of the discourse, irony, metaphors, and the exploitation of weak implicatures. It also helps one to understand how James builds his ethics of poverty and wealth.

Chapter 5

James 4:13–5:11

James lays out the foundation of his thoughts on poverty and wealth in chapters 1 and 2 of his letter. In 1:9–11, he presents the eschatological reversal of fortunes. This theme will reappear in his exhortations in chapters 4 and 5. God's concern for the poor (2:5) is also foundational in his denunciation of the crimes of the wealthy in chapter 5. Similarly, James develops several themes in 3:1–4:12 that are essential to an understanding of his ideas here: poverty and wealth, human speech, arrogance.[1] James advances his discourse by evoking earlier parts of it to strengthen his global teaching and to give his discourse coherence. In this chapter, the topic of poverty and wealth guides the study of the use of the OT in 4:13–17 and 5:1–6 and 7–11. The RT method of discourse analysis and evaluation of possible allusions helps in this process. The previous chapters of this research show that when using the OT, James tends to combine interpretive with metalinguistic metarepresentations of the OT. That is, he does not only evoke OT texts or mention them literally, but also appropriates them for use in his own discourse. As in the sections of the letter considered in previous chapters, James continues to build his ethics of poverty and wealth by interpretively metarepresenting the OT and Jesus's teachings in the present section.

Methodology Applied to 4:13–17

James aims his admonitions at the wealthy businessmen of the Christian community. It is hard to establish how wealthy they are. As mentioned in chapter 3, it is probable that these rich merchants are between categories ES_4 and ES_5 in Longenecker's scale. Many scholars think that these wealthy merchants are non-Christians.[2] Blomberg and Kamell summarize the main points of that argument as follows:

1. These themes are developed later, when analyzing the co-text of 4:13–17.

2. See, e.g., Dale C. Allison, *A Critical and Exegetical Commentary on the Epistle of James*, ICC (New York: Bloomsbury, 2013), 647–8; David H. Edgar, *Has God Not Chosen the Poor? The Social Setting of the Epistle of James*, JSNTSup 206 (Sheffield: Sheffield Academic, 2001), 198–9; Patrick J. Hartin, *James*, SP 14 (Collegeville, Minn.: Liturgical Press, 2003), 232; Sophie S. Laws, *A Commentary on the Epistle of James*, BNTC 16 (San Francisco: Harper & Row, 1980), 190;

> (1) "Come now" (ἄγε νῦν)... definitely brusque and not a friendly greeting; (2) "we will do business" (ἐμπορευσόμεθα) elsewhere in the NT... only in 2 Pe 2:3, where it means to cheat or deceive;... (3) the bulk of trading and commercial activities... limited to the native aristocracy of large landowners (thus linking this group in 4:13–17 to the group in 5:1–6);... (4) the repetition of "Come now" in 5:1, more clearly addressed to absent unbelievers (by the literary device of apostrophe); (5) the lack of any reference to "brothers" or "sisters" (fellow Christians);... (6) the profit motive of the ungodly plans.[3]

However, James seems to reserve the word πλούσιοι to refer to the wicked rich (1:10–11, 2:6, 5:1). He does not use this word to depict these merchants. Furthermore, James assumes these addressees have several Christian ideals: (1) they see life from a Christian perspective (2:14), (2) they include the Lord in their plans (4:15), (3) they know what they ought to do (4:17), and (4) they agree with James's Christian perception of the concepts of "arrogance" and "sin."[4] Furthermore, there is early testimony of wealthy Christians, such as Chloe (1 Cor 1:11) and Lydia (Acts 16:14), who were merchants. It is not necessary to have a large group of these people in order to address them. The wealthy were very influential in the life of any community. In this case, their example could be a bad model for the rest of the congregation. That is reason enough to move James to deal with their arrogance. Also, the word group ἐμπορεύομαι/ἐμπόρος refers to merchants and their activity of buying and selling (cf. Matt 22:5; Gen 34:10, 42:34; 2 Chr 9:14; Ezek 27:13; Plato, *Lg.* 952e; *Ep.* 7, 8; Thucydides, *Hist.* 7.13). Even though in 2 Peter 2:3 (the other occurrence of the verb in the NT) the verb is used metaphorically, its literal meaning is well attested. Finally, although both 4:13–17 and 5:1–6 begin the same, the tone of the latter is harsher than that of the former and their focus and content are different (as shown later). For these reasons, it is likely that James focuses on two different groups: in 4:13–17, he emphasizes the wealthy Christians; in 5:1–6, he highlights the sin of the wicked rich.[5]

Pedrito U. Maynard-Reid, *Poverty and Wealth in James* (Eugene, Ore.: Wipf & Stock, 1987, 2004), 70–5; Scot McKnight, *The Letter of James*, NICNT (Grand Rapids, Mich.: Eerdmans, 2011), 369.

3. Craig L. Blomberg and Mariam J. Kamell, *James*, ZECNT 16 (Grand Rapids, Mich.: Zondervan, 2008), 206 n. 8.

4. McKnight, *James*, 369; Douglas J. Moo, *The Letter of James*, PNTC (Grand Rapids, Mich.: Eerdmans, 2000), 201.

5. For supporters of this view, see, e.g., James B. Adamson, *The Epistle of James*, NICNT (Grand Rapids, Mich.: Eerdmans, 1976), 180; Blomberg and Kamell, *James*, 206–11; William F. Brosend II, *James and Jude*, NCBC (Cambridge: Cambridge University Press, 2004), 126; Peter H. Davids, *The Epistle of James: A Commentary on the Greek Text*, NIGTC (Grand Rapids, Mich.: Eerdmans, 1982), 171; Simon J. Kistemaker, *Exposition of James and the Epistles of John*, BNTC (Grand Rapids, Mich.: Baker, 1986), 146; Moo, *James*, 201; Joseph B. Mayor, *The Epistle of St. James: The Greek Text with Introduction, Notes, and Comments*, 2nd ed. (London: Macmillan, 1897), 153.

In issuing these admonitions, James manages to address the problem of arrogance that seems to be present in other segments of the congregation as well. Next, study of the use of the OT in 4:13–17 will show that James uses the OT interpretively to reinforce his teaching.

Establishment of the Text

This pericope has several textual issues. In v. 13, some manuscripts changed the strongly supported reading σήμερον ἢ αὔριον to the more common σήμερον καὶ αὔριον. The former is preferred.[6] It is probable that some copyists changed the conjunction to conform the text to a more frequent phrase. Another problem in this verse is the change of the future tense to the aorist subjunctive in the verbs πορευσόμεθα, ποιήσομεν, ἐμπορευσόμεθα, and κερδήσομεν.[7] The same change appears in 4:15 (ζήσωμεν and ποιησώμεθα instead of ζήσομεν and ποιησόμεθα respectively). The future indicative is the most probable reading.

In v. 14, there are three main issues. The first is the presence or absence of the neuter article in the syntagma τὸ τῆς αὔριον. The inclusion of the article is well supported.[8] Another difficult problem is the inclusion or exclusion of γάρ in ποία ἡ ζωὴ ὑμῶν. Its inclusion turns the phrase into an independent question: ποία γὰρ ἡ ζωὴ ὑμῶν; However, the omission of γάρ is

6. A, P, 307, 442, 642, 1175, 1243, 1448, 1611, 1852, 2492, Byz, the Syriac versions, some MSS of the Bohairic version, Jerome, and Cyril of Alexandria read σήμερον καὶ αὔριον. However, there is strong support of σήμερον ἢ αὔριον. The papyrus P74, ℵ, B, Ψ, 5, 33, 81, 436, 1735, 1739, 2344, the Latin tradition, syp, and the Coptic versions support the disjunctive conjunction. As Allison mentions, the expression σήμερον καὶ αὔριον is common. He mentions Exod 19:10 (LXX); 2 Kgdms 11:12; Sir 10:10; Luke 12:28, 13:32, 33. Allison, *James*, 653 n. 62.

7. Several manuscripts (mainly A, Ψ, 5, 33, 81, and Byz) include the aorist subjunctive πορευσώμεθα, ποιήσωμεν, ἐμπορευσώμεθα, and κερδήσωμεν, instead of the verbs πορευσόμεθα, ποιήσομεν, ἐμπορευσόμεθα, and κερδήσομεν, all of them in future indicative (4:13). The future indicative is supported by important Alexandrian testimony (mainly p100, ℵ, A, B, P) and some ancient versions. Allison points out: "One guesses ο was misheard as ω [in πορευσόμεθα] or vice versa and that scribes then assimilated the tenses of the other verbs." Ibid. For Dibelius, "it seems obvious that all the subjunctives are due to recension." Martin Dibelius, *James: A Commentary on the Epistle of James* (Philadelphia: Fortress, 1976), 232 n. 10. Comfort comments: "[I]t appears that the changes in verb tense (from future indicative to aorist subjunctive) were done so as to emphasize that the businessmen's plans were tentative." He thinks "the businessmen were making definite plans for the future. And this is what troubled James and led to his admonition." Philip W. Comfort, *New Testament Text and Translation Commentary: Commentary on the Variant Readings of the Ancient New Testament Manuscripts and How They Relate to the Major English Translations* (Carol Stream, Ill.: Tyndale House, 2008), 731.

8. B omits the article. A, P, 33, 81, and few others read the plural neuter τά. The inclusion of the neuter singular is well supported by Alexandrian and Byzantine traditions (ℵ, Ψ, 5, 307, 436, 442, 642, 173, Byz, ff, vg, and Jerome). As Metzger points out, the plural neuter "though supported by several good witnesses . . . is suspect as a scribal assimilation to Pr 27:1." Bruce M. Metzger, *A Textual Commentary on the Greek New Testament*, 2nd ed. (Stuttgart: Deutsche Bibelgesellschaft, 1994), 613.

the best reading.[9] The third problem revolves around the beginning of the last segment of the verse: ἀτμὶς γάρ ἐστε ἡ πρὸς ὀλίγον φαινομένη, ἔπειτα καὶ ἀφανιζομένη. א omits the first three words. Some manuscripts change the tense and person of ἐστε. Some include the article before ἀτμὶς. It is hard to decide the most probable reading. Here, NA^{28} is followed.[10] Minor variants appear in vv. 16–17. So, the text under study is the following:

> 13 ἄγε νῦν οἱ λέγοντες· σήμερον ἢ αὔριον πορευσόμεθα εἰς τήνδε τὴν πόλιν καὶ
> ποιήσομεν ἐκεῖ ἐνιαυτὸν καὶ ἐμπορευσόμεθα καὶ κερδήσομεν· 14 οἵτινες οὐκ
> ἐπίστασθε τὸ τῆς αὔριον ποία ἡ ζωὴ ὑμῶν· ἀτμὶς γάρ ἐστε ἡ πρὸς ὀλίγον φαινομένη,
> ἔπειτα καὶ ἀφανιζομένη. 15 ἀντὶ τοῦ λέγειν ὑμᾶς· ἐὰν ὁ κύριος θελήσῃ καὶ ζήσομεν
> καὶ ποιήσομεν τοῦτο ἢ ἐκεῖνο. 16 νῦν δὲ καυχᾶσθε ἐν ταῖς ἀλαζονείαις ὑμῶν· πᾶσα
> καύχησις τοιαύτη πονηρά ἐστιν. 17 εἰδότι οὖν καλὸν ποιεῖν καὶ μὴ ποιοῦντι, ἁμαρτία
> αὐτῷ ἐστιν.

Elucidation of the Co-text

As in the rest of the epistle, scholars differ in how they locate this text in James's discourse. In Osborne's outline, James 4:13–5:11 is the fifth main point, "Admonitions to the Worldly and the Godly." He divides the section into three main paragraphs: 4:13–17, 5:1–6, entitled "Warnings to the Worldly," and 5:7–11, "Challenges to the Believers–Patience in Suffering."[11]

9. Important manuscripts include the conjunction (p74, p100, א^{2}, A, P, Ψ, 5, 33, 81, Byz, vg, syp, bo). A few omit it (א*, B, 1448, 1611, 1852, l, syh, bo mss). Metzger points out: "[T]he connective appears to have been inserted (perhaps under the influence of the following clause) in order to prevent ambiguity." Metzger, *A Textual Commentary*, 613. In the same vein, Comfort thinks the inclusion is "an editorial fix intended to relieve ambiguity or perceived anacoluthon, both created by the word ποία ('what')." He explains that this word may modify the verb ἐπίστασθε ("you do not know what will be tomorrow, what your life will be like") or as a feminine form of ποίος may modify the syntagma ἡ ζωὴ ὑμῶν (as an apposition: "you have not knowledge of tomorrow—what your life will be"). Comfort, *New Testament Text*, 731–2.

10. Several manuscripts read the future singular ἔσται (A, P, Ψ, 307, 436, 442, 1448, 1611, and Byz^{pt}). Few manuscripts read the present singular ἔστιν (Byz^{pt}, sa, and bo mss). Few manuscripts support the text of NA^{28} (B, 81, 642, 1175, 1243, 1739, 1852, 2492, syh, and Jerome). Comfort thinks it is more probable that "the article ἡ was added to introduce the following expression as an appositive, rather than deleted." He prefers the WH edition. Comfort, *New Testament Text*, 732. For including the article, Metzger points out: "Although several important witnesses (including B and 1739) lack the article, the Committee considered it more probable that scribes would have accidentally omitted ἡ than added it." Metzger, *A Textual Commentary*, 613. In any case, Blomberg and Kamell point out: "[T]he presence or lack of the article does not change the meaning." Regarding the third person of the verb, they comment that this "was more likely to be introduced by a copyist after interpreting the previous clause as a question." Blomberg and Kamell, *James*, 208 n. 14. For Martin, no one of the variants has sufficient evidence to challenge the reading ἀτμὶς γάρ ἐστε. Ralph P. Martin, *James*, WBC 48 (Waco, Tex.: Word Books, 1988), 158.

11. Grant R. Osborne, "James," in *James, 1–2 Peter, Jude, Revelation*, CBC 18 (Carol Stream, Ill.: Tyndale House, 2011), 18. Vouga similarly divides 4:13–17; 5:1–6; 5:7–11. François Vouga, *L'épître de saint Jacques*, CNT XIIIa (Geneva: Labor et Fides, 1984), 20.

Sophie Laws splits it into two groups: 4:13–17 and 5:1–11.[12] Blomberg and Kamell divide the section into two groups as well: 14:13–17 and 5:1–12.[13] Many others separate 4:13–5:6 into one section and consider 5:7–11 as part of the final section or as part of the closing statements.[14] Here, in our outline, 4:13–5:11 is considered a unit that proposes that "the daily Christian life should reflect a correct attitude toward wealth." It is subdivided into three related segments focused on merchants' arrogance (4:13–17), farmers' sin (5:1–6), and Christian patient endurance (5:7–11).

Although there is no agreement on the outline, scholars agree that this section exhibits thematic connections with earlier sections of the letter. James intertwines key themes presented in earlier parts of his letter by resuming and advancing those themes. The main links are poverty and wealth, speech control, and arrogance.

Poverty and Wealth

As the previous chapters in the present work show, the first explicit mention of the issue of poverty and wealth is in 1:9–11. James presents "the correct boast" of both the humble brother and the wealthy. In an eschatological reversal, James calls on the humble to boast in their imminent exaltation (1:9). Conversely, he warns the wealthy about their imminent humiliation. He invites them to boast in their humiliation (1:10–11). He builds his calling upon Isaiah 40:6–7 (LXX), emphasizing the ephemeral life of the rich. Now, in 4:13–17, he resumes both themes of boasting and the ephemeral life to warn the Christian merchants about their sinful boasting.

Next, there is a shift in focus. In 1:26–2:26, James focuses on the correct attitude every Christian should have toward the poor. In 4:13–5:6, he focuses on the sinful actions and attitudes of the wealthy. In 1:26–27, James urges the main group of addressees to consider their responsibility to visit orphans and widows as an integral part of their worship of God. In 2:1–26, he focuses on how true faith should look. This faith in the glorious Lord Jesus Christ should be without discrimination against the poor (2:1–13). In 2:5, James points out that Christians should honor the poor as God does. He has chosen them to be heirs of his kingdom. Discrimination against the poor is a clear violation of the love command, and as heinous as adultery or murder (2:8–11). In 5:1–6,

12. Laws, *James*, 189, 94.

13. Blomberg and Kamell, *James*, 26.

14. Davids, *James*, 28–9; George H. Guthrie, "James," in *The Expositor's Bible Commentary: Hebrews-Revelation*, ed. Tremper Longman III and David E. Garland, EBC (Grand Rapids, Mich.: Zondervan, 2006), 206–7; Hartin, *James*; Dan G. McCartney, *James*, BECNT (Grand Rapids, Mich.: Baker, 2009); Wiard Popkes, *Der Brief des Jakobus*, THKNT 14 (Leipzig: Evangelische Verlagsanstalt, 2001), IX-X; Mark E. Taylor, *A Textlinguistic Investigation into the Discourse Structure of James*, LNTS 311 (New York: T&T Clark, 2006), ix. McCartney includes 5:7–11 in a fourth discourse (5:7–18). McCartney, *James*, 67. For other outlines, see Martin, *James*, c-cii; McKnight, *James*, 50–5.

James confronts the actions and attitudes of the impious wealthy against the poor. In 2:6–7, the wealthy drag Christians into human tribunals. In 5:1–6, the wealthy appear in God's tribunal.

Furthermore, James emphasizes that a genuine faith performs good deeds (2:14–26). In particular, he mentions merciful deeds toward brothers and sisters in need in the community (2:14–17). It is not enough to know essential creeds; a genuine faith is accompanied by deeds (2:19). Now, in 4:13–17, he resumes this idea by insisting that if someone knows the good he/she ought to do and doesn't do it, he/she sins (4:17).

Human Speech

Another precursor theme of this section is the control of one's speech.[15] James begins the theme in 1:19. Everyone should be quick to listen but slow to speak. In 1:26, the correct use of one's tongue is part of a pure and undefiled religion before God the Father. A person who does not control his tongue, James says, has a vain religion (1:26). James fully develops the theme in 3:1–12.[16] He begins his discourse with a warning to those who want to be teachers (3:1). He recognizes that all people have problems with the control of their own speech (3:2–3). Control of speech permits the control of the whole body, James says; however, an uncontrolled tongue is tremendously dangerous (3:4–6). He echoes language of the creation narrative to emphasize that even though human beings are able to control nature, the tongue is untamable (3:7–8). With their tongue, people could bless God instead of insulting other human beings (3:9–12). Speech control comes from the correct source of wisdom. James presents two types of wisdom: earthly wisdom and heavenly wisdom (3:13–18).[17] Human attitudes and actions reflect one of them.

15. Some scholars see the control of one's speech as the unifier theme of this section from 3:1 to 5:6. See, e.g., Martin, *James*, 159; Moo, *James*, 200; Taylor, *Discourse Structure of James*, 117. McKnight sees the tongue and teachers as the unifier theme but just from 3:1 to 4:12. He sees 4:13–5:11 as another section centered on wealth. McKnight, *James*, 264–8, 318–21, 58–60, 66–67. Guthrie sees a similar progression. However, he is right in the transitional role 4:11–12 plays. In one way, this paragraph closes the section 3:1–4:12, which is centered on speech control. At the same time, 4:11–12 anticipates God's judgment on the wicked rich (5:1–6) and echoes the themes presented in 2:12–13. Guthrie, "James," 257.

16. For a good analysis of the section, see Dale C. Allison, Jr., "Blessing God and Cursing People: James 3:9–10," *JBL* 130 (2011): 397–405; Allison, *James*, 509–60; William R. Baker, *Personal Speech-Ethics in the Epistle of James*, WUNT 68 (Tübingen: J. C. B. Mohr, 1995), 123–34; Pheme Perkins, "James 3:16–4:3," *Int* 36 (1982): 283–7; Huub van de Sandt, "James 4,1–4 in the Light of the Jewish Two Ways Tradition 3,1–6," *Bib* 88 (2007): 38–63; Leif E. Vaage, "Cuídate la boca: La palabra indicada, una subjetividad alternativa y la formación social de los primeros cristianos según Santiago (3,1–4,17)," *RIBLA* 31 (1998): 110–21; Duane F. Watson, "The Rhetoric of James 3:1–12 and a Classical Pattern of Argumentation," *NovT* 35 (1993): 48–64.

17. See a good discussion on wisdom in James in William R. Baker, "Searching for the Holy Spirit in the Epistle of James: Is 'Wisdom' Equivalent?," *TynBul* 59 (2008): 293–315; Richard Bauckham, *James: Wisdom of James, Disciple of Jesus the Sage* (London: Routledge, 1999);

Contrary to what wisdom from heaven evidences in human relationships, the addressees manifest interpersonal problems that reflect earthly wisdom (4:1–3). They have adopted a worldly standard instead of friendship with God (4:4–5). James calls them to repentance, to be humble before God (4:6–10). In 4:11–12, he warns those who speak against their brothers and sisters. Now, in 4:13–17, James criticizes "those who say" (4:13). What they say reflects their arrogance (4:16). Instead, they "should say" what reflects humbleness before God (4:15).

Arrogance

The theme of arrogance is not present in the first two chapters of the letter. James, however, develops it from the theme of the use and abuse of human speech.[18] In 3:1–12, James presents the dangers of uncontrolled speech. One characteristic of the personified tongue in 3:5 is that it makes great boasts. Quarrels and fights among James's addressees reflect a problem of pride (4:1–3).[19] Quoting Proverbs 3:34, James emphasizes that God resists and opposes the proud. He calls his addressees to repentance and humility before God

Bauckham, "The Wisdom of James and the Wisdom of Jesus," in *The Catholic Epistles and the Tradition*, ed. J. Schlosser, BETL 176 (Leuven: Leuven University Press, 2004), 75–92; John A. Burns, "James, the Wisdom of Jesus," *CTR* 1 (1986): 113–35; Robert F. Chaffin, Jr., "The Theme of Wisdom in the Epistle of James," *ATJ* 29 (1997): 23–49; Cain Hope Felder, "Wisdom, Law, and Social Concern in the Epistle of James" (Ph.D. diss., Columbia University, 1982); Donald E. Gowan, "Wisdom and Endurance in James," *HBT* 15 (1993): 145–53; Matt A. Jackson-McCabe, "A Letter to the Twelve Tribes in the Diaspora: Wisdom and 'Apocalyptic' Eschatology in the Letter of James," *SBLSP* 35 (1996): 504–17; Mariam J. Kamell, "The Soteriology of James in Light of Earlier Jewish Wisdom Literature and the Gospel of Matthew" (Ph.D. diss., University of Saint Andrews, 2010); Darian Lockett, "The Spectrum of Wisdom and Eschatology in the Epistle of James and 4QInstruction," *TynBul* 56 (2005): 131–48; Dan G. McCartney, "The Wisdom of James the Just," *SBJT* 4.3 (2000): 52–64; Christopher W. Morgan, *A Theology of James: Wisdom for God's People*, EBT (Phillipsburg, N.J.: P&R, 2010); David W. Perkins, "The Wisdom We Need: James 1:5–8, 3:13–18," *ThEd* 34 (1986): 12–25.

18. Some scholars think this is the unifying theme of 4:11–5:6. See, e.g., Luke Timothy Johnson, *The Letter of James: A New Translation with Introduction and Commentary*, AB 37A (New Haven: Yale University Press, 1995), 291–2; Laws, *James*, 211–2; Robert W. Wall, *Community of the Wise: The Letter of James*, NTC (Valley Forge, Pa.: Trinity, 1997), 189. Even though this is an important theme in this section, and in effect it gives some cohesion, poverty and wealth is a stronger theme in 4:13–5:11. Hubert Frankemölle, *Der Brief des Jakobus, Kapitel 2–5*, GTB 518 (Gütersloh: Echter, 1994), 234–6.

19. For an analysis of James 4 besides the commentaries on James, see Baker, *Personal Speech-Ethics*, 222–48; William L. Blevins, "A Call to Repent, Love Others, and Remember God: James 4," *RevExp* 83 (1986): 419–26; C. B. Carpenter, "James 4.5 Reconsidered," *NTS* 47 (2001): 189–205; Mark E. Gaskins, "Looking to the Future: James 4:13–5:11," *RevExp* 97 (2000): 237–42; J. William Johnston, "James 4:5 and the Jealous Spirit," *BibSac* 170.679 (2013): 344–60; Sophie S. Laws, "Does Scripture Speak in Vain? A Reconsideration of James 4:5," *NTS* 20 (1974): 210–5; Perkins, "James 3:16–4:3," 283–7; Sandt, "James 4,1–4," 38–63; John J. Schmitt, "You Adulteresses! The Image in James 4:4," *NovT* 28 (1986): 327–37; Thomas C. Urrey, "An Exposition of James 4," *SJT* 29 (1986): 37–42.

(4:7–10). One action that evidences this arrogance is their καταλαλία (4:13). This slander or bad speech against one another evidences the attitude of judgment that some addressees have when speaking against their brothers and sisters (4:11). With these actions, says James, they usurp God's role as judge (4:12). Another example of arrogance is the attitude of Christian merchants who make plans without taking God seriously in their lives (4:13–17). A third example of arrogance is the hedonist life of the impious wealthy, which James more strongly condemns in 5:1–6. Mark Taylor identifies two types of arrogance in these paragraphs: arrogant presumption (4:13–17) and arrogant oppression (5:1–6).[20] So the theme of arrogance is an important thread in the fabric of this epistle.

Other Connections

Other minor themes are repeated as well. Some scholars see continuity in the issue of friendship with the world/worldly disposition.[21] Also, the tension of knowing versus doing in 4:17 recalls the discussion of a real faith in 2:1–26 and the exhortation to be doers of the word (1:22–25). In the same vein, there is a development of the concept of ἁμαρτία. In 1:15, James points out that sin has its origin in human desires, and consummated sin gives birth to death. Discrimination against the poor is one type of sin; it is a clear violation of the law (2:9). In 4:17, James goes a step further by saying that omission of doing good is also sin.

Finally, there are a couple of contrasts between 4:1–12 and 4:13–5:6. In 4:9, James calls grieving, mourning, and wailing signals of repentance. In 5:1, weeping and wailing are symbols of the inevitability of punishment for the wicked wealthy. In 4:8, James calls for a cleansing of the heart. In 5:5, the wicked rich have fattened their hearts for the day of slaughter.

Description of the General Cognitive Environment

James 4:13–17 assumes some knowledge of first-century commerce. James also uses some common metaphors in this section. So, it is necessary to explore these issues before analyzing the text. The discussion turns next to some information about businessmen and traders and presents a couple of metaphors.

Businessmen and Traders

William Brosend finds a similarity with a model business plan in the text of 4:13–17. The text includes (1) a time frame (today or tomorrow), (2) a travel plan (we will go), (3) a destination (such and such city), (4) a duration (spend

20. Taylor, *Discourse Structure of James*, 117.

21. Dibelius, *James*, 230; Hartin, *James*, 223; Popkes, *Der Brief des Jakobus*, 238–43.

a year there), (5) an activity (doing business), and (6) a goal (making money).[22] This characteristic of the text illustrates that James assumes that his readers/hearers would be acquainted with this type of businessman (i.e., traveling trader, merchant, etc.), and some of his audience might even be described as such a businessman (2:15, ἀντὶ τοῦ λέγειν ὑμᾶς).

James provides a general description of traveling traders.[23] Traveling traders used the numerous roads and shipping lanes of the Roman world to do business.[24] They could take advantage of these intricate commercial routes to plan their business.[25] Maritime and land routes were safer and faster in Roman times than before.[26] Nevertheless, the unpredictability of travel and multiple variables, such as security, illness, and weather, made it difficult to precisely determine business plans (cf. Acts 27–28).

Common Metaphors

In 4:14, James uses two images common in the Jewish and Greco-Roman world in the first century. The first is in the sentence οἵτινες οὐκ ἐπίστασθε τὸ τῆς αὔριον. The expression τὸ τῆς αὔριον depicts the uncertainty and fragility of life. Johnson comments that "the sentiment concerning the fragility and uncertainty of life is a commonplace in moral literature." He quotes Plutarch, *A Letter to Apollonius* 11; Marcus Aurelius, *Meditations* 11, 17; Seneca, *To Marcia on Consolation* 10:1–5; and *On the Shortness of Life* 1:1–4, 9:1–10:1. The theme is also common in the LXX (Prov 16:9, 27:1; Sir 11:18–19).[27] Popkes also finds this idea in Pseudo-Phocylides 116–20 and Philo, *Legatio ad Gaium* 3:226–27. For him, James works with a cultural commonplace.[28]

The second expression is the metaphor ἀτμίς. McKnight highlights that "[a]grarian cultures watch the weather, and few things are as noticeable as vaporous clouds that bring no rain. These puffs of mist appear for a while

22. Brosend, *James and Jude*, 126.

23. Matthias Ahrens, *Der Realitäten Widerschein oder Arm und Reich im Jakobusbrief: Eine sozialgeschichtliche Untersuchung*, AH (Berlin: Alektor-Verlag, 1995), 122–4.

24. Allison, *James*, 653.

25. Maynard-Reid, *Poverty and Wealth*, 71. Malina argues that the practices of merchants were considered a type of usury. The merchant, as the lender and the tax collector, was considered an impious. Bruce J. Malina, *El mundo del Nuevo Testamento: Perspectivas desde la antropología cultural*, Αγορα 1 (Navarra: Verbo Divino, 1995), 131–2. However, James does not point out this problem. He highlights the arrogance of their planning.

26. Maynard-Reid, *Poverty and Wealth*, 73. In this regard, Edd Noell argues: "The extent to which market exchange became dominant in first-century Palestine under Roman rule is suggested by research pointing to growing intra-regional and inter-regional market trade." Edd S. Noell, "A 'Marketless World'? An Examination of Wealth and Exchange in the Gospels and First-Century Palestine," *JMM* 10 (2007): 93.

27. Johnson, *James*, 296.

28. Popkes, *Der Brief des Jakobus*, 290. Allison also mentions Instruction of Amen-em-Opet 19:11–13; the Eloquent Pesant 183; b.Sanh. 100b; Philodemus, *Mort.* 37:26–27; Seneca, *Ep.* 101:4–5; and Stobaeus, *Ecl.* 4:41 as examples that the uncertainty of the future is "a common place of all wisdom literature." Allison, *James*, 655–6.

and then disappear."[29] The idea of mist or smoke suggests transitoriness and lack of solidity (cf. Hos 13:3; Wis 2:4–5). "It is a fitting symbol of human temporality and frailty: such a column never lasts for long."[30] Johnson points out that "in Jewish apocalyptic literature, the wicked are compared to a mist or smoke that will disappear (see 4 Ezra 7:61; 2 Bar. 82:3; 1 En. 97:8–10; 1QM 15:10)." It is also used in Christian literature as "a symbol of nothingness" (1 Clem. 17:6).[31]

Identification of Possible OT Texts and Traditions Evoked

Some scholars see an allusion to Proverbs 27:1 (LXX) in James 4:14.[32] The verse has several textual variants, as shown above. Scribal changes in the neuter article in the syntagma τὸ τῆς αὔριον in 4:14 suggest that at least some copyists seemed to conform James's words to Proverbs 27:1 by changing τό to τά.[33] Other manuscripts omit the article. The text of Proverbs 27:1 (LXX) reads: μὴ καυχῶ τὰ εἰς αὔριον, οὐ γὰρ γινώσκεις τί τέξεται ἡ ἐπιοῦσα.

Hays's four criteria could help to determine the probability of James's intentionality: (1) availability, (2) volume, (3) recurrence, and (4) thematic coherence. Regarding availability, James directly quotes Proverbs 3:34 (LXX) in 4:6. Johnson thinks that "the influence of the original context of Prov 3:34 can be found throughout James 3:13–4:6."[34] James also contains an allusion to Proverbs 10:12 in 5:20 (also alluded to in 1 Pe 4:8). So, it is highly probable that Proverbs 27 is part of James's and his addressees' shared encyclopedic knowledge. Regarding volume, James 4:14 and Proverbs 27:1 (LXX) share just one word: αὔριον. So, although there seems to be a thematic relationship,

29. McKnight, *James*, 373.

30. Allison, *James*, 657. Blomberg and Kamell points out that mist "was a prevalent OT metaphor for the transitory, drawn from the world of nature (along with others like grass, shadow, cloud, and smoke)." Blomberg and Kamell, *James*, 208.

31. Johnson, *James*, 296. See also Popkes, *Der Brief des Jakobus*, 290. Allison offers a long list of examples of biblical and extrabiblical uses of this metaphor of "world-wide wisdom." Allison, *James*, 657.

32. Arnold G. Fruchtenbaum, *The Messianic Jewish Epistles: Hebrews, James, First Peter, Second Peter, Jude*, ABC, 1st ed. (Tustin, Calif.: Ariel Ministries, 2005), 296; David A. Jones, *Old Testament Quotations and Allusions in the New Testament*, (Bellingham, Wash.: Logos Research Systems, 2009), Logos edition, Proverbs, "chapter 27"; C. Jeanne Orjala Serrão, *James: A Commentary in the Wesleyan Tradition*, NBBC (Kansas City: Beacon Hill, 2010), 155. Commenting on this textual variant, Allison considers that the change here "may mark assimilation to LXX Prov 27:1." But he is conscious of the plural also in Luke 20:25; Rom 14:19; 2 Cor 11:30. Allison, *James*, 655 n. 81. On his part, Dibelius points out that the catenae and scholia adduce Prov 27:1 in this context. Dibelius, *James*, 232 n. 14. Robert Wall argues that Ecclesiastes's use of ἀτμίς "informs the merchant illustration in James." However, he builds his case on a weak basis. He thinks that the use of the masculine form ἀτμός in a variant reading of Eccl 9:9 (LXX) (B and Aquila) justifies his inference that James is thinking of the concept of "vanity." Wall, *Community of the Wise*, 220–1.

33. Metzger, *A Textual Commentary*, 613.

34. Johnson, *James*, 33.

the volume is low. As a result, based on the criterion of volume, the probability that James wants his readers/hearers to make the connections is low. Regarding recurrence, although James quotes Proverbs, his language is close to wisdom tradition. As Johnson says, "James's appropriation of the wisdom tradition needs little demonstration."[35] So, it is hard to know, from this perspective, whether James is consciously evoking this passage in particular or if he is using "wisdom language." Finally, regarding thematic coherence, Proverbs 27:1 fits well in James's criticism. James points out the problem of arrogant planning, which does not take God into account. James mentions the same uncertainty of tomorrow and life in general. However, although James is in the same vein as Proverbs 27:1, it is not possible to discern with Hays's criteria if he wants his readers/hearers to make the connection.

As shown above, the image of mist/smoke and the concept of transitoriness are so spread out that the cognitive benefits obtained by making the connection with Proverbs 27:1 (LXX) are almost the same as not making it at all, while the processing effort in making the connection is higher. So, in RT terms, it is less relevant making the connection than not doing so. In a similar way, as is observed in the use of the OT in James 1:26–27, one could at least infer that biblical content is embedded in James's language.

Interpretation of the Text in James

In order to interpret the text of 4:13–17, it is necessary to perform several tasks at the level of explicature. The text of 4:13–14 is problematic, as the numerous textual variants reveal. The paragraph begins with the expression ἄγε νῦν (4:13, 5:1). The expression is a constraint on implicatures in the entire paragraph.[36] Hart and Hart call the phrase "a *prominence orienter*. . . . It implies disapproval and marks the transition to a new step in the discourse."[37] Allison calls it "an insistent . . . brusque address with scoffing tone." It is attested in Greco-Roman literature. It is equivalent to the Hebrew לכו־נא (cf. Isa 1:18).[38] So, with this phrase James shows disapproval. What James disapproves of is not what a person says, but what his/her saying implies.

James addresses his criticism to "those who say today or tomorrow we will go into such and such city and stay/spend a year there and trade, and make a profit." As mentioned above, these verbs depict businessmen's planning. The use of "today or tomorrow" and the verbs in the future indicative imply

35. Ibid.

36. For procedural meaning and procedural/lexical meaning distinction, see Diane Blakemore, *Relevance and Linguistic Meaning: The Semantics and Pragmatics of Discourse Markers*, CSL 99 (Cambridge: Cambridge University Press, 2002).

37. George Hart and Helen Hart, *A Semantic and Structural Analysis of James*, SSA (Dallas: SIL International, 2001), 127.

38. Allison, *James*, 651; contra Dibelius, who thinks that ἄγε begins a rhetorical question; Dibelius, *James*, 231.

clarity regarding the future.[39] A sequence of implicatures of this might be the following:

1. A person who makes such an assertion has complete clarity regarding the future.
2. A person who makes such an assertion has clear confidence in his/her plans.[40]
3. Someone who says "today or tomorrow" will do something, but he/she has not decided yet when he/she will do it. Only he/she decides, and no one else will decide when he/she will go, and he/she has not yet decided.[41]
4. Someone who says "today or tomorrow" is looking for what is better for business.[42]
5. Someone who describes in detail what he/she will do in a whole year shows overconfidence in him/herself and overconfidence in the predictability of external circumstances.

James criticizes this overconfidence. Through an anacoluthon in vv. 13–14,[43] he shows that this overconfidence is based upon incorrect assumptions about life. The pronoun οἵτινες refers to those businessmen who make plans with such confidence. Hartin understands it as "of such a nature," and translates: "You are people of such a nature who do not know what will happen tomorrow."[44] The adverb αὔριον comes from v. 13, so, "here James turns the words of the merchants against themselves: they do not know what they think they know."[45] They do not know what will happen tomorrow. There is some irony; they are planning a year, but they do not even know the day after. Davids synthesizes vv. 13–14: "Come now, you who make plans—you don't even understand how little control you have over life itself."[46] So, in vv. 13–14, James, at the level of explicatures says:

1. Come now! You who [arrogantly] say "today or tomorrow we will go into such and such city and we will spend a year there and we will

39. In this regard, Osborne points out: "The future tenses demonstrate their absolute assurance that their infallible itineraries will work." Osborne, "James," 96.

40. Ibid.

41. Allison, *James*, 653.

42. Elsa Tamez, *No discriminen a los pobres: Lectura latinoamericana de la carta de Santiago* (Estella: Verbo Divino, 2008), 93.

43. The vocative is explicit: "those who say." However, there is no main verb. So, one solution is to consider the relative pronoun in v. 14 in apposition to οἱ λέγοντες, the main verb as ἐπίστασθε, and the subject implicit.

44. Hartin, *James*, 224. Moo paraphrases the idea: "How can you, being the kind of creatures that you are, presume to dictate the course of future events?" Moo, *James*, 203.

45. Allison, *James*, 655.

46. Davids, *James*, 172.

> trade, and we will make a profit," [ironically] such persons, you do not know about tomorrow–what your life will be. For you are a mist which appears for a little while, and then disappears.

In his confrontation of the wealthy merchants' attitude, James presents to them the uncertainty of the future and the fragility of life. In doing that, he uses language that could guide his addressees toward the OT. However, as shown above, the connections are weak. Maybe an echo of a passage such as Proverbs 27:1 (LXX) could be present. Nevertheless, the processing effort to make the connections does not result in much cognitive effect. In fact, the metaphor is common in the OT and in Second Temple and Greco-Roman literature.[47] The idea that life is as ephemeral as smoke is common in the Psalter (Pss 37:20, 39:11, 90:10, 102:3) and other OT texts (1 Chr 19:15; Hos 13:3). In Second Temple literature, the metaphor depicts the transience of life (1 En. 108:9; Wis 2:2–5). But it is also associated with eschatological punishment (4 Ezra 7:61; 2 Bar. 82:3, 6; 1 En. 97:8–10; 1QM 15:10). So, it is highly probable that James and his addressees could derive cognitive effects via weak implicatures without making the connection to any specific OT text. In this case, some implicatures might be the following:

2. Nobody knows what will happen tomorrow.
3. Nobody knows what his/her life will be like tomorrow.
4. Someone who plans, as if he/she knows the future, is arrogant.

Also, if James intends his addressees to make the connection with Proverbs 27:1 [LXX] (or some similar text), other implicatures might be these:

5. The Scriptures teach that this kind of person is arrogant.
6. The Scriptures teach not to make such an assertion.
7. James teaches what the Scriptures say.

The reason James gives for not making those overconfident statements echoes his first warning to the wealthy in 1:10–11. James 1:9–11 is salient in the discourse. So, when his addressees read/hear the metaphor of the ephemeral mist, they could make the connections with the ephemeral grass. In that case, some implicatures could associate brevity with God's punishment and with the eschatological reversal. As Allison points out, James presents a similar idea in 1:10–11 but using a different metaphor.[48] In contrast to these arrogant merchants, James knows the imminent future. Allison adds: "He [James] knows what tomorrow will bring—'the coming of the Lord'

47. Allison, *James*, 657; Johnson, *James*, 296.
48. Allison, *James*, 657. See also Tamez, *No discriminen a los pobres*, 93–4.

(5:7), the judgment (4:12; 5:9), punishment (3:6; 5:1–3), reward (1:12)."[49] One difference in the impact of this last metaphor, points out Krüger, is that the mist, "in comparison with the flower and grass (Jas 1:10–11), has a frighteningly short life. Furthermore, the vapor completely vanishes."[50] Arrogance is the opposite attitude of that in 1:10–11. In these verses, James exhorts the wealthy to boast in their humiliation. Here, he criticizes them for their permanent arrogance that leads them away from helping the needy, from doing what is correct.

Instead of having this arrogant attitude, James puts the right words in their mouths. The construction is complex, in part because James uses another anacoluthon. The prepositional phrase ἀντι τοῦ λέγειν ὑμᾶς assumes a previous main verb. However, the previous clause is also an anacoluthon. Davids thinks James considers the participle in v. 13, λέγοντες, as conjugated: "You say... instead of saying...."[51] In this way, v. 14 seems to be parenthetical.[52] Most commentators and English and Spanish translations understand the infinitive as an imperative and translate ἀντὶ τοῦ λέγειν ὑμᾶς as "instead, you ought to say" or something similar. Allison says that "one can also... regard v. 14 as an interruption and see v. 15 as the continuation of v. 13: 'Come now, you who say... instead of saying, 'if the Lord wishes, we will both live and do this or that.'"[53] In any case, at the level of explicature, the illocutionary force of the sentence seems to be an exhortation. In the new and correct saying, they should recognize God's control of their lives and their plans. As McCartney paraphrases it, "If the Lord wills, we will live in accordance with God's righteous revealed will, and in conformity to it we will do this or that."[54]

In v. 16, James clearly exposes the deep problem of these wealthy merchants. He points out: "But you now boast in your arrogance"; or as Hart and Hart translate: "But now you are boasting about all the things that you arrogantly plan to do."[55] "All such boasting is evil," says James. Although Toby Ziglar is commenting on the practices of the wealthy in 2:6–7, his words apply here too. He says: "This passage helps distinguish the 'rich' and 'poor'

49. Allison, *James*, 658.

50. René Krüger, *Pobres y ricos en la epístola de Santiago: El desafío de un cristianismo profético* (Buenos Aires: Lumen, 2005), 262.

51. Davids, *James*, 172. McKnight proposes to connect this infinitive with καυχᾶσθε in v. 15, instead of with λέγοντες, v. 13. He translates: "Instead of your saying... you are now boasting." McKnight, *James*, 374–5. Although it is grammatically possible, the use of νῦν δέ in v. 16 seems to contrast this sentence with the entire segment of vv. 13–15, and not with just v. 15.

52. Allison, *James*, 659; Johnson, *James*, 296; Popkes, *Der Brief des Jakobus*, 286, 9.

53. Allison, *James*, 659. In Spanish, la Biblia de Jerusalén opts for this translation.

54. McCartney, *James*, 228.

55. Hart and Hart, *Analysis of James*, 130. Blomberg and Kamell translate the noun "repeated acts of arrogance." Blomberg and Kamell, *James*, 210.

in James, not only as economic classes but as competing value systems and habitual behaviors";[56] in this case, the arrogance of the wealthy.

The correct boasting they should have is in their humiliation (1:10–11). Allison sees in 4:16 some echoes of Proverbs 27:1 (LXX) and Jeremiah 9:23, but he is conscious that there are many biblical and extrabiblical examples with the connection between wealth and pride or boasting.[57] Again, it is possible that James follows a language that permits his addressees to loosely associate his words with the OT. In this case, in RT terms, James would interpretively metarepresent OT teaching such as Proverbs 27:1 (LXX); Psalms 37:20, 39:11, 90:10, 102:3; 1 Chronicles 19:15; or Hosea 13:3. Nevertheless, the connection with James 1:10–11 is strong. The word group καυχάομαι/καύχησις appears three times in James: twice here in 4:15 and once in 1:9. The verb is implicit in 1:10–11. So, probably, by using boasting language and a similar metaphor, James is warning his addressees, guiding them to derive implicatures regarding God's punishment and the eschatological reversal.

He reinforces his exhortation with the proverbial sentence, moving "from a particular problem to a general principle."[58] In 4:17, he concludes: "Anyone, therefore, who knows the good thing to do yet fails to do it, commits sin."[59] In light of the previous verses, James seems to imply that the problem of the merchants was not only making plans without taking God into consideration, but also making them apart from what God considers proper. Allison understands the participle εἰδότι as "be able" and comments: "[I]f one is able to help and does not, it is sin. On this reading, James exhorts merchants to put their resources to good use."[60] Throughout his letter, James shows what he considers these good things before God. In particular, they include deeds of compassion and caring for the poor.[61]

The different addressees read this segment in diverse ways. Those who are merchants are directly alluded to, but the rest of the congregation receives it as a warning to not follow the merchants' attitude. For James, the issue here is not whether the merchants are believers or not; rather, the problem he addresses is the severity of their sin. The exhortation to this first group of wealthy, however, is less severe than the exhortation to the second group in 5:1–6. James presents several implicatures strongly implied in this segment:

56. Toby Ziglar, "Profit or People First? An Examination of Jas 4:13–16," *RevExp* 108 (2011): 454.

57. Allison lists as examples Ps 49:6; Prov 16:18–19; Isa 2:7, 11; 13:11, 17; Ezek 28:5; Wis 5:8; Ecclus 13:20; 1 En. 46:7; 94:8; 97:8–9; 1 QH 18(10):25; 1QpHab 8:3, 9–12; 1 Tim 6:17; Josephus, *Ant.* 1.194; 4.223–24; Tg. 1 Sam 2:5. It is a widespread concept both in biblical and in Jewish literature. Allison, *James*, 662 and n. 128. For McCartney, James "clearly echoes Prov 27:1." McCartney, *James*, 228.

58. McCartney, *James*, 229.

59. Hart and Hart, *Analysis of James*, 133.

60. He gives as examples T. Job 11:3; Prov 3:27–28 (LXX); 1 John 3:17. Allison, *James*, 665.

61. Blomberg and Kamell, *James*, 210–1.

8. Someone who says in detail what he/she will do in a whole year reflects overconfidence in him/herself and overconfidence in the predictability of external circumstances.
9. Nobody knows what will happen tomorrow.
10. Nobody knows what his/her life will be like tomorrow.
11. Someone who plans, as if he/she knows the future, is arrogant.

If James echoes an OT passage such as Proverbs 27:1 (LXX) (or some similar text), other weakly implied implicatures are the following:

12. The Scriptures teach that this kind of person is arrogant.
13. The Scriptures teach not to make such an assertion.
14. James teaches what the Scriptures say.

If the eschatological overtones in some examples of the use of the metaphor of smoke/mist in Second Temple literature are also present in James's words, another weak implicature might be this:

15. As the mist disappears, the arrogant rich will perish.

Summary of How James Uses the OT in 4:13–17

In a similar way to what happens in 1:26–27, James addresses his readers/hearers with a language impregnated with the OT. Even though there is no clear allusion, some scholars think James echoes passages such as Proverbs 27:1 (LXX). If this is the case, then James interpretively metarepresents the OT. Furthermore, this metarepresentation could be a loose resemblance of OT teaching.

In his rhetorical strategy here, James seems to evoke earlier sections of his discourse, in particular 1:9–11 and 4:6. If this is the case, he brings the concepts of eschatological reversal and punishment of the rich from Isaiah 40:6–7 (LXX), for example, into this part of the discourse via weak implicatures. The same would be true of Proverbs 3:34 (LXX), which is quoted in 4:6. In that section, there is a clear calling for repentance from arrogance (4:7–12). If James's readers/hearers make the connections, they may derive implicatures such as the following:

1. One should not act arrogantly in his/her plans, because life is short and God will punish the impious wealthy in the eschatological reversal.
2. The wealthy should instead boast in their humiliation.
3. Sinners should repent from their arrogance.
4. God is the judge who can save those who repent from their arrogance and destroy those who do not.

Methodology Applied to 5:1–6

This pericope is the strongest address to the wealthy in the letter. James charges his language with eschatological energy. The study of the OT in 5:1–6 shows closeness with the OT in almost every sentence. James interpretively uses the OT in order to evoke in his readers hope and warning.

Elucidation of the Co-text

James 5:1–6 is closely connected with the paragraphs before and after it. Both 4:13–17 and 5:1–6 begin with the expression ἄγε νῦν. The subject matter is similar, although the rhetoric of 5:1–6 is stronger than that of 4:13–17.[62] "[B]oth paragraphs condemn a pursuit of wealth that fails to take into account the reality of God and his will for humanity."[63] Also, 5:7–11 is related to 5:1–6 by the inferential conjunction οὖν. In 5:1–6, James presents his denunciation of the wealthy landlords, and in 5:7–11, he encourages his addressees who suffer the oppression of the rich. As Hart and Hart point out, 5:1–6 is the expository basis for the hortatory paragraph 5:7–11.[64]

However, like earlier sections, 5:1–6 continues the theme of poverty and wealth. It is the last time James addresses the wealthy. In 1:10–11, James exhorts them concerning the humiliation they should boast about. Now, he is more explicit. He presents the causes and the imminence of their eschatological humiliation. Furthermore, there are some echoes of the earlier sections with some important reversals.[65] In 1:26–27, widows and orphans live with afflictions. Here, the wealthy are about to weep and wail (5:1). In 2:2, a rich man with fine clothing and a golden ring enters their synagogue. Here, the clothing, gold, and silver rot and are witnesses against the rich in God's tribunal. In 2:1–13, the wealthy are those who drag some of the addressees into human tribunals (2:6). Here, they are in front of God's tribunal. In 2:1–13, the wealthy enjoy impunity. Here, God's punishment is imminent; his verdict is already pronounced.

James 5:1–6 also has connections with 4:1–10. William Varner finds that not only is the theme of selfish pleasure (4:1–3) common to both (5:1), there are also several shared words: φονεύετε/ἐφονεύσατε; ταλαιπωρήσατε/ταλαιπωρίαις; κλαύσατε/κλαύσατε; πενθός, πενθήσατε/ὀλολύζοντες; ἀντιτάσσεται/ἀντιτάσσεται. However, the passages differ in that 4:1–10 ends with an explicit call to repentance, but 5:1–6 does not.[66] It is shown later that the call for repentance is implicit in this section.[67]

62. Allison, *James*, 649.

63. Moo, *James*, 209.

64. Hart and Hart, *Analysis of James*, 133–44.

65. Johnson also detects these reversals. Johnson, *James*, 299–300.

66. William Varner, *The Book of James: A New Perspective; A Linguistic Commentary Applying Discourse Analysis* (Woodlands, Tex.: Kress Biblical Resources, 2010), 168.

67. It is argued later that the different implied audiences perceive the text in different ways. Thus, the same text could be read/heard as hope or warning. See, in this regard, for example,

Description of the General Cognitive Environment

The text of 5:1–6 is James's final address to the wealthy. He denounces landowners and their treatment of their workers. He does this in an eschatological framework. A brief analysis of the theme of farmers, landlords, and laborers, and of the eschatological language used follows.

Farmers, Landlords, and Laborers

In 5:1–6, James depicts an agrarian scene. Maynard-Reid presents an exhaustive analysis of the issues behind this text.[68] In 5:4, workers and harvesters have mowed τὰς χώρας. Χώρα "designates large farms or tracts of land—a whole estate under one ownership."[69] The concentration of lands in few hands was not unique to Palestine. It is a phenomenon known in other parts of the Roman Empire. One of the reasons for this accumulation of land is that small farmers were more vulnerable to bad harvests and taxation.[70] Although many landlords worked their fields with slaves, during harvest season they hired laborers (ἐργάται, μισθότοι).[71] Given the economy of scale, the great landlords gradually pushed out the small farmers. Many of these small farmers stopped working as laborers of those wealthy landlords.[72] The wealthy depicted here could be in the ES_4 or even ES_3 category in Longenecker's scale.

The laborers were poor, maybe in the lower category ES_7 in Longenecker's scale. They depended exclusively on a daily salary to survive. In Palestine, the unemployment rate was critical. Day laborers had to work for any amount of money (cf. Matt 20:1–7). In that region, "the fact that there were slaves, as well as a great unemployed 'reserve army,' made it very easy for the large landowners to keep down (or hold back) the wages and depress the economic level of the free laborer."[73] This situation of precariousness was exacerbated by intentional retention of salaries. Robbery and debt were two ways the poor farmers tried to solve their scarcity of food and clothing. In fact, in the Jewish revolt of A.D. 66, one of the first things the Zealot did was to "burn contracts belonging to their creditors, and thereby dissolve their obligation for paying their debts" (*War* 2.17.6).[74] In this context, James points out the sin of the wealthy with eschatological language.

David P. Nystrom, *The NIV Application Commentary: James* (Grand Rapids, Mich.: Zondervan, 1997), 268; Kurt A. Richardson, *James*, NAC 36 (Nashville: Broadman & Holman, 2001), 205.

68. Here only a summary is presented. See Maynard-Reid, *Poverty and Wealth*, 81–98.

69. James Hardy Ropes, *A Critical and Exegetical Commentary on the Epistle of St. James*, ICC (New York: C. Scribner's Sons, 1916), 288; James B. Adamson, *James: The Man and His Message* (Grand Rapids, Mich.: Eerdmans, 1989), 241; Maynard-Reid, *Poverty and Wealth*, 85.

70. "Landlords and Tenants," *LBD*, Logos version, "Wealth."

71. Adamson, *James: The Man and His Message*, 241.

72. Hartin, *James*, 236.

73. Maynard-Reid, *Poverty and Wealth*, 91.

74. Quoted by Maynard-Reid, *Poverty and Wealth*, 90.

Eschatological Language

Eschatological language is embedded in 5:1–6. In 5:1, James says: "Weep and wail, you rich, for the miseries that are coming upon you." He describes the deterioration of their wealth in 5:2–3. Their own wealth will be a witness against them in God's tribunal (5:3). This judgment is in the latter days (5:3). They have fattened their hearts for the day of slaughter (5:5). This language connects James's addressees with their eschatological hope and with the great eschatological themes of reversal of fortunes and God's judgment, which have been present in the letter from the beginning. This language guides the interpretation both at the level of explicatures and at the level of implicatures. Regarding the eschatological language in 5:1–6, Hartin points out, "James's rhetorical function is to use these descriptions to encourage the poor and the oppressed: he wishes to give his readers/hearers the assurance that God hears the cry of the poor."[75] In this way, James builds his exhortation in a language that permits him to guide his addressees toward other implicatures by combining prophetic denunciation and eschatology.

The concept of God's last judgment of human beings is well attested in the OT. It becomes synonymous with "the day of the Lord," another rich OT metaphor. Also it is present in Second Temple literature and Jesus's teachings.[76] The theme is clearest in the OT prophets and developed later mainly in apocalyptic literature. In this last judgment, God will punish the disobedient within Israel and also the nations that oppose God (Isa 1:1–31; Dan 12:2–3; Jdt 16:17; Add Esth 10:11; 1 En. 1:1–9, 10:12, 22:11, 13; 4 Ezra 7:70–74). This last judgment involves the vindication of the righteous and punishment of the wicked (Isa 61–66; Zech 12–14; Mal 4:1–6; 2 Esd 7:38, 102, 104, 113; 12:34; Jub. 30:19–23; 1 En. 89:70, 98:8; 2 En. 52:15; 2 Bar. 24:1; CD 20:19–20).

The apocalyptic literature develops the concept of the final judgment. The military scene where God is a mighty warrior who defeats his enemies is present (1 En. 1:3–9; 1QM 1:4–5, 14–15; T. Levi 3:3). A judicial scene is also present; God is the great judge who punishes the wicked (1 En. 47:3, 90:20–26; 4 Ezra 7:33; 2 Bar. 83:1–3; Sir 35:14–15; T. Abr. 13–15). Kent Yinger presents a good summary of a variety of judgment scenes (earthly or heavenly judgment)

75. Patrick J. Hartin, "James and Eschatology: Place and Function of Eschatology within a Letter to the 'Twelve Tribes in the Dispersion,'" in *Eschatology of the New Testament and Some Related Documents*, ed. J. G. Van der Watt, WUNT 2 315 (Tübingen: Mohr Siebeck, 2011), 463.

76. The theme by itself would demand another book. Here, some examples, references, and main ideas are presented. For a good summary of the issue, see Richard Bauckham, "Covenant, Law, and Salvation in the Jewish Apocalypses," in *The Jewish World around the New Testament* (Grand Rapids, Mich.: Baker, 2010), 269–323; J. Julius Scott, Jr., *Jewish Backgrounds of the New Testament* (Grand Rapids, Mich.: Baker, 1995), 283–305; Mark A. Seifrid, "Judgment," *DLNTD* 621–5; Stephen H. Travis, "Judgment," *DPL* 516–7; Stephen H. Travis, "Judgment," *DJG* 408–11; Klaus Wengst, "Aspects of the Last Judgment in the Gospel according to Matthew," in *Eschatology in the Bible and in Jewish and Christian Tradition*, ed. Henning Graf Reventlow, JSOTSup 243 (Sheffield: Sheffield Academic Press, 1997), 233–45; Kent L. Yinger, "Judgment," *EDEJ* 853–5.

and agents of judgment (God, angels, the watchers, Melchizedek). There are scenes of individual or collective judgment. The objects of judgment normally are the wicked, the enemies of God, and "inhabitants of cosmic realms."[77]

God is represented as king and judge. He is a victorious warrior king in a last battle against the evil (Joel 2:1, 11; Isa 13:6, 9; cf. Rev 16:14; 1 En. 1:3–9; 1QM 1:4–5, 14–15; T. Levi 3:3). Also, he is the supreme judge in a tribunal (Lam 3:58–59; Isa 51:5; Joel 4:2, 12; Eccl 12:14; Sir 35:14–15; 1 En. 47:3, 90:20–26; 4 Ezra 7:33–44; 2 Bar. 83:1–3; T. Abr. 13–15). His judgment is presented as a sacrifice (Jer 46:10; Zeph 1:7; cf. Isa 30:33)—a day of slaughter (Jer 12:3, 25:30–38; 1 En. 94:7–9).

In Jesus's teaching, God is the judge, but Jesus is also the judge alongside his Father (Matt 7:22, 10:28–33, 19:27–20:16; Luke 17:30–35). The theme of vindication and punishment is also present (Matt 7:24–27, 13:38, 25:31–46; Mark 9:42–48). The objects of the judgment are more or less the same ones observed in apocalyptic literature. The resurrection of the dead becomes central. Yinger points out that "the major shift involves the inaugurated or 'realized' eschatology of the New Testament, whereby divine judgment has in one sense already occurred... but in another sense is yet to come."[78]

These images are present in James 5:1–6. James depicts the wicked rich in God's tribunal receiving God's condemnation on "the day of slaughter." This scene is similar to different passages in 1 Enoch (94:8–9, 97:8–9, 98:10–11, 99:15) that portray God's judgment of the wicked wealthy for almost the same crimes. In James God is also the Lord of Hosts, the warrior king. So, it is highly probable that not only the concept of final judgment but also the imagery used by James was part of the shared knowledge between him and his addressees.

Identification of Possible OT Texts and Traditions Evoked

James's language in this pericope is highly charged with OT "aroma." As Brosend hyperbolically points out, "[i]t is also the passage with perhaps the thickest intertexture, virtually every noun and verb resonating throughout the biblical tradition."[79] Before analysis of the possible OT texts here, the argument of some scholars that Jesus's words are behind James's text will be considered.

Jesus's Words

Allison makes a strong case that Jesus's words are behind James 5:2 in a pre-Matthean form.[80] He builds his case on Davids, Kloppenborg, and others

77. Yinger, *EDEJ* 854–5.

78. Ibid., 855.

79. Brosend, *James and Jude*, 131.

80. Allison, *James*, 670–1. He seems to be more cautious in his recent analysis, in Dale C. Allison, Jr., "The Audience of James and the Sayings of Jesus," in *James, 1 and 2 Peter, and Early*

Table 5.1. Allison's comparison of James 4:14–5:5 and the synoptic tradition

Jas 4:14–5:5	Matt 6:19–21//Luke 12:33–34
ἀφανιζομένη	ἀφανίζει (Matthew, *bis*)
σέσηπεν, σητόβρωτα	σῆς (Matthew and Luke)
σητόβρωτα	βρῶσις (Matthew)
τὰ ἱμάτια	clothing is implicit in the Synoptics
ἐθησαυρίσατε ἐν	θησαυρίζετε . . . ἐν, θησαυρούς (Matthew)
	θησαυρόν (Luke)
	θησαυρός (Matthew and Luke)
ἐπὶ τῆς γῆς	ἐπὶ τῆς γῆς (Matthew)
καρδίας ὑμῶν	καρδία ὑμῶν (Luke), καρδία σου (Matthew)
Eschatological application	Eschatological application

who observe similarities between James 4:13–5:5 and Matthew 6:19–21//Luke 12:33–34.[81] Allison presents a comparison of these texts (see table 5.1).[82]

Differences between James and the Synoptic texts could be intentional adaptations of James to the new urban situation. The majority of Jesus's teachings have an agrarian setting. James seems to address people in urban areas with close nearness to agrarian lands. So, it is possible that some differences between James's text and the Synoptic material evoked in his letter are intentional modifications of the Jesus tradition due to the new context.[83] In Hartin's words, "James is not quoting the Q tradition directly, but is using

Jesus Traditions, ed. Alicia J. Batten and John S. Kloppenborg, LNTS 478 (London: Bloomsbury, 2015), 58–77.

81. Allison quotes several scholars. Among them are Peter H. Davids, "James and Jesus," in *Jesus Tradition outside the Gospels*, ed. David Wenham, GP 5 (Sheffield: JSOT, 1984), 63–84; Peter H. Davids, "Palestinian Traditions in the Epistle of James," in *James the Just and Christian Origins*, ed. Bruce Chilton and Craig A. Evans, SupNovT 98 (Leiden: Brill, 1999), 33–57; Dean B. Deppe, "The Sayings of Jesus in the Epistle of James" (Th.D. thesis, Free University of Amsterdam, 1989); Patrick J. Hartin, *James and the Q Sayings of Jesus*, JSNTSup 47 (Sheffield: JSOT, 1991), 179–81; Steven R. Johnson, *Seeking the Imperishable Treasure: Wealth, Wisdom, and a Jesus Saying* (Eugene, Ore.: Wipf and Stock, 2010), 97–100; John S. Kloppenborg, "The Emulation of Jesus Tradition in the Letter of James," in *Reading James with New Eyes*, ed. Robert L. Webb and John S. Kloppenborg, LNTS 342 (London: T&T Clark, 2007), 121–50; John S. Kloppenborg, "The Reception of the Jesus Tradition in James," in *Catholic Epistles and Apostolic Tradition*, ed. Karl-Wilhelm Niebuhr and Robert W. Wall (Waco: Baylor University Press, 2009), 71–100.

82. Allison, *James*, 671.

83. Alicia J. Batten, "The Urbanization of Jesus Traditions in James," in *James, 1 and 2 Peter, and Early Jesus Traditions*, ed. Alicia J. Batten and John S. Kloppenborg, LNTS 478 (London: Bloomsbury, 2015), 78–96. For Bauckham, this phenomenon shows that James does not necessarily resemble Jesus's sayings, but rather that he appropriates Jesus's wisdom as his own. Bauckham, *James*, 82–3. Kloppenborg follows Bauckham's argument and applies it to Jas 2:7 and Luke 6:20b. He shows that James emulates Jesus's teachings. In this way, his addressees can identify the intertext and appreciate his artistry. Kloppenborg, "The Jesus Tradition," 71–100.

it according to his usual method of working it into his argument."[84] If James is intentionally evoking Jesus's teachings, he is reinforcing his own teachings and authority with Jesus's thoughts and authority. A similar situation has already been discussed in the analysis of 2:6 in the chapter 4. If this conclusion is right, then James builds his indictment against the wealthy landlords on the basis of Jesus, and he expects his addressees to make the same connections.

OT in James 5:1–6

James builds this discourse with a language close to the wisdom, prophetic, and Torah traditions. Given the high degree of similarity between almost every sentence and these traditions, each verse is analyzed in detail. In 5:2, James mentions two figures that appear is wisdom, prophetic and apocalyptic literature. He says: ὁ πλοῦτος ὑμῶν σέσηπεν καὶ τὰ ἱμάτια ὑμῶν σητόβρωτα γέγονεν. The idea of rotted wealth or moth-eaten clothing appears in Greek texts like Job 13:28; Proverbs 25:20a; Isa 51:8; Sirach 14:19, 29:9–12, 42:13; Bar 6:72 (Ep Jer LXX 71). Clothing is an external reflection of wealth and status (Jas 2:2–3; cf. Matt 6:28–31; Luke 7:25). So, moth-eaten clothing is a signal of impermanence and God's judgment upon men (cf. Isa 50:9, 51:8). In the case of Job 13:28, Hartin points out that although it is possible that James's text is influenced by Job's text, "it is more likely that he is using a traditional image."[85] (Cf. Prov 25:20; Isa 33:1, 50:9; Sib Or. frag. 3.26.)

In 5:3, James's words are close to passages like Psalms 20:10 and 21:9 or Judith 16:17. In fact, OT and Jewish literature mention the metaphors of the rusting gold (Sir 12:11; Bar 6:11–12, 24 [Ep Jer LXX 10, 23]) and an eating flesh fire (Ps 20:10). In 5:4, there are two separated OT alluded concepts: a violation of Law (Lev 19:13b; Deut 24:14–15) and an invocation of the Lord of Hosts that seems to come from Isaiah 5:9. Both concepts are analyzed separately.

Deuteronomy 24:14–15 in James 5:4

In his denunciation in 5:4, James points out that the landlords have kept back by fraud the salary of their workers. This salary serves as a testimonial against the landlords in God's court. James is appealing to Torah. Both Leviticus 19:13 and Deuteronomy 24:14–15 speak against this common practice. Deuteronomy 24:15 is closer to James's text. In both Deuteronomy 24:15 and James 5:4, ὁ μισθός is personified and cries to God. In Deuteronomy 24:14–15 what is implicit in James is explicit, the poverty of the workers and their hope of receiving their salaries.

84. Hartin, *James and the Q Sayings of Jesus*, 180.

85. Hartin, *James*, 227. Johnson points out: "The image itself is widespread." Johnson, *James*, 299.

Table 5.2. Comparison of James 5:4, Leviticus 19:13b, and Deuteronomy 24:14–15[a]

Jas 5:4	Lev 19:13b	Deut 24:14–15
ἰδοὺ ὁ μισθὸς τῶν ἐργατῶν τῶν ἀμησάντων τὰς χώρας ὑμῶν ὁ ἀπεστερημένος ἀφ᾽ ὑμῶν κράζει, καὶ αἱ βοαὶ τῶν θερισάντων εἰς τὰ ὦτα κυρίου σαβαὼθ εἰσεληλύθασιν.	οὐ κοιμηθήσεται ὁ μισθὸς τοῦ μισθωτοῦ παρὰ σοὶ ἕως πρωί	14 οὐκ ἀπαδικήσεις μισθὸν πένητος καὶ ἐνδεοῦς ἐκ τῶν ἀδελφῶν σου ἢ ἐκ τῶν προσηλύτων τῶν ἐν ταῖς πόλεσίν σου· 15 αὐθημερὸν ἀποδώσεις τὸν μισθὸν αὐτοῦ, οὐκ ἐπιδύσεται ὁ ἥλιος ἐπ᾽ αὐτῷ, ὅτι πένης ἐστὶν καὶ ἐν αὐτῷ ἔχει τὴν ἐλπίδα· καὶ οὐ καταβοήσεται κατὰ σοῦ πρὸς κύριον, καὶ ἔσται ἐν σοὶ ἁμαρτία.

[a]The Greek text of Lev 19:13b and Deut 24:14–15 comes, respectively, from John William Wevers, ed., *Leviticus*, VTG, Auctoritate Academiae Scientiarum Gottingensis editum (Göttingen: Vandenhoeck & Ruprecht, 1986); John William Wevers, ed., *Deuteronomium*, VTG, Auctoritate Academiae Scientiarum Gottingensis editum (Göttingen: Vandenhoeck & Ruprecht, 2006).

Again, Hays's four criteria of validation help to decide the possible use of the OT text: (1) availability, (2) volume, (3) recurrence, and (4) thematic coherence. Regarding availability, both Leviticus 19:13b and Deuteronomy 24:14–15 are part of the cognitive environment of James and his addressees. Concerning the criterion of volume, parallels between the texts are more thematic than textual, as table 5.2 shows. But, as mentioned above, Deuteronomy 24:14–15 is closer to James's text than Leviticus 19:13b is. Regarding the criterion of recurrence, both Leviticus 19 and Deuteronomy 24 are quoted in the NT.[86] Finally, regarding thematic coherence, Deuteronomy 24 is closer to James's emphasis on the eschatological tone of the prohibition.

Deuteronomy 24:14–15 is "the first of three laws protecting the poor and the vulnerable" in chapter 24.[87] The other two are 24:17–18 and 19–22. The connection between laws protecting poor workers (24:14–15) and laws in favor of widows and orphans (24:17–22) is noticeable; these are the same groups about whom James manifests concern. J. A. Thompson observes that in the entire twenty-fourth chapter, the humanitarian motive is strong (24:6, 7, 10–13, 17, 18, 19–22). He comments: "It was fundamental to Israel's

86. Lev 19 was mentioned when dealing with Jas 2:1–13. Deut 24 is quoted or alluded to in several texts: Deut 24:1, 3 in Matt 5:31, 19:7; Mark 10:4; Deut 24:7 in 1 Cor 5:13; Deut 24:14 in Matt 20:18.

87. Duane L. Christensen, *Deuteronomy 21:10–34:12*, WBC 6B (Dallas: Word, 2002), 585.

understanding of the covenant family that he who delivered Israel from Egypt had a special concern for the underprivileged and the weak."[88] The discussion of this law in 24:14–15 is addressed to the landowners. It gives the rationale behind the commandment. The laborers under consideration here are poor, and they depend on being paid for their own subsistence and that of their families, no matter their nationality. If a landlord retains their salary, his workers could cry to God, and God would consider this fault against him as a sin of the landlord.

Prophetic and wisdom literature seems to build warnings and advice on Deuteronomy 24:14–15/Leviticus 19:13b. For example, in Jeremiah 22:13, the prophet criticizes Jehoahaz (Shallum in 22:11) for not giving wages to his workers (cf. Isa 58:3b). In Malachi 3:5, God accuses his people of cheating laborers of their wages. Malachi 3:25 (LXX) reads: ἔσομαι μάρτυς ταχὺς… ἐπὶ τοὺς ἀποστεροῦντας μισθὸν μισθωτοῦ. Also the image appears in wisdom literature. For example, Sirach 34:22 points out: "He slays his neighbor who deprives him of his living: he sheds blood who denies the laborer his wages" (NAB). Other texts that reflect on these passages are Job 7:2 and 24:10 and Tobit 4:14.

So, in RT terms, it is highly probable that James intends his addressees to make the connection with Deuteronomy 24:14–15. If James is alluding to Deuteronomy 24:14–15, he emphasizes the poverty of the laborers, the need for salary, the hope for salary, the desperation of the workers, and the act of sin before God via implicatures. The sin of the landlords in James, though, is greater than what is depicted in Deuteronomy 24:14–15. The latter text concerns the severity of withholding the salary from an evening, but in James, the laborers are τῶν ἐργατῶν τῶν ἀμησάντων τὰς χώρας ὑμῶν. As Kruger points out, "[i]n James, the situation of the mowers is even worse than what is present in the text of Deut or Lev. While the Old Testament texts demand a daily payment, in James the harvest ended…; namely, the wealthy not only owe the salary of yesterday, but several or maybe a lot of continuous salaries."[89] This desperate crying in James 5:4 is addressed not just toward the Lord (Deut 24:15) but toward "the Lord of Hosts." This last phrase is common in the OT, but it seems to come from Isaiah 5:9.

Isaiah 5:9a in James 5:4

Carson is right when he says: "The notion of God hearing the cries (*boai*) of the oppressed is a common one."[90] Texts like Exodus 22:23–26 are close to the scene here in James 5:4. Abel's blood crying to God is frequently quoted

88. J. A. Thompson, *Deuteronomy: An Introduction and Commentary*, TOTC 5 (Downers Grove, Ill.: InterVarsity Press, 1974), 270.

89. Krüger, *Pobres y ricos en la epístola de Santiago*, 294.

90. D. A. Carson, "James," in *Commentary on the New Testament Use of the Old Testament*, ed. G. K. Beale and D. A. Carson (Grand Rapids, Mich.: Baker, 2007), 1009.

(Gen 4:10).[91] However, the sentence αἱ βοαὶ τῶν θερισάντων εἰς τὰ ὦτα κυρίου σαβαὼθ εἰσεληλύθασιν is close to Isaiah 5:9a, ἠκούσθη γὰρ εἰς τὰ ὦτα κυρίου σαβαωθ ταῦτα.

Again, Hays's four criteria of validation help to discern the presence of the OT. Regarding the criterion of availability, Isaiah is a well-known book in the first-century church, as mentioned in relation to Isaiah 40 in James 1:9–11. Concerning the criterion of volume, in the LXX, the title κυρίου σαβαώθ is used almost exclusively of Isaiah (fifty-one of fifty-eight occurrences), although in the Hebrew text יהוה צְבָאוֹת is a common title of God. This title elsewhere in the NT appears only in Romans 9:26, which is a quotation of Isaiah 1:9. In the LXX, the only other place where the expression εἰς τὰ ὦτα κυρίου σαβαωθ appears is Odes 10:9, which seems to be a commentary on Isaiah 5 (cf. a similar expression in Isa 22:14: καὶ ἀνακεκαλυμμένα ταῦτά ἐστιν ἐν τοῖς ὠσὶ κυρίου σαβαωθ). The comparison of James 5:4 and Isaiah 5:9a in table 5.3 shows the closeness of James's text to the OT text.

Regarding the criterion of recurrence, the best-known section of Isaiah 5 quoted or alluded to is the vineyard canticle (5:1–7). It is present in Matthew 22:33, Mark 12:1, and Luke 13:6 and 20:9. Nevertheless, the expression εἰς τὰ ὦτα κυρίου σαβαὼθ appears only here in the NT.[92] Regarding the criterion of global coherence, the content of Isaiah 5:9 fits well with James's denunciation. Isaiah 5:8–10 is the first of several complaints of YHWH against his people (Isa 5:8–24), mainly the wealthy.[93] Each complaint is introduced by הוֹי (5:8, 11, 18, 20, 21, and 22). Some themes are similar. For example, there is a complaint about banquets and debauchery (5:11–13, 22; cf. Jas 5:5), about the privation of justice for the righteous (5:23; cf. Jas 5:6), about the accumulation of goods at the expense of the poor (5:8; cf. Jas 5:2), and about God's coming judgment (5:13–15, 24–25; cf. Jas 5:1, 3, 5).

The literary form of the text of Isaiah 5:8–10 is an accusation (5:8) and an announcement of judgment (5:9–10).[94] Isaiah criticizes the "latifundialization" of the land to the deprivation of the peasantry.[95] Desolation and low productivity of the land are God's punishment for these landlords (5:9–10). In the Hebrew text, the prophet hears God's judgment, בְּאָזְנָי. In the LXX, however, God is the one who directly hears the sin of accumulation of goods at the expense of the poor, ἠκούσθη γὰρ εἰς τὰ ὦτα κυρίου σαβαωθ

91. See the analysis of J. Byron, "Living in the Shadow of Cain: Echoes of a Developing Tradition in James 5:1–6," *NovT* 48 (2006): 261–74.

92. 1 Pet 3:12 presents a similar expression coming from Ps 33:16 (LXX), ὅτι ὀφθαλμοὶ κυρίου ἐπὶ δικαίους καὶ ὦτα αὐτοῦ εἰς δέησιν αὐτῶν.

93. Robert B. Chisholm, Jr., "Structure, Style, and the Prophetic Message: An Analysis of Isaiah 5:8–30," *BibSac* 143.569 (1986): 46–60.

94. The rest of Isa 5:8–30 follows the same pattern. Chisholm, "Isaiah 5:8–30," 50.

95. D. N. Premnath, "Latifundialization and Isaiah 5:8–10," *JSOT* 40 (1988): 49.

Table 5.3. Comparison of Jas 5:4 and Isa 5:9[a]

Jas 5:4	**Isa 5:9**
ἰδοὺ ὁ μισθὸς τῶν ἐργατῶν τῶν ἀμησάντων τὰς χώρας ὑμῶν ὁ ἀπεστερημένος ἀφ᾽ ὑμῶν κράζει, καὶ αἱ βοαὶ τῶν θερισάντων εἰς τὰ ὦτα κυρίου σαβαὼθ εἰσεληλύθασιν.	ἠκούσθη γὰρ εἰς τὰ ὦτα κυρίου σαβαωθ ταῦτα· ἐὰν γὰρ γένωνται οἰκίαι πολλαί, εἰς ἔρημον ἔσονται μεγάλαι καὶ καλαί, καὶ οὐκ ἔσονται οἱ ἐνοικοῦντες.

[a]The Greek text of Isa 5:9 comes from Joseph Ziegler, ed., *Septuaginta*, vol. 14, *Isaias*, VTG, Auctoritate Academiae Scientiarum Gottingensis editum (Göttingen: Vandenhoeck & Ruprecht, 1983).

ταῦτα. So, in the Isaianic text, God's intervention in favor of the oppressed is highlighted via implicatures.[96]

The title Lord of Hosts is important in James's claim. The title יהוה צְבָאוֹת appears 284 times in the OT, and 251 in the prophets. Its meaning is much debated.[97] "Hosts has reference to any group, human or divine, called upon by God to mediate a divine objective, which may or may not be military in nature."[98] However, the title Lord of Sabaoth emphasizes God as a warrior.[99] In Isaiah 5, the Lord of Hosts is the Holy One of Israel (5:19), the owner of the vineyard (5:1–7), the one who observes the evil (5:7, 9), the one who does justice, and the one who punishes those who oppress and do evil (5:16, 24) but brings peace and blessings (5:17). God as the Lord of Sabaoth is the one who punishes the evildoers. In Isaiah, this title is related to God's judgments and vindication.[100] So, on RT terms, it is highly probable that James intends his addressees to make the connection with Isaiah 5:9a and the Isaianic Lord of Hosts. There are more cognitive benefits that compensate the higher processing effort in making the connection. James could trigger some of the above-mentioned characteristics associated with the title Lord of Hosts via weak implicatures.

The Day of Slaughter in James 5:5

In 5:5, James depicts the problem with eschatological language. He expresses that the landlords have accumulated wealth; they have fattened their hearts

96. Johnson points out that this phrase "emphasizes God's power to act." Johnson, *James*, 303. McCartney comments: "God is a warrior who will bring disaster upon those who oppress the poor." McCartney, *James*, 234.

97. Terence Fretheim, "Yahweh," *NIDOTTE* 4:1297.

98. Ibid., 1298.

99. Tremper Longman III, "צָבָא," *NIDOTTE* 3:733.

100. James Crenshaw arrives at a similar conclusion in his analysis of the title in the prophets in general. James L. Crenshaw, "YHWH tseba'ôt šemô Form-Critical Analysis," *ZAW* 81 (1969): 156–75.

Table 5.4. Comparison of James 5:5 and Jeremiah 12:3[a]

Jas 5:5	**Jer 12:3**
ἐτρυφήσατε ἐπὶ τῆς γῆς καὶ ἐσπαταλήσατε, ἐθρέψατε τὰς καρδίας ὑμῶν ἐν ἡμέρᾳ σφαγῆς	καὶ σύ, κύριε, γινώσκεις με, δεδοκίμακας τὴν καρδίαν μου ἐναντίον σου· ἅγνισον αὐτοὺς εἰς ἡμέραν σφαγῆς αὐτῶν.

[a]The Greek text of Jer 12:3 comes from Joseph Ziegler, ed., *Jeremias, Baruch, Threni, Epistula Jeremiae*, VTG, Auctoritate Academiae Scientiarum Gottingensis editum (Göttingen: Vandenhoeck & Ruprecht, 2006).

ἐν ἡμέρᾳ σφαγῆς. Many scholars associate this last syntagma with Jeremiah 12:3.[101] The word σφαγή appears twenty-two times in the LXX. However, the expression ἡμέρα σφαγῆς appears just once in Jeremiah 12:3. In Jeremiah, the concept of σφαγή as judgment is recurrent (12:3, 15:3, 19:6, 27:27, 28:40, 31:15, 32:34). In Second Temple literature, the expression appears in 1 Enoch 16:1 and 32:6 (καιροῦ σφαγῆς).

Hays's four criteria of validation help to discern the presence of the OT. Regarding the criterion of availability, Jeremiah is a well-known prophet in the NT.[102] Regarding the criterion of volume, there are just two similar words in James's text and Jeremiah 12:3, as table 5.4 shows. From this perspective, it is hard to decide James's dependence. Regarding the criterion of recurrence, Jeremiah 12 is seemingly alluded to mainly in the Gospels, although this passage is not quoted or alluded to elsewhere.[103] Regarding the criterion of global coherence, Jeremiah's claim to God in Jeremiah 12:1–6 fits well into James's proclamation.

In Jeremiah 12:1–6, Jeremiah presents his second lament. As Marvin Sweeny says, "the prophet employs legal language to charge that God has failed to do justice."[104] In v. 1, he asks God why the evildoers prosper, and God seems to not show concern about it (at least for rhetorical purposes). In vv. 2–3a, he contrasts the prosperity of the evildoers as God's action and his own situation even in spite of his faithfulness. For that reason, he says to God in 12:3b: "Pull them out like sheep for the slaughter, and set them apart for the day of slaughter" (ESV). This may mean, says Carson, "that Jeremiah wants the wicked to receive their due punishment, without much thought being given to the question of when this will take place; he may imagine

101. Almost any commentary on James would serve as an example.

102. Almost every chapter of Jeremiah is quoted or alluded to in the *Loci citati vel allegati* given by NA[28]. Barbara Aland et al., *Nestle-Aland Novum Testamentum Graece*, 28th ed. (Stuttgart: Deutsche Bibelgesellschaft, 2012), 861–3.

103. NA[28] listed 12:6 in Mark 3:21; 12:7 in Matt 23:38; Luke 13:35; Rev 20:9; 12:11 in Luke 9:44; 12:12 in Mark 13:27; 12:15 in Acts 15:16; and 12:17 in Luke 13:3. Ibid., 862.

104. Marvin A. Sweeney, "Jeremiah," in *The Jewish Study Bible*, ed. Adele Berlin, Marc Zvi Brettler, and Michael A. Fishbane (New York: JPS, 2004), 950.

specific temporal punishment; alternatively, he may have final judgment in mind."[105] It becomes apparent throughout Jeremiah's use of the concept of slaughter (12:3, 15:3, 19:6, 27:27, 28:40, 31:15, 32:34) that this is not an either/or, but a both/and concept. Finally, in v. 4, he asks: "How long God?" In vv. 5–6, God answers: surely, there will be more hardship for you.

So, in RT terms, the evidence of Jeremiah 12:3 behind James's expression is divided. Hays's criteria slightly support James's use. Allison thinks that in the expression ἅγνισον αὐτοὺς εἰς ἡμέραν σφαγῆς αὐτῶν, James has substituted "fatten your hearts" for "purify them," "probably in part because he wants to reserve the language of purity for positive statements."[106] There are some implicatures that could be derived from the connection with the eschatological echo of Jeremiah's concept of the "day of slaughter":

1. God will punish the wicked on the eschatological day of slaughter.
2. Although the wicked prosper today, there will be vindication for the oppressed when God punishes the wicked.
3. There is hope for those who are oppressed today, because there will be a day of slaughter.
4. There is a warning for those who live like the wicked in Jeremiah 12:1–3. God will punish them if they do not repent.

Of these implicatures, only the last one is derived exclusively from this passage. The other three could also be derived from the eschatological encyclopedic knowledge of James's addressees. If James wants his readers/hearers to make the connections with this passage, the connection would be an echo more than an allusion.

Interpretation of the Text in James

In this paragraph, James addresses οἱ πλούσιοι (5:1). He uses this adjective to refer to the wealthy in 1:10–11 and 2:6. Many scholars argue that the wealthy here are unbelievers, outsiders. A few others think they are rich Christians.[107] However, as mentioned in the analysis of 1:9–11, James is concerned with the rich qua rich.[108] In this way, he manages to confront his different audiences via implicatures.

The text of 5:1–6 has a more or less discernible literary structure. In 5:1, James presents an announcement of the condemnation of the wealthy. As Witherington says, "the rich are invited to view their funeral

105. Carson, "James," 1011.

106. Allison, *James*, 683.

107. Frankemölle, *Der Brief des Jakobus*, 630–2.

108. Ben Witherington III, *Letters and Homilies for Jewish Christians: A Socio-Rhetorical Commentary on Hebrews, James, and Jude* (Downers Grove, Ill.: IVP Academic, 2007), 524.

in advance."[109] In 5:2–6, James explains the charges against them in God's eschatological tribunal. There are four discernible charges: (1) they have selfishly hoarded wealth (vv. 2–3); (2) they have defrauded their workers (v. 4); (3) they follow a self-indulgent lifestyle (v. 5); and (4) they oppress "the righteous" (v. 6).[110]

The announcement of the condemnation of the wealthy is embedded in eschatological language (5:1). James begins with ἄγε νῦν, the same expression as in 4:13. As mentioned in the analysis of that passage above, James uses it to constrain implicatures. It implies condemnation. Next, James says to the rich: κλαύσατε ὀλολύζοντες ἐπὶ ταῖς ταλαιπωρίαις ὑμῶν ταῖς ἐπερχομέναις. In 4:9–10, he uses similar language in a call to repentance. Here, there is no such call, although, a call to repentance is probably implicated. If James's addressees are familiar with eschatological literature, probably this language could evoke passages like 1 Enoch 94:8–9, a similar pronouncement against the rich (cf. 1 En. 97:1–10, 98:1–16, 99:11–16, 100:7–9, 102:1–11). The onomatopoetic verb ὀλολύζω is a hapax legomenon in the NT. In the LXX, it appears nineteen times, exclusively in the prophets (mainly in Isaiah, twelve times), "in the context of laments in response to the disasters visited on the people by Yahweh for their apostasy"[111] (Hos 7:14; Amos 8:3; Zech 11:2; Isa 10:10; 13:6; 14:31; 15:2–3; 16:7; 23:1, 6, 14; 24:11; 52:5; 65:14; Jer 2:23; 31:20, 31; Ezek. 21:17). The verb ταλαιπωρέω and the noun ταλαιπωρία are associated in the LXX with prophetic laments; these words frequently allude "to the miseries suffered by those who have resisted God" (Pss 13:3, 139:6; Hos 9:6, 10:2; Amos 3:10, 5:9; Mic 2:4; Joe 1:10, 15; Hab 1:3; Zeph 1:15; Zech 11:2–3; Isa 16:4, 47:11, 59:7, 60:18; Jer 4:13, 20; 6:7; 9:18; 10:20; 12:12).[112] James describes these miseries as being about to come upon them, ἐπερχομέναις.

Therefore, again, if the addressees are familiar with apocalyptic language and the genre, these words could trigger a lot of eschatological associations. Almost every word in the verse reinforces eschatological associations already present in the discourse since the beginning.[113] James's readers/hearers recall the eschatological reversal of 1:9–11. That is the first time James addresses the wealthy, οἱ πλούσιοι. On this second occasion, he is more critical and specific. In 1:10–11, he says that the wealthy will wither away in the midst of their πορείαις. Here, they must mourn for their punishment. In 1:9–11, the causes of their humiliation are not explained. Here, James makes explicit what there was implicit. The reversal of their situation is due to their own sin.

109. Ibid.

110. Moo, *James*, 210.

111. Johnson, *James*, 298–9.

112. Ibid., 285, 99.

113. Allison points out that κλαίω + ὀλολύζω "was not a traditional Greek combination. The background probably lies in LXX prophetic oracles, in which both words address those confronting divine judgment." Allison, *James*, 669.

The first accusation appears in 5:2–3: accumulating wealth. James's words are close to Jesus's teachings reflected on Matthew 6:19–21 and Luke 12:33. If James intends his addressees to make the connection, then the accusation is worse because the rich are doing the opposite of what Jesus commanded his disciples to do. James says: your wealth is rotted and your clothing moth-eaten, and your gold and silver rusted. James uses the perfect tense to depict these three characteristics. Many scholars consider these prophetic perfects.[114] It is not aspectually clear, however, what James wants to emphasize.[115] Maybe he emphasizes the prominence of these three characteristics in the eschatological judgment.[116] Everything that the wealthy consider important, and accumulate, is now fading away. At this point, readers/hearers could derive some weak implicatures from the metaphors that contradict the confidence in possessions, such as the following:

5. If wealth deteriorates then it is ephemeral.
6. Wealth is transitory and unreliable.[117]

These contradict a traditional understanding of wealth:

7. Wealth and prosperity are signals of God's blessing.

But the negative associations triggered by the eschatological language of v. 1 guide the hearers/readers to think about why what is supposedly good (possessions) is under God's punishment. This raises the expectation of relevance in the discourse. The next sentence clarifies that there is something sinful in these material possessions. James uses personification to depict a tribunal scene. In this courtroom, instead of the wealthy dragging the poor into court, their own wealth bears testimony against them and acts as the means of punishment: "Their rust will witness against you and will eat your flesh like fire" (5:3). At the end of the day, what they have done in hoarding all

114. Essentially, they follow *Aktionsart* theory, which indicates that the perfect tense is an action in the past with repercussions in the present. So, if the actions have not yet happened, then they have to be future referring, prophetic. In fact, a future tense verb, ἔσται, follows them. See, e.g., Dibelius, *James*, 236; Mayor, *St. James*, 154.

115. McKnight, following Porter's understanding of the aspect of the perfect tense, thinks that James "depicts the act of rotting [and for extension, the other two verbs] as complete and as having brought into being a state of affairs." McKnight, *James*, 386; Moo, *James*, 213. However, if one follows Campbell's understanding of the perfect tense, these three verbs depict imperfective aspect. Constantine R. Campbell, *Basics of Verbal Aspect in Biblical Greek* (Grand Rapids, Mich.: Zondervan, 2008), 103. In an eschatological context, this makes more sense, because the action of these three verbs enters into the already and not-yet eschatological tension. James also used the perfect to depict the prominence of the actions.

116. Constantine R. Campbell, *Verbal Aspect, the Indicative Mood, and Narrative: Soundings in the Greek of the New Testament*, SBG 13 (New York: Peter Lang, 2007), 195–209.

117. Moo, *James*, 523.

this wealth is to store up treasure for the latter days (5:3). For Allison, "this is blunt irony."[118] Instead of laying up treasures in heaven, as Jesus encouraged them, they have accumulated wealth on earth. Jesus ends his teaching saying: "for where your treasure is, there your heart will be also" (Matt 6:21). Some possible implicatures here might be the following:

8. If someone puts his/her trust in wealth, he/she is fool.
9. In light of the eschatological latter days, it is unwise to lay up treasures on earth.
10. If accumulated wealth witnesses against a person in the eschatological tribunal, that person acted sinfully.
11. If wealth eats the flesh of its owner, wealth is dangerous. It is God's instrument of punishment.

The progression of James's thoughts is apparent. First, he announces the verdict (5:1). Then, he evidences the already-but-not-yet fulfillment of that sentence through the decay of the wealth of the rich (5:2–3a). This deterioration is witness against them in the eschatological courtroom, and again the sentence is confirmed: "You have laid up treasure in the last days" (5:3b). Now in vv. 4–5, he opens the veil of what is wrong with this wealth. The wealth of the rich serves as witness against them, says James, for the way they obtained it (5:4) and the manner in which they use it (5:5). Upon all this evidence against them, they add another crime; they oppress the righteous (5:6).

In 5:4, James presents his second accusation: defrauding workers. James reinforces this eschatological scene with the OT. First, he shows their clear violation of God's law, and second, he highlights the character of God. Again, he uses the perfect tense to emphasize both the crime and God's character. He introduces this accusation with ἰδού. James uses this interjection "to call attention to important images and examples" (3:4, 5; 5:4, 7, 9, 11);[119] in this case, a clear and reiterative infringement of the law.

He personifies the salary of the workers. This salary cries. It is a standard way of speaking, says Allison, "in which inanimate objects cry out for truth or justice when people do not or cannot" (cf. Gen 4:10; Job 31:38; Hab 2:11; Luke 19:40; Heb 12:24; 1 En. 47:1).[120] This salary pertains to the workers who harvested the estates of the wealthy landlords. The salary cries. Why does it cry? James says: ὁ μισθὸς τῶν ἐργατῶν τῶν ἀμησάντων τὰς χώρας ὑμῶν ὁ ἀπεστερημένος ἀφ' ὑμῶν κράζει. The prepositional syntagma ἀφ' ὑμῶν could modify the participle or the main verb. Understanding the preposition ἀπό as indicating source and modifying the verb, Blomberg and Kamell suggest

118. Allison, *James*, 677.
119. Davids, *James*, 177.
120. Allison, *James*, 679.

that the salary cries from "the pocket" of these landlords. They translate the sentence: "The wages... that were defrauded cry out from you."[121] However, most scholars understand the clause modifying the participle as the agent of the passive voice: "were defrauded by you." Although either option makes sense in the passage, given the semantic nature of the verb ἀποστερέω, the idea of agent, "by you," is preferred.[122] In this way, the strongly implied accusation is this:

12. You defrauded your workers by not paying them their wages.

The emphasis seems to be on the person who defrauded and not on the place from which the cry comes.

In any case, this charge is a clear violation of Leviticus 19:13, or more probably Deuteronomy 24:14–15. As mentioned above, Hays's criteria permit one to infer that James's text is closer to Deuteronomy 24:14–15 than to Leviticus 19:13. It is highly probable that James guides his addressees to make connections with Deuteronomy 24:14–15. There is a violation of the law, and people cry. By using the personification, James highlights the seriousness of the fault. God considers this fraud a sin against the workers and against himself. By evoking this text, James criticizes the action on a strong basis. He not only shows appreciation for what was a common practice of his first-century context. He builds his accusation on solid ground, the Torah. The following are some strongly communicated implicatures:

13. Their wealth is witness against them because they have illegally obtained it.
14. They have defrauded their workers.
15. If someone cheats his workers and does not pay them, he/she violates God's law.
16. As Torah teaches, if a defrauded worker cries to God, he will hear and act in his favor.

James joins together Deuteronomy 24:14–15 and Isaiah 9:5 and adapts both texts to fit his own discourse. In doing so, he implies that these workers are poor, and depicts God as the Lord of Hosts. Clearly, the use of this title for God triggers several implicatures for James's addressees. James Ropes thinks this "term is here used (after Isa 5:9) to suggest the almighty power and majesty of Him who will make the cause of the labourers his own" (cf. 3 Macc 6:17).[123] As mentioned above, other implicatures triggered by this title might be the following:

121. Blomberg and Kamell, *James*, 223.
122. "ἀποστερέω," *DGENT* 3:955.
123. Ropes, *James*, 289.

17. The Lord of Hosts is the Lord of justice.
18. The Lord of Hosts is the one who punishes the evildoers.
19. The Lord of Hosts is the one who vindicates the poor and oppressed.

James criticizes that they not only have illegitimately obtained their wealth but also have used it egotistically. In 5:5, he presents the third accusation: living in luxury and self-indulgence. James points to ἐτρυφήσατε ἐπὶ τῆς γῆς καὶ ἐσπαταλήσατε. Allison thinks that the phrase "on earth" adds no information but connects with Jesus's saying in Matthew 6:19–21.[124] They have laid up treasure on earth instead of in heaven. James has already pointed out that his addressees do not pray correctly because they are thinking of satisfying their own pleasures (4:2–4). In 5:5, this attitude is reflected in the verbs τρυφάω and σπαταλάω, which depict self-indulgence. Even the metaphor "you have fattened your hearts" emphasizes this self-indulgence. Now James changes the tense of the verbs. He uses the aorist to depict the action perfectively. They have lived on earth without thinking about eternity. They have lived in luxury and self-indulgence as if this life were an eternal present. So, in the case of these wealthy landowners, this wrong attitude has been their characteristic for a long period of time. While some believers are almost naked and lacking in daily food, they have lived without any concern for the situation of others. Their workers are without the necessities of life, but they have fattened their hearts. Ironically, however, they have fattened their hearts in the day of slaughter (5:5).

The eschatological tone of this last phrase makes it difficult to decide whether James wants his addressees to connect "the day of slaughter" with Jeremiah 12:3, or at least with Jeremiah's concept of "day of slaughter." In apocalyptic literature some texts depict a similar situation for the wealthy. For example, 1 Enoch 98:3 is very close to what James says: "For this reason, they [the foolish rich] are devoid of knowledge and wisdom, so they shall perish thereby together with their goods and together with all their glory and honor. Then in dishonor, in slaughter, and in great misery, their spirits shall be cast away."[125]

As Johnson points out, this common agricultural image of slaughtering animals, in the prophetic contexts "bec[omes] the image for divine judgment on evildoers" (cf. Zech 11:4, 7; Isa 34:2, 6; 65:12; Jer 15:3, 19:6, 32:34).[126] So, it is possible that James evokes in his addressees this image without any passage in particular. In this case, he is loosely metarepresenting the OT. He interpretively metarepresents an OT concept.

124. Allison, *James*, 682.

125. James H. Charlesworth, *The Old Testament Pseudepigrapha*, vol. 1 (New York: Yale University Press, 1983), 78.

126. Johnson, *James*, 304.

Finally, in 5:6 James presents the fourth and last accusation: oppressing the righteous. Depicting the actions with the aorist, James points out: κατεδικάσατε, ἐφονεύσατε τὸν δίκαιον. The verb καταδικάζω is derived from forensic contexts.[127] Louw and Nida indicate that the word group means "to judge someone as definitely guilty and thus subject to punishment."[128] This denunciation evokes the act already mentioned in 2:6. These landowners have dragged the poor into courts, they have used their influence on judges, and these have declared the poor guilty.[129] As a result, they have murdered the righteous one. Probably, the referent of this δίκαιος is a collective noun for those oppressed, the righteous, innocent poor.[130] Here, it is possible to understand the verb φονεύω metaphorically, as in Sirach 34:21–22: ἄρτος ἐπιδεομένων ζωὴ πτωχῶν, ὁ ἀποστερῶν αὐτὴν ἄνθρωπος αἱμάτων. φονεύων τὸν πλησίον ὁ ἀφαιρούμενος ἐμβίωσιν, καὶ ἐκχέων αἷμα ὁ ἀποστερῶν μισθὸν μισθίου. Or it could be literal, and some believers have actually died as a result of this oppression. It is hard to decide which of these two options is meant here. In fact, it is not difficult to see both situations in the Latino American reality.

James ends this accusation saying: οὐκ ἀντιτάσσεται ὑμῖν. Some scholars connect this phrase with 4:6, ὁ θεὸς ὑπερηφάνοις ἀντιτάσσεται; consider 4:7–5:6 as a literary unit, a commentary on Proverbs 3:34 in 4:6; and understand the tacit subject in 5:6b as God and the clause as a rhetorical question: "Does God not oppose you?"[131] However, as Allison mentions, "although it is an intriguing suggestion, 4.11–12 does not fit the scheme very well, and it is not clear to this writer that either 4.7–10 or 4.13–5.6 is really commentary on Prov 3.34. Moreover, one can hardly decide whether οὐκ ἀντιτάσσεται ὑμῖν is a question."[132] In light of the previous verses, at the level of implicature, this last charge is an aggravation of God's verdict. So, the condemnation is

127. Ibid.

128. "καταδικάζω," *L&N* 56.31.

129. Osborne points out that the language here "is a forensic language for the misuse of the courts against the poor, who had no means of defending themselves in a system controlled by the powerful." Osborne, "James," 105.

130. Ibid., 106. There have been different proposals regarding the identity of the righteous one here. Allison gives a list of seven possibilities: (i) Jesus, (ii) James, (iii) those killed during the Bar Kokba war, (iv) an individual or event already forgotten, (v) the singular noun is collective, referring to a class of individuals, and the verb refers to the mistreatment, not literal murder, (vi) a collective noun, but the verb is not purely figurative, and (vii) whichever option one selects, one might detect an allusion to Abel, who was murdered by Cain. The most supported by commentaries are options v and vi. Allison, *James*, 685–7.

131. Luis Alonso Schökel, "James 5:2 and 4:6," *Bib* 54 (1973): 73–6; Edgar, *Has God Not Chosen the Poor?* 203; Johnson, *James*, 305; Todd C. Penner, *The Epistle of James and Eschatology: Re-reading an Ancient Christian Letter*, JSNTSup 121 (Sheffield: Sheffield Academic Press, 1996), 155–8.

132. Allison, *James*, 688. Still another possibility is to consider the clause a question, but with the implicit subject "the righteous": Should they not resist you? Davids, *James*, 180; Ropes, *James*, 292. But, as Osborne rightly points out, the nonresistance of the poor fits better in the context. Osborne, "James," 101. This nonresistance of the poor, says Allison, "magnifies the guilt of the rich." Allison, *James*, 688.

worse. Their actions against the righteous are so overwhelming that he is totally defenseless; he cannot resist them. For that reason, they aggravate their case before God's tribunal.

At a high level of explicitness, this entire paragraph has at least two illocutionary forces. On one hand, for the poor and oppressed among James's addressees, these words are a source of hope. They can rest on God's vindication, as the next paragraph (5:7–11) will explicitly show. Also, they can rest on God's justice. On the other hand, for those rich Christians, this is clearly a warning. If the rich depicted in this paragraph are outsiders, unbelievers, what is about to come upon them is God's punishment, which is already in operation. So, if wealthy Christians are tempted to imitate the common conduct of their social class they must know what God thinks about it. Instead, all of them should lay up treasures in heaven, as Jesus taught them. Also, there is a warning for those believers who are tempted to look for patronage in the wrong place. There is a similar warning in 2:1–13, but here James shows the end of those rich to whom these Christians are showing favoritism. Here, he unmasks them.

So, in this paragraph, James communicates several strong implicatures:

1. God will punish the wicked on the eschatological day of slaughter.
2. Although the wicked prosper today, there will be vindication for the oppressed when God punishes the wicked.
3. There is hope for those who are oppressed today, because there will be a day of slaughter.
4. There is a warning for those who live like the wicked in Jeremiah 12:1–3. God will punish them if they do not repent.
5. If wealth deteriorates then it is ephemeral.
6. Wealth is transitory and unreliable.
7. If someone puts his/her trust in wealth, he/she is a fool.
8. In light of the eschatological latter days, it is unwise to lay up treasures on earth.
9. If accumulated wealth witnesses against a person in the eschatological tribunal, that person acted sinfully.
10. If wealth eats the flesh of its owner, wealth is dangerous. It is God's instrument of punishment.
11. Rich landlords defrauded their workers by not paying them their wages.
12. Their wealth is witness against them because they have illegally obtained it.
13. If someone cheats his workers and does not pay them, he/she violates God's law.
14. As Torah teaches, if a defrauded worker cries to God, he will hear and act in his favor.

15. The Lord of Hosts is the Lord of justice.
16. The Lord of Hosts is the one who punishes the evildoers.
17. The Lord of Hosts is the one who vindicates the poor and oppressed.

Summary of How James Uses the OT in 5:1–6

James embroiders this section on an OT tapestry. Almost every sentence evokes eschatological imagery and prophetic jargon. In this way, James manages to communicate more than the sin he wants to denounce. The eschatological tone of this section permits him to trigger in his readers/hearers several emotions and concepts associated with the OT. At the level of explicature, hope and warning go hand in hand. At the level of implicature, James builds his discourse for his different audiences.

Two clear allusions are interwoven in 5:4. James seems to apply to Deuteronomy 24:14–15 and Isaiah 5:9 something similar to the fourth Hillel's rule, *Binyan ab mishene kethubim*, where the connection of both texts is through the theme of the oppressive wealthy landlords. In both cases, he does not quote the text directly. Instead, he uses some key words from the text, combining interpretive and metalinguistic metarepresentation. He uses enough words in both cases to lead his addressees to make the connections. But he also uses them interpretively. He evokes from Deuteronomy 24:14–15 the concepts of the wealthy's oppressive abuse of poor laborers, the crying to God as an alternative for those oppressed, and the certainty of God's answer in favor of them. From Isaiah 5:9, he evokes the concept of God as the Lord of Hosts and all that the Isaianic image implies. In joining both texts, he strongly and simultaneously communicates hope to the oppressed and a warning to those who sympathize with the oppressors. Furthermore, he communicates God's unchangeable disposition toward the needy. He says that God has chosen the poor, and here he demonstrates one implication of that election: God's commitment to them.

A less clear allusion, or, maybe better, an echo of Jeremiah 12:3 in 5:5 helps James strengthen his case against the wealthy. James interpretively metarepresents Jeremiah's concept of the day of slaughter. In this way, James uses eschatological language to build the evocation of the great reversal, and in particular the punishment of the wicked.

No less important is James's evocation of Jesus's words. James's denunciation is built on Jesus's teaching on wealth. By using Jesus's words interpretively, James reinforces his teaching. In this case, these are not just James's thoughts but Jesus's as well. Jesus teaches where our treasure should be, but these wealthy disobey that teaching. If, in effect, James wants his readers/hearers to make the connection with Jesus's teachings, then the crime he denounces is worse, because it is not only a violation of the Torah, but also disobedience of Jesus himself.

Methodology Applied to 5:7–11

After two paragraphs of warnings, James closes this section with a touch of hope. He encourages his readers/hearers with a calling to an active patience, perseverance in the midst of suffering, in light of the imminent coming of the Lord. The next section shows how James uses the OT exemplars to guide his readers in models of endurance. He interpretively evokes those images in order to illustrate his discourse.

Elucidation of the Co-text

As mentioned above, this paragraph is grammatically connected to the former with the inferential conjunction οὖν (5:7). James 5:1–6 is the expository basis for the hortatory paragraph 5:7–11.[133] This paragraph is a kind of hinge between 5:1–6 and 5:12–20. As Painter points out, "the tirade threatening judgment on the rich is now replaced by instruction";[134] or more specifically, by "instructions to the wider community."[135]

Thematically, 5:7–11 is the logical continuation of the former paragraph, but recalls other important themes of the epistle. The eschatological expectation is the main link. The text in 5:1–6 presents the eschatological reversal for the wealthy that echoes the negative part of the reversal in 1:9–11. In the same way, the text in 5:7–11 presents the positive side of the reversal, emphasizing endurance, as in 1:12.[136] Instead of fattening their hearts as the wicked rich (5:5), they must strengthen them (5:8). "The final day that will bring judgment upon the rich will be a day of salvation for the just."[137]

Other minor themes also connect with this paragraph. This text returns to the topic of patient endurance under trials (1:2–4, 12). Furthermore, James's call to not grumble against one another continues his concern about judging one another in 4:11–12, the last time he calls his addressees ἀδελφοί (cf. κριτής 4:12, 5:9).

The closing section of the letter begins in 5:12. Our outline entitled it "The daily Christian life should reflect care for one another" (5:12–20). However, there has been much debate about the nature of 5:12 and its relationship to the surrounding verses.[138] The phrase πρὸ πάντων at the beginning of the verse seems to suggest a transition. As Hartin proposes, the

133. Hart and Hart, *Analysis of James*, 133–44.

134. John Painter, "James," in *James and Jude*, ed. Mikeal C. Parsons and Charles H. Talbert, Paideia (Grand Rapids, Mich.: Baker, 2012), 161.

135. Brosend, *James and Jude*, 141.

136. Johnson, *James*, 312.

137. Allison, *James*, 696.

138. Some scholars consider 5:12 part of 5:7–11. See, e.g., Blomberg and Kamell, *James*, 218; Wall, *Community of the Wise*, 259–60. For a good discussion of this problem, see Allison, *James*, 723–8.

translation "finally" "would capture the meaning of *pro pantōn* better."[139] Or better, as Vouga suggests, with this phrase James is summarizing in some way the general content of the letter.[140] The topic changes from patience in the midst of suffering (5:7–11) to oath (5:12) to prayer (5:13–18) to communal restoration (5:19–20). For that reason many scholars prefer to see 5:12–20 as several closing exhortations.[141]

Description of the General Cognitive Environment

James continues with agricultural imagery. Now, he illustrates his point with small farmers and their attitudes and practices. Next, some ideas on small agriculture and early and latter rain are explored.

Small Agriculture

James uses the farmer as an example of patience (5:7). Instead of the landlords and the big-scale farming depicted in 5:1–6, here James speaks about the small farmer in Palestine. Comparing both scenes, Allison points out: "[W]e have moved from large estates to small farms, and from workers being mistreated to workers doing their job."[142] So, in terms of Longenecker's scale, this farmer is on the ES_5 or ES_6 level, or even ES_7. This type of farming is almost subsistence cultivation.[143] Davids illustrates well the conditions of this type of agriculture:

> The small farmer plants his carefully saved seed and hopes for a harvest, living on short rations and suffering hunger during the last weeks. The whole livelihood, indeed the life itself, of the family depends on a good harvest: the loss of the farm, semistarvation, or death could result from a bad year.[144]

Early and Latter Rain

In the illustration, the farmer patiently waits for rain. This is particularly true in Palestine agriculture. This type of irrigation is proper of "the east end of the Mediterranean," "from the Taurus Mountains south to the

139. Hartin, *James*, 258.

140. Vouga, *L'épître de saint Jacques*, 138. For Martin this is the best solution. Martin, *James*, 203.

141. See, e.g., Allison, *James*, 726–8; Brosend, *James and Jude*, 148–9; Hartin, *James*, 258; Johnson, *James*, 325; Laws, *James*, 218; McKnight, *James*, 423. Popkes sees the end section 5:7–20. Popkes, *Der Brief des Jakobus*, 314.

142. Allison, *James*, 700.

143. This was the same in the entire Roman Empire. See, e.g., Helen Rhee, *Loving the Poor, Saving the Rich: Wealth, Poverty, and Early Christian Formation* (Grand Rapids, Mich.: Baker, 2012), 2–5.

144. Davids, *James*, 183.

Judean Negeb."[145] There were two main rainy seasons. At the beginning of the grain-sowing season in October to December, there was the early rain, or just πρόϊμος. At the end of the citrus harvest and preceding the wheat and barley harvest in late March to early April, there was the latter rain, or just ὄψιμος.[146] This type of irrigation seems to have been unknown in Alexandria.[147]

Identification of Possible OT Texts and Traditions Evoked

Possible allusions and clear examples are present in this paragraph. Some see allusions in both 5:7 and 5:9. In 5:7, McCartney sees connections with Joel 2:23–24. In 5:9, Johnson sees a thematic allusion to Leviticus 19:18a. Furthermore, James expressly alludes to the prophets and Job in 5:10–11. Also, many scholars see a close connection between 5:9 and Jesus's words in Matthew 7:1, and between 5:11a and Matthew 5:11–12. An analysis of these cases and an evaluation of the accessibility of the cognitive environment are presented next.

Possible Allusions

McCartney thinks James is alluding to Joel 2:23–24 in 5:7, when mentioning the early and latter rain.[148] This expression πρόϊμον καὶ ὄψιμον appears in the LXX five times (Deut 11:14; Hos 6:3; Joel 2:23; Zech 10:1; Jer 5:24). Following Hays's criteria for validation of allusions, regarding availability, it could be possible that Joel is part of the cognitive environment of James and his addressees. Joel 3:1–5 is quoted in Acts 2, and Joel 3:5 in Romans 10:13.[149] Regarding the criterion of volume, there are just three words in common: πρόϊμον καὶ ὄψιμον. The two adjectives are very specialized terms not used except in very limited contexts. The three words also appear in the other four passages. See table 5.5.

Regarding the criterion of recurrence, no other NT author quotes or alludes to Joel 2:23–24 (LXX). Finally, regarding the criterion of global coherence, McCartney says: "James's allusion to it thus reminds the readers that the Lord has indeed promised, in Scripture, to restore all things in righteousness."[150] However, this does not seem to be the point of James. Rather, he encourages his audience to be patient until the Lord's coming,

145. Ibid.

146. "Latter Rain," *TBD* 804; "πρόϊμος, ον (also πρωΐμος)," *ALGNT* 329.

147. This could explain the changes or additions in some manuscripts. McCartney, *James*, 244.

148. Ibid., 241.

149. McCartney says: "Joel 2 was especially significant to the early Christian community. According to Acts 2, Peter quoted it in reference to the phenomena of Pentecost." Ibid. However, technically, Peter's quotation comes from Joel 3:1–5 (LXX).

150. Ibid., 241.

Table 5.5. Comparison of "early and latter rain" in James 5:7 and in the LXX[a]

Jas 5:7	**Deut 11:14**	**Hos 6:3**
μακροθυμήσατε οὖν, ἀδελφοί, ἕως τῆς παρουσίας τοῦ κυρίου. ἰδοὺ ὁ γεωργὸς ἐκδέχεται τὸν τίμιον καρπὸν τῆς γῆς μακροθυμῶν ἐπ᾽ αὐτῷ ἕως λάβῃ πρόϊμον καὶ ὄψιμον.	καὶ δώσει τὸν ὑετὸν τῇ γῇ σου καθ᾽ ὥραν πρόιμον καὶ ὄψιμον, καὶ εἰσοίσεις τὸν σῖτόν σου καὶ τὸν οἶνόν σου καὶ τὸ ἔλαιόν σου,	καὶ γνωσόμεθα διώξομεν τοῦ γνῶναι τὸν κύριον, ὡς ὄρθρον ἕτοιμον εὑρήσομεν αὐτόν, καὶ ἥξει ὡς ὑετὸς ἡμῖν πρόιμος καὶ ὄψιμος τῇ γῇ.
Joel 2:23	**Zech 10:1**	**Jer 5:24**
καὶ τὰ τέκνα Σιων, χαίρετε καὶ εὐφραίνεσθε ἐπὶ τῷ κυρίῳ θεῷ ὑμῶν, διότι ἔδωκεν ὑμῖν τὰ βρώματα εἰς δικαιοσύνην καὶ βρέξει ὑμῖν ὑετὸν πρόιμον καὶ ὄψιμον καθὼς ἔμπροσθεν	αἰτεῖσθε ὑετὸν παρὰ κυρίου καθ᾽ ὥραν πρόιμον καὶ ὄψιμον, κύριος ἐποίησεν φαντασίας, καὶ ὑετὸν χειμερινὸν δώσει αὐτοῖς, ἑκάστῳ βοτάνην ἐν ἀγρῷ.	καὶ οὐκ εἶπον ἐν τῇ καρδίᾳ αὐτῶν φοβηθῶμεν δὴ κύριον τὸν θεὸν ἡμῶν τὸν διδόντα ἡμῖν ὑετὸν πρόιμον καὶ ὄψιμον κατὰ καιρὸν πληρώσεως προστάγματος θερισμοῦ καὶ ἐφύλαξεν ἡμῖν.

[a]The LXX text does not have a diaeresis in πρόιμον. The Greek text of the different OT verses comes respectively from Wevers, *Deuteronomium*; Ziegler, *Septuaginta: Isaias*; Joseph Ziegler, ed., *Duodecim Prophetae*, VTG, Auctoritate Academiae Scientiarum Gottingensis editum (Göttingen: Vandenhoeck & Ruprecht, 1984); Ziegler, *Jeremias, Baruch, Threni, Epistula Jeremiae*.

like the farmer waits for the rain. In this regard, Hosea 6:3 would have more affinity with James's emphasis in 5:7–11.[151] Therefore, Hays's four criteria for evaluating allusions make McCartney's case improbable. An evaluation of the accessibility of the cognitive environment reaffirms this point. If the readers/hearers know the rain cycles of Palestine, or at least are familiar with the image,[152] they could easily access that encyclopedic knowledge in order

151. This is precisely Laws's proposal. Laws, *James*, 212–3. But her arguments have the same problems as McCartney's proposal. Although there is a closer affinity between Hos 6:3 and Jas 5:7–11, James's point is not a call for repentance, but a call for the believers' perseverance. Richardson sees an allusion to Exod 2:24, but the theme is different. In Exod 2:23–25 the grumbling is against their oppressors, and it is heard by God. In James, the grumbling is against one another. Kurt A. Richardson, "Job as Exemplar in the Epistle of James," in *Hearing the Old Testament in the New Testament*, ed. Stanley E. Porter (Grand Rapids, Mich.: Eerdmans, 2006), 221–2. Patrick Gray presents an even weaker case by relating grumbling in James to Job's friends grumbling. Patrick Gray, "Points and Lines: Thematic Parallelism in the Letter of James and the Testament of Job," *NTS* 50 (2004): 423. As Allison correctly points out, the verb στενάζω does not appear in Job or in T. Job. Allison, *James*, 705.

152. Dibelius argues that James uses "a proverbial expression from the Old Testament." He gives as an example Deut 11:14, which is recited in the second part of the daily Jewish confession. Dibelius, *James*, 244.

to make James's appeal relevant. In RT terms, one input is more relevant than another when it gives more cognitive benefits for the same processing effort, or when it gives more cognitive benefits with the same processing effort. In this case, their extra effort in connecting James's text with Joel 2:23–24 would not give more cognitive benefits, so it would be less relevant to make the connection than not to make it. As Blomberg and Kamell point out, "James's analogy would have resonated deeply with his audience, many of whom were clearly farmers."[153] Therefore, from the RT perspective, the connection with Joel 2:22–23 is unlikely.

Johnson argues that it is possible to see a thematic allusion to Leviticus 19:18a in 5:9. In particular, he sees Leviticus 19:18a behind James's exhortation μὴ στενάζετε, ἀδελφοί, κατ᾽ ἀλλήλων.[154] Although Leviticus 19 is present in other sections of the letter, it is not so clear that it is present here. There are no closely related words, nor is the topic similar. Johnson admits: "It must be granted that this argument for a thematic allusion in 5:9 is the most fragile of those I am suggesting."[155] From the RT perspective, the processing effort to make the connections does not represent a major cognitive benefit. So, the allusion is highly improbable. The expression seems to have a better candidate behind it, namely, Jesus's words in Matthew 7:1.

Explicit Mentions

As he does in 2:20–26, here James uses two examples to strengthen his exhortation: the prophets (5:10) and Job (5:11). He assumes that his addressees are pretty familiar with both examples. "The prophets who spoke the name of the Lord" (5:10) is the first example. Various texts (2 Macc 6:18–31; Heb 11:33–38; Matt 5:10–12; Luke 6:22–23, 11:49–51; Acts 7:52; 1 Thess 2:15; *Mart. Ascen. Isa.*) illustrate that it is highly probable that a tradition of prophets' patience in suffering was part of the encyclopedic knowledge shared by James and his addressees. As Moo points out, "[r]eference to the fortitude of martyrs as a model for others to imitate became very popular in the wake of the Maccabean Revolt in the early to middle second century B.C."[156] The reason these prophets suffered is that they spoke the word of God. The same is true of early Christian proclamation. Although James does not specify in what ways they should imitate these prophets, via weak implicatures, he guides his addressees to derive examples. Allison presents some strongly communicated implicatures of James's exhortation in 5:10–11:[157]

153. Blomberg and Kamell, *James*, 227.

154. Luke Timothy Johnson, "The Use of Leviticus 19 in the Letter of James," *JBL* 101 (1982): 396–7.

155. Ibid., 397. Other scholars who see the presence of Lev 19:10–18 in James do not agree with Johnson's proposal either. See, e.g., McCartney, *James*, 44–5.

156. Moo, *James*, 226.

157. Allison, *James*, 708.

1. Suffering will come to the saints.
2. Saints have shown that they can persevere.
3. Those who persevere will receive reward from God, who abounds in compassion and mercy.

These implicated premises and conclusions build on James's exhortations on endurance, as in 1:12. From these conclusions they could derive ad hoc implicatures such as the following:

1. We should endure under our current situation like those prophets.
2. As God blessed them, if we endure, we will receive God's crown of life.

The other example is Job (Jas 5:11). James assumes his addressees have heard and have seen Job's narrative. It is not surprising that James cites Job, says Davids, because "[t]he story of Job was a favorite in Jewish and Christian circles, so it is not in the least surprising that Job was often used as an example (e.g. Ezk. 14:14, 20; Test. Abr. 15:10; 1 Clem. 17; Clem. Alex. Strom. 2.103–104)."[158] James's succinct mention of Job highlights his endurance/patience. However, many scholars have noted that the canonical Job is not precisely depicted as patient (cf. Eliphaz's criticism of Job's impatience in Job 4:1–5, and Job's recognition of it in 6:1–13). So, they conclude that James uses or depends on the Testament of Job.[159] However, as Gray correctly argues, there is not adequate evidence to prove literary dependence between James and the Testament of Job.[160] Allison points out: "Even though the chief protagonist of canonical Job is scarcely an exemplar of patient endurance, ὑπομένω occurs over a dozen times in the LXX version of the book (for several different Hebrew verbs); and while sometimes the meaning is simple 'remain,' there are instances where the word is used by or of Job in interesting and perhaps laded ways. No doubt this contributed to associating him with patience."[161] Later, he concludes: "We should then not explain Jas 5:11 by suggesting the author's ignorance of canonical chapters but by positing his knowledge of extracanonical traditions."[162] So, it is highly probable that both James and his addressees were familiar with Job traditions that emphasize Job's patience in the midst of suffering, in particular, the canonical Job.

158. Davids, *James*, 187.

159. Moo, *James*, 228–9; Richardson, "Job as Exemplar," 213–29. Johnson thinks that James perhaps refers "to apocryphal traditions transmitted in assemblies such as the synagogue." Johnson, *James*, 319. Davids has a similar opinion. Davids, *James*, 187.

160. Gray, "Points and Lines," 422. In this sense, Ghantous erroneously sees James's literary dependence on T. Job and on Qur'anic and Islamic references to Job. Hadi Ghantous, "Was Job 'Patient'? Is God 'Just'?," *TR* 33 (2012): 22–38.

161. Allison, *James*, 714.

162. Ibid., 716.

There is not anything in James 5:11 that precludes seeing James as alluding to the canonical Job, except the emphasis the exegete has on "patience." But as shown below, the canonical Job evidences a "militant patience."

In RT terms, James loosely metarepresents Job tradition. In this case, this would be an interpretive metarepresentation. In this way, he guides his readers/hearers to derive weak implicatures. For example, Elsa Tamez argues that James includes Job as an exemplar of "militant patience." This patience "is a question of doing everything possible not to despair in spite of the desperate situation, relying on the future that will put an end to the sufferings."[163] At the first moments, Job seemed to show resignation, but from Job 3 on "all his verbal fury erupted against his situation and he did not desist until the Almighty came onto the scene. Job did not succumb to pain; on the contrary, the more he experienced attacks, isolation, and suffering, the more he was strengthened, the greater his self-confidence. Job resisted unto death and God vindicated him."[164] In this sense, James uses Job's ὑπομονή "as an example of how to live faithfully through suffering with much resolve and commitment to persevere and to provide a witness to the world of God's compassion and mercy."[165]

Jesus's Words

Many scholars have noted the closeness of James's exhortation in 5:9 to Jesus's words reflected in Matthew 7:1: μὴ κρίνετε, ἵνα μὴ κριθῆτε. He seems to allude to this same segment of the Jesus tradition in James 4:11–12. In this regard, Allison points out: "This [use of the Jesus tradition here] is indeed close to certain, because the precise phrase, ἵνα μὴ κριθῆτε, is unattested outside of Christian Greek texts; and it occurs only in the saying of Jesus, James, and quotations of those texts."[166] Also, James seems to be familiar with the traditions attested in the Sermon on the Mount, as mentioned before. If James wants his addressees to make the connection with Jesus's words, then, anew, he strengthens his exhortation appealing to Jesus's authority. In this case, at least, James interpretively metarepresents Jesus's teaching. That is, he uses and adapts it in his own discourse.[167] The processing effort in making the connection is compensated with extra cognitive benefits. For example, the

163. Elsa Tamez, *The Scandalous Message of James: Faith without Works Is Dead*, rev. ed. (New York: Crossroad, 2002), 46.

164. Ibid., 44.

165. L. Gay Byron, "James," in *True to Our Native Land: An African American New Testament Commentary*, ed. Brian K. Blount et al. (Minneapolis: Fortress, 2007), 469. In a similar way, Solomon Andria comments regarding Job's example: "Anyone who loves God may have to face suffering, but by the end of it they will know God better, and have a far deeper understanding of his love and mercy." Salomon Andria, "James," in *Africa Bible Commentary*, ed. Tokunboh Adeyemo (Grand Rapids, Mich.: Zondervan, 2006), 1515.

166. Allison, *James*, 706.

167. Contra Ropes, who thinks that in James there is "nothing of the idea that judging brings judgment." Ropes, *James*, 297.

exhortation is strengthened with the severity Jesus places on judging others. Also, if the entire pericope of Matthew 7:1–5 is behind the allusion, the idea of looking first at the plank in one's own eye before seeing the speck in one's brother's eye should reinforce James's exhortation via implicatures.

Another possible allusion to Jesus's teaching reflected in the Sermon on the Mount is in James 5:10–11. James gives the prophets as examples of patience in the midst of suffering. After presenting the example, he says: ἰδοὺ μακαρίζομεν τοὺς ὑπομείναντας. These two ideas together seem to evoke Jesus's words reflected in Matthew 5:11–12. There, Jesus says: "Blessed are you when others revile you and persecute you and utter all kinds of evil against you falsely on my account. Rejoice and be glad, for your reward is great in heaven, for so they persecuted the prophets who were before you" (ESV). If this is the case, James reverses the order. First, he presents the prophets as examples, and then expresses the macarism. In this way, he reinforces his own discourse by interpretively metarepresenting Jesus's words.

Interpretation of the Text in James

James 5:7–11 has a discernible structure. It has four imperatives (5:7, 8, 9, and 10). The first two are immediately followed by a rationale; the last two are immediately followed by two rationales. The complete paragraph has the pattern *aba*. The main concern is patient endurance in the midst of suffering. In order to convey this, in 5:7–8 he uses μακροθυμέω/μακροθυμία, and in 5:10–11, ὑπομένω/ὑπομονή. At the center, in 5:9, he exhorts his addressees to not grumble or complain against one another.

Like 5:1–6, this section of the text is embroidered on an eschatological tapestry. James frames his exhortation with perseverance ἕως τῆς παρουσίας τοῦ κυρίου (5:7). In 5:8, he ends his exhortation with ὅτι ἡ παρουσία τοῦ κυρίου ἤγγικεν. In 5:9, he warns his readers/hearers: ἵνα μὴ κριθῆτε· ἰδοὺ ὁ κριτὴς πρὸ τῶν θυρῶν ἕστηκεν. So, he clearly continues his eschatological discourse from 5:1–6, as a direct counterpart to that section.[168] Now, he emphasizes the nearness of the Lord's vindication of the righteous, the other side of the great reversal in 5:1–6. So, through this eschatological language, James guides his readers/hearers to connect the exhortation to perseverance in the midst of suffering with hope and the imminence of their salvation. Their suffering is coming to an end. They are about to receive the crown of life (1:12).

This section is grammatically linked to the former by the inferential conjunction οὖν (5:1). As McCartney points out, "this section is the response of faith to the wickedness of the unjust landowner presented in the preceding section."[169] He seems to use the term "brothers" for different and

168. Vouga, *L'épître de saint Jacques*, 132.

169. McCartney, *James*, 240. Vouga sees this paragraph as the "contrapartie directe" of the invective against the "spéculateurs" (4:13–17) and the rich (5:1–6). Vouga, L'épître de saint

complimentary reasons (5:7, 9, 10): to differentiate his focus here from the previous paragraphs, to show a change of tone, to show closeness to and affection for his addressees, and to motivate them to heed his warning.[170] He also uses the interjection ἰδοὺ three times (5:7, 9, 11) to capture the audience's attention to what he is saying.[171]

Instead of arrogance, selfish living, exploitation of the needy, and mistreatment of the righteous, James calls them to live in light of the Lord's coming. In this sense, he continues the theme already presented in 1:12, 2:12–13, and 4:11–12. The addressees should manifest an internal disposition of the heart. James calls them to be patient and persevere: μακροθυμήσατε. Because of its semantic/pragmatic nature, this verb may communicate divergent implicatures. Some scholars understand this verb with both a passive sense, "to wait," and an active sense, "to trust";[172] as the opposite of "wrath and revenge";[173] to be close in meaning to ὑπομένω/ὑπομονή, to indicate "passivity toward the activity of another," "enduring/endurance,"[174] and even "resignation."[175] However, as seen above, James's example guides his audience to a more active sense of "waiting," to not give up.[176] This patience is what Elsa Tamez calls "a militant patience."[177]

This patience has a goal and a time frame, ἕως τῆς παρουσίας τοῦ κυρίου. The referent of κυρίου has been a topic of debate. Παρουσία is used for "the arrival of an important person, especially a king or emperor as well as the manifestation of a hidden deity."[178] In the LXX (Jdt 10:18; 2 Macc 8:12, 15:21; 3 Macc 3:17; and Codex Alexandrinus of Neh 2:6) it is used in the secular sense of "arrival"

Jacques, 132. Allison does not see a clear function of this conjunction. As presented here, the conjunction guides the readers/hearers to make inferences about the relationship between the admonition in 5:1–6 and the hope in 5:7–11. He agrees with Laws in that "the threat to the rich is an indication that there will be an end to oppression, and that the readers should therefore be patient." Allison, *James*, 697–8; Laws, *James*, 208.

170. Allison, *James*, 698; Hartin, *James*, 241; Johnson, *James*, 312; Tamez, *No discriminen a los pobres*, 105.

171. Witherington, *Letters and Homilies*, 536.

172. Osborne, "James," 106.

173. Allison, *James*, 696.

174. Johnson, *James*, 312–3.

175. Moo's comment illustrates this approach: "The attitude that James calls on us to adopt here, then, includes resignation in the face of suffering along with confident expectation of a day when the fortunes of this life will be reversed." Moo, *James*, 222. This way of understanding patience has led to the concept of redemptive suffering among African American Christians, "who have understood the words of James . . . as a mandate to tolerate evil in its various manifestations of injustice and oppression." Byron, "James," 469–70.

176. Blomberg and Kamell, *James*, 226. As Johnson says, μακροθυμία/μακροθυμεῖν means "the active adoption of an attitude of 'forbearance' and 'putting up with' another." Johnson, *James*, 313.

177. Tamez, *The Scandalous Message*, 43. She uses another Spanish expression to communicate this idea, sadly it is not equivalent to the English translation for what it implies, "aguante inquebrantable" (close to unbreakable endurance). Tamez, *No discriminen a los pobres*, 104.

178. Allison, *James*, 698; Hartin, *James*, 243.

or "presence." Allison points out that Testament of Judah 22:2, Testament of Moses 10:12, 2 Baruch 30:1, and Testament of Abraham RecLng. 13:4 "raise the possibility that, in pre-Christian times, some already used the noun of the eschatological coming of God or a divine intermediary."[179] Very similar is the language of Testament of Judah 22:2, ἕως παρουσίας τοῦ θεοῦ. However, as many scholars observe, in early Christian literature, and elsewhere in the NT, the expression παρουσίας τοῦ κυρίου is a technical expression for the second coming of Jesus (Matt 24:3, 27, 37, 39; 1 Cor 15:23; 1 Thess 2:19, 3:13, 4:15, 5:23; 2 Thess 2:1; 2 Pet 1:16; 3:4, 12; 1 John 2:28).[180] James uses κύριος with Jesus as referent in 1:1 and 2:1. Nevertheless, God the Father is the clear referent, almost everywhere else in the letter (1:7; 3:9; 4:10, 15; 5:4, 10–11, 14–15?). So, some scholars see God the Father as the referent here and in 5:8.[181] However, it is more probable that James and his addressees would have understood this expression in its Christian connotation, Jesus's coming as vindicator of the righteous and judge of the wicked (cf. Matt 24:3, 27, 37, 39).

To guide his addressees in deriving the implicatures that he wants, James uses the farmer as an illustration of what he means by "be patient" (5:7). The farmer, and in particular a subsistence farmer, is in no way an example of resignation and passivity. Even though he has no control over rain, he does all that is possible to prepare the field in order to receive rain.[182] This could even be considered a heroic patience because of the extreme conditions farmers faced.[183] James's point is to highlight "waiting without losing patience."

Following the example, then, says James, they also should be patient. They must strengthen their hearts. Commenting on this expression, Johnson points out: "James's language evokes a Septuagintal idiom, 'strengthening the heart,' which, depending on context, can mean to gain physical strength, as for a journey (Judg 19:5, 8; Ps 104:15), or courage that comes from trust in the Lord (Ps 111:18), or firmness of intention (Sir 6:37; 22:16; . . .). It is undoubtedly one of these latter two meanings James intends."[184] So, instead of fattening their hearts as the wicked rich do (5:5), they should strengthen their hearts by knowing that the coming of the Lord is near (5:8). This awareness of the imminence of Jesus's coming permits them to have the right

179. Allison, *James*, 698.

180. See, e.g., Dibelius, *James*, 242; Hartin, *James*, 241–2; Johnson, *James*, 314; Laws, *James*, 208–9; Osborne, "James," 108; Ropes, *James*, 293.

181. J. Cantinant, *Les épîtres de Saint Jacques et de Saint Jude*, SB (Paris: Gabalda, 1973), 232; McKnight, *James*, 408. Allison does not decide with clarity; he concludes: "[W]e have here a line that Christians could have read one way, Jews another." Allison, *James*, 699.

182. As Blomberg and Kamell explain, farmers of this type "work hard in weeding, hoeing, fertilizing, and doing whatever they could to bring their crops to full fruition." Blomberg and Kamell, *James*, 227.

183. Tamez highlights this point, saying, "[I]f they only depend on the fruit of the land to survive. They would experience hunger, but they know that in the end, they will get the fruit." Tamez, *No discriminen a los pobres*, 105.

184. Johnson, *James*, 315.

attitude. Their hope is twofold, the Lord's coming brings with it vindication for the righteous, but also punishment for the wicked. For James, this waiting implies that they should not reproduce those actions and attitudes of oppression witnessed inside the community. They must visit orphans and widows. They must help the needy. They must eradicate discrimination against the poor among them, if not τί τὸ ὄφελος;

However, they seem to have forgotten this eschatological perspective. One wrong attitude could turn them against one another. For that reason, at the center of this paragraph, James exhorts them to not grumble, complain against one another (5:9). In the midst of consolation, there is a warning. It is not clear what kind of complaining James has in mind or how this verse fit in the surrounding texts. James deals with problems of speech control in 1:26–27, 3:1–12, and 4:1–3. He asks them to not curse others (3:1–12) and to not judge others (4:11). But, here, it is hard to know why or about what they are complaining. As Blomberg and Kamell say, "[p]erhaps they project their frustrations at the landlords onto each other. Or perhaps they disagree on how they ought to deal with the oppression, and the different factions complain about each other in their anger. Maybe they are blaming one another for the problems they are facing as a congregation, or maybe they are accusing each other to avoid problems themselves."[185]

What is clear, however, is that for James, their complaining is a serious problem. Complaining against one another is a type of καταλαλέω (4:11). If they complain against one another, they are taking on the role of judges. However, the real judge is at the gates. They should stop complaining and wait for the judge's verdict. But if they do not change their attitude in the community, they must know that they could be judged. As a matter of fact, the judge is at the gates (cf. Mark 13:29; Matt 24:33). In 4:11, God is the judge. But here, James seems to be intentionally ambiguous. The judge could be God the Father or Jesus. Jesus is also known early in the church as the eschatological judge (Matt 25:31–46; John 5:22; Acts 17:31; 2 Cor 5:10; Rev 9:11).[186] The nearness of the expression "the Lord's coming" (twice in 5:7–8) makes Jesus the most probable referent. In RT terms, in the context, Jesus is more salient than God the Father as the referent for "the judge."[187] The apocalyptic imagery of being at the door seems to imply that not only is the Lord about to come but he is also watching believers' actions.[188] Therefore, instead of this sinful attitude, they should be patient with one another and support and encourage one another. Jesus's teachings behind Matthew 7:1

185. Blomberg and Kamell, *James*, 228.

186. Allison, *James*, 707.

187. Johnson, *James*, 317; Martin, *James*, 192; Moo, *James*, 225; Osborne, "James," 106–7. Contra Hartin, *James*, 243; Laws, *James*, 213; McKnight, *James*, 415.

188. Dibelius, *James*, 244.

resonate here. If this is the case, and James wants his addressees to make the connections, then, they could derive implicatures such as the following:

1. James exhorts us to stop complaining against one another.
2. James is reminding us about what Jesus has already taught us.
3. If we do not stop grumbling against one another, Jesus will judge us.
4. Jesus is at the gates, about to come, watching us.
5. Jesus is at the gates, about to come, so we must change our attitude and be patient with one another.

In the last two verses (5:10–11), he again emphasizes active patience. This time, he appeals to two biblical examples. In 2:20–26, James presents two exemplars (Abraham and Rahab). There, he implicitly calls his addressees to imitate them. Here, in contrast, James explicitly calls his addressees to imitate these exemplars. In 2:20–26, the imitation is implied. In 5:10, James says through a double accusative, Consider the prophets who spoke in the name of the Lord as examples τῆς κακοπαθίας καὶ τῆς μακροθυμίας. This hendiadys emphasizes patience in the midst of suffering.[189] No specific prophet is mentioned. However, one could think of prophets like Jeremiah or Elijah, who suffered precisely because of their proclamation and denunciation of sin. So, what James is encouraging them to imitate is not precisely a passive patience, a resignation and waiting for better times. James strongly implies that his addressees should be prepared to suffer because of Christ, in light of Jesus's imminent coming, as these OT prophets did. As Osborne implies, "[t]he message to James's readers is simple: No matter what the consequences, live for God and proclaim his word."[190]

This implication could be strengthened if James has in mind Jesus's teachings, such as those reflected in Matthew 5:11–12, behind the macarism ἰδοὺ μακαρίζομεν τοὺς ὑπομείναντας (5:11a). If this is the case, as mentioned above, James, anew, is interpretively metarepresenting Jesus's teachings in order to strengthen his own discourse with Jesus's authority. As shown in other passages in the epistle, James seems to strengthen his teaching by appealing to Jesus's teaching, in particular that reflected in the Sermon on the Mount. However, it is hard to know whether James wants his addressees to make the connection with this specific saying here.

Those who endure are the prophets of the past, but it is not only they who persevere.[191] The aorist depicts perfective aspect, but not the chronological

189. Contra McKnight, who thinks the hendiadys is not as clear. He prefers to maintain both terms "suffering and patience." McKnight, *James*, 417. But, probably, James is not inviting his addressees to imitate suffering; the ὑπόδειγμα is the prophets' perseverance/patience in the midst of their sufferings. See McCartney, *James*, 242.

190. Osborne, "James," 110.

191. Contra Adamson and Martin, who limit the macarism to the OT prophets. Adamson, *The Epistle of James*, 192–3; Martin, *James*, 193.

time. In this case, it includes Christians who, like those OT prophets, have also persevered in trials, afflictions, and persecution. These believers are part of the first generations of Christians. It is possible that some of them were in Palestine with James before departing for their current homes. So, it is highly probable that they have in their encyclopedic knowledge Christians like Stephen (Acts 7). Their encyclopedic knowledge also could include experiences of the believers in their own community.

The last example James gives is Job. He assumes his addressees have enough knowledge of the story to evoke it with just the phrases τὴν ὑπομονὴν Ἰώβ and τὸ τέλος κυρίου (5:11b). They surely know Job's story and how at the end of his story God restored him.[192] He showed his kindness to Job by restoring his family and everything. God at the end showed Job ὅτι πολύσπλαγχνός ἐστιν ὁ κύριος καὶ οἰκτίρμων. These characteristics of God are well attested in the OT (Exod 34:6; Pss 103:8; 111:4), but James seems to form the adjective πολύσπλαγχνός, unattested before him. As Allison points out, "[h]ere then we seemingly have again James' fondness for new variations on old ways of speaking."[193] If the canonical Job is in view, as shown above, Tamez's description of Job's patience illustrates how James conceives ὑπομένω/ὑπομονή.[194] This patience relies on a deep trust in God and his son Jesus, and on a total confidence in Jesus's imminent coming. Paraphrasing McKnight, it is an eschatological patience.[195]

At a higher level of explicitness, it is possible to detect at least two illocutionary forces. The main purpose of this paragraph is encouragement. The case of the oppressive landlords in 5:1–6 is one illustration of the kind of problems the Christian community is facing. So, James encourages his addressees with the great eschatological reversal and the imminent coming of Jesus. In light of this coming, he animates his addressees to persevere, to endure in the midst of their suffering. At the same time, he warns them not to complain/grumble against one another. The following are some of the most strongly implied implicatures in this paragraph:

6. Suffering will come to the saints.
7. Saints have shown that they can persevere.

192. The expression has had different interpretations. McCartney presents a good summary of the main four alternatives derived from the semantic range of τέλος (purpose or result) and the referent of κύριος (Jesus or the Father): (1) the end of the Lord's (Christ's) life and earthly ministry, (2) the end of history, (3) the end result of Job's story, and (4) God's purpose in subjecting Job to suffering. The more common understanding and that supported by the text of Job and the context in James is alternative 3. McCartney, *James*, 243. Allison sees some connections between this phrase and Job 23:3. He concludes: "One could reasonably read Job so that its conclusion brings to Job the τέλος he spoke of and desired earlier." Allison, *James*, 719.

193. Allison, *James*, 720–1.

194. Tamez, *The Scandalous Message*, 44.

195. McKnight, *James*, 405.

8. Those who persevere will receive reward from God, who abounds in compassion and mercy.
9. We should endure under our current situation like those prophets.
10. As God blessed them, if we endure, we will receive God's crown of life.
11. James exhorts us to stop complaining against one another.
12. James is reminding us of what Jesus has already taught us.
13. If we do not stop grumbling against one another, Jesus will judge us.
14. Jesus is near to us, about to come, watching us.
15. Jesus is near to us, about to come, so we must change our attitude and be patient with one another.

Summary of How James Uses the OT in 5:7–11

This section closes James's thoughts on poverty and wealth. He closes the theme with a touch of hope for those who suffer. As he does in 5:1–6, James paints his message on an eschatological canvas. Thus, his use of the OT is framed in eschatological language. His language and use of the OT is not as "baroque" as in 5:1–6. In 5:1–6, almost every word alludes to the OT. Here, he uses the OT to support his exhortations to have an active patience. He evokes the OT via examples. He uses a loose interpretive resemblance of the OT. He rests on his shared encyclopedic knowledge with his addressees. He interpretively metarepresents the prophets' lives of proclamation and patience in the midst of suffering, and Job's story of "militant patience." In this way, he manages to guide his readers/hearers in their derivation of implicatures. He builds his ethics of poverty and wealth by interpretively metarepresenting the OT.

Also, as in other parts of his discourse, James seemingly evokes Jesus's teachings in order to strengthen his own words. He warns them not to complain against one another by evoking Jesus's teaching reflected in Matthew 7:1–5. He seemingly evokes Jesus's teachings on Christian suffering reflected in Matthew 5:11–12, in order to reinforce his OT example of the prophets' patience in suffering.

Conclusions

As in previous chapters, the aim here was to study how James uses the OT in several passages where he deals with the issue of poverty and wealth. An RT approach is used in the discourse analysis. Also Hays's first four criteria of validation are used to evaluate possible allusions. This chapter analyzes James 4:13–17 and 5:1–6 and 7–11. The use of the OT and Jesus's words in these passages confirms the thesis that James builds his ethics of poverty and wealth by interpretively metarepresenting the OT and Jesus's teachings.

In 4:13–17, James uses OT language, but seemingly does not appeal to any specific text. On one hand, there is a possible echo of Proverbs 27:1 in 4:16. If James intends his addressees to make the connection, he is interpretively metarepresenting that text. It would be a loose resemblance of the OT. On the other hand, he seems to evoke earlier parts of his discourse, in particular 1:9–11. If this is the case, he guides his addressees to evoke the theme of the eschatological reversal, and the warning against the wealthy there. In this way, his metaphor of the mist is recovered with the eschatological warning of the Isaianic text.

James 5:1–6 is the greatest intertext with the OT anywhere in the letter and also alludes to Jesus's teachings. Both allusions and eschatological language contribute to James's rhetoric. There are two clear allusions in 5:4: Deuteronomy 24:14–15 and Isaiah 5:9. There is also a possible echo of Jeremiah 12:3 in James 5:5. In both allusions, James considers the OT context of his citations. Both OT contexts help him to build his message of warning and hope. He metalinguistically uses enough words of each text to trigger in his addressees a connection with the OT, but also uses those texts interpretively in his own discourse. The echo of Jeremiah 12:3 contributes in a similar way. It helps James to strengthen his case against the rich.

His eschatological language, already present since 1:9–11, gives James a very useful instrument to communicate via implicatures more than what he could communicate via explicatures. He may evoke a series of themes, sentiments, hope, and warning via implicatures triggered by the eschatological imagery. He uses the great reversal and God's tribunal where the rich are punished, but the cry of the laborers is finally heard. The powerful image of God as the Lord of Hosts cooperates to the same end, to communicate via implicatures more than what he could communicate via explicatures. The accumulation of powerful metaphors gives to James great freedom of action. He manages to communicate hope to the oppressed but at the same time warns those who sympathize with the oppressor. He evokes earlier sections of his discourse to highlight this reversal already in operation on the rich. Shiny clothing, gold, the rich abusing their social position in human tribunals against those who cannot oppose them—these are reversed by the eschatological judgment. Moth-eaten clothing and corroded gold are evidence that God's tribunal has dictated a sentence against the wealthy.

James takes two OT passages and recovers them with an eschatological ethos. Deuteronomy 24:14–15 has a forensic initial context. Isaiah 5:9 is a prophetic ethical denouncement in the midst of a woe oracle. However, James interpretively uses both of them. He applies Deuteronomy 24:14–15 to the situation some of his addressees are experiencing, and transforms the Deuteronomic "Lord" into the Isaianic "Lord of Hosts." He uses both texts in a scene of God's eschatological tribunal. In this way, he guides his readers/hearers to understand these texts in this new eschatological setting, the last judgment. As a result, other implicatures appear. For example, the images of God as a judge and a warrior are combined, the hope for God's vindication of the righteous and the punishment of the wicked is strengthened, and the imminence of the Lord's coming is implied. He respects the OT context. However, through this new setting and interpretive use, he adds new implicatures to those texts. As a result, he strengthens his discourse by appealing to the OT's authority.

In 5:7–11, James's evocation of Jesus's words is also important. If James wants his readers/hearers to make the connection with Jesus's teaching reflected in Matthew 6:19–21, his denunciation of the wealthy landlords is strengthened. In this way, the crime James denounces is worse. Instead of laying up treasures in heaven, these wicked rich are storing up treasures on earth, in evil ways and for egotistic purposes.

In 5:7–11, James centers his discourse on those who are suffering. He encourages them to be patient. James exemplifies the model of patience he has in mind with three models: the small farmer, the OT prophets, and Job. These last two examples evoke the OT. James assumes his addressees know them well. So, in that way, he interpretively metarepresents the OT. This permits him to guide his readers/hearers in the derivation of implicatures. Also here, he seems to evoke Jesus's teaching. He seemingly evokes Jesus's words reflected in Matthew 5:11–12 and 7:1–5. With Jesus, James exhorts them to not grumble against one another so that they may not be judged. Instead, they must be patient with one another. Also with Jesus, James encourages them to face suffering with patience in light of Jesus's imminent coming.

The use of the RT methodology in this chapter helps to confirm the presence of allusions, but also to discard others. The use of Hays's criteria of validation and the evaluation of the accessibility of the cognitive environment help to confirm the presence of clear allusions to Deuteronomy 24:14–15 and Isaiah 5:9 in James 5:4 and possible echoes of Proverbs 27:1 in James 4:14 and Jeremiah 12:3 in James 5:5. At the same time, this methodology helps to discard Joel 2:23–24 and Hosea 6:3 in James 5:7 and Leviticus 19:18a in James 5:9 as improbable allusions.

In synthesis, James uses the OT in different ways throughout 4:13–5:11. On a couple of occasions he metalinguistically uses the OT, in particular in 5:1–6. However, in general, he tends to use it interpretively. Even in 5:5, he uses a combination of metalinguistic and interpretive resemblance. He uses and adapts the OT context to his own discourse. He mainly preserves the OT context but uses it for his own purposes. The main example of his interpretive use here is his eschatological language. By using eschatological language, he manages to guide his readers/hearers to evoke OT eschatological concepts and themes. This language permits him to build his allusions on a strong basis. Thus, he may evoke OT passages and give them an eschatological flavor. Furthermore, this loose metarepresentation of the

OT permits James to guide his readers/hearers to derive weak implicatures constrained by two eschatological themes: the great reversal and God's judgment. To these OT themes, he adds here Jesus's coming. In this way, James builds his ethics of poverty and wealth by interpretively metarepresenting the OT and Jesus's teachings.

Chapter 6

Conclusion

The epistle of James is submerged in OT language. It also reflects Jesus's words and teachings. At the same time, James shows great concern for the spiritual health of his addressees. For that reason, he uses both the OT and Jesus's words throughout the epistle to expound upon different aspects of the Christian life. In particular, he corrects his addressees' attitudes and values concerning poverty and wealth. A wrong basis for these attitudes and values results in incongruence between his addressees' faith and their practice. Following is a summary of the main conclusions in each chapter of the present work, a synthesis of how James uses the OT, a synopsis of James's ethics of poverty and wealth, and a consideration of the contributions of RT to the discussion of these issues. Then, final conclusions are presented.

Chapter 1

Chapter 1 broadly presents the main ideas that develop in the present research. One of the major concerns of James in his epistle is the issue of poverty and wealth. This theme occupies around 45% of the epistle. Each time James addresses the topic, he uses imagery alluding to or quoting the OT. So, how does James use the OT in those passages? This question guides the research. In a review of the literature about the issue of poverty and wealth, some ideas stand out. Dibelius's commentary and his ideas of the pious poor were very influential. For him, and for many after him, the poor in the letter are Christians. "Poor" and "Christian" are almost synonymous terms. The rich, on their part, are the enemies of Christians. So, for Dibelius, poor and rich are not financial/social categories, but religious distinctions. Another influential author, Peter Davids, adapts the concept of poor and rich slightly and permits socioeconomic aspects to enter into the discussion. In more recent decades, however, this idea of *Armenfrömmigkeit* has been set aside for all practical purposes, and clearer socioeconomic categories now dominate the analysis of the issue. Today there are some more balanced approaches to the issue. Scholars such as Allison, Blomberg and Kamell, Johnson, and McKnight deal with the issue of poverty in their commentaries, taking into account social science as one factor in the equation.

Studies analyzing the OT in James have been fewer in number, but no less important. These works have focused on specific passages or topics. However, there has been no study as yet on how James uses the OT in passages where he deals with poverty and wealth. Thus, the present work is a contribution in this area.

This study assumes that James, the brother of Jesus, is the author of the letter and that he is writing mainly to Jewish Christians living in the diaspora in the late 40s and early 50s A.D.

Chapter 2

In order to do the analysis, this investigation proposes a method based on Relevance Theory. Chapter 1 presents a synthesis of RT and its potential for the research. In chapter 2, a précis of RT is presented. RT takes into account the inferential nature of language. It considers the meaning of any utterance to be a combination of explicit and implicit information. This information is highly context-dependent. Furthermore, RT sees the locus of meaning in the dialogue among the author, the text, the reader/hearer, and the context. In RT, "relevance" is a technical concept. It relates to the modifications of a reader's/hearer's cognitive environment and the cognitive effort invested in that change. In this sense, any stimulus is relevant to an individual when it connects with his context to yield conclusions that matter to him. Also "context" is seen as the information accessed in the communication process. Each utterance triggers different components of the cognitive environment. These components become the context of that utterance.

RT focuses on both sides of communication: author and reader/hearer. The principle of relevance guides the interpretive process. The author communicates ostensively, and the reader/hearer infers from the evidence provided and the context what the author's intent is. In doing so, he invests cognitive processing effort to understand the author. Cognitive effects compensate this effort. The greater the cognitive effects, the greater the relevance, and the less the processing effort to obtain those effects, the greater the relevance.

In order to recover the author's meaning, a reader/hearer uses the utterance, and guided by the search for relevance, he recovers explicatures and implicatures. At the explicit level, he looks for ambiguities to clarify, references to assign, ellipses to interpret, and so on. At a higher level of explicitness, such as the level where irony functions, he infers attitudes, resolves illocutionary indeterminacies, and so on. These tasks are called the recovery of explicatures. The reader/hearer also discerns implicit premises and derives implicated conclusions. These tasks are called the recovery of implicatures. Traditional exegetical methods tend to focus more on the recovery of explicatures. RT gives a more balanced approach to the recovery of the author's meaning.

RT notes that one of the characteristics of human communication is the ability to represent the thoughts of other persons or oneself at another time and ascribe intentions to them. The representation of another's thoughts is called metarepresentation. Quotations, allusions, and echoes are types of metarepresentation—linguistic metarepresentation.

In RT terms, an author may metarepresent another's thoughts or words in at least two ways. She may provide a metalinguistic resemblance of the other person's thoughts. This type of metarepresentation is a resemblance in form. She may also exploit a resemblance in content. This is an interpretive resemblance. In a discourse, an author could metarepresent another's thoughts or words with either of these resemblances or combine both. That is, she takes from her source some phrases or words and uses them in her own discourse. This is what is regularly observed in James's discourse. Even in those few cases where James metalinguistically metarepresents the OT, he uses those texts interpretively in his own discourse by exploiting implicatures from the source text. In fact, James builds his ethics of poverty and wealth by interpretively metarepresenting the OT and Jesus's teachings.

An author guides her readers/hearers in the search for explicatures and implicatures. She uses different tropes and rhetorical devices in order to accomplish this. Metarepresentations are one of these literary resources. When an author intentionally uses them, she guides her reader/hearer to make connections with the other's thoughts or words. In this way, she shares the implicatures of the other's thoughts or words, and uses them in her own discourse. If the reader/hearer detects the metarepresentation, he may derive more cognitive effects that compensate for the extra processing effort.

This last characteristic of metarepresentations helps in the evaluation of possible allusions and echoes. Current readers of the biblical text are secondary readers. As such, in order to interpret the biblical text, a person today needs to evaluate different aspects of the cognitive environment shared by the biblical author and his first audience. Among these aspects are the OT text and traditions. In order to detect a possible allusion and its contribution to the discourse, it is necessary to evaluate whether the NT author intended his audience to make the connection with the OT or they could understand the NT text without making the connection. The methodology applied in this research is built on this characteristic.

This methodology consists of seven steps: (1) establishment of the text, (2) elucidation of the co-text, (3) description of the general cognitive environment, (4) identification of the possible OT texts and traditions evoked, (5) evaluation of the accessibility of the cognitive environment, (6) interpretation of the text within a prioritized cognitive environment, and (7) summary of how James uses the OT. In step 4, Hays's first four criteria of validation help in discerning possible allusions. These criteria are in total agreement with an RT perspective: (1) availability, (2) volume, (3) recurrence, and (4) thematic coherence. Therefore, they are used in the identification of the possible OT texts and traditions evoked. These potential texts are later compared with other elements of the cognitive environment in order to discern whether James uses the OT in his own discourse.

RT is a good companion to the historical-critical and literary methods. As this research shows, RT is an aid in exegesis. It is not a method that replaces the others. In particular, it is a robust model that integrates context and text in the interpretive process. Also, it gives balance to the search for meaning at both the explicit level and the implicit level. It takes into account both the author and his/her readers/hearers. In the case of allusions, it gives balanced criteria to discern the presence of OT texts or to discard unlikely candidates.

Chapter 3

In the study of James's use of the OT, this research focuses on those passages where James deals with poverty and wealth. James 1:9–11, 26–27; 2:1–13, 14–26; 4:13–17; and 5:1–6, 7–11 are the texts considered. Purely for pragmatic reasons, these texts are grouped in three blocks. Chapter 3 studies 1:9–11 and 26–27. Chapter 4 focuses on 2:1–13 and 14–26. Chapter 5 deals with 4:13–17 and 5:1–6 and 7–11.

The first time James explicitly deals with poverty and wealth is in 1:9–11. He alludes to Isaiah 40:6–7 (LXX). He presents an eschatological reversal of fortunes for the humble and the rich. This reversal is the basis for what he argues in the rest of the letter. He leaves some assumptions implicit in the text that later he explicitly develops. In this way, he manages to evoke eschatological themes when dealing with other aspects of the theme of poverty and wealth.

He uses enough words from Isaiah 40:6–7 to guide his addressees to make the connection with the Isaianic passage. In this way, he metalinguistically metarepresents the OT text. But he also uses the text in his own discourse. In this sense, he combines metalinguistic and interpretive resemblance. As a result, he guides his addressees to derive implicatures related to vindication of the righteous and punishment of the wicked. The Isaianic text reinforces this theme by evoking the ideas of God bringing his people back to Zion and punishing his adversaries. The use of Isaiah 40:6–7 not only gives him the opportunity to strengthen his own discourse with OT authority, but also permits James to reinforce the idea of eschatological reversal and lay the foundations of his ethics of poverty and wealth.

In 1:9–11, James instructs the humble and the rich. He gives the same direction to both of them. They should boast for different reasons: exaltation and humiliation. At this point in the discourse, however, James does not explain why the humble should exalt and what this exaltation looks like. He also does not explain the humiliation of the rich. The eschatological flavor of the reversal permits one to infer that James refers to the final exaltation of the righteous and the condemnation of the wicked. In the same vein, the ephemeral life of the rich reflects God's punishment of them. Later in his letter, however, James expands these two ideas.

Here, James does not explain whether these rich are or are not part of the Christian community. He presents the rich *qua* rich. This ellipsis permits him to address different illocutionary forces in his discourse: hope and warning. He encourages the poor among his addressees. At the same time, he warns those rich believers who are tempted to imitate the wicked wealthy. There is vindication, but there is also a certain punishment imminent. In the next passages, James is more explicit in his message to those believers who are socially between these extremes.

The second text is 1:26–27. Here, James does not use any explicit allusions. Nevertheless, his language is charged with OT concepts. Also, the eschatological language present in 1:9–11 continues as a fabric of his discourse. With this tapestry, he encourages his addressees to have a genuine worship before their God and Father. This worship includes speech control, caring for orphans and widows in the midst of their afflictions, and ethical purity. If James wants his readers/hearers to make connections with the OT, he is using language that guides his addressees to link his discourse with OT teachings. In this passage, James shows how some of these humble brothers and sisters live. He shows the current position of humiliation from which God is about to exalt them.

In this chapter, the method helps to discern the presence of Isaiah 40:6–7 in James 1:10–11. Also it offers a more objective way to dismiss other LXX texts: Job 14:1–2; Psalms 89:3–6; 101:5, 12; and 102:14–15. Furthermore, it is useful to note that no specific text is alluded to in James 1:26–27, but rather there is a general agreement with OT teaching regarding the care for widows and orphans. A possible echo of Malachi 3:1–5 could be behind James 1:26–27. The method also shows that James interpretively metarepresents the OT.

Chapter 4

This chapter deals with 2:1–23. The entire chapter is one literary unit subdivided into two segments, 2:1–13 and 14–23. In 2:1–13, James confronts his addressees with the incongruence between their faith in Jesus Christ the glorious Lord and their discrimination against the poor in favor of the rich. In 2:14–26, he shows that one cannot have faith without deeds, in particular merciful deeds in favor of the poor.

In order to demonstrate this incongruence, James appeals to Jesus's words, alludes to Deuteronomy 6:5 and Leviticus 19:5(?), and explicitly quotes Leviticus 19:18b and Deuteronomy 5:17–18/Exodus 20:13, 15. He interpretively metarepresents Jesus's words reflected in Luke 6:20. The poor in the world's perspective are heirs of the kingdom of God (Jas 2:5), so subject to highest honor. But the addressees in their search for patronage have humiliated them, instead of giving them their due honor. This kingdom is promised to all of those who love God, an echo of Deuteronomy 6:5. This discrimination is an overt violation of the royal law reflected in Leviticus 19:18b. It is as heinous as murder or adultery, two clear commandments. By appealing to Leviticus 19:18b, James seems to evoke Jesus's words reflected in the Synoptic Gospels. In this way, James not only is in line with Jesus's teaching, but also includes Jesus's teachings as part of the royal law, the law of freedom. Although James metalinguistically metarepresents Leviticus 19:18b and the two commandments, he interpretively uses them in his discourse, as he does with the other alluded texts. In each metarepresentation, James introduces the OT implicatures. He respects the OT context but at the same time uses it in his own discourse. He presents Leviticus 19:18b as the distinctive law of the kingdom of God. He sees Leviticus 19:18b through Jesus's eyes. James strongly implies that discrimination against the poor is a clear violation of this law. It is as severe as murder or adultery. Also he implies that God, the giver of the law, is vigilant in its obedience.

In 2:14–26, James demonstrates that a congruent faith in Jesus is a faith that works. In particular, he seems to have in mind merciful deeds, as the example in 2:14–17 reveals. James alludes to Deuteronomy 6:4 to shows that a mere confession that is not accompanied by deeds is dead faith, which is useless. He supports his claim that one cannot have faith without deeds by appealing to two emblematic OT figures: Abraham (in the *Aqedah* and Gen 15:6 [LXX]) and Rahab. In both cases, deeds are the key element. Regarding his use of the OT, he metalinguistically metarepresents Genesis 15:6 (LXX), but at the same time, he uses the quotation in his own discourse interpretively. In James's discourse, God's declaration of Abraham's righteousness is fulfilled in the *Aqedah*. Also, James interpretively uses Rahab's story. He highlights her deeds that revealed her genuine faith. From an RT perspective, his use of examples permits James to guide his addressees to derive weak implicatures. He implicitly calls them to imitate both Abraham and Rahab in their faith that works.

In both segments of this unit (2:1–13, 14–26), James seems to focus on the middle group of believers. They are neither poor nor rich. However, by looking for patronage of the rich, they have discriminated against the poor. Instead of visiting orphans and widows, they do not pay enough attention to the poor and their extremely urgent needs. More important, they have not given the poor the honor that they deserve. They are not in tune with Jesus's teachings in this regard. Thus, at a higher level of explicitness, James exhorts his addressees to have a genuine and congruent faith in Jesus Christ, a faith that does not discriminate but cares for the poor. For the poor in the congregation, this text again will bring hope and consolation. For the wealthy in the congregation, this is an alert. Maybe they have some attitudes that here depict the unbelieving rich. It could even be possible that some of them have committed the same crimes against their fellow believers.

At this point, RT permits one to see how James builds his ethics of poverty and wealth mainly from what is implicit in the text. Rhetorical questions and examples permit James to influence and lead his addressees toward a correct attitude toward and concept of the poor and the needy in a broader way than the explicit language of assertions. It is clear from this chapter that James derives his teaching from the OT and the Jesus tradition. In particular, besides the use of the explicit OT texts quoted, the method helps one to see an allusion to Deuteronomy 6:5 in James 2:5 and a possible echo of Leviticus 19:5 in 2:1 and 9. James 2:5 alludes to Jesus's teachings reflected in Luke 6:20b. The Jesus tradition also seems to be behind James's use of Leviticus 19:18b.

Chapter 5

This chapter presents the research on 4:13–17 and 5:1–6 and 7–11. Themes and the nature of the use of the OT are slightly different from the findings for chapters 3 and 4 of the present work. James's focus is mainly on the rich, except in 5:7–11. In 4:13–17, the word πλούσιοι does not appear, but the text depicts wealthy businessmen and merchants. James uses the noun in 5:1–6, and it seems to depict the rich outsider. Furthermore, the eschatological language saturates the environment, in particular 5:1–11. In this way, James manages to guide his addressees to evoke eschatological themes alongside his main discourse. His own language evokes earlier parts of the discourse. In this way, he integrates all his teaching regarding poverty and wealth. The great reversal of 1:9–11 surfaces in the section. Several echoes of the actions and attitudes of the rich from 2:1–13 appear here.

In 4:13–17, James does not use any explicit OT allusions. There is a possible echo of Proverbs 27:1 in 4:14, but the evidence is inconclusive. James seems to evoke his warning to the rich in 1:10–11 and the call to be humble before God given in 4:6. If this is the case, James guides his addressees to connect his teaching with the OT via weak implicatures. The reversal and punishment of the wicked from Isaiah 40:6–7 and God's resistance toward the arrogant from Proverbs 3:34 could be behind James's exhortation to the wealthy merchants.

The text of 5:1–6 is the richest in OT imagery and evocations in the entire letter. James uses language close to the wisdom, prophetic, and Torah traditions. The eschatological language permits James to tack OT allusions onto his discourse and guide his readers/hearers to derive more implicatures. Two clear allusions appear in 5:4. James combines interpretive and metalinguistic metarepresentations of Deuteronomy 24:14–15 and Isaiah 5:9. He seems to echo Jeremiah 12:3 in 5:5. With his allusion to Deuteronomy 24:14–15, James manages to guide his addressees toward the derivation of implicatures, such as the poverty of the workers, the need for a salary, and the desperation of workers heard by God. With his allusion to Isaiah 5:9, James strengthens the former allusion, presenting God as the Lord of Hosts, who is about to act in vindication of the oppressed and punishment of the oppressors. In the case of the echo of Jeremiah 12:3, James strengthens the irony of the reversal of the rich by appealing to Jeremiah's eschatological concept of "the day of slaughter." If he is making an intentional echo, he guides his addressees toward implicatures related to eschatological reversal of the wicked. As noted above, RT emphasizes not only the explicit side of the communication process but also the implicit side. This permits one to see that James builds his ethics centered more on the implicit side. James's teaching definitely goes deeper than what is explicitly communicated. James gives hope and warning, but also guides his addresses to build their ethics of poverty and wealth in line with biblical teaching.

OT eschatological themes are also present in this passage and permit other illocutionary forces in the discourse. In 1:9–11, in a succinct way, James presents a reversal of fortunes for the humble and the rich. In 5:1–6, he develops the side of the rich, their humiliation. God's tribunal is central. The wicked rich are judged. Their own wealth witnesses against them, and is an instrument of God's punishment. These images help James build his discourse in order to give his addressees hope, in particular those poor among his addressees. At the same time, he may communicate another illocutionary force to the middle group of the congregation. Their confidence and trust must be in God and not in the wealthy. In 2:1–13, James points out the problem of patronage. Here, he exposes the sin of the wealthy, the same people whom they look to for patronage.

In 5:7–11, James closes the theme of poverty and wealth. He presents the other side of the reversal. In 1:9, he invites the humble to boast in their exaltation. Now, he connects this exaltation with Jesus's second coming as judge and savior. He invites them to be patient in light of the imminence of this coming. In order to do this, he uses three examples. The first comes from the daily agricultural life. The other two are clear allusions to the OT. He uses biblical examples to strengthen his discourse, but also to illustrate what he means by patience. He uses the life of the OT prophets who proclaimed the word of the Lord and were patient in the midst of their suffering. The other example is Job. In both cases, a loose interpretive resemblance permits James to guide his readers/hearers to derive weak implicatures related to perseverance in their own situation. In these three examples, the invitation is to imitate an active patience.

In this segment, he seems to evoke Jesus's words reflected in Matthew 7:1–5 in 5:9, and in Matthew 5:10–11 in 5:11. If this is the case, in 5:9, he guides his readers to derive weak implicatures associated with Jesus's concerns regarding judgment between brothers. In 5:11, he strengthens the connection between the example of the suffering of the prophets and his addressees' suffering as Christians. In both cases, James interpretively metarepresents Jesus's teaching.

James's Use of the OT

Several characteristics of James's discourse are recurrent, both in his use of the OT and in his evocation of Jesus's words. First, James intertwines the OT and Jesus's teachings with his own discourse. He rarely uses introductory formulas in his discourse. Rather, he metalinguistically metarepresents the necessary words of the OT, in order to trigger the connection in his addressees. At the same time, he interpretively uses the resemblance for his own purposes in his discourse. In this way, his own words are fully integrated with the teachings of the OT and Jesus.

Second, he seems to respect the OT context when he consciously uses it. In this sense, he reinforces his own discourse with themes and implicatures linked with those OT texts. Something similar is observed in the way the book of Revelation embeds the OT allusions right into the narrative. For example, in the case of Isaiah 40:6–7 in 1:10–11, James uses the eschatological imagery and themes that surface in the Isaianic text. The return to Zion, the vindication of God's people, and the punishment of the wicked are in line with James's own description of the reversal of fortunes of the humble and the wealthy (1:9–11). Another good example is Deuteronomy 24:14–15/Isaiah 5:9 in James 5:4. James uses Deuteronomy imagery of the harvesters' crying and God's answer, and combines them with the Lord of Hosts of Isaiah 5:9 in an eschatological scene of God's tribunal. In this way, he highlights the sin of the wealthy landlords, and God's promptness to defend the defenseless by interpretively metarepresenting the OT.

Third, James adopts and adapts the OT. As mentioned above, he interpretively uses the OT. In general, he loosely resembles the OT text. This is clearest when evoking examples. The four times James uses examples he loosely resembles the OT. With Abraham, he loosely metarepresents Genesis 22, with Rahab, Joshua 2, and with Job, the entire book. In the case of his use of the prophets, he evokes an entire tradition. The same is true of Elijah's example in 5:17–18 (although that passage is outside the scope of this research).

Fourth, in his use of the OT, James does not show a marked influence of Second Temple literature. Although he coincides with the method and interpretation of some trends in Second Temple literature, he does not seem to be influenced by any particular trend. There is not enough evidence to prove James's literary dependence.[1] For example, when appealing to Isaiah

1. Although some scholars, as Allison, argue "James does not know biblical text in isolation but received and understood them via Jewish tradition," parallels do not prove dependence. His

40:6–7 in 1:10–11, James is in line with the interpretation found in diverse sources (Tg. Isa. 40:6–8; 2 Bar 82:7; 4Q185). In other cases, he differs from them. When using Leviticus 19:18b, he is in line with Jesus's interpretation of the verse.

Fifth, both James and his addressees are familiar with the OT. That is what one can infer from the way James uses the OT. For example, in his illustrations of OT people, a few words and names are enough to trigger in his audience a range of weak implicatures. The same is true with regard to OT quotations. James points out, for example, in chapter 2 "the one who said . . . also said," assuming his addressees know whom he is talking about. With a high level of confidence, this characteristic of known references permits one to infer he is doing something similar with less explicit allusions. This familiarity with the OT permits him to interpretively metarepresent the OT, evoking in his addressees the OT teachings mainly via weak implicatures.

Sixth, the socioeconomic context of James and his addressees influences the way he addresses them. Several topics, examples of daily life, and OT-related themes flow from a heart deeply concerned about its reality. James reflects on the OT and Jesus's teaching from his and his addressees' context of exploitation and exclusion. James not only reinforces his discourse with both the OT and Jesus's authority. He also appeals to the OT and Jesus's teaching in order to find hope, vindication, and strength in the midst of his addressees' suffering. He exhorts them to conform not to the world's mentality but to the OT and Jesus's teachings. Perhaps these are the main purposes of his use of the OT.

James's Ethics of Poverty and Wealth

James's ethics of poverty and wealth presents three front lines depending on his audience. He shows three simultaneous and complementary views: the poor, the rich, and those in between. James builds his ethics on the OT and Jesus's teachings. In this way, he appeals to the authority of the OT and Jesus's words. He intertwines his own discourse with different OT texts and Jesus's teaching by interpretively metarepresenting them. He presents his ethics in eschatological language rich in imagery that permits one to derive a wide range of implicatures.

He begins to delineate his ethics of poverty and wealth with his eschatological exhortation in 1:9–11. This exhortation reveals that God has given a

examples of parallelism with Philo are inconclusive, as he himself admits it. He asserts: "James and Philo have so much in common because they draw from the common river of Hellenistic-Jewish tradition." The same is true about his possible relation with the Testament of the Twelve Patriarchs and other literature. Dale C. Allison, *A Critical and Exegetical Commentary on the Epistle of James* (ICC; New York: Bloomsbury, 2013), 54–55.

high position to the poor. Their poverty is just in worldly standards, but in God's eye, they have honor (2:5). They are heirs of God's kingdom. However, there is a tension between their eschatological reality and their current situation. The poor, laborers, widows, and orphans live in afflictions. Some of them do not have food or clothing. Some of them live in economic despair because of their lack of a salary. This situation of vulnerability is aggravated by the conduct of some rich, who drag them into court.

James exhorts the poor to hope in God. He is the Lord of Hosts, who is about to judge the wicked and vindicate them. Patience and endurance are results of their hope in light of Jesus's coming. This is anything but passivity. He calls them to show an active patience like the OT prophets or Job. He also exhorts the rest of the congregation to care for the needy. They have to visit widows and orphans in their afflictions (1:26–27). They have to show a congruent faith by providing what the poor need, food and clothing (2:14–17). The hospitality of Rahab is worthy of imitation. The wealthy in the congregation have a greater responsibility (4:17). Words of blessing are not enough (2:16).

The other side of the coin, James's ethics of wealth, is also present in 1:9–11. Something is wrong with the wealthy. They should be aware of their imminent humiliation. The causes of this judgment are apparent in the rest of the letter. Arrogance is an evil pattern even among rich Christians (4:13–17). The world's code of honor and patronage also permeate the congregation (2:1–13). The selfishness of the wealthy is denounced before God. James criticizes their exploitation of the poor (5:1–6). At the same time, he warns about their already/not yet punishment. God has begun to act in vindication of the poor.

This strong denunciation is a call to Christians. For the rich, it is a severe warning. The world's standard of conduct is not God's. There is imminent punishment if they do not abandon their friendship with the world. At the same time, there is a warning for those believers who are looking for patronage. That wrong search led them to discrimination toward the poor (2:1–7). God is their benefactor (1:16–18); they do not need to look for patronage. Instead, they must show a genuine faith in Jesus, a pure and undefiled worship of God the Father. Finally, there is a sense of God's justice in regard to the oppressed. They can find peace and hope. They are not alone. God is in control. He is the Lord of Hosts, who defends them. Jesus, the judge, is at the doors, ready to vindicate them.

In synthesis, James builds his ethics of poverty and wealth by interpretively metarepresenting primarily the OT and on several occasions also Jesus's teachings. He guides his readers/hearers to make the connections with the OT and Jesus's teaching, sometimes with explicit examples. For instance, he invites his readers/hearers to imitate Abraham, Rahab, Job, and the prophets. He implicitly invites his addressees to be friends of God, as Abraham was. On other occasions, he uses explicit OT texts to emphasize his point. For example, he uses two commandments in 2:11 to highlight how heinous discrimination is. Furthermore, he enriches his language with eschatological evocations. His accusation against the rich farmers in 5:1–6 is a good example of how eschatological language strengthens his discourse. Sometimes, he uses a few words from the OT, just enough to bring the OT implicatures into his discourse. The great reversal in 1:9–11 is a clear example of this. James evokes Isaiah 40:6–7 and with it brings the Isaianic reversal into his own discourse. On some occasions, James evokes Jesus's teachings with the same purpose. Maybe, the clearest example is 2:5. James seems to allude to Jesus's beatitude reflected in Luke 6:20 to reinforce his own teaching against discrimination and patronage. Therefore, in variegated ways, James builds his ethics of poverty and wealth by interpretively metarepresenting the OT and Jesus's teachings.

Contributions of Relevance Theory Methodology to the Research

As noted in chapter 2, RT contributes to the discussion of the NT use of the OT in at least two ways: its understanding of context and the way it deals with intertextuality. Throughout the analysis of the different texts, both of these contributions manifest themselves. RT strengthens the awareness of the close relationship between text and context. In this sense, RT adds to historical-critical and literary methods by emphasizing that the writer's meaning is more than what is explicitly communicated. It includes also what is implicit, and both aspects should be contextually recovered. For these reasons, RT is a very good complement to the traditional historical-critical and literary methods of exegesis.

This methodology helps in understanding not only what is explicit but also what is implicit in the text. In particular, it helps in discerning how an author guides his addressees in the derivation of implicatures, the illocutionary forces of the discourse, and so on. In James's case, he embroiders his discourse on an eschatological tapestry. He uses brief metalinguistic resemblance, but interpretively metarepresents the OT and Jesus's words. In this way, he inserts OT imagery and Jesus's teachings into his own discourse. This permits him to evoke different eschatological themes, OT teaching, and Jesus's words. He guides his readers/hearers to make the connections and derive weak implicatures. Different segments of his addressees derive different implicatures. James can use different illocutionary forces at the same time. He uses them to give hope to the poor and to warn wealthy Christians. On some occasions he warns those believers socially in between; on others, he encourages them.

The way RT deals with intertextuality also contributes to the discussion. The methodology, applied to different potential allusions, helps in discerning what OT texts are probably being used, but it also helps discard other proposed candidates. In this way, RT helps to frame the discourse analysis. The method *per se* does not eliminate all the subjectivity in the task, but it considerably diminishes it.

Final Conclusions

A question guides this research: How does James use the OT when dealing with the issue of poverty and wealth? In order to answer this question, Relevance Theory is used as a tool for discourse analysis. This method permits one to see that James adopts and adapts the OT and Jesus's teachings when addressing the issue. He builds his ethics of poverty and wealth by interpretively metarepresenting the OT and Jesus's teachings. His addressees' socio-economic situation influences the focus of James's teaching. He respects the OT context but also interpretively resembles the text. Furthermore, he assumes his addressees' knowledge of those texts and traditions when evoking them. In this way, he not only builds his ethic of poverty and wealth on the OT and Jesus's teachings, but he also strengthens his teaching by appealing to the OT and Jesus's authority. The method also permits one to see how James uses different illocutionary forces simultaneously, guiding his addressees to the derivation of implicatures depending on their situation. James wants his addressees to have a genuine and congruent faith in Jesus Christ, and to worship God the Father with a pure and undefiled religion.

Bibliography

Abegg, Martin G. “Exile and the Dead Sea Scrolls.” Pages 111–25 in *Exile: Old Testament, Jewish, and Christian Conceptions*, edited by James M. Scott. Leiden: Brill, 1997.

Adamson, James B. *The Epistle of James*. NICNT. Grand Rapids, Mich.: Eerdmans, 1976.

———. *James: The Man and His Message*. Grand Rapids, Mich.: Eerdmans, 1989.

Ahrens, Matthias. *Der Realitäten Widerschein oder Arm und Reich im Jakobusbrief: Eine sozialgeschichtliche Untersuchung*. AH. Berlin: Alektor-Verlag, 1995.

Aichele, George, and Gary A. Phillips. “Intertextuality and the Bible.” *Semeia* 69–70 (1995): 1–305.

Aland, Barbara, Kurt Aland, Ioannis Karavidopoulos, Carlo Maria Cardinal Martini, Bruce Manning Metzger, Holger Strutwolf, Eberhard Nestle, and Erwin Nestle. *Nestle-Aland Novum Testamentum Graece*. 28th ed. Stuttgart: Deutsche Bibelgesellschaft, 2012.

Allbee, Richard A. “Asymmetrical Continuity of Love and Law between the Old and New Testaments: Explicating the Implicit Side of a Hermeneutical Bridge, Leviticus 19:11–18.” *JSOT* 31 (2006): 147–66.

Allison, Dale C. *A Critical and Exegetical Commentary on the Epistle of James*. ICC. New York: Bloomsbury, 2013.

Allison, Dale C., Jr. “The Audience of James and the Sayings of Jesus.” Pages 58–77 in *James, 1 and 2 Peter, and Early Jesus Traditions*, edited by Alicia J. Batten and John S. Kloppenborg. LNTS 478. London: Bloomsbury, 2015.

———. “Blessing God and Cursing People: James 3:9–10.” *JBL* 130 (2011): 397–405.

———. “The Fiction of James and Its *Sitz im Leben*.” *RB* 108 (2001): 529–70.

Allison, Dale C., Jr., and W. D. Davies. *Introduction and Commentary on Matthew 1–7*. Vol. 1 of *A Critical and Exegetical Commentary on the Gospel according to Saint Matthew*. ICC. Edinburgh: T&T Clark, 2004.

Alonso Schökel, Luis. “James 5:2 and 4:6.” *Bib* 54 (1973): 73–6.

Andria, Salomon. “James.” Pages 1509–16 in *Africa Bible Commentary*, edited by Tokunboh Adeyemo. Grand Rapids, Mich.: Zondervan, 2006.

Arlandson, James Malcolm. *Women, Class, and Society in Early Christianity: Models from Luke-Acts*. Peabody, Mass.: Hendrickson, 1997.

Baasland, Ernst. “Der Jakobusbrief als Neutestamentliche Weisheitsschrift.” *ST* 36.2 (1982): 119–39.

Baker, William R. *Personal Speech-Ethics in the Epistle of James*. WUNT 68. Tübingen: J. C. B. Mohr, 1995.

———. “Searching for the Holy Spirit in the Epistle of James: Is ‘Wisdom’ Equivalent?” *TynBul* 59 (2008): 293–315.

Bark, Franziska. “‘Listen Your Way in with Your Mouth’: A Reading of Leviticus.” *Judaism* 48 (1999): 198–208.

Barry, John D., Lazarus Wentz, Douglas Mangum, Carrie Sinclair-Wolcott, Rachel Klippenstein, David Bomar, Elliot Ritzema, Wendy Widder, and Derek R. Brown, eds. *The Lexham Bible Dictionary*. Bellingham, Wash.: Lexham, 2014.

Bartholomew, Craig G. *Introducing Biblical Hermeneutics: A Comprehensive Framework for Hearing God in Scripture*. Grand Rapids, Mich.: Baker Academic, 2015.

Batten, Alicia J. "An Asceticism of Resistance in James." Pages 355–70 in *Asceticism and the New Testament*. New York: Routledge, 1999.

———. *Friendship and Benefaction in James*. ESEC 15. Dorset: Deo, 2010.

———. "God in the Letter of James: Patron or Benefactor?" *NTS* 50 (2004): 257–72.

———. "Ideological Strategies in the Letter of James." Pages 6–26 in *Reading James with New Eyes*, edited by Robert L. Webb and John S. Kloppenborg. LNTS 342. London: T&T Clark, 2007.

———. "The Jesus Tradition and the Letter of James." *RevExp* 108 (2011): 381–90.

———. "The Urbanization of Jesus Traditions in James." Pages 78–96 in *James, 1 and 2 Peter, and Early Jesus Traditions*, edited by Alicia J. Batten and John S. Kloppenborg. LNTS 478. London: Bloomsbury, 2015.

———. *What Are They Saying about the Letter of James?* WATSA. New York: Paulist Press, 2009.

Bauckham, Richard. "Covenant, Law, and Salvation in the Jewish Apocalypses." Pages 269–324 in *The Jewish World around the New Testament*. Grand Rapids, Mich.: Baker, 2010.

———. "For Whom Were Gospels Written?" Pages 9–48 in *Gospels for All Christians: Rethinking the Gospel Audiences*. Grand Rapids, Mich.: Eerdmans, 1998.

———. "James, 1 and 2 Peter, Jude." Pages 303–17 in *It Is Written: Scripture Citing Scripture*, edited by D. A. Carson and H. G. M. Williamson. Cambridge: Cambridge University Press, 1988.

———. *James: Wisdom of James, Disciple of Jesus the Sage*. London: Routledge, 1999.

———. "The Spirit of God in Us Loathes Envy: James 4:5." Pages 270–81 in *Holy Spirit and Christian Origins: Essays in Honor of James D. G. Dunn*, edited by Graham N. Stanton, Bruce W. Longenecker, and Stephen C. Barton. Grand Rapids, Mich.: Eerdmans, 2004.

———. "The Wisdom of James and the Wisdom of Jesus." Pages 75–92 in *The Catholic Epistles and the Tradition*, edited by J. Schlosser. BETL 176. Leuven: Leuven University Press, 2004.

Bauer, Walter, Frederick W. Danker, William Arndt, and F. Wilbur Gingrich, eds. *A Greek-English Lexicon of the New Testament and Other Early Christian Literature.* 3rd ed. Chicago: University of Chicago Press, 2000.

Beale, G. K. *The Book of Revelation: A Commentary on the Greek Text*. NIGTC. Grand Rapids, Mich.: Eerdmans, 1999.

———. *Handbook on the New Testament Use of the Old Testament: Exegesis and Interpretation*. Grand Rapids, Mich.: Baker, 2012.

———. *John's Use of the Old Testament in Revelation*. JSNTSup 166. Sheffield: Sheffield Academic, 1998.

———. "Questions of Authorial Intent, Epistemology, and Presuppositions and Their Bearing on the Study of the Old Testament in the New: A Rejoinder to Steve Moyise." *IBS* 21 (1999): 152–80.

———, ed. *The Right Doctrine from the Wrong Texts? Essays on the Use of the Old Testament in the New*. Grand Rapids, Mich.: Baker Academic, 1994.

Beale, G. K., and D. A. Carson, eds. *Commentary on the New Testament Use of the Old Testament*. Grand Rapids, Mich.: Baker, 2007.

———. “Introduction.” Pages xxiii–xxviii in *Commentary on the New Testament Use of the Old Testament*, edited by G. K. Beale and D. A. Carson. Grand Rapids, Mich.: Baker, 2007.

Beek, Martinus Adrianus. “Rahab in the Light of Jewish Exegesis.” Pages 37–44 in *Von Kanaan bis Kerala: Fest, Prof Mag Dr J O M van der Pleog zur Vollendung des siebzigsten Lebensjahres am 4, juli 1979*, edited by W. C. Delsman, J. R. T. M. Peters, and J. T. Nelis. AOAT 211. Kevelaer: Butzon und Bercker, 1982.

Belli, Filippo. *Argumentation and Use of Scripture in Romans 9–11*. AnBib 183. Rome: Gregorian & Biblical Press, 2010.

Benson, George. *A Paraphrase and Notes on the Seven (Commonly Called) Catholic Epistles*. London: J. Waugh and W. Fenner, 1756.

Berges, Ulrich, and Rudolf Hoppe. *Arm und Reich*. NEchtB 10. Würzburg: Echter, 2009.

Berthelot, K. *L'‘humanité de l'autre homme’ dans la pensée juive ancienne*. JSJSup 87. Leiden: Brill, 2004.

Betz, Hans Dieter. *The Sermon on the Mount: A Commentary on the Sermon on the Mount, Including the Sermon on the Plain (Matthew 5:3–7:27 and Luke 6:20–49)*. Hermeneia. Minneapolis: Fortress, 1995.

Blackburn, Perry L. *The Code Model of Communication: A Powerful Metaphor in Linguistic Metatheory*. Dallas: SIL International, 2007.

Blakemore, Diane. *Relevance and Linguistic Meaning: The Semantics and Pragmatics of Discourse Markers*. CSL 99. Cambridge: Cambridge University Press, 2002.

———. *Understanding Utterances: An Introduction to Pragmatics*. BTL 6. Oxford: Blackwell, 1992.

Blass, Regina. *Relevance Relations in Discourse: A Study with Special Reference to Sissala*. CSL 55. Cambridge: Cambridge University Press, 1990.

Blevins, William L. “A Call to Repent, Love Others, and Remember God: James 4.” *RevExp* 83 (1986): 419–26.

Blomberg, Craig L. “The Gospels for Specific Communities and All Christians.” Pages 111–33 in *Audience of the Gospels: The Origin and Function of the Gospels in Early Christianity*, edited by Edward W. Klink. LNTS 353. London: T&T Clark, 2010.

———. *Matthew*. NAC 22. Nashville: Broadman & Holman, 1992.

———. “Matthew.” Pages 1–109 in *Commentary on the New Testament Use of the Old Testament*, edited by G. K. Beale and D. A. Carson. Grand Rapids, Mich.: Baker, 2007.

———. *Neither Poverty Nor Riches: A Biblical Theology of Material Possessions*. NSBT. Grand Rapids, Mich.: Eerdmans, 1999.

Blomberg, Craig L., and Mariam J. Kamell. *James*. ZECNT 16. Grand Rapids, Mich.: Zondervan, 2008.

Bock, Darrel L. *9:51–24:53*. Vol. 2 of *Luke*. BECNT. Grand Rapids, Mich.: Baker, 1996.

Boggan, Charlie W. “Wealth in the Epistle of James.” Ph.D. diss., The Southern Baptist Theological Seminary, 1982.

Brooks, Oscar S. “The Function of the Double Love Command in Matthew 22:34–40.” *AUSS* 36 (1998): 7–22.

Brosend, William F, II. *James and Jude*. NCBC. Cambridge: Cambridge University Press, 2004.

Brown, Francis, Samuel Rolles Driver, and Charles Augustus Briggs. *The Enhanced Brown-Driver-Briggs Hebrew and English Lexicon*. Oak Harbor, Wash.: Logos Research Systems, 2000.

Brown, Jeannine K. *The Disciples in Narrative Perspective: The Portrayal and Function of the Matthean Disciples*. SBLAB 9. Leiden: Brill, 2002.

———. *Scripture as Communication: Introducing Biblical Hermeneutics*. Grand Rapids, Mich.: Baker, 2007.

Bruce, F. F., Peter H. Davids, Walter C. Kaiser, Jr., and M. T. Baruch. *Hard Sayings of the Bible*. Downers Grove, Ill.: InterVarsity Press, 1996.

Bruno, Christopher R. "Readers, Authors, and the Divine Author: An Evangelical Proposal for Identifying Paul's Old Testament Citations." *WTJ* 71 (2009): 311–21.

Buell, Denise Kimber. "'Be Not One Who Stretches Out Hands to Recieve but Shuts Them When It Comes to Giving': Envisioning Christian Charity When Both Donors and Recipients Are Poor." Pages 37–47 in *Wealth and Poverty in Early Church and Society*, edited by Susan R. Holman. HCSPTH. Grand Rapids, Mich.: Baker, 2008.

Burns, John A. "James, the Wisdom of Jesus." *CTR* 1 (1986): 113–35.

Byron, J. "Living in the Shadow of Cain: Echoes of a Developing Tradition in James 5:1–6." *NovT* 48 (2006): 261–74.

Byron, L. Gay. "James." Pages 461–75 in *True to Our Native Land: An African American New Testament Commentary*, edited by Brian K. Blount, Cain Hope Felder, Clarice Jannette Martin, and Emerson B. Powery. Minneapolis: Fortress, 2007.

Caetano da Silveira, Jane Rita. "Cognição, relevância e textualidade." Pages 68–95 in *Tópicos em teoria da relevância*, edited by Jorge Campos and Fábio José Rauen. Porto Alegre, Brazil: EDIPUCRS, 2008.

Campbell, Constantine R. *Basics of Verbal Aspect in Biblical Greek*. Grand Rapids, Mich.: Zondervan, 2008.

———. *Verbal Aspect, the Indicative Mood, and Narrative: Soundings in the Greek of the New Testament*. SBG 13. New York: Peter Lang, 2007.

Cantinant, J. *Les épîtres des Saint Jacques et de Saint Jude*. SB. Paris: Gabalda, 1973.

Cappelen, Herman, and Ernie Lepore. *Language Turned on Itself: The Semantics and Pragmatics of Metalinguistic Discourse*. Oxford: Oxford University Press, 2007.

———. "Using, Mentioning, and Quoting: A Reply to Saka." *Mind* 108 (1999): 741.

———. "Varieties of Quotation." *Mind* 106 (1997): 429–50.

Cargal, Timothy B. *Restoring the Diaspora: Discursive Structure and Purpose in the Epistle of James*. SBLDS 144. Atlanta: Scholars, 1993.

Carpenter, C. B. "James 4.5 Reconsidered." *NTS* 47 (2001): 189–205.

Carson, D. A. "James." Pages 997–1013 in *Commentary on the New Testament Use of the Old Testament*, edited by G. K. Beale and D. A. Carson. Grand Rapids, Mich.: Baker, 2007.

———. "Matthew." Pages 3–599 in *Mathew, Mark, and Luke*. EBC 8. Grand Rapids, Mich.: Zondervan, 1984.

Carson, D. A., and Douglas J. Moo. *An Introduction to the New Testament*. 2nd ed. Grand Rapids, Mich.: Zondervan, 2005.

Carson, D. A., and H. G. M. Williamson, eds. *It Is Written: Scripture Citing Scripture; Essays in Honour of Barnabas Lindars*. Cambridge: Cambridge University Press, 1988.

Carston, Robyn. "Lexical Pragmatics, Ad Hoc Concepts and Metaphor: From a Relevance Theory Perspective." *IJL* 22 (2010): 153–80.

———. "Relevance Theory and the Saying/Implicating Distinction." Pages 633–56 in *Handbook of Pragmatics*, edited by Gregory Ward and Laurence Horn. BHL 16. Oxford: Blackwell, 2004.

———. *Thoughts and Utterances: The Pragmatics of Explicit Communication*. Oxford: Blackwell, 2002.

———. "XIII—Metaphor: Ad Hoc Concepts, Literal Meaning, and Mental Images." *PAS* 110 (2010): 295–321.

Carston, Robyn, and Alison Hall. "Implicature and Explicature." Pages 1–30 in *Cognitive Pragmatics*, edited by H-J. Schmid and D. Geeraerts. Berlin: Mount de Gruyter, 2011.

Carter, Warren. "Love Your Enemies." *WW* 28 (2008): 13–21.

Chaffin, Robert F., Jr. "The Theme of Wisdom in the Epistle of James." *ATJ* 29 (1997): 23–49.

Charles, Ronald. "Rahab: A Righteous Whore in James." *Neot* 45 (2011): 206–20.

Charlesworth, James H. *The Old Testament Pseudepigrapha*. Vols. 1 and 2. New York: Yale University Press, 1983, 1985.

Cheung, Luke L. *The Genre, Composition, and Hermeneutics of the Epistle of James*. Eugene, Ore.: Wipf & Stock, 2006.

Childs, Brevard S. *Isaiah*. OTL. Louisville: Westminster John Knox, 2001.

Chisholm, Robert B., Jr. "Structure, Style, and the Prophetic Message: An Analysis of Isaiah 5:8–30." *BibSac* 143.569 (1986): 46–60.

Christensen, Duane L. *Deuteronomy 21:10–34:12*. WBC 6B. Dallas: Word, 2002.

Ciampa, Roy E. *The Presence and Function of Scripture in Galatians 1 and 2*. WUNT 2 102. Tübingen: Mohr Siebeck, 1998.

Cohick, Lynn H. *Women in the World of the Earliest Christians: Illuminating Ancient Ways of Life*. Grand Rapids, Mich.: Baker, 2009.

Collins, John J., and Daniel C. Harlow, eds. *The Eerdmans Dictionary of Early Judaism.* Grand Rapids, Mich.: Eerdmans, 2010.

Comfort, Philip W. *New Testament Text and Translation Commentary: Commentary on the Variant Readings of the Ancient New Testament Manuscripts and How They Relate to the Major English Translations*. Carol Stream, Ill.: Tyndale House, 2008.

Cotterell, Peter, and Max Turner. *Linguistics and Biblical Interpretation*. Downers Grove, Ill.: InterVarsity Press, 1989.

Crenshaw, James L. "YHWH tseba'ôt šemô Form-Critical Analysis." *ZAW* 81 (1969): 156–75.

Crotty, Robert B. "The Literary Structure of the Letter of James." *ABR* 40 (1992): 45–57.

Davids, Peter H. *The Epistle of James: A Commentary on the Greek Text*. NIGTC. Grand Rapids, Mich.: Eerdmans, 1982.

———. "The Epistle of James in Modern Discussion." Pages 3621–45 in *Principat 25,5*. New York: Walter de Gruyter, 1988.

———. "James and Jesus." Pages 63–84 in *Jesus Tradition outside the Gospels*, edited by David Wenham. GP 5. Sheffield: JSOT, 1984.

———. "James's Message: The Literary Record." Pages 66–87 in *The Brother of Jesus: James the Just and His Mission*, edited by Bruce Chilton and Jacob Neusner. Louisville: Westminster John Knox, 2001.

——. "Palestinian Traditions in the Epistle of James." Pages 33–57 in *James the Just and Christian Origins*, edited by Bruce Chilton and Craig A. Evans. SupNovT 98. Leiden: Brill, 1999.
——. "The Poor Man's Gospel." *Them* 1 (1976): 36–41.
——. "The Test of Wealth." Pages 355–84 in *Missions of James, Peter, and Paul: Tensions in Early Christianity*, edited by Bruce Chilton and Craig A. Evans. SupNovT 115. Leiden: Brill, 2005.
——. *A Theology of James, Peter, and Jude: Living in the Light of the Coming King*. BTNT 6. Grand Rapids, Mich.: Zondervan, 2014.
——. "Tradition and Citation in the Epistle of James." Pages 113–26 in *Scripture, Tradition, and Interpretation: Essays Presented to Everett F. Harrison by His Students and Colleagues in Honor of His Seventy-Fifth Birthday*, edited by W. Ward Gasque and William Sanford LaSor. Grand Rapids, Mich.: Eerdmans, 1978.
——. "Why Do We Suffer? Suffering in James and Paul." Pages 435–66 in *Missions of James, Peter, and Paul*, edited by Bruce Chilton and Craig A. Evans. SupNovT 115. Leiden: Brill, 2005.
Davidson, Robert. "The Imagery of Isaiah 40:6–8 in Tradition and Interpretation." Pages 37–55 in *Quest for Context and Meaning: Studies in Biblical Intertextuality in Honor of James A. Sanders*, edited by Craig A. Evans and Shemaryahu Talmon. Leiden: Brill, 1997.
Deppe, Dean B. "The Sayings of Jesus in the Epistle of James." Th.D. thesis, Free University of Amsterdam, 1989.
deSilva, David A. "Final Topics: The Rhetorical Functions of Intertexture in Revelation 14:14–16:21." Pages 215–41 in *Intertexture of Apocalyptic Discourse in the New Testament*, edited by Duane F. Watson. SBLSymS 14. Atlanta: Society of Biblical Literature, 2002.
——. *Honor, Patronage, Kinship, and Purity: Unlocking New Testament Culture*. Downers Grove, Ill.: InterVarsity Press, 2000.
——. *An Introduction to the New Testament: Contexts, Methods, and Ministry Formation*. Downers Grove, Ill.: InterVarsity Press; Apollos, 2004.
Dibelius, Martin. *James: A Commentary on the Epistle of James*. Philadelphia: Fortress, 1976.
Dimant, Devorah. "Use and Interpretation of Mikra in the Apocrypha and Pseudepigrapha." Pages 379–419 in *Mikra: Text, Translation, Reading, and Interpretation of the Hebrew Bible in Ancient Judaism and Early Christianity*, edited by Martin J. Mulder and Harry Sysling. CRINT 2. Philadelphia: Fortress, 1988.
Douglas, Mary. "Justice as the Cornerstone: An Interpretation of Leviticus 18–20." *Int* 53 (1999): 341–50.
Dyrness, William. "Mercy Triumphs over Justice: James 2:13 and the Theology of Faith and Works." *Them* 6.3 (1981): 11–6.
Eberhart, Christian. "The Term 'Sacrifice' and the Problem of Theological Abstractions: A Study of the Reception History of Genesis 22:1–19." Pages 47–66 in *Multivalence of Biblical Texts and Theological Meanings*, edited by Christine Helmer and Charlene T. Higbe. SBLSymS 37. Atlanta: Society of Biblical Literature, 2006.
Eddinger, Terry W. "An Analysis of Isaiah 40:1–11 (17)." *BBR* 9 (1999): 119–35.
Edenburg, Cynthia. "Intertextuality, Literary Competence, and the Question of Readership: Some Preliminary Observations." *JSOT* 35 (2010): 131–48.

Edgar, David H. *Has God Not Chosen the Poor? The Social Setting of the Epistle of James*. JSNTSup 206. Sheffield: Sheffield Academic, 2001.

———. "The Use of the Love-Command and the Shema' in the Epistle of James." *PIBA* 23 (2000): 9–22.

Ego, Beate. "Abraham's Faith in the One God: A Motif of the Image of Abraham in Early Jewish Literature." Pages 337–54 in *Biblical Figures in Deuterocanonical and Cognate Literature*, edited by H. Lichtenberger and U. Mittmann-Richert. DCL. Berlin: de Gruyter, 2009.

Elliott, John Hall. "The Epistle of James in Rhetorical and Social Scientific Perspective: Holiness-Wholeness and Patterns of Replication." *BTB* 23 (1993): 71–81.

Elwell, Walter A., and Barry J. Beitzel, eds. *Baker Encyclopedia of the Bible*. Grand Rapids, Mich.: Baker, 1988.

Elwell, Walter A., and Philip Wesley Comfort. *Tyndale Bible Dictionary*. Wheaton, Ill.: Tyndale House, 2001.

Enns, Peter. "Apostolic Hermeneutics and an Evangelical Doctrine of Scripture: Moving beyond a Modernist Impasse." *WTJ* 65 (2003): 263–87.

———. *Inspiration and Incarnation: Evangelicals and the Problem of the Old Testament*. Grand Rapids, Mich.: Baker Academic, 2005.

Evans, Craig A., ed. *From Prophecy to Testament: The Function of the Old Testament in the New*. Peabody, Mass.: Hendrickson, 2004.

———. "Listening for Echoes of Interpreted Scripture." Pages 47–51 in *Paul and the Scriptures of Israel*, edited by Craig A. Evans and James A. Sanders. JSNTSup 83. Sheffield: JSOT Press, 1993.

Evans, Craig A., and James A. Sanders, eds. *Paul and the Scriptures of Israel*. JSNTSup 83. Sheffield: JSOT Press, 1993.

Evans, Craig A., and H. Daniel Zacharias, eds. *Early Christian Literature and Intertextuality*. Vol. 1, *Thematic Studies*. LNTS 391. London: T & T Clark, 2009.

———, eds. *Early Christian Literature and Intertextuality*. Vol. 2, *Exegetical Studies*. LNTS 392. London: T & T Clark, 2009.

Fantin, Joseph D. *The Greek Imperative Mood in the New Testament: A Cognitive and Communicative Approach*. SBG 12. New York: Peter Lang, 2010.

———. *Lord of the Entire World: Lord Jesus, a Challenge to Lord Caesar?* Sheffield: Sheffield Phoenix Press, 2011.

Felder, Cain Hope. "Partiality and God's Law: An Exegesis of James 2:1–13." *JRT* 39.2 (1983): 51–69.

———. "Wisdom, Law, and Social Concern in the Epistle of James." Ph.D. diss., Columbia University, 1982.

Filho, José Adriano. "El pobre y el rico en Santiago y en el Pastor de Hermas." *RIBLA* 31 (1998): 144–58.

Fish, Stanley E. "Interpreting the Variorum." Pages 164–84 in *Reader-Response Criticism: From Formalism to Post-structuralism*, edited by Jane P. Tompkins. Baltimore: Johns Hopkins University Press, 1980.

Fishbane, Michael A. "Types of Biblical Intertextuality." Pages 39–44 in *Congress Volume: Oslo 1998*, edited by André Lemaire and Magne Sæbø. VTSup 80. Leiden: Brill, 2000.

Fitzmyer, Joseph A. "The Interpretation of Genesis 15:6: Abraham's Faith and Righteousness in a Qumran Text." Pages 257–68 in *Emmanuel: Studies in the*

Hebrew Bible, Septuagint, and Dead Sea Scrolls in Honor of Emmanuel Tov, edited by Shalom M. Paul, Robert A. Kraft, Eva Ben-David, Lawrence H. Schiffman, and Weston W. Fields. Leiden: Brill, 2003.

Ford, J. Massynbaerde. "Bookshelf on Prostitution." *BTB* 23.3 (1993): 128–34.

Fowler, Robert M. "Who is 'The Reader' in Reader Response Criticism." *Semeia* 31 (1985): 5–23.

France, R. T. *The Gospel of Matthew*. NICNT. Grand Rapids, Mich.: Eerdmans, 2007.

——. *Matthew: An Introduction and Commentary*. TNTC 1. Downers Grove, Ill.: InterVarsity Press, 1985.

Frankemölle, Hubert. "Das semantische Netz des Jakobusbriefes: Zur Einheit eines umstrittenen Briefes." *BZ* 34 (1990): 161–97.

——. *Der Brief des Jakobus, Kapitel 1*. GTB 517. Gütersloh: Echter, 1994.

——. *Der Brief des Jakobus, Kapitel 2–5*. GTB 518. Gütersloh: Echter, 1994.

——. "Zum Thema des Jakobusbriefes im Kontext der Rezeption von Sir 2,1–18 und 15,11–20." *BN* 48 (1989): 21–49.

Friberg, Timothy, Barbara Friberg, and Neva F. Miller. *Analytical Lexicon of the Greek New Testament.* Grand Rapids, Mich.: Baker, 2000.

Friesen, Steven J. "Injustice or God's Will: Explanations of Poverty in Proto-Christian Texts." Pages 240–60 in *Christian Origins*, edited by Richard A. Horsley. PHC 1. Minneapolis: Fortress, 2005.

Fruchtenbaum, Arnold G. *The Messianic Jewish Epistles: Hebrews, James, First Peter, Second Peter, Jude*. ABC. 1st ed. Tustin, Calif.: Ariel Ministries, 2005.

Fuller, Reginald H. "Double Commandment of Love: Test Case for the Criteria of Authenticity." Pages 41–56 in *Essays on the Love Commandment*, edited by Luise Schottroff. Philadelphia: Fortress, 1978.

Furlong, Anne M. "Relevance Theory and Literary Interpretation." Ph.D. diss., University College London, 1995.

Furnish, Victor Paul. *The Love Command in the New Testament*. Nashville: Abingdon, 1972.

García Martínez, Florentino. *Textos de Qumrán*. 6th ed. Madrid: Trotta, 2009.

Gaskins, Mark E. "Looking to the Future: James 4:13–5:11." *RevExp* 97 (2000): 237–42.

Gerstenberger, Erhard. *Leviticus: A Commentary*. OTL. 1st American ed. Louisville: Westminister John Knox Press, 1996.

Geyser, Albert S. "The Letter of James and the Social Condition of His Addressees." *Neot* 9 (1975): 25–33.

Ghantous, Hadi. "Was Job 'Patient'? Is God 'Just'?" *TR* 33 (2012): 22–38.

Gillmayr-Bucher, Sussane. "Intertextuality: Between Literary Theory and Text Analysis." Pages 13–23 in *The Intertextuality of the Epistles: Explorations of Theory and Practice*, edited by Thomas L. Brodie, Dennis R. MacDonald, and Stanley E. Porter. Sheffield: Sheffield Phoenix, 2006.

Goldingay, John, and David Payne. *Introduction and Commentary on Isaiah 40:1–44:23*. Vol. 1 of *A Critical and Exegetical Commentary on Isaiah 40–55*. ICC. New York: T&T Clark, 2006.

Goldsworthy, Graeme. *Gospel-Centered Hermeneutics: Foundations and Principles of Evangelical Biblical Interpretation*. Downers Grove, Ill.: InterVarsity Press, 2006.

González, Justo L. *Faith and Wealth: A History of Early Christian Ideas on the Origin, Significance, and Use of Money*. San Francisco: Harper Collins, 1990.

Goppelt, Leonhard. *Typos: The Typological Interpretation of the Old Testament in the New*. Grand Rapids, Mich.: Eerdmans, 1982.

Gowan, Donald E. "Wisdom and Endurance in James." *HBT* 15 (1993): 145–53.

Gray, Patrick. "Points and Lines: Thematic Parallelism in the Letter of James and the Testament of Job." *NTS* 50 (2004): 406–24.

Green, Gene L. *The Letters to the Thessalonians*. PNTC. Grand Rapids, Mich.: Eerdmans, 2002.

———. "Lexical Pragmatics and Biblical Interpretation." *JETS* 50 (2007): 799–812.

———. "Relevance Theory and Biblical Interpretation." Pages 266–73 in *The Oxford Encyclopedia of Biblical Interpretation*, edited by Steve L. McKenzie. Oxford: Oxford University Press, 2013.

———. "Relevance Theory and Biblical Interpretation." Pages 217–40 in *Linguist as Pedagogue*. Sheffield: Sheffield Phoenix, 2009.

———. "Relevance Theory and Theological Interpretation: Thoughts on Metarepresentation." *JTI* 4 (2010): 75–90.

Green, Joel B., Scot McKnight, and I. Howard Marshall, eds. *Dictionary of Jesus and the Gospels.* Downers Grove, Ill.: InterVarsity Press, 1992.

Grice, H. P. "Meaning." *PhR* 66 (1957): 377–88.

Grice, Paul. *Studies in the Way of Words*. Cambridge, Mass.: Harvard University Press, 1989.

Gundry, Robert H. *Commentary on the New Testament*. Grand Rapids, Mich.: Baker, 2010.

Guthrie, George H. "James." Pages 198–273 in *The Expositor's Bible Commentary: Hebrews-Revelation*, edited by Tremper Longman III and David E. Garland. EBC. Grand Rapids, Mich.: Zondervan, 2006.

Gutt, Ernst-August. *Translation and Relevance: Cognition and Context*. Cambridge: Cambridge University Press, 1991.

Hagner, Donald A. *Matthew 1–13*. WBC 33a. Dallas: Word, 1993.

———. *Matthew 14–28*. WBC 33b. Dallas: Word, 1995.

Hahn, F., and P. Müller. "Der Jakobusbrief." *TRu* 63 (1998): 1–73.

Hanson, Anthony T. *The Living Utterances of God: The New Testament Exegesis of the Old*. Darton, England: Darton, Longman and Todd, 1983.

———. "Rahab the Harlot in Early Christian Tradition." *JSNT* 1 (1978): 53–60.

———. "Seminar Report: Report on Working Group on 'The Use of the Old Testament in the Epistle of James,' Tübingen, 1977; Châtenay-M, 1978." *NTS* 25 (1979): 526–7.

Hart, George, and Helen Hart. *A Semantic and Structural Analysis of James*. SSA. Dallas: SIL International, 2001.

Hartin, Patrick J. "Call to Be Perfect through Suffering (James 1,2–4): The Concept of Perfection in the Epistle of James and the Sermon on the Mount." *Bib* 77 (1996): 477–92.

———. "'Come Now, You Rich, Weep and Wail . . .' (James 5:1–6)." *JTSA* 84 (1993): 57–63.

———. *James*. SP 14. Collegeville, Minn.: Liturgical Press, 2003.

———. "James and Eschatology: Place and Function of Eschatology within a Letter to the 'Twelve Tribes in the Dispersion.'" Pages 451–71 in *Eschatology of the New Testament and Some Related Documents*, edited by J. G. Van der Watt. WUNT 2 315. Tübingen: Mohr Siebeck, 2011.

———. "James and the Jesus Tradition: Some Theological Reflections and Implications." Pages 55–70 in *Catholic Epistles and Apostolic Tradition*, edited by Karl-Wilhelm Niebuhr and Robert W. Wall. Waco: Baylor University Press, 2009.

———. *James, First Peter, Jude, Second Peter*. NCBCNT 10. Collegeville, Minn.: Liturgical Press, 2006.

———. *James of Jerusalem: Heir to Jesus of Nazareth*. Collegeville, Minn.: Liturgical Press, 2004.

———. *James and the Q Sayings of Jesus*. JSNTSup 47. Sheffield: JSOT, 1991.

———. "The Letter of James: Its Vision, Ethics, and Ethos." Pages 445–71 in *Identity, Ethics, and Ethos in the New Testament*, edited by J. G. Van der Watt and F. S. Malan. BZNW 141. Berlin: Walter de Gruyter, 2006.

———. "The Poor in the Epistle of James and the Gospel of Thomas." *HTS* 53 (1997): 146–62.

———. "The Religious Context of the Letter of James." Pages 203–31 in *Jewish Christianity Reconsidered: Rethinking Ancient Groups and Texts*, edited by Matt Jackson-McCabe. Minneapolis: Fortress, 2007.

———. "'Who Is Wise and Understanding among You?' (James 3:13): An Analysis of Wisdom, Eschatology, and Apocalypticism in the Letter of James." Pages 149–68 in *Conflicted Boundaries in Wisdom and Apocalypticism*, edited by Benjamin G. Wright III and Lawrence M. Wills. SBLSymS 35. Atlanta: Society of Biblical Literature, 2006.

Hartley, John E. *Leviticus*. WBC 4. Dallas: Word, 1992.

Hatina, Thomas R. *The Gospel of Luke*. Vol. 3 of *Biblical Interpretation in Early Christian Gospels*. LNTS. New York: T & T Clark, 2010.

Hawthorne, Gerald F., Ralph P. Martin, and Daniel G. Reid, eds. *Dictionary of Paul and His Letters.* Downers Grove, Ill.: InterVarsity Press, 1993.

Hays, Richard B. *Echoes of Scripture in the Letters of Paul*. New Haven: Yale University Press, 1989.

———. *Reading Backwards: Figural Christology and the Fourfold Gospel Witness*. Waco: Baylor University Press, 2014.

Hays, Richard B., Stefan Alkier, and Leroy Andrew Huizenga. *Reading the Bible Intertextually*. Waco: Baylor University Press, 2009.

Hernández Iglesias, Manuel. "*Ad Hoc* Concepts and Metaphor." Pages 173–82 in *Explicit Communication: Robyn Carston's Pragmatics*, edited by Belén Soria and Esther Romero. PSPLC. Basingstoke, England: Palgrave Macmillan, 2010.

Hiebert, D. Edmond. *James*. Chicago: Moody Press, 1979.

———. "Unifying Theme of the Epistle of James." *BibSac* 135 (1978): 221–31.

Hill, Harriet. *The Bible at Cultural Crossroads: From Translation to Communication*. Manchester, England: St Jerome, 2006.

Hill, Harriet, Ernst-August Gutt, Margaret Hill, Christoph Unger, and Rick Floyd. *Bible Translation Basics: Communicating Scriptures in a Relevant Way*. Dallas: SIL International, 2011.

Hill, Harriet, and Margaret Hill. *Translating the Bible into Action: How the Bible Can Be Relevant in All Languages and Cultures*. Carlisle, England: Piquant Editions, 2008.

Hoe, David H. K. "Apocalyptic Discourse in Second Peter." Ph.D. diss., Dallas Theological Seminary, 2008.

Hollander, Harm W. "The Words of Jesus: From Oral Traditions to Written Record in Paul and Q." *NovT* 42 (2000): 340–57.
Holman, Susan R., ed. *Wealth and Poverty in Early Church and Society*. HCSPTH. Grand Rapids, Mich.: Baker, 2008.
Horsley, Richard A. "Ethics and Exegesis: 'Love Your Enemies' and the Doctrine of Nonviolence." Pages 72–101 in *Love of Enemy and Nonretaliation in the New Testament*, edited by Willard M. Swartley. SPS. Louisville: Westminster/John Knox, 1992.
Hultgren, Arland J. "Double Commandment of Love in Mt 22:34–40: Its Sources and Compositions." *CBQ* 36 (1974): 373–8.
Isaacs, Marie E. *Reading Hebrews and James: A Literary and Theological Commentary*. Macon, Ga.: Smyth and Helwys, 2002.
Jackson-McCabe, Matt A. "The Law of Freedom (James 1:25): Light from Early Exegesis." *PEGLMBS* 21 (2001): 33–44.
———. "A Letter to the Twelve Tribes in the Diaspora: Wisdom and 'Apocalyptic' Eschatology in the Letter of James." *SBLSP* 35 (1996): 504–17.
———. *Logos & Law in the Letter of James: The Law of Nature, the Law of Moses, & the Law of Freedom*. SupNovT Leiden: Brill, 2001.
Jacobs, Irving. "Midrashic Background for James 2:21–3." *NTS* 22 (1976): 457–64.
James, Arthur. "James." Pages 1731–7 in *South Asia Bible Commentary*, edited by Brian C. Wintle. Rajasthan, India: Open Door, 2015.
Jensen, Robin M. "The Offering of Isaac in Jewish and Christian Tradition: Image and Text." *BibInt* 2 (1994): 85–110.
Jobes, Karen H. *Letters to the Church: A Survey of Hebrews and the General Epistles*. Grand Rapids, Mich.: Zondervan, 2011.
———. "The Minor Prophets in James, 1 & 2 Peter, and Jude." Pages 135–53 in *Minor Prophets in the New Testament*, edited by Maarten J. J. Menken and Steve Moyise. LNTS 377. London: T & T Clark, 2009.
———. "Relevance Theory and the Translation of Scripture." *JETS* 50 (2007): 773–97.
Jodłowiec, Maria. "How the Context Emerges." Pages 134–46 in *In the Mind and across Minds: A Relevance-Theoretic Perspective on Communication and Translation*, edited by Ewa Wałaszewska, Marta Kisielewska-Krysiuk, and Agnieszka Piskorka. Cambridge: Cambridge Scholars Publishing, 2010.
———. "Relevance Theory and Degrees of Understanding." Pages 23–42 in *Relevance Round Table I*, edited by Ewa Mioduszewska and Agnieszka Piskorka. Warsaw: Warsaw University Press, 2008.
Johnson, Luke Timothy. *The Acts of the Apostles*. SP 5. Collegeville, Minn.: Liturgical Press, 1992.
———. *Among the Gentiles: Greco-Roman Religion and Christianity*. AYBRL. New Haven: Yale University Press, 2009.
———. *Brother of Jesus, Friend of God: Studies in the Letter of James*. Grand Rapids, Mich.: Eerdmans, 2004.
———. "An Introduction to the Letter of James." *RevExp* 97 (2000): 155–67.
———. "James 3:13–4:10 and the Topos ΠΕΡΙ ΦΘΟΝΟΥ." *NovT* 25 (1983): 327–47.
———. *The Letter of James: A New Translation with Introduction and Commentary*. AB 37A. New Haven: Yale University Press, 1995.

——. *The Literary Function of Possessions in Luke-Acts*. SBLDS 39. Missoula, Mont.: Scholars Press, 1977.
——. "Making Connections: The Material Expression of Friendship in the New Testament." *Int* 58 (2004): 158–71.
——. "The Mirror of Remembrance (James 1:22–25)." *CBQ* 50 (1988): 632–45.
——. *Sharing Possessions: What Faith Demands*. 2nd ed. Grand Rapids, Mich.: Eerdmans, 2011.
——. "The Social World of James: Literary Analysis and Historical Reconstruction." Pages 178–97 in *Social World of the First Christians: Essays in Honor of Wayne A. Meeks*, edited by L. Michael White and O. Larry Yarbrough. Minneapolis: Fortress, 1995.
——. "The Use of Leviticus 19 in the Letter of James." *JBL* 101 (1982): 391–401.
——. *The Writings of the New Testament: An Interpretation; Revised Edition*. Minneapolis: Fortress, 1999.
Johnson, Steven R. *Seeking the Imperishable Treasure: Wealth, Wisdom, and a Jesus Saying*. Eugene, Ore.: Wipf and Stock, 2010.
Johnston, J. William. "James 4:5 and the Jealous Spirit." *BibSac* 170.679 (2013): 344–60.
Jones, David A. *Old Testament Quotations and Allusions in the New Testament*. Bellingham, Wash.: Logos Research Systems, 2009. Logos edition.
Kamell, Mariam J. "The Economics of Humility: The Rich and the Humble in James." Pages 157–75 in *Engaging Economics: New Testament Scenarios and Early Christian Reception*, edited by Bruce W. Longenecker and Kelly D. Liebengood. Grand Rapids, Mich.: Eerdmans, 2009.
——. "Incarnating Jeremiah's Promised New Covenant in the 'Law' of James." *EvQ* 83 (2011): 19–28.
——. "The Soteriology of James in Light of Earlier Jewish Wisdom Literature and the Gospel of Matthew." Ph.D. diss., University of Saint Andrews, 2010.
Kaminsky, Joel S. "Loving One's (Israelite) Neighbor: Election and Commandment in Leviticus 19." *Int* 62 (2008): 123–32.
Kaveny, M. Cathleen. "The Order of Widows: What the Early Church Can Teach Us about Older Women and Health Care." *CB* 11 (2005): 11–34.
Keener, Craig S. *Acts: An Exegetical Commentary, 3:1–14:28*. Grand Rapids, Mich.: Baker Academic, 2013.
——. *A Commentary on the Gospel of Matthew*. Grand Rapids, Mich.: Eerdmans, 1999.
Keerankeri, G. *The Love Commandment in Mark: An Exegetico-Theological Study of Mk 12,28–34*. AnBib 150. Rome: Editrice Pontificio Istituto Biblico, 2003.
Keith, Pierre. "La citation de Lv 19,18b en Jc 2,1–13." Pages 227–48 in *The Catholic Epistles and the Tradition*, edited by J. Schlosser. BETL 176. Leuven: Leuven University Press, 2004.
Kelly, Francis X. "Poor and Rich in the Epistle of James." Ph.D. diss., Temple University, 1973.
Kistemaker, Simon J. *Exposition of James and the Epistles of John*. BNTC. Grand Rapids, Mich.: Baker, 1986.
Klassen, William. "The Authenticity of the Command: 'Love Your Enemies.'" Pages 385–407 in *Authenticating the Words of Jesus*. Leiden: Brill, 1999.
——. *Love of Enemies: The Way to Peace*. OBT 15. Philadelphia: Fortress, 1984.

Klein, Daniel A. "Who Counted Righteousness to Whom? Two Clashing Views by Shadal on Genesis 15:6." *JBQ* 36 (2008): 28–32.
Klein, William W., Craig L. Blomberg, and Robert L. Hubbard. *Introduction to Biblical Interpretation*. Nashville: Thomas Nelson, 2004.
Kloppenborg, John S. "The Emulation of Jesus Tradition in the Letter of James." Pages 121–50 in *Reading James with New Eyes*, edited by Robert L. Webb and John S. Kloppenborg. LNTS 342. London: T&T Clark, 2007.
———. "Patronage Avoidance in James." *HTS* 55 (1999): 755–94.
———. "The Reception of the Jesus Tradition in James." Pages 71–100 in *Catholic Epistles and Apostolic Tradition*, edited by Karl-Wilhelm Niebuhr and Robert W. Wall. Waco: Baylor University Press, 2009.
———. "The Reception of the Jesus Traditions in James." Pages 93–142 in *The Catholic Epistles and the Tradition*, edited by J. Schlosser. BETL 176. Leuven: Leuven University Press, 2004.
Koch, D. A. *Die Schrift als Zeuge des Evangeliums: Untersuchungen zur Verwendung und zum Verständnis der Schrift bei Paulus*. BHT 69. Tübingen: Mohr Siebeck, 1986.
Konradt, Matthias. *Christliche Existenz nach dem Jakobusbrief: Eine Studie zu seiner soteriologischen und ethischen Konzeption*. SUNT. Gottingen: Vandenhoeck & Ruprecht, 1998.
———. "The Love Command in Matthew, James, and the Didache." Pages 271–88 in *Matthew, James, and Didache: Three Related Documents in Their Jewish and Christian Settings*, edited by Huub van de Sandt and Jürgen K. Zangenberg. SBLSymS 45. Atlanta: Society of Biblical Literature, 2008.
Köstenberger, Andreas J., and Richard D. Patterson. *Invitation to Biblical Interpretation: Exploring the Hermeneutical Triad of History, Literature, and Theology*. ITSS. Grand Rapids, Mich.: Kregel, 2011.
Krause, Jens-Uwe. *Witwen und Waisen im romischen Reich.* HABES 16. Stuttgart: F. Steiner, 1994.
Krüger, René. *Der Jakobusbrief als prophetische Kritik der Reichen: Eine exegetische Untersuchung aus lateinamerikanischer Perspektive*. BVB 12. Münster: Lit, 2005.
———. "El vuelco irritante y definitivo: Santiago 1:9–11 y el anuncio de la inversión total de la situación." *CuadT* 23 (2004): 45–77.
———. *Pobres y ricos en la epístola de Santiago: El desafío de un cristianismo profético*. Buenos Aires: Lumen, 2005.
Lange, Armin. "The Shema Israel in Second Temple Judaism." *JAJ* 1 (2010): 207–14.
Lange, Armin, and Matthias Weigold, eds. *Biblical Quotations and Allusions in Second Temple Jewish Literature*, JAJSup 5. Göttingen: Vandenhoeck & Ruprecht, 2011.
Laws, Sophie S. *A Commentary on the Epistle of James*. BNTC 16. San Francisco: Harper & Row, 1980.
———. "Does Scripture Speak in Vain: A Reconsideration of James 4:5." *NTS* 20 (1974): 210–5.
Lenski, Gerhard Emmanuel. *Power and Privilege: A Theory of Social Stratification*. Chapel Hill: University of North Carolina Press, 1984.
Lenski, R. C. H. *The Interpretation of the Epistle to the Hebrews and the Epistle of James*. Minneapolis: Augsburg, 1966.
Levine, Baruch A. *Leviticus: The Traditional Hebrew Text with the New JPS Translation*. JPSTC. Philadelphia: JPS, 1989.

Lima Vasconcellos, Pedro. "Los pobres y el reino: Santiago y la recreación de las sentencias de Jesús." *RIBLA* 31 (1998): 136–43.

Lockett, Darian R. "God and 'the World': Cosmology and Theology in the Letter of James." Pages 144–56 in *Cosmology and New Testament Theology*, edited by Jonathan T. Pennington and Sean M. McDonough. LNTS 355. London: T & T Clark, 2008.

———. *An Introduction to the Catholic Epistles*. TTCABS. New York: T&T Clark, 2012.

———. *Purity and Worldview in the Epistle of James*. LNTS 366. London: Clark, 2008.

———. "The Spectrum of Wisdom and Eschatology in the Epistle of James and 4QInstruction." *TynBul* 56 (2005): 131–48.

———. "Strong and Weak Lines: Permeable Boundaries between Church and Culture in the Letter of James." *RevExp* 108 (2011): 391–405.

———. "Structure or Communicative Strategy? The 'Two Ways' Motif in James' Theological Instruction." *Neot* 42 (2008): 269–87.

———. "'Unstained by the World': Purity and Pollution as an Indicator of Cultural Interaction in the Letter of James." Pages 49–74 in *Reading James with New Eyes*, edited by Robert L. Webb and John S. Kloppenborg. LNTS 342. London: T&T Clark, 2007.

Longenecker, Bruce W. *Remember the Poor: Paul, Poverty, and the Greco-Roman World*. Grand Rapids, Mich.: Eerdmans, 2010.

Longenecker, Richard N. *Biblical Exegesis in the Apostolic Period*. 2nd ed. Grand Rapids, Mich.: Eerdmans; Regent College, 1999.

———. "'Faith of Abraham' Theme in Paul, James, and Hebrews: A Study in the Circumstantial Nature of New Testament Teaching." *JETS* 20 (1977): 203–12.

Longman, Tremper, III. "Literary Approaches to Biblical Interpretation." Pages 91–192 in *Foundations of Contemporary Interpretation*, edited by Moisés Silva. Grand Rapids, Mich.: Zondervan, 1996.

López, Ediberto. "Relecturas de Génesis 22: El temprano judaísmo y el cristianismo primitivo y el sacrificio de Isaac." *RIBLA* 40 (2001): 62–83.

Louw, Johannes P., and Eugene Albert Nida. *Greek-English Lexicon of the New Testament: Based on Semantic Domains.* New York: United Bible Societies, 1996.

Lunde, Jonathan, and Kenneth Berding, eds. *Three Views on the New Testament Use of the Old Testament*. Grand Rapids, Mich.: Zondervan, 2007.

Lust, Johan, Erik Eynikel, and Katrin Hauspie. *A Greek-English Lexicon of the Septuagint: Revised Edition.* Stuttgart: Deutsche Bibelgesellschaft, 2003.

Luz, Ulrich. *Matthew 8–20: A Commentary*. Hermeneia. Minneapolis: Augsburg, 1989.

Mackenzie, Ian. *Paradigms of Reading: Relevance Theory and Deconstruction*. New York: Palgrave Macmillan, 2002.

Makujina, J. "The Second Greatest Commandment and Self-Esteem." *MSJ* 8 (1997): 211–25.

Malamat, Abraham. "'Love Your Neighbor as Yourself': What It Really Means." *BAR* 16.4 (1990): 50–1.

Malik, Rachel. "Fixing Meaning: Intertextuality, Inferencing, and Genre in Interpretation." Ph.D. diss., Middlesex University, 2003.

Malina, Bruce J. *El mundo del Nuevo Testamento: Perspectivas desde la antropología cultural*. Αγορα 1. Navarra: Verbo Divino, 1995.

Manns, Frédéric. "Luc 7,47 et les traditions juives sur Rahab." *RSR* 61 (1987): 1–16.

Marcus, David. "Prolepsis in the Story of Rahab and the Spies (Joshua 2)." Pages 149–62 in *Bringing the Hidden to Light: Essays in Honor of Stephen A. Geller*, edited by Kathryn F. Kravitz and Diane M. Sharon. Winona Lake, Ind.: Eisenbrauns, 2007.

Marshall, I. Howard, and Philip H. Towner. *A Critical and Exegetical Commentary on the Pastoral Epistles*. London: T&T Clark International, 1999.

Martin, Brice L. "Matthew on Christ and the Law." *TS* 44 (1983): 53–70.

Martin, Ralph P. *James*. WBC 48. Waco, Tex.: Word Books, 1988.

Martin, Ralph P., and Peter H. Davids, eds. *Dictionary of the Later New Testament and Its Developments.* Downers Grove, Ill.: InterVarsity Press, 2000.

Martínez, Aquiles Ernesto. "Imágenes feministas en Santiago: Óptica de género y destellos de liberación." *Apuntes* 18.3 (1998): 67–79.

Mateos, Juan, and Jesús Peláez, eds. *Diccionario Griego-Español del Nuevo Testamento.* Córdoba: El Almendro, 2007.

Mathys, Hans-Peter. *Liebe deinen Nächsten wie dich selbst: Untersuchungen zum alttestamentlichen Gebot der Nächstenliebe (Lev 19,18)*. OBO 71. Göttingen: Vandenhoeck & Ruprecht, 1986.

Matthews, K. A. *Genesis 11:27–50:26*. NAC 1B. Nashville: Broadman & Holman, 2005.

Maynard-Reid, Pedrito U. *James: True Religion in Suffering*. ALBA. Boise: Pacific, 1996.

———. *Poverty and Wealth in James*. Eugene, Ore.: Wipf & Stock, 1987, 2004.

Mayor, Joseph B. *The Epistle of St. James: The Greek Text with Introduction, Notes, and Comments*. 2nd ed. London: Macmillan, 1897.

McCartney, Dan G. *James*. BECNT. Grand Rapids, Mich.: Baker, 2009.

———. "Self-Deception in James." *CTR* 8.2 (2011): 31–43.

———. "The Wisdom of James the Just." *SBJT* 4.3 (2000): 52–64.

McComiskey, Douglas S. "Exile and Restoration from Exile in the Scriptural Quotations and Allusions of Jesus." *JETS* 53 (2010): 673–96.

McGinn, T. A. J. "Widows, Orphans, and Social History." *JRA* 12 (1999): 617–32.

McKnight, Scot. *The Letter of James*. NICNT. Grand Rapids, Mich.: Eerdmans, 2011.

———. "A Parting within the Way: Jesus and James on Israel and Purity." Pages 83–129 in *James the Just and Christian Origins*, edited by Bruce Chilton and Craig A. Evans. SupNovT 98. Leiden: Brill, 1999.

Meadowcroft, Tim. "Relevance as a Mediating Category in the Reading of Biblical Texts: Venturing beyond the Hermeneutical Circle." *JETS* 45 (2002): 611–27.

Menken, Maarten J. J., and Steve Moyise, eds. *Deuteronomy in the New Testament*. LNTS 358. London: T&T Clark, 2007.

Metzger, Bruce M. *A Textual Commentary on the Greek New Testament*. 2nd ed. Stuttgart: Deutsche Bibelgesellschaft, 1994.

Míguez, Nestor. "Ricos y pobres: Relaciones clientelares en la carta de Santiago." *RIBLA* 31 (1998): 86–98.

Milavec, Aaron. "The Social Setting of 'Turning the Other Cheek' and 'Loving One's Enemies' in Light of the Didache." *BTB* 25 (1995): 131–43.

Milgrom, Jacob. *Leviticus 17–22: A New Translation with Introduction and Commentary*. AB 3A. New York: Doubleday, 2000.

Moberly, R. W. L. "Abraham's Righteousness (Genesis 15:6)." Pages 103–30 in *Studies in the Pentateuch*, edited by John A. Emerton. VTSup 41. Leiden: Brill, 1990.

Moo, Douglas J. *The Letter of James*. PNTC. Grand Rapids, Mich.: Eerdmans, 2000.

Morgan, Christopher W. *A Theology of James: Wisdom for God's People*. Phillipsburg, N.J.: P&R, 2010.

Morris, Leon. *The Gospel according to Matthew*. PNTC. Grand Rapids, Mich.: Eerdmans, 1992.

Moyise, Steve. *Evoking Scripture: Seeing the Old Testament in the New*. London: T&T Clark, 2008.

———. "How Does Paul Read Scripture?" Pages 184–96 in *Early Christian Literature and Intertextuality,* vol. 1, *Thematic Studies*, edited by Craig A. Evans and H. Daniel Zacharias. LNTS 391. London: T&T Clark, 2009.

———. "Intertextuality and Biblical Studies: A Review." *VE* 23 (2002): 418–31.

———. "Intertextuality and Historical Approaches to the Use of Scripture in the New Testament." *VE* 26 (2005): 447–58.

———. "Intertextuality and the Study of the Old Testament in the New Testament." Pages 14–41 in *Old Testament in the New Testament: Essays in Honour of J. L. North*. Sheffield: Sheffield Academic Press, 2000.

———. "Intertextuality, Historical Criticism, and Deconstruction." Pages 24–34 in *The Intertextuality of the Epistles: Explorations of Theory and Practice*, edited by Thomas L. Brodie, Dennis R. MacDonald, and Stanley E. Porter. Sheffield: Sheffield Phoenix Press, 2006.

———. *Jesus and Scripture: Studying the New Testament Use of the Old Testament*. Grand Rapids, Mich.: Baker, 2010.

———. "The Old Testament in the New: A Reply to Greg Beale." *IBS* 21 (1999): 54–8.

———. *The Old Testament in the New: An Introduction*. ContBS. London: Continuum, 2001.

———. *Paul and Scripture: Studying the New Testament Use of the Old Testament*. Grand Rapids, Mich.: Baker Academic, 2010.

———. "Quotations." Pages 15–28 in *As It Is Written: Studying Paul's Use of Scripture*, edited by Stanley Porter and Christopher D. Stanley. SBLSymS 50. Atlanta: Society of Biblical Literature, 2008.

———. "Respect for Context Once More." *IBS* 27 (2006): 24–31.

Mussner, Franz. *Der Jakobusbrief*. 3rd expanded ed. Freiburg: Herder, 1975.

Myllykoski, Mati. "James the Just in History and Tradition: Perspectives of Past and Present Scholarship (Part I)." *CBR* 5 (2006): 73–122.

———. "James the Just in History and Tradition: Perspectives of Past and Present Scholarship (Part II)." *CBR* 6 (2007): 11–98.

Neudecker, Reinhard. "'And You Shall Love Your Neighbor as Yourself—I Am the Lord' (Lev 19:18) in Jewish Interpretation." *Bib* 73 (1992): 496–517.

Ng, Esther Yue L. "Father-God Language and Old Testament Allusions in James." *TynBul* 54 (2003): 41–54.

Nida, Eugene Albert. "The Role of Context in the Understanding of Discourse." Pages 20–7 in *Discourse Analysis and the New Testament: Approaches and Results*, edited by Stanley E. Porter and Jeffrey T. Reed. JSNTSup 170. Sheffield: Sheffield Academic, 1999.

Noack, Bent. "Jakobus wider die Reichen." *ST* 18 (1964): 10–25.

Noell, Edd S. "A 'Marketless World'? An Examination of Wealth and Exchange in the Gospels and First-Century Palestine." *JMM* 10 (2007): 85–114.

Nogueira, Pablo. "La dignidad del pobre en una sinagoga cristiana de la diáspora: Un ejemplo de seguimiento de la Torá en el cristianismo primitivo." *RIBLA* 31 (1998): 99–109.

———. "O grito do salário: Conflito no mundo do trabalho en Tiago 4,13–5,6." *EB* 44 (1994): 77–86.

Noh, Eun-Ju. *Metarepresentation: A Relevance-Theory Approach*. PBNS 69. Amsterdam: John Benjamins, 2000.

Nolland, John. *The Gospel of Matthew: A Commentary on the Greek Text*. NIGTC. Grand Rapids, Mich.: Eerdmans, 2005.

———. *Luke 9:21–18:34*. WBC 35b. Dallas: Word, 1993.

Nystrom, David P. *The NIV Application Commentary: James*. Grand Rapids, Mich.: Zondervan, 1997.

Obermüller, Rodolfo. "¿Contaminación? En torno a una definición de religión (Sant 1,27)." *RevistB* 34 (1972): 13–9.

———. "Hermeneutische Themen im Jakobusbrief." *Bib* 53 (1972): 234–44.

———. "Santiago: La iglesia en minoría." *CuadT* 1.4 (1972): 11–31.

Oegema, G. S. *Für Israel und die Völker: Studien zum alttestamentlich-jüdischen Hintergrund der paulinischen Theologie*. NovTSup 95. Leiden: Brill, 1999.

———. "'Love Your Neighbor as Yourself': Jesuanic or Mosaic?" *BN* 116 (2003): 77–86.

Oeming, Manfred. *Contemporary Biblical Hermeneutics: An Introduction*. Translated by Joachim Vette. Aldershot, England: Ashgate, 2006.

———. "Der Glaube Abrahams: Zur Rezeptionsgeschichte von Gen 15,6 in der Zeit des zweiten Tempels." *ZAW* 110 (1998): 16–33.

Ogletree, Thomas W. "The Essential Unity of the Love Commands: Moving beyond Paradox." *JRE* 35 (2007): 695–700.

Oishi, Etsuko, and Anita Fetzer, eds. *Context and Contexts: Parts Meet Whole?* PBNS 209. Amsterdam: John Benjamins, 2011.

Ong, Siow-Heng. *A Strategy for a Metaphorical Reading of the Epistle of James*. Lanham, Md.: University Press of America, 1996.

Osborne, Grant R. *The Hermeneutical Spiral: A Comprehensive Introduction to Biblical Interpretation*. 2nd ed. Downers Grove, Ill.: InterVarsity Press, 2006.

———. "James." Pages 3–127 in *James, 1–2 Peter, Jude, Revelation*. CBC 18. Carol Stream, Ill.: Tyndale House, 2011.

———. *Matthew*. ZECNT 1. Grand Rapids, Mich.: Zondervan, 2010.

———. "Recent Trends in the Study of the Apocalypse." Pages 473–504 in *The Face of New Testament Studies: A Survey of Recent Research*, edited by Scot McKnight and Grant R. Osborne. Grand Rapids, Mich.: Baker, 2004.

———. *Revelation*. BECNT. Grand Rapids, Mich.: Baker, 2002.

Oswalt, John N. *Isaiah*. NIVAC. Grand Rapids, Mich.: Zondervan, 2003.

Painter, John. "James." Pages 1–174 in *James and Jude*, edited by Mikeal C. Parsons and Charles H. Talbert. Paideia. Grand Rapids, Mich.: Baker, 2012.

Pao, David W., and Eckhard J. Schnabel. "Luke." Pages 251–414 in *Commentary on the New Testament Use of the Old Testament*, edited by G. K. Beale and D. A. Carson. Grand Rapids, Mich.: Baker, 2007.

Pattemore, Stephen W. *The People of God in the Apocalypse: Discourse, Structure, and Exegesis*. SNTSMS 128. Cambridge: Cambridge University Press, 2004.

Paulien, Jon. "Dreading the Whirlwind: Intertextuality and the Use of the Old Testament in Revelation." *AUSS* 39 (2001): 5–22.

———. "Elusive Allusions in the Apocalypse: Two Decades of Research into John's Use of the Old Testament." Pages 61–8 in *The Intertextuality of the Epistles: Explorations of Theory and Practice*, edited by Thomas L. Brodie, Dennis R. MacDonald, and Stanley E. Porter. Sheffield: Sheffield Phoenix, 2006.

———. "Elusive Allusions: The Problematic Use of the Old Testament in Revelation." *BR* 33 (1988): 37–53.

———. "New Testament Use of the Old Testament." Pages 167–88 in *"For You Have Strengthened Me": Biblical and Theological Studies in Honor of Gerhard Pfandl in Celebration of His Sixty-Fifth Birthday*, edited by Martin Pröbstle. St Peter am Hart, Austria: Seminar Schloss Bogenhofen, 2007.

Pehrson, Benjamin J. "Mitigation and Intensitifaction of Persuasive Discourse in a Koine Greek Letter: Coherent Macrostructure in the Letter of James." Master's thesis, Graduate Institute of Applied Linguistics, 2010.

Penner, Todd C. *The Epistle of James and Eschatology: Re-reading an Ancient Christian Letter*. JSNTSup 121. Sheffield: Sheffield Academic Press, 1996.

———. "The Epistle of James in Current Research." *CurBS* 7 (1999): 257–308.

Perkins, David W. "The Wisdom We Need: James 1:5–8, 3:13–18." *ThEd* 34 (1986): 12–25.

Perkins, Pheme. "James 3:16–4:3." *Int* 36 (1982): 283–7.

Pilkington, Adrian. "Metaphor Comprehension: Some Questions for Current Accounts in Relevance Theory." Pages 156–72 in *Explicit Communication: Robyn Carston's Pragmatics*, edited by Belén Soria and Esther Romero. PSPLC. Basingstoke, England: Palgrave Macmillan, 2010.

———. *Poetic Effects: A Relevance Theory Perspective*. PBNS 75. Amsterdam: John Benjamins, 2000.

Pimentel, Frank. "Codicia, resistencia y proyecto alternativo: Un acercamiento socio-lingüístico y actualizante a la carta de Santiago." *RIBLA* 31 (1998): 68–85.

Piper, John. *"Love Your Enemies": Jesus' Love Command in the Synoptic Gospels and the Early Christian Paraenesis*. Grand Rapids, Mich.: Baker, 1991.

Popkes, Wiard. *Adressaten, Situation und Form des Jakobusbriefes*. SBS 125/126. Stuttgart: Katholisches Bibelwerk, 1986.

———. *Der Brief des Jakobus*. THKNT 14. Leipzig: Evangelische Verlagsanstalt, 2001.

———. "James and Scripture: An Exercise in Intertextuality." *NTS* 45 (1999): 213–29.

———. "Two Interpretations of 'Justification' in the New Testament Reflections on Galatians 2:15–21 and James 2:21–25." *ST* 59 (2005): 129–46.

Porter, Stanley E. "Allusions and Echoes." Pages 29–40 in *As It Is Written: Studying Paul's Use of Scripture*, edited by Stanley E. Porter and Christopher D. Stanley. SBLSymS 50. Atlanta: Society of Biblical Literature, 2008.

———. "Assessing Translation Theory: Beyond Literal and Dynamic Equivalence." Pages 117–45 in *Translating the New Testament: Text, Translation, Theology*, edited by Stanley E. Porter and Mark J. Boda. MNTS. Grand Rapids, Mich.: Eerdmans, 2009.

———. “Further Comments on the Use of the Old Testament in the New Testament.” Pages 98–110 in *The Intertextuality of the Epistles: Explorations of Theory and Practice*, edited by Thomas L. Brodie, Dennis R. MacDonald, and Stanley E. Porter. 16. Sheffield: Sheffield Phoenix, 2006.

———. “Is Critical Discourse Analysis Critical? An Evaluation Using Philemon as a Test Case.” Pages 47–70 in *Discourse Analysis and the New Testament: Approaches and Results*, edited by Stanley E. Porter and Jeffrey T. Reed. JSNTSup 170. Sheffield: Sheffield Academic Press, 1999.

———. *Sacred Tradition in the New Testament: Tracing Old Testament Themes in the Gospels and Epistles*. Grand Rapids, Mich.: Baker Academic, 2016.

———. “The Use of the Old Testament in the New Testament: A Brief Comment on Method and Terminology.” Pages 79–96 in *Early Christian Interpretation of the Scriptures of Israel*, edited by Stanley E. Porter. Sheffield: Sheffield Academic, 1997.

———. *Verbal Aspect in the Greek of the New Testament: With Reference to Tense and Mood*. New York: P. Lang, 1989.

Porter, Virgil V., Jr. “The Use of the Sermon on the Mount in the Epistle of James.” Ph.D. diss., Dallas Theological Seminary, 2003.

Powell, Mark Allan. “Expected and Unexpected Readings of Matthew: What the Reader Knows.” *AsTJ* 48.2 (1993): 31–51.

Powery, Emerson B. *Jesus Reads Scripture: The Function of Jesus’ Use of Scripture in the Synoptic Gospels*. BI 63. Leiden: Brill, 2003.

———. “Under the Gaze of the Empire: Who Is My Neighbor?” *Int* 62 (2008): 134–44.

Premnath, D. N. “Latifundialization and Isaiah 5:8–10.” *JSOT* 40 (1988): 49–60.

Rahlfs, Alfred, ed. *Septuaginta: Psalmi Cum Odis*. VTG 10. Göttingen: Vandenhoeck & Ruprecht, 1979.

Ranieri, Aldo Adriano. “La intertextualidad como perspectiva hermenéutica: Un desafío para la exégesis bíblica.” Pages 99–111 in *Palabra viva y actual*, edited by Carlos Galli and Héctor Fernández. Buenos Aires: San Benito, 2005.

Recanati, François. *Oratio Obliqua, Oratio Recta: An Essay on Metarepresentation*. Cambridge, Mass.: MIT Press, 2000.

———. *Truth-Conditional Pragmatics*. Oxford: Oxford University Press, 2010.

Reicke, Bo. *The Epistles of James, Peter, and Jude: Introduction, Translation, and Notes*. AB. Garden City, N.Y.: Doubleday, 1963.

Reiser, Marius. “Love of Enemies in the Context of Antiquity.” *NTS* 47 (2001): 411–27.

Rhee, Helen. *Loving the Poor, Saving the Rich: Wealth, Poverty, and Early Christian Formation*. Grand Rapids, Mich.: Baker, 2012.

Richardson, Kurt A. *James*. NAC 36. Nashville: Broadman & Holman, 2001.

———. “Job as Exemplar in the Epistle of James.” Pages 213–29 in *Hearing the Old Testament in the New Testament*, edited by Stanley E. Porter. Grand Rapids, Mich.: Eerdmans, 2006.

Rivera, Luis Fernando. “La epístola de Santiago como modelo de halakha cristiana.” *CuadT* 1.4 (1972): 32–48.

———. “Sobre el socialismo de Santiago (Sant 2,1–13).” *RevistB* 34 (1972): 3–9.

Roberts, J. W. *A Commentary on the General Epistle of James*. Austin, Tex.: R. B. Sweet, 1963.

Rogland, Max. "Abram's Persistent Faith: Hebrew Verb Semantics in Genesis 15:6." *WTJ* 70 (2008): 239–44.

Rooker, M. F. "The Best-Known Verse in Leviticus." *FM* 21.2 (2004): 3–16.

Ropes, James Hardy. *A Critical and Exegetical Commentary on the Epistle of St. James*. ICC. New York: C. Scribner's Sons, 1916.

Ruzer, S. "From 'Love your Neighbor' to 'Love Your Enemy': Trajectories in Early Jewish Exegesis." *RB* 109 (2002): 371–89.

Saka, Paul. "Quotation: A Reply to Cappelen & Lepore." *Mind* 108 (1999): 751–4.

Saldarini, Anthony J. *Pharisees, Scribes, and Sadducees in Palestinian Society: A Sociological Approach*. BRS. Grand Rapids, Mich.: Eerdmans, 2001.

Sandt, Huub van de. "James 4,1–4 in the Light of the Jewish Two Ways Tradition 3,1–6." *Bib* 88 (2007): 38–63.

Sänger, D., ed. *Gottessohn und Menschensohn: Exegetische Studien zu zwei Paradigmen biblischer Intertextualität*. BTS 67. Neukirchen-Vluyn: Neukirchener, 2004.

Sartor Bressan, Roberto. "Culto y compromiso social según la epístola de Santiago." *RevistB* 34 (1972): 21–32.

Saussure, Ferdinand de. *Course in General Linguistics*. Translated by Wade Baskin. New York: Philosophical Library, 1957.

Schliesser, Benjamin. *Abraham's Faith in Romans 4: Paul's Concept of Faith in Light of the History of Reception of Genesis 15:6*. WUNT 2 224. Tübingen: Mohr Siebeck, 2007.

Schmitt, John J. "You Adulteresses! The Image in James 4:4." *NovT* 28 (1986): 327–37.

Schwartz, Baruch J. "Leviticus." In *The Jewish Study Bible*, edited by Adele Berlin, Marc Zvi Brettler, and Michael A. Fishbane. New York: JPS, 2004.

Scott, J. Julius. *Jewish Backgrounds of the New Testament*. Grand Rapids, Mich.: Baker, 1995.

Scott, James M. "Exile and the Self-Understanding of Diaspora Jews in the Greco-Roman Period." Pages 173–218 in *Exile: Old Testament, Jewish, and Christian Conceptions*, edited by James M. Scott. Leiden: Brill, 1997.

Seitz, Christopher R. "The Divine Council: Temporal Transition and New Prophecy in the Book of Isaiah." *JBL* 109 (1990): 229–47.

Seitz, Oscar Jacob Frank. "Love Your Enemies: The Historical Setting of Matthew 5:43f, Luke 6:27f." *NTS* 16 (1969): 39–54.

Serrão, C. Jeanne Orjala. *James: A Commentary in the Wesleyan Tradition*. NBBC. Kansas City: Beacon Hill, 2010.

Sim, Margaret G. "Particles and Participles: A Helpful Partnership." Pages 226–44 in *Discourse Studies & Biblical Interpretation: A Festschrift in Honor of Stephen H. Levinsohn*, edited by Steven E. Runge. Bellingham, Wash.: Lexham, 2011.

———. "A Relevance Theoretical Approach to the Particle [*sic*] ἵνα in Koine Greek." Ph.D. diss., University of Edinburgh, 2006.

Smith, Steve. *The Fate of the Jerusalem Temple in Luke-Acts: An Intertextual Approach to Jesus' Laments over Jerusalem and Stephen's Speech*. LNTS 553. London: T&T Clark, 2016.

Söding, T. "Nächstenliebe bei Jesus Sirach: Eine Notiz zur weisheitlichen Ethik." *BZ* 42 (1998): 239–47.

Sommer, Benjamin D. "Isaiah." Pages 780–916 in *The Jewish Study Bible*, edited by Adele Berlin and Marc Zvi Brettler. Oxford: Oxford University Press, 2004.

Sperber, Dan, and Deirdre Wilson. "Introduction: Pragmatics." Pages 1–27 in *Meaning and Relevance*, edited by Deirdre Wilson and Dan Sperber. Cambridge: Cambridge University Press, 2012.

———. *Relevance: Communication and Cognition*. 2nd ed. Oxford: Blackwell, 1995.

Stamps, Dennis L. "The Use of the Old Testament in the New Testament as a Rhetorical Device: A Methodological Proposal." Pages 9–37 in *Hearing the Old Testament in the New Testament*, edited by Stanley Porter. Grand Rapids, Mich.: Eerdmans, 2006.

Stanley, Christopher D. *Arguing with Scripture: The Rhetoric of Quotations in the Letters of Paul*. New York: T&T Clark, 2004.

———. *Paul and the Language of Scripture: Citation Technique in the Pauline Epistles and Contemporary Literature*. SNTSMS 74. Cambridge: Cambridge University Press, 1992.

———. "Paul's 'Use' of Scripture: Why the Audience Matters." Pages 125–55 in *As It Is Written: Studying Paul's Use of Scripture*, edited by Stanley E. Porter and Christopher D. Stanley. SBLSymS 50. Atlanta: Society of Biblical Literature, 2008.

———. "'Pearls before Swine': Did Paul's Audiences Understand His Biblical Quotations?" *NovT* 41 (1999): 124–44.

Stulac, George M. *James*. IVPNTC 16. Downers Grove, Ill.: InterVarsity Press, 1993.

———. "Who Are 'the Rich' in James?" *Presb* 16.2 (1990): 89–102.

Swart, Gerhard. "Rahab and Esther in Josephus: A Comparative Analysis." Pages 471–86 in *Biblical Figures in Deuterocanonical and Cognate Literature*, edited by Ulrike Mittmann-Richert and Hermann Lichtenberger. DCL. Berlin: de Gruyter, 2009.

Sweeney, Marvin A. "Jeremiah." Pages 917–1041 in *The Jewish Study Bible*, edited by Adele Berlin, Marc Zvi Brettler, and Michael A. Fishbane. New York: JPS, 2004.

Tamez, Elsa. "Elementos que iluminan el camino de la comunidad cristiana: Un ejercicio hermenéutico de la carta de Santiago." *RIBLA* 1 (1988): 59–66.

———. "I Timothy and James on the Rich, Women, and Theological Disputes." *Conc* 1 (2002): 49–58.

———. "James: A Circular Letter for Immigrants." *RevExp* 108 (2011): 369–80.

———. *No discriminen a los pobres: Lectura latinoamericana de la carta de Santiago*. Estella: Verbo Divino, 2008.

———. *The Scandalous Message of James: Faith without Works Is Dead*. Rev. ed. New York: Crossroad, 2002.

Tate, W. Randolph. *Biblical Interpretation: An Integrated Approach*. 3rd ed. Peabody, Mass.: Hendrickson, 2008.

———. *Handbook for Biblical Interpretation: An Essential Guide to Methods, Terms, and Concepts*. Grand Rapids, Mich.: Baker, 2012.

Taylor, Mark E. "Recent Scholarship on the Structure of James." *CurBS* 3 (2004): 86–115.

———. *A Textlinguistic Investigation into the Discourse Structure of James*. LNTS 311. New York: T&T Clark, 2006.

———. "A Textlinguistic Investigation into the Discourse Structure of James." Ph.D. diss., Southwestern Baptist Theological Seminary, 2001.

Taylor, Mark E., and G. H. Guthrie. "The Structure of James." *CBQ* 68 (2006): 681–705.

Tendahl, Markus, and Raymond W. Gibbs, Jr. "Complementary Perspectives on Metaphor: Cognitive Linguistics and Relevance Theory." *JPrag* 40 (2008): 1823–64.

Terry, Ralph Bruce. "Some Aspects of the Discourse Structure of the Book of James." *JOTT* 5 (1992): 106–25.

Thomas, Robert L. "The New Testament Use of the Old Testament." *MSJ* 13 (2002): 79–98.

———. "The Principle of Single Meaning." *MSJ* 12 (2001): 33–47.

Thompson, J. A. *Deuteronomy: An Introduction and Commentary*. TOTC 5. Downers Grove, Ill.: InterVarsity Press, 1974.

Thompson, Michael. *Clothed with Christ: The Example and Teaching of Jesus in Romans 12:1–15:13*. JSNTSup 59. Sheffield: JSOT, 1991.

Thurén, Lauri. "Risky Rhetoric in James?" *NovT* 37 (1995): 262–84.

Tiller, Patrick A. "The Rich and Poor in James: An Apocalyptic Ethic." Pages 169–79 in *Conflicted Boundaries in Wisdom and Apocalypticism*, edited by Benjamin G. Wright III and Lawrence M. Wills. SBLSymS 35. Atlanta: Society of Biblical Literature, 2005.

———. "The Rich and Poor in James: An Apocalyptic Proclamation." Pages 909–20 in *SBL Seminar Papers*, edited by David J. Lull. SBLSP 37. Atlanta: Scholars, 1998.

Tsuji, Manabu. *Glaube zwischen Vollkommenheit und Verweltlichung: Eine Untersuchung zur literarischen Gestalt und zur inhaltlichen Kohärenz des Jakobusbriefes*. WUNT 2 93. Tübingen: J. C. B. Mohr, 1997.

———. "Zwischen Ideal und Realität: Zu den Witwen in 1 Tim 5.3–16." *NTS* 47 (2001): 92–104.

Uchida, Seiji. "Text and Relevance." Pages 161–78 in *Relevance Theory: Applications and Implications*, edited by Robyn Carston and Seiji Uchida. PBNS. Amsterdam: John Benjamins, 1998.

Unger, Christoph. *Genre, Relevance, and Global Coherence: The Pragmatics of Discourse Type*. PSPLC. Basingstoke, England: Palgrave Macmillan, 2006.

Urrey, Thomas C. "An Exposition of James 4." *SJT* 29 (1986): 37–42.

Vaage, Leif E. "Cuídate la boca: La palabra indicada, una subjetividad alternativa y la formación social de los primeros cristianos según Santiago (3,1–4,17)." *RIBLA* 31 (1998): 110–21.

VanderKam, James C. "Exile in Jewish Apocalyptic Literature." Pages 89–109 in *Exile: Old Testament, Jewish, and Christian Conceptions*, edited by James M. Scott. Leiden: Brill, 1997.

van Dijk, Teun A. "Algunos principios de una teoría del contexto." *RLED* 1 (2001): 69–81.

———. *Discourse and Context: A Sociocognitive Approach*. Cambridge: Cambridge University Press, 2008.

———. *Sociedad y discurso: Cómo influyen los contextos sociales sobre el texto y la conversación* Barcelona: Editorial Gedisa, 2011.

———. *Studies in the Pragmatics of Discourse*. JL 101. Mouton: The Hague, 1981.

VanGemeren, Willem, ed. *New International Dictionary of the Old Testament Theology & Exegesis.* Grand Rapids, Mich.: Zondervan, 1997.

Vanhoozer, Kevin J. *Is There a Meaning in This Text? The Bible, the Reader, and the Morality of Literary Knowledge*. Grand Rapids, Mich.: Zondervan, 1998.

Vanhoozer, Kevin J., Craig G. Bartholomew, Daniel J. Treier, and N. T. Wright, eds. *Dictionary for Theological Interpretation of the Bible.* Grand Rapids, Mich.: Baker, 2005.

Varner, William. *The Book of James: A New Perspective; A Linguistic Commentary Applying Discourse Analysis.* Woodlands, Tex.: Kress Biblical Resources, 2010.

Vermès, Géza. *The Complete Dead Sea Scrolls in English.* Rev. ed. PengC. London: Penguin, 2004.

Verseput, Donald. "James 1:17 and the Jewish Morning Prayers." *NovT* 39 (1997): 177–91.

Vouga, François. *L'épître de saint Jacques.* CNT XIIIa. Geneva: Labor et Fides, 1984.

Vyhmeister, Nancy J. "The Rich Man in James 2: Does Ancient Patronage Illumine the Text?" *AUSS* 33 (1995): 265–83.

Wachob, Wesley Hiram. "The Apocalyptic Intertexture of the Epistle of James." Pages 165–85 in *Intertexture of Apocalyptic Discourse in the New Testament*, edited by Duane F. Watson. Atlanta: Society of Biblical Literature, 2002.

———. "'The Rich in Faith' and 'the Poor in Spirit': The Socio-Rhetorical Function of a Saying of Jesus in the Epistle of James." Ph.D. diss., Emory University, 1993.

———. *The Voice of Jesus in the Social Rhetoric of James.* SNTSMS 106. Cambridge: Cambridge University Press, 2000.

Wachob, Wesley Hiram, and Luke Timothy Johnson. "The Sayings of Jesus in the Letter of James." Pages 431–50 in *Authenticating the Words of Jesus*, edited by Bruce D. Chilton and C. F. Evans. Boston: Brill, 2002.

Wacholder, Ben Zion. "Rules of Testimony in Qumranic Jurisprudence: CD9 and 11Q Torah 64." *JJS* 40 (1989): 161–74.

Waldow, Hans Eberhard von. "Social Responsibility and Social Structure in Early Israel." *CBQ* 32 (1970): 182–204.

Wall, Robert W. *Community of the Wise: The Letter of James.* NTC. Valley Forge, Pa.: Trinity, 1997.

———. "The Intertextuality of Scripture: The Example of Rahab (James 2:25)." Pages 217–36 in *Bible at Qumran: Text, Shape, and Interpretation*, edited by Peter W. Flint. SDSSRL. Grand Rapids, Mich.: Eerdmans, 2001.

———. "James as Apocalyptic Paraenesis." *ResQ* 32 (1990): 11–22.

Walsh, Efthalia Makris. "Wealthy and Impoverished Widows in the Writings of St. John Chrysostom." Pages 176–86 in *Wealth and Poverty in Early Church and Society*, edited by Susan R. Holman. HCSPTH. Grand Rapids, Mich.: Baker, 2008.

Waltke, Bruce K., and Michael Patrick O'Connor. *An Introduction to Biblical Hebrew Syntax.* Winona Lake, Ind.: Eisenbrauns, 1990.

Walton, John H. *Genesis.* NIVAC. Grand Rapids, Mich.: Zondervan, 2001.

Wanamaker, Charles A. *The Epistles to the Thessalonians: A Commentary on the Greek Text.* NIGTC. Grand Rapids, Mich.: Eerdmans, 1990.

Ward, Roy B. "Partiality in the Assembly: James 2:2–4." *HTR* 62 (1969): 87–97.

———. "Works of Abraham: James 2:14–26." *HTR* 61 (1968): 283–90.

Warden, Duane. "The Rich and Poor in James: Implications for Institutionalized Partiality." *JETS* 43 (2000): 247–57.

Watson, Duane F. "James 2 in Light of Greco-Roman Schemes of Argumentation." *NTS* 39 (1993): 94–121.

———. "The Rhetoric of James 3:1–12 and a Classical Pattern of Argumentation." *NovT* 35 (1993): 48–64.

Watts, John D. W. *Isaiah 34–66*. WBC 25. Rev. ed. Nashville: Thomas Nelson, 2005.

Wendland, E. R. "On the Relevance of 'Relevance Theory' for Bible Translation." *BT* 47 (1996): 126–37.

———. "A Review of 'Relevance Theory' in Relation to Bible Translation in South-Central Africa, Part 1." *JNSL* 22 (1996): 91–106.

———. "A Review of 'Relevance Theory' in Relation to Bible Translation in South-Central Africa, Part 2." *JNSL* 23 (1997): 83–108.

Wengst, Klaus. "Aspects of the Last Judgment in the Gospel according to Matthew." Pages 233–45 in *Eschatology in the Bible and in Jewish and Christian Tradition*, edited by Henning Graf Reventlow. JSOTSup 243. Sheffield: Sheffield Academic Press, 1997.

Wenham, Gordon J. "The Date of Deuteronomy: Linch-Pin of Old Testament Criticism." *Them* 10 (1985): 15–20.

———. *Genesis 1–15*. WBC 1. Dallas: Word, 2002.

Wevers, John William, ed. *Deuteronomium*. VTG 3, 2. Göttingen: Vandenhoeck & Ruprecht, 2006.

———, ed. *Leviticus*. VTG 2, 2. Göttingen: Vandenhoeck & Ruprecht, 1986.

White, Hugh C. "The Joseph Story: A Narrative Which 'Consumes' Its Content." *Semeia* 31 (1985): 49–69.

Whitlark, Jason A. "Ἔμφυτος Λόγος: A New Covenant Motif in the Letter of James." *HBT* 32 (2010): 144–65.

Wilkinson, Bruce, and Kenneth Boa. *Talk thru the Bible*. Nashville: T. Nelson, 1983.

Williams, H. H. D. "Of Rags and Riches: The Benefits of Hearing Jeremiah 9:23–24 within James 1:9–11." *TynBul* 53 (2002): 273–82.

Williams, Robert Lee. "Piety and Poverty in James." *WTJ* 22 (1987): 37–55.

Wilson, Deirdre. "Metarepresentation in Linguistic Communication." *UCLWPL* 11 (1999): 127–62.

———. "Relevance Theory," Pages 719–20 in *MIT Encyclopedia of the Cognitive Sciences*, edited by Robert A. Wilson and Frank C. Keil. Cambridge, MA: MIT Press, 2001.

———. "Relevance Theory and the Interpretation of Literary Works." *UCLWPL* 23 (2011): 47–68.

Wilson, Deirdre, and Dan Sperber. "Linguistic Meaning and Relevance." Pages 149–68 in *Meaning and Relevance*, edited by Deirdre Wilson and Dan Sperber. Cambridge: Cambridge University Press, 2012.

———. "Outline of Relevance Theory." *Hermes* 5 (1990): 35–56.

———. "Relevance Theory." *UCLWPL* 14 (2002): 249–90.

———. "Relevance Theory." Pages 607–31 in *Handbook of Pragmatics*, edited by Gregory Ward and Laurence Horn. BHL 16. Oxford: Blackwell, 2004.

———. "Truthfulness and Relevance." Pages 47–83 in *Meaning and Relevance*, edited by Deirdre Wilson and Dan Sperber. Cambridge: Cambridge University Press, 2012.

Wimsatt, W. K., and Monroe C. Beardsley. "The Intentional Fallacy." Pages 3–20 in *The Verbal Icon: Studies in the Meaning of Poetry*, edited by W. K. Wimsatt. Lexington: University Press of Kentucky, 1954.

Winbery, Carlton L. "The Attitude toward Wealth in the Letter of James." *ThEd* 34 (1986): 26–34.

Winter, Bruce W. *Roman Wives, Roman Widows: The Appearance of New Women and the Pauline Communities*. Grand Rapids, Mich.: Eerdmans, 2003.
Witherington, Ben, III. *Letters and Homilies for Jewish Christians: A Socio-Rhetorical Commentary on Hebrews, James, and Jude*. Downers Grove, Ill.: IVP Academic, 2007.
Wright, N. T. *The New Testament and the People of God*. London: SPCK, 1992.
Young, F., and D. F. Ford. *Meaning and Truth in 2 Corinthians*. BFT. London: SPCK, 1987.
Yus, Francisco. "Misunderstandings and Explicit/Implicit Communication." *Prag* 9 (1999): 487–517.
——. "Relevance Theory Online Bibliographic Service." http://www.ua.es/personal/francisco.yus/rt.html.
Ziegler, Joseph, ed. *Duodecim Prophetae*. VTG 13. Göttingen: Vandenhoeck & Ruprecht, 1984.
——, ed. *Jeremias, Baruch, Threni, Epistula Jeremiae*. VTG 15. Göttingen: Vandenhoeck & Ruprecht, 2006.
——, ed. *Septuaginta: Iob*. VTG 11, 4. Göttingen: Vandenhoeck & Ruprecht, 1982.
——, ed. *Septuaginta: Isaias*. VTG 14. Göttingen: Vandenhoeck & Ruprecht, 1983.
Ziglar, Charles Frank. "The Social Orientation of the Implied Community in James." Ph.D. diss., The Southern Baptist Theological Seminary, 1994.
Ziglar, Toby. "Profit or People First? An Examination of Jas 4:13–16." *RevExp* 108 (2011): 453–58.

Index of Authors

Index of Scripture